Johnnie Gough, V.C.

Johnnie Gough, V.C. c.1910

Ian F. W. Beckett

Johnnie Gough, V.C.

A Biography of Brigadier-General
Sir John Edmond Gough, V.C., K.C.B.

TOM DONOVAN
LONDON

First published in 1989 by
TOM DONOVAN PUBLISHING LTD
52 Willow Road
Hampstead
London NW3 1TP

© Ian F. W. Beckett, 1989

ISBN: 1–871085–01–2

Photoset in Linotron Sabon
by Northern Phototypesetting Co, Bolton
Printed in Great Britain
by Bookcraft (Bath) Ltd

For Hugh Francis Gordon Carey (1923–1984)

Contents

Preface and Acknowledgements

For many historians Johnnie Gough has remained a shadowy figure. Widely known as an outstanding soldier, his achievements nevertheless have been obscured by an early death, the greater fame of his elder brother Hubert Gough and by the apparent absence of surviving personal papers. In reality, however, there was an extensive collection of papers in family hands and, through the efforts of Johnnie Gough's daughter, Mrs Diana Pym, and the encouragement of his former regiment, the Rifle Brigade, a biography was begun in 1983. Sadly the author, Hugh Carey, a former officer of the Rifle Brigade, died suddenly some six months after starting work. At the time of his death, Hugh Carey had completed drafts of five chapters (approximating to chapters 2, 3, 4, 6 and 8 of the present volume). My own work on the Curragh Incident on behalf of the Army Records Society had meanwhile put me on the trail of Johnnie Gough's papers and Mrs Pym and her son John Pym were kind enough to allow me to consult material relevant to the Curragh for the ARS volume published in 1986. Moreover, as a result of the contacts made and to my delight, Mrs Pym invited me to complete the biography of her father. Hugh Carey's chapters were an immediate starting point and I am grateful to his brother, Canon Adrian Carey, for permission to make full use of material that would in the normal course have been copyrighted in Hugh Carey's name. However, our literary styles were not compatible and I felt it necessary to rewrite totally those portions of the manuscript which Hugh Carey had completed, retaining only occasionally a particularly apt phrase from his original typescript. Rewriting also enabled me to incorporate material from other archives. Nevertheless, I freely acknowledge the debt I owe to Hugh Carey's essential spadework and this volume is dedicated to his memory.

I have received the utmost support from Mrs Pym and her son, who was kind enough to transcribe the East African letters of Johnnie and Dorothea Gough. Both Mrs Pym and John Pym have also allowed me total freedom as to the interpretation I cared to place upon Johnnie Gough's character and career. Valuable assistance has also been rendered by other members of the Gough family including Mrs Pym's daughter, Mrs Jill Hoare, who undertook research in the Ashmolean Museum on Johnnie's period in Crete; her daughter, Miss Joanna Hoare, who transcribed material from the F. S. Oliver collection in the National Library of Scotland; and to Mrs Pym's grandson, Alex Taylor, not least for putting me into contact with the publisher of this volume, Tom Donovan. Lefkothea Manoura, the mother of Mrs Pym's godchild Diana, was indefatigable in the search for Cretan connections and the publication of a letter and photograph in the Greek newspaper *Alaghi* resulted in contact being made with Dr Michael S. Macrakis of Belmont, Massachussetts, who identified several of the Cretans photographed with Johnnie Gough in 1899 and produced deeds initialled by Johnnie at that time. Considerable help was also given by the daughters of Hubert Gough: Mrs Myrtle Dutton, Mrs Denise Boyes, Anne Gough and Joyce Gough. In particular, Mrs Boyes was kind enough to allow me to take away material from Hubert's papers for more detailed study. The history of the Gough family written by Brenda Gough was also invaluable.

Members of the Keyes family, of whom Johnnie's wife, Dorothea, was one, were of equal assistance. Mrs Rosemary Fellowes, Patrick and Michael Keyes were all helpful on matters of Keyes family history, but my especial thanks goes to Lord Keyes for being kind enough to invite me to his home on a number of occasions to work on family papers in his possession. Two of Johnnie Gough's godsons, Professor Sir John Pope-Hennessy and Vice-Admiral Sir Peter Dawnay, were also more than willing to search for additional material relating to their fathers' close friendship with Johnnie. Tony Allen, who saved many of the papers of the Bloomfield Gough branch of the family from dispersion, was informative on Johnnie's beloved cousin, Lucy Gough. I also had the privilege of interviewing Mrs Beatrix Rabagliati, the daughter of F. S. Oliver, on her memories of Johnnie and other members of her father's circle of friends. Previously, the late Mark Oliver had shared his recollections with Mrs Pym.

I also wish to acknowledge the help Mrs Pym and/or myself have received from Colonel J. R. Baker and the trustees of the Royal Greenjackets Museum at Winchester; General Sir Anthony Farrar-Hockley; Major-General David Alexander-Sinclair; Brigadier J. S. Ryder; Colonel F. G. Robson; Major A. C. J. Congreve; J. G. Gathirimu of the Kenyan Department of Defence; W. Alister Williams; and George Stevenson, who as a member of 25th Field Ambulance witnessed Johnnie Gough's funeral. I also extend my thanks to Oliver Everett, the Librarian and Keeper of the Royal Archives at Windsor and his staff; Paul Quarrie, the Librarian and Keeper of College Collections at Eton College; Mrs Jane Hogan of the Sudan Archive of the University of Durham; Ann Brown of the Ashmolean Museum, Oxford; Boris Mollo and the staff of the Department of Records at the National Army Museum; Rod Suddaby and the staff of the Department of Documents at the Imperial War Museum; and the staff of the Staff College Library and the Library of the Royal Military Academy, Sandhurst.

As always I have benefitted from the knowledge and advice of my colleagues in the Department of War Studies at Sandhurst, notably those doyens of
Great War scholarship, John Keegan, Richard Holmes and Keith Simpson.
Unfortunately, events have conspired to deprive Sandhurst of the talents of all
three of the former while I have been working on this volume but I have still
been able to draw on their expertise and that of a younger colleague, Gary
Sheffield. In any case, there is no better climate in which to study the pre-war
military mind.

None of the foregoing are responsible, of course, for any errors of interpretation or fact on my part.

Quotations from material in the Royal Archives appears by gracious
permission of Her Majesty the Queen. Other use of Crown copyright material in the Public Record Office, India Office Library or other repositories is by
permission of Her Majesty's Stationery Office. I also gratefully acknowledge
the generosity of the following in enabling me to consult and/or quote from
archive material in their possession or copyright: Lord Keyes; Lord Mottis-
tone; Lord Robertson of Oakridge; Lieutenant Colonel the Viscount
Allenby; Lady Patricia Kingsbury; Sir Charles Fergusson, Bt and Adam
Ferguson; Sir Hector Monro, M.P.; Mrs Myrtle Dutton; Mrs Denise Boyes;
Mrs Beatrix Rabagliati; M. A. F. Rawlinson; William Bell; Lord Bonham
Carter; Sir John Pope-Hennessy; Vice-Admiral Sir Peter Dawnay; Tony
Allen; the Trustees of the Royal Greenjackets Museum and of the Rifle
Brigade Museum; the Queen's Royal Irish Hussars; the Trustees of the
Imperial War Museum; the Trustees of the Beaverbrook Foundation; the
Trustees of the British Library Board; the Trustees of the Liddell Hart Centre
for Military Archives, King's College; the Clerk of the Records and the House
of Lords Record Office; the Trustees of the National Library of Scotland; the
National Register of Archives (Scotland) and the Scottish Record Office; the
Public Record Office; the National Army Museum; the Ashmolean Museum;
the Bodleian Library; the Provost and Fellows of Eton College; Nuffield
College, Oxford; the Master, Fellows and Scholars of Churchill College,
Cambridge; the Warden and Fellows of New College, Oxford; the Sudan
Archive of the University of Durham; Birmingham University Library; the
Army Museums Ogilby Trust; Earl Haig; R. Farquhar-Oliver; the Rifle
Brigade Club Committee; Lt. Commander David Verney; Captain Dugald
Malcolm.

IFWB
RMAS, May 1988

Johnnie Gough: A Biographical Sketch

25.10.1871	Born at Murree, India
1881	Entered Buckland's private school, Laleham (Middx)
1885	Entered Eton College
12. 4.1890	Commissioned Second Lieutenant, Westmeath Militia
18. 2.1891	Resigned from militia and entered Royal Military College, Sandhurst
12. 3.1892	Commissioned Second Lieutenant, Rifle Brigade
23. 5.1892	Joined First Battalion, Rifle Brigade in India
6.12.1893	Promoted to First Lieutenant
12. 3.1895	Transferred to Second Battalion, Rifle Brigade in Ireland
26. 8.1896	Seconded to special service in British Central Africa
9.12.1897	Returned to regimental duty at Malta
12. 7.1898	Battalion left Malta for Sudan
10. 9.1898	Battalion ordered from Sudan to Crete
5.12.1898	Promoted to Captain
1.10.1899	Battalion ordered to South Africa
30.10.1899	Battalion cut off in Ladysmith
28. 2.1900	Relief of Ladysmith
19. 7.1900	Became Temporary ADC to Major-General Francis Howard, 8th Brigade
10. 9.1900	Became Signalling Officer, 8th Brigade
31.10.1900	Became District Commissioner at Lydenburg, Transvaal
29.11.1900	Promoted to Brevet Major
7. 7.1902	Left Lydenburg and proceeded to England
27.10.1902	Seconded to special service in Somaliland
18.12.1903	Returned to England
16. 1.1904	Gazette announced award of Victoria Cross for action at Dara-toleh in Somaliland (22.4.1903) and backdated promotion to Brevet Lieutenant Colonel
1.1904	Entered Staff College, Camberley
22.12.1905	Graduated from Staff College
23.12.1905	Appointed DAAG, Irish Command

29. 6.1907 Married Dorothea Keyes
14. 8.1907 Promoted Brevet Colonel and appointed ADC to the King
 1.10.1907 Appointed Inspector-General, King's African Rifles
 6. 5.1908 Promoted Major in Rifle Brigade
18.10.1908 Birth of daughter, Diana
19. 1.1909 Appointed Officer Commanding, Troops in Somaliland
14. 6.1909 Invalided home from Somaliland
23.12.1909 Appointed GSO1, Staff College as Substantive Colonel
21. 1.1913 Went on half-pay
 9.10.1913 Appointed BGGS, Aldershot Command
24. 5.1914 Collapsed with severe abdominal problem
14. 8.1914 Embarked as BGGS, I Corps
26.12.1914 Became BGGS, First Army
18. 2.1915 Gazetted C.B.
20. 2.1915 Fatally wounded by sniper near Fauquissart, France
22. 2.1915 Died at Estaires, France
22. 4.1915 Posthumously gazetted K.C.B.

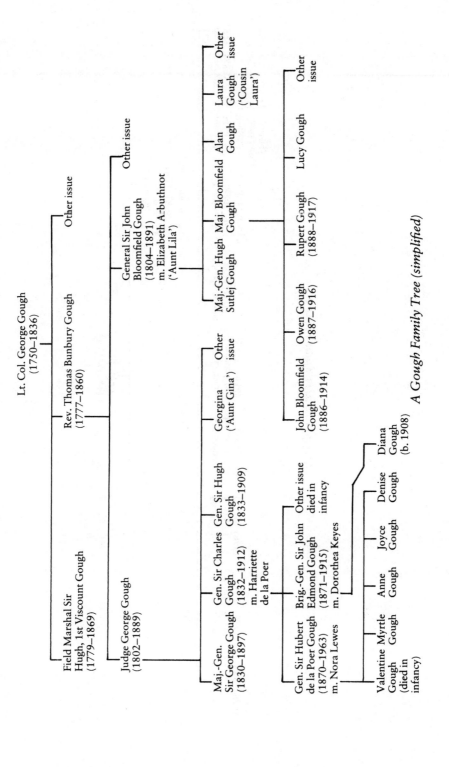

A Gough Family Tree (simplified)

Lt. Col. George Gough
(1750–1836)

Field Marshal Sir
Hugh, 1st Viscount Gough
(1779–1869)

Rev. Thomas Bunbury Gough
(1777–1860)

Other issue

Judge George Gough
(1802–1889)

General Sir John
Bloomfield Gough
(1804–1891)
m. Elizabeth Arbuthnot
('Aunt Lila')

Other issue

Maj.-Gen.
Sir George Gough
(1830–1897)

Gen. Sir Charles
Gough
(1832–1912)
m. Harriette
de la Poer

Gen. Sir Hugh
Gough
(1833–1909)

Georgina
('Aunt Gina')

Other
issue

Maj.-Gen. Hugh
Sutlej Gough

Maj. Bloomfield
Gough

Alan
Gough

Laura
Gough
('Cousin
Laura')

Other
issue

Gen. Sir Hubert
de la Poer Gough
(1870–1963)
m. Nora Lewes

Brig.-Gen. Sir John
Edmond Gough
(1871–1915)
m. Dorothea Keyes

Other issue
died in
infancy

John Bloomfield
Gough
(1886–1914)

Owen Gough
(1887–1916)

Rupert Gough
(1888–1917)

Lucy Gough

Other
issue

Valentine Myrtle
Gough
(died in
infancy)

Anne
Gough

Joyce
Gough

Denise
Gough

Diana
Gough
(b. 1908)

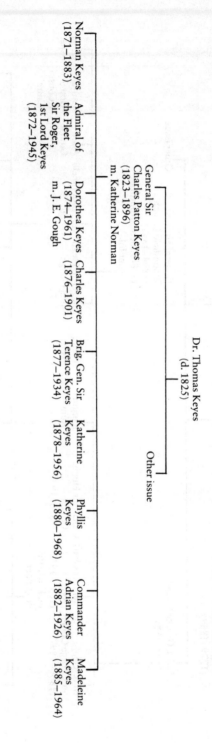

Dr. Thomas Keyes
(d. 1825)

General Sir
Charles Patton Keyes
(1823–1896)
m. Katherine Norman

Other issue

Norman Keyes
(1871–1883)

Admiral of
the Fleet
Sir Roger,
1st Lord Keyes
(1872–1945)

Dorothea Keyes
(1874–1961)
m. J. E. Gough

Charles Keyes
(1876–1901)

Brig. Gen. Sir
Terence Keyes
(1877–1934)

Katherine
Keyes
(1878–1956)

Phyllis
Keyes
(1880–1968)

Commander
Adrian Keyes
(1882–1926)

Madeleine
Keyes
(1885–1964)

A Keyes Family Tree (simplified)

Illustrations

All illustrations are from the Johnnie Gough MSS except where stated otherwise

Maps

All maps, apart from Johnnie's sketch of the action at Daratoleh, drawn by Nicole Woodman

1

Early Life, 1871–1896

DURING Wednesday 25 February 1915, the Commander-in-Chief of the British Expeditionary Force in France and Flanders, Field Marshal Sir John French, returned to a letter he had begun the previous day to his confidante, Mrs Winifred Bennett. Seven months of warfare had taken its toll of his emotions:

Alas, alas! Another dear friend gone. The Chief of the Staff of the First Army – General Gough was caught near the trenches by a stray bullet and died of his wounds on Sunday last. My room is becoming thick with the spirits of my friends. God bless & keep them all!

It was not the only occasion upon which French expressed such feelings and the phenomenon of being visited by the dead or the dying was far from uncommon in the Great War. Indeed, Gough's young daughter had experienced the presence of her father in her bedroom at South Terrace, Littlehampton on the very night – 20 February – that he lay critically wounded in the 25th Field Ambulance at Estaires. Taken off to Checkendon in Oxfordshire while her mother hurried to France, Diana Gough sensed that her father was dead before the news reached England.[1]

In fact, Johnnie Gough, as Brigadier-General John Edmond Gough, V.C. was universally known, was not a close friend of French. Almost a year earlier, Johnnie and his elder brother Hubert, now commanding the 2nd Cavalry Division on the Western Front, had played leading roles in the Curragh Incident that led to French's resignation as Chief of the Imperial General Staff. There were many who believed that, by failing to stand up to politicians, French had betrayed the army and Hubert's correspondence in the months following the affair had described French in such uncompromising terms as 'that rogue and buck stick'. Moreover, in November 1914 French had refused to promote Johnnie to Major-General as he was low on the Colonel's list, Brigadier-General being an appointment rather than a rank.[2] That French could now refer to Johnnie as a 'dear friend' reflected not only the unifying effect of war upon personal relationships within the army but also Johnnie's popularity and the tremendous sense of loss that pervaded the British army at his death.

In a subsequent despatch French recorded his belief that Johnnie had been 'one of our most promising military leaders of the future', an opinion echoed after the war both by Field Marshal Sir William Robertson, who wrote of Johnnie as 'a brilliant and accomplished soldier', and by Major-General Sir George Aston, who believed that Johnnie had been killed 'too early in the war to reach the high position in which his sterling character and transcendent qualities would undoubtedly have placed him'. Aston had met Johnnie when an instructor at the Staff College in 1904. Johnnie later served as one of Robertson's divisional directors at the Staff College where his lectures were credited with inspiring the future Field Marshal Earl Wavell's book on generalship. Certainly, the book Johnnie wrote, *Fredericksburg and Chancellorsville* published in 1913, was still a set book for promotion examinations in the 1930s.[3]

More immediately, Johnnie's death came at a crucial time in the preparation for the first significant British offensive on the Western Front at Neuve Chapelle, an operation for which First Army was responsible. Johnnie's brother-in-law, Roger Keyes, firmly believed that the initial success at Neuve Chapelle on 10 March 1915 – one of only four comparable breakthroughs by the British army during the entire course of the war on this front – would not have been wasted had Johnnie lived. According to Douglas Haig's intelligence chief and later biographer, Brigadier-General John Charteris, Johnnie's death was 'almost the only time in the war' when Haig, then commanding First Army, 'allowed a personal incident to interfere with the normal routine of his work'.[4] Johnnie was undoubtedly important to Haig and, even though he was in the process of taking his leave of Haig's staff to go home to command a division, the consequences of his loss for the future course and military direction of the war is almost incalculable

That Johnnie should have raised such high expectations for his future was not perhaps surprising given the astonishing military pedigree of the Goughs. Resident in Wiltshire in the fifteenth and sixteenth centuries, the Goughs moved to County Limerick in Ireland during the early seventeenth century. Three sons of George Gough (1750–1836), Lieutenant Governor of Limerick in the troubled year of 1798, entered the British army. One became Field Marshal Hugh, First Viscount Gough (1779–1869), Commander-in-Chief in India from 1843 to 1849 and victor of the Sikh wars. A fourth of George's sons – Thomas Bunbury (1777–1860) – entered the church but, of his six children, three sons also joined the army. Another of Thomas Bunbury's sons, George (1802–1889), became a judge of the High Court of the East India Company. In turn, three of the judge's sons served in the military forces of the Company – George (1830–1897), Charles John Stanley (1832–1912) and Hugh Henry (1833–1909). All three achieved general rank and both Charles and Hugh won the Victoria Cross during the Indian Mutiny, Charles for four specific acts of gallantry which included the saving of Hugh's life at Khurkowdah on 15 August 1857. Thus, when Johnnie won his Victoria Cross in Somaliland in 1903, it was held by father, son and uncle simultaneously.

Charles Gough, who went on to serve on the Bhootan expedition of 1864–5, eventually returned to his father's house at Rathronan near Clonmel in County Tipperary. In 1869 he married Harriette, the daughter of Edmond de la Poer (sometimes rendered in the anglicised version of Edmond Power), Liberal M.P. for Waterford from 1866 to 1873, who resided at Gurteen a few miles across the river Suir in County Waterford. Their first child, christened Hubert de la Poer, was born in London on 12 August 1870. Shortly afterwards, Charles returned to India with his wife and infant son and a second son, John Edmond – Johnnie – was born at Murree near Rawalpindi on 25 October 1871.

For the families in the service of the Raj, separation was a fact of life. The whole family returned to England on 'home leave' in 1877; went back to India and then, a little earlier than might otherwise have been the case due to the imminent outbreak of hostilities with the Amir of Afghanistan, Harriette again returned with the brothers to England in 1879. Two other children born in India also accompanied her, as they had on the previous occasion – Annie Frances, born in 1873, and Charles Arnold born in 1876. Sadly, Annie and Charles Arnold caught scarlet fever in London, the latter dying first on 23 February 1880 at 84 Cadogan Place and his sister on 14 March 1880. Harriette's physical health was permanently impaired by the same epidemic but, fortunately, Hubert and Johnnie escaped. The death of Annie and Charles Arnold was recounted by Hubert in his memoirs and has been repeated in subsequent accounts. In fact, it was not the first tragedy to strike the family for there had been two other daughters, whose brief lives are omitted even from the Gough family history. Harriette Charlotte had died at Delhi on 12 January 1876 at the age of eighteen months and Kathleen Maud had died at Nowgong in Assam on 10 October 1878 at just 3½ months old.

For Charles, isolated on campaign in Afghanistan, the loss of 'our four children Angels in Heaven' was a bitter blow. Writing to his cousin Laura from Kabul on 4 May 1880, Charles was concerned greatly for his wife when Hubert and Johnnie must soon go to school:

I cannot bear the idea of her attempting to set up Home by herself now, even if she kept Hubert and Johnnie with her they could not be companions to her like Annie and Charlie. They must be at their lessons a good deal and then boys of that age are of boisterous spirits and must be out a good deal. Properly I think they should now go to school as they are of that age now. Then, where is Harrie left. How is she to spend her time, where is her society? This picture of poor Harriette's loneliness is ever present in my mind – and I cannot be with her. I am obliged to remain at my post, and even that must cause her anxiety, poor thing.[5]

Since Charles had not received any word from his own father at Rathronan on the subject of his family's immediate future, he was particularly grateful for an invitation extended to Harriette by her father to go to Gurteen. He was also full of thanks to Laura for taking care of the 'poor little fellows', Hubert and Johnnie.

Although Hubert and Johnnie were to spend time at Rathronan with the judge, considerably more time was spent at the nearby Knockeevan home of their great uncle, General Sir John Bloomfield Gough, and in the company of his daughters, Margaret and Laura. Sir John's wife, Elizabeth ('Aunt Lila'), and his unmarried niece, Georgina ('Aunt Gina'), completed the Knockeevan household which, according to Hubert, was to form 'the most important influence' on the lives and characters of the two brothers in their formative years. That this should be so was due to Harriette's decision to rejoin Charles in India although it is apparent that she was torn between her duties as mother and wife. In September 1885, for example, Charles was to write to Laura that Harriette was 'most anxious to see the boys again' but, as Harriette had written to Johnnie five months previously, she did 'not quite like leaving Father behind all by himself'. Both parents returned home in April 1886 but Charles, who had been knighted in 1881 for his services during the 2nd Afghan War and promoted to Major-General in 1885, returned to India after six months to command a division in Bengal. Harriette stayed to supervise the brothers' education then, three years later, returned to India from where Sir Charles wrote to Johnnie:

it will be very pleasant for me having her with me again, and as you boys have had that advantage so long, it is only fair I should have my innings. It will not be very long however I hope before we both get back again.

For Harriette, writing to Johnnie from Bombay on 28 October 1889, it was 'not in the nature of things that mother and sons should always be together'.[6]

Separated as they were so frequently by thousands of miles, Hubert and Johnnie were made aware constantly of the devotion and interest of both parents. In turn, Harriette was disappointed if the mails did not bring letters from her sons. In the words of her letter to Johnnie from Bombay, she wished to ensure that the boys would 'always as long as we live have a loving home to turn to'. In the meantime, the holidays spent at Gurteen, Rathronan and especially Knockeevan were particularly happy for Hubert and Johnnie. Both boys 'ran wild' in the hills around Clonmel, becoming firm friends with the gamekeepers of the de la Poer and Gough estates. The boys would 'borrow' the carriage horses to go hunting and, many years later, Hubert's eldest daughter would be shown bullet holes in a wall made by Hubert, who only narrowly missed Johnnie standing on the lawn nearby. All the Gough clan were fine horsemen and women and one letter to Johnnie from Harriette in May 1885 expressed her delight that her thirteen-year-old son had 'got some shooting at Rathronan, and riding too I hope' during the Easter holidays. Both the Gough and de la Poer households were also keen churchgoers, providing Hubert and Johnnie with a 'solid religious atmosphere'. Although Edmund de la Poer was a Catholic, Harriette's mother was a Protestant and both households were 'anti Home Rulers', Hubert recalling in his memoirs the tales of 'murders, ambushes . . . and midnight raids' which contributed to the boyhood excitement of life at Knockeevan and Rathronan.[7]

Apart from their cousin, Laura, Knockeevan was also home for her four elder brothers. Of these, Alan who was seven years older than Hubert and commissioned into the Royal Welch Fusiliers in 1882, was especially ready to be 'sympathetic with them and enter into their little amusements and sports'. Sir Charles was similarly pleased to hear from Laura in May 1885 that both Hubert and Johnnie were 'so able to win friends for themselves'. Yet, the two brothers suffered understandable loneliness and became very close to one another. The loneliness manifested itself most in their lack of progress at school, Johnnie following Hubert in 1881 to the private school at Laleham near Staines run by 'Mat' Buckland. In February 1883 Sir Charles wrote to Laura that he was pleased with Johnnie's report from Laleham which 'when not contrasted with that of Hubert is for such a young child very fair'. However, he hoped that Johnnie would soon settle down 'more steadfastly to his work'. Two years later, on 14 May 1885, Harriette was writing to Johnnie that,

Mr Buckland does not give a very good account of you, which is very disappointing, as I had hoped, now that you were growing into such a big Boy, that you would see the necessity of working.

A week later Harriette again exhorted Johnnie to greater effort for,

I am all anxious about you and Hubert, neither of you seem to be working well, and what is to become of you if you cannot pass your exams. You ought to be the head of the school at Laleham by this, as you must be one of the oldest boys and certainly have been the longest there; and yet I do not hear of you being even in the first class.

Just ten days later, on 1 June, came yet another letter from Harriette advising Johnnie to 'make friends with your French master' in order to improve his grasp of the language. The letters may have worked for Johnnie received a watch from Sir Charles as a reward for a good report and a prize in his last term at Laleham.[8]

Sir Charles and Harriette gave some thought to separating the brothers for, while Hubert had proceeded to Eton from Laleham in 1884, it was intended that Johnnie should attend Winchester. In the event, the scheme fell through and Johnnie went to Eton in the Michaelmas term of 1885. Sir Charles wrote to Hubert to ask him to look after Johnnie 'a little bit when he first comes and until he has made his own friends'. At the same time Johnnie received letters from his father urging the necessity of securing a good place in the entrance examination and of obtaining early admission to the 'Remove'. However, like Hubert before him, Johnnie took only a moderate place in the examination before joining the same house as Hubert under the direction of A. C.

James. Entering one of the fourth form classes, Johnnie's weekly fare comprised Latin, Greek, Mathematics, French, Geography and History. Both Hubert and Johnnie played for their house in the Lower Boy Football Cup, one of them distinguishing himself 'in the bully' during the final held on St Andrew's Day, 1885, a match won by James' house by one goal and two rouges to nil.

Little else survives of the mark made by either brother on Eton, although Johnnie was fined for 'violating House Library rules' on 16 July 1887, by which time he had progressed to the Remove. In an obituary of Johnnie in the *Liverpool Daily Post* in 1915, an anonymous correspondent who had obviously been at Eton with him wrote of Johnnie's 'dare-devil high spirits, and in those days it must be confessed he was unmerciful to nervous and delicate boys. But there was no harm in him even then, and he played football with desperate keenness'. This seems somewhat curious given Johnnie's reserved nature and it is more than possible that the writer was confusing Johnnie with Hubert after the lapse of thirty years.[9] In any case, neither brother remained long at Eton.

Hubert left at the end of the Lent term of 1886 to prepare for entrance to the Royal Military College, Sandhurst through a period of intensive language instruction in France and then with a crammer in London. A number of the public schools, including Eton, had special 'army classes' to take a boy on from the 'preliminary' examination, usually taken at the age of fifteen or sixteen in March or July, to the 'further' examination which consisted of compulsory papers in Mathematics, Latin, French or German, English Composition, and both Freehand and Geometrical Drawing plus at least one further subject chosen from a number of options. The competition was such that, in the case of Sandhurst, only one in four of the candidates secured a place since it was necessary to gain a high position on the list to ensure entrance. Thus, even where schools had 'modern' departments capable of tutoring for Sandhurst and Woolwich (for candidates wishing to enter the Royal Artillery or Royal Engineers), it was more usual for aspiring cadets to attend a cramming establishment. In 1885, for example, 79 per cent of the successful candidates for Sandhurst entrance had attended a crammer, such as the celebrated Captain James in Lexham Gardens whose classes were attended not only by Hubert but, later, by the young Winston Churchill. Having secured a high mark sufficient for entrance, Hubert entered the college in January 1888.

By comparison with the exuberant Hubert, Johnnie was a rather more reserved boy although one with a dry wit. He enjoyed riding and shooting but he also shared his mother's interest in wild flowers and in sketching, both parents remarking in letters to Johnnie in May 1885 how he would have appreciated the orchids and other flowers at Mahableshwar where they were staying temporarily. Nevertheless, Johnnie had expressed the same desire as Hubert to enter the army and it was intended that he should also attend a crammer if his schooling did not improve. In fact, Johnnie became ill with typhoid fever in early 1887, which left him weak and with periodic swelling in his legs. He left Eton therefore at the end of the Michaelmas term of 1887 to attend a special clinic in Paris while continuing his preparation for Sandhurst with a crammer in France. Separated from both Hubert and his mother, Johnnie reported from his residence at Neuilly near the French capital in February 1888 that 'it is most awfully lonely'. But he was understanding French much better, had mastered all the Euclid he required to pass the Sandhurst 'Prelim', which he had been unable to work for through his illness at Eton, and was now beginning to work on his Geography, another 'Prelim' subject together with French, Geometrical Drawing, Arithmetic and Algebra. At some expense, he had been 'quite cured' in the legs, though he would never lose white marks on them .[10]

Apparently, Johnnie remained abroad for almost two years. Certainly he was at Biarritz and Pau in the autumn of 1889, his mother writing of his 'new life' and being anxious concerning the 'arrangements you have made about masters'. Sir Charles promised to do all in his power to obtain a cadetship for Johnnie at Sandhurst but, in return, expected 'plenty of good work' and particular attention to History, Mathematics and French. As the correspondence on the cadetship indicated, the thoughts of both parents and presumably those of Johnnie were turning already to his future military career. Sir Charles, now promoted to Lieutenant-General, advised Johnnie not to come out to India for some years even though he would appreciate the sport. Harriette, an accomplished artist herself, had shown some of Johnnie's sketches of France to a Captain Norman who had connections with *The Times* and some of the illustrated periodicals. Determined that 'from the *very* beginning' Johnnie should 'stand out a little from the common herd', she believed that he should offer his services as an artist to the *Graphic* or *Illustrated London News* since 'this would always ensure your going on service even if your Regiment was not going and put a good round sum into your pockets!'.[11]

The cadetship for which Sir Charles and Johnnie aimed was evidently that of Honorary Queen's Cadet. Each year a total of ten sons of British officers and three sons of Indian Army officers of distinguished service received the nomination of the Commander-in-Chief for a place at Sandhurst. Honorary Queen's Cadet did not qualify for free places as did Queen's Cadets, usually the sons of impoverished officers or officers' orphans, but shared the advantage of not being subjected to the competitive entrance examination. However, they were required to satisfy the examiners by gaining sufficient marks to demonstrate a 'competent amount of general proficiency'. It would appear that Sir Charles was unsuccessful initially in having Johnnie nominated through the Military Secretary of the India Office for, on 12 April 1890, Johnnie was commissioned a Second Lieutenant in the Westmeath Militia, nominally the 9th Battalion of the Rifle Brigade. Revived in 1852, the militia was designed primarily for home defence but, increasingly, it was being employed to supplement the Regular army through embodiment at times of crisis. During the Crimean War, for example, a number of battalions had served in Mediterranean garrisons while others had been embodied during the Indian Mutiny and again in the threatened international or Imperial crises of 1882 and 1885. In the process, the militia was becoming little more than a draft finding body for the Regular army, approximately a third of all Regular recruits deriving from the militia between 1882 and 1904. Moreover, the possession of a militia commission was a recognised 'back door' in that militia officers could be commissioned directly into the army without passing through Sandhurst at all. Since 1872 each militia battalion had been able to nominate one subaltern annually for a regular commission, provided that he was between the ages of 19 and 22 and had served two annual training periods; the militia came out for 'permanent training' for 28 days each summer.

Henry Wilson and Hugh Trenchard were two later celebrities who entered the army's commissioned ranks by the militia route and it would appear that Johnnie probably joined the Westmeath Militia by way of insurance. In fact, he attended only one annual training of his battalion, which had its headquarters at Mullingar in County Westmeath, for he secured his Honorary Queen's India Cadetship and resigned from the militia on 18 February 1891. Therefore, whereas Hubert had entered Sandhurst at the age of only seventeen, Johnnie did not begin his course there until after his nineteenth birthday. However, his period abroad and his practical, if limited, military experience in the militia would have given him a far greater maturity than many of his contemporaries.

Like Hubert, Johnnie clearly adapted well to the work at Sandhurst. Hubert – gazetted to the 16th Lancers in March 1889 – had met with some success at the college in securing 924 marks in his preliminary examination after the first half of the course and 2,215 marks in his final examination. Unfortunately, the surviving college records for this period give no indication of the order of merit of the 180 cadets who joined the RMC at the same time as Johnnie. However, few of them were to make such a mark on the army. Only thirteen including Johnnie attained the rank of Brigadier-General of whom only two – Archibald Eden and Herbert Trevor – apart from him were to exercise that rank in brigade appointments during the Great War. The remainder reached that rank only after the war. Just four of Johnnie's contemporaries were to reach the higher rank of Major-General. Three of them – George Farmar, Percy Hazelton and Hugh Herdan – did so only after the Great War, although Frederick Maurice was Director of Military Operations at the War Office and provoked the celebrated 'Maurice debate' in May 1918 by publicly challenging David Lloyd George's honesty with regard to manpower strengths in France and Flanders. While not attaining high rank, a number of Johnnie's other fellow cadets were to earn their reputations in quasi-military appointments including Randal Feilden in the Sudan, John Greig in Bombay, Beauchamp Kerr-Pearse in Australia and Hugh (Protheroe) Smith as a long-serving Chief Constable of Cornwall. One other distinguished future soldier was the Hon. George Morris who was to serve alongside Johnnie as a Staff College instructor and to find an even earlier grave in Flanders.

In so far as the records do survive, Johnnie clearly showed some promise although he did not represent the college in any sports nor take part in any of the amateur dramatic performances. His conduct in the first half of his course up to July 1891 was 'very good' and he scored 821 marks in Military Administration, Military Law, Tactics, Fortification and Military Topography. In the second part of the course, Johnnie's conduct was 'exemplary' and, in the final examination of December 1891, his marks in the same subjects with the addition of Drill, Gymnastics, Riding and those awarded by professors totalled 2,405.[12] He had also been a Cadet Corporal in the company – E Company – to which he had been attached. Retiring from Sandhurst in February 1892, Johnnie was gazetted Second Lieutenant in the Rifle Brigade on 12 March 1892.

A year after Johnnie left Sandhurst, the course was extended to eighteen months in duration. Additional time was given over to more practical outdoor work while a number of new subjects such as French or German, Geography and Military History were introduced progressively to the syllabus over the course of the next decade. Within the army as a whole, changes were also being contemplated. The late 1880s and 1890s were years of almost unremitting European tensions arousing fears for the safety of Britain itself and leading to major reviews of British defence capabilities. But the resulting preoccupation with home defence was not without its critics within the political and military establishments and there were bitter disputes between Eurocentric and Indocentric strategists. To some extent the difficulties stemming from the administrative legacy of Edward Cardwell's tenure at the War Office between 1868 and 1874 were solved at this time, but conflict still raged within the army between proponents and opponents of Cardwell's reforms.

The Royal Commission chaired by Lord Hartington, which presented reports in July 1889 and February 1890, focused attention on the deficiencies in the higher organisation of defence and there was at least a tentative beginning of a more systematic defence structure in the War Office Council of 1890 and the Joint Naval and Military Committee of 1891. Through the Stanhope Memorandum of 1888, reissued three years later, the army also received a definitive statement of the purposes for which it existed, which had been lacking for more than twenty years. Moreover, the perennial problems of finding sufficient reinforcing drafts to maintain British garrisons in India and the colonies and of stimulating recruitment at home were tackled by the Wantage Committee, reporting in 1892. An impressive barracks construction programme was begun in the 1890s to replace the Crimean vintage wooden huts still occupied at Aldershot and elsewhere, and long overdue recommendations were adopted with regard to such matters as better sanitation and diet for the rank and file.

Yet, for all that there was some progress, it must be recognised that it was limited both through financial retrenchment and the parsimony that governed military expenditure and, also, through the entrenched attitudes and fundamental conservatism even of supposed military reformers such as Lord Wolseley. Thus, the majority recommendation of the Hartington Commission for the abolition of the office of Commander-in-Chief and for the creation of a continental-style General Staff foundered, the War Office Council falling far short of Hartington's original design. The Duke of Cambridge, who had dominated affairs as Commander-in-Chief for forty years, was replaced by Wolseley in 1895, but it would take the shocks of the South African War to promote more far-reaching change. Before that conflict, the kind of colonial campaigning undertaken by the Victorian army throughout the Empire merely reinforced the refusal to concede that warfare was being transformed increasingly by technological change. The anachronistic tactics which served to dispose of most native opponents led only to complacency and belief in the immutable character of war and the supremacy of traditional military values.

At the heart of those values lay the concept of regimental esprit de corps. For a young subaltern such as Johnnie embarking on a military career, the regiment projected a robust sense of corporate and cohesive identity shared by officers and men alike. Essentially, it was a private family, differentiated by its own peculiar traditions from all the other equally unique manifestations of the country's military culture. Many officers would never move beyond the narrow confines of their regiments and, in any case, the loyalties thus fashioned would last a lifetime. It was while Johnnie was visiting his old battalion that he was hit in February 1915 and it was his old company that provided the firing squad at his funeral. But, at the same time, the army's officers naturally displayed common characteristics and ones not altogether far removed from their contemporaries in landed society. Indeed, the club-like atmosphere of the mess; the social and financial exclusiveness, in which the possession of a private income was still a practical necessity; and the unbridled opportunities for sport sustained the army's appeal among the scions of county society. Quite simply, an officer must be a gentleman.

The merit of the public schools, which produced the overwhelming majority of the candidates for commission, was that their pupils from whatever background were inculcated with precisely the qualities most suited to the perpetuation of the ideal of the officer gentleman. Loyalty, obedience, courage, honour, an uncomplicated patriotism, a love of team games and a concern for subordinates were all values prized as much in the public school as in the regiment. The public schools were not in themselves overtly military institutions and they did not teach 'leadership'. What they did do was to mould character and, above all, that was what was required of an officer in such a pre-technological army. The regimental tradition had undeniable virtues but it had the inevitable effect of encouraging conformity and, through the accepted life style of the officer, it also militated against professionalism. 'Shop' was never to be discussed in the mess and to be seen to be too diligent in the study of the military profession was still likely to result in 'ragging' or, conceivably, much worse. It was therefore a special world into which Johnnie now moved, but one for which both his education and his own family tradition had equipped him.

A kind of 'pair bonding'[13] usually occurred at Sandhurst, if not before, by which there was a mutual decision on admission to a particular regiment between cadet and the regiment. Wealth or status alone did not guarantee acceptance in a chosen regiment. As a family, the Goughs had shown no especial loyalty to one regiment in the past, although the family motto *Faugh-a-Ballagh* ('Clear the Way') was shared with the 87th Foot (later the Royal Irish Fusiliers), which the First Viscount Gough had led at the battle of Barossa in 1811: Johnnie was to attend the centenary celebrations. There is no indication, however, as to why Hubert had gone to the 16th Lancers in 1889 or why Johnnie went to the Rifle Brigade three years later. One of cousin Laura's brothers, Bloomfield, had entered the Rifle Brigade in 1870 but had transferred to the 9th Lancers in 1873. On the other hand, the Westmeath Militia was affiliated to the corps and this may have been the catalyst. Both Hubert and Johnnie's regiments were fashionable, however, and well towards the top of the recognised 'pecking order' in the army.

The Rifle Brigade, of course, was more distinct than most as a rifle regiment. Raised as an experimental corps of riflemen in 1800, all ranks were expected to use their initiative in the context of the highly mobile light infantry operations for which the corps was intended. It carried no colours, marched at the trail instead of the slope and used a series of bugle calls, or 'horns', all its own, which varied from battalion to battalion and even between companies. A second battalion of what had become the 95th Rifle Regiment was raised in 1805 and a third in 1809 and all three battalions won a fine reputation in the Peninsular War and at Waterloo. Uniquely removed from the numbered regiments of the line in 1816 and styled the Rifle Brigade, the regiment was reduced to two battalions but the third was raised anew in 1855 and a fourth in 1857. Riflemen saw service in most parts of the Empire and participated in the First and Second Kaffir Wars, the Crimean War, the Indian Mutiny, the Second Ashanti War, the Second Afghan War, the Third Burma War and detachments with the Camel Corps on the Gordon Relief Expedition.

But there were other aspects to the Rifle Brigade. As a self-confessed 'sporting regiment' to quote the annual *Rifle Brigade Chronicle* for 1893, it was admirably suited to Johnnie's tastes at this early stage of his career, but it also maintained its reputation in the 1890s for excellent marksmanship. Moreover, although it was a close-knit family community in which junior officers were not required to address their seniors in the mess as 'Sir', it encouraged its officers towards a broader contact with civilian society than was normal and in the pursuit of activities far removed from either the sports field or conventional soldiering. Thus, one of the pioneers of electricity. R. E. Compton, had begun his experimentation in science while with the Rifle Brigade in India in the 1870s. Others such as the Hon. E. Noel, who had served in the regiment in the 1870s and 1880s, and Boyd Alexander, who served in the Rifle Brigade after the South African War, won reputations in the field of exploration.[14]

Despite Sir Charles' advice of three years previously, Johnnie found himself joining the 1st Battalion of the Rifle Brigade in India in the company of a Sandhurst contemporary, George Paley. On arrival his height was recorded in the battalion record of officers as 5' 9¼" compared to the 5' 7⁴⁄₁₀" recorded in the Sandhurst records a year earlier. His first station was Ranikhet in the foothills of the Himalayas which he reached on 23 May 1892, the battalion as a whole having returned there from its cold weather camp at Bareilly a month before. Almost immediately Johnnie threw himself into his new life for, at the annual sports meeting on 10/11 June, he won the officers' race. However, the battalion was not long at Ranikhet. In October, it began the long journey east to Calcutta. Much of the distance was covered on the march, two men dying en route, and the battalion did not reach Calcutta until 26 December. There it was to remain for two years.

Its quarters were situated in the Old Fort William on the left bank of the Hughli river, a far cry from the hill station at Ranikhet with its limited facilities. In particular, the officers were expected to fulfil a large number of social duties in the 'whirl of excitement' that marked the Calcutta season of racing, polo, cricket, balls and banquets from November through to March. Johnnie was an active participant. He played cricket for the battalion against the Calcutta cricketers. In November 1893 he again represented the battalion number nine in a team total of 209 for 9, which proved too great a target for the Calcutta cricketers. In November 1893 he again represented the battalion against Calcutta, scoring 21 runs on this occasion. But his real contribution was in polo. In December 1893 he played for the 2nd Lieutenants against Calcutta then, in February 1894, won a single polo match against McCleod, a leading Calcutta sportsman, by 5–0 over three chukkas played without changing horses. In February 1894 he also represented the battallion in the Infantry Polo Tournament at Lucknow and played in the Calcutta Monsoon Polo Tournament for both the battalion and a team led by his first cousin, Captain Charles Gough, then serving in the 12th Bengal Lancers. Another favoured pastime was participation in the paperchase cups held every Thursday from December to March. Johnnie was only an occasional competitor in 1893 but on 24 February 1894 he won the Captain Grimstone Trophy for his second place on 'Sir Charles' in the Pony Paper Chase Cup.

Each March the leave season began. In 1893 Johnnie accompanied 2nd Lieutenant Lord C. A. Conyngham on a ten-day pigsticking and shooting expedition in the Kulu district of Assam, which was marred by an accident in which Conyngham broke his arm. Johnnie also managed a shooting expedition for blackbuck while the battalion was on a march near Kirwe, fifty miles south east of Allahabad. On 14 April 1894 his second leave took him on an expedition into the Central Provinces with Major A. R. Pemberton. They were turned away from a Government Reserve Forest at Jharsuguda, forty miles north of Sumbelpoor, into which they strayed and, as a result, the bag was poor. No tigers were encountered, Johnnie missed a bison, and he returned to the battalion on 13 June with only ten head of game of which two blackbuck, three sambur and a nelgai were the largest. Nevertheless, Johnnie was a member of the battalion's leading snipe shooting syndicate for 1894.

Life in Calcutta was not all sport for the British battalion at Fort William had a large number of static guard duties to perform and there was even an officers' guard. The Calcutta season also included a camp of exercise. Between 30 December 1893 and 18 January 1894, for example, the battalion took part in divisional exercises with the 6th Bengal Infantry and 21st Garrison Battery of the Royal Artillery with which it shared Fort William, as well as two other native battalions, two English batteries, a squadron of native cavalry and the Royal Sussex Regiment. During 1893, too, Johnnie obtained a signalling certificate at the Central School of Signalling at Kasauli, taking a total of four examination papers in June and October. He was promoted to Lieutenant on 6 December.

In November 1894 the period at Calcutta came to an end and the battalion embarked for Hong Kong, arriving at the island on 15 December. It was altogether cloudier and wetter in the cold season at Hong Kong and, in March, the battalion was employed as labour during a general strike by coolies in protest against restrictions placed on them as a precaution to prevent plague in overcrowded lodgings. Johnnie, however, did not remain long with the battalion for on 12 March 1895 he went home, the *Rifle Brigade Chronicle* for the year remarking that '*mirabile dictum*' he preferred Dublin to Hong Kong as he joined the 2nd Battalion of the regiment there on 7 May 1895. Whatever his real reasons for changing battalions, he quickly became a trusted member of the new battalion. Just before coming back to Ireland he had played once more for the 1st Battalion cricket team against the Royal Navy in Hong Kong and cricket was a highly popular sport in the 2nd Battalion. Indeed, in the following 1896 season, he played regularly, although averaging only 11.4 with the bat in seven innings.

From the point of view of Johnnie's new commanding officer, Lieutenant Colonel Francis Howard, Dublin was a most unsatisfactory station through the difficulty of finding adequate space for training. Nonetheless, Howard contrived to hold as many exercises as possible including practising night outposts. After one such night exercise, Johnnie together with the Adjutant, Lieutenant George Thesiger, and Captain Arthur Acland-Hood wrote a letter to Howard purporting to be from a farmer claiming damages against the battalion for frightening his cow. Howard sent the mythical farmer £5 and the affair ended in the battalion 'lie book'.[15] After performing ceremonial duties for the state entry of the new Lord Lieutenant of Ireland, Earl Cadogan, in October 1895, the battalion moved to Corunna Barracks, Aldershot. There, Howard was far happier, as the *Rifle Brigade Chronicle* phrased it, route marching came in 'with severity'. In 1896 there were manoeuvres and the annual musketry course but, like Calcutta, Aldershot offered the 'vortex of society' with easy access to London. Johnnie again took up riding, falling in the regimental point-to-point on his mount 'Roebuck' but finishing sixth in the Divisional Light Weight point-to-point. It was at Aldershot, too, that he became a firm friend of a newly arrived subaltern, the Honourable Hugh Dawnay, who was also to find an early grave in Flanders.

In November 1895 volunteers had been called for from the battalion for a special service company for the 3rd Ashanti War. Acland-Hood was among those selected, the men eventually returning to the battalion in February 1896. Conceivably, this may have fired Johnnie's own imagination to seek service beyond the bounds of the regiment that had consumed his interest for five years. At short notice, in late August 1896, he set off for the British Central African Protectorate for which he had volunteered earlier. It meant greater responsibility than that of a platoon commander and, of course, Johnnie's first taste of active service at the age of twenty-five.

2

British Central Africa, 1896–1898

PROMOTED to full general in April 1894, Sir Charles had retired from the Indian Army in May 1895. Sir Charles and Harriette then settled at Innislonagh House in the village of Marlfield, near Clonmel in County Tipperary and close to the river Suir. The house became a haven for both Johnnie and Hubert when on leave. Having missed their parents for so much of their boyhood, Johnnie and Hubert were happiest with them and were to enjoy life among the horses and dogs at Innislonagh far more than the social round in London in succeeding years. It was from Innislonagh that Johnnie set out for his new appointment in British Central Africa: BCA in contemporary nomenclature, the protectorate would be known as Nyasaland after 1907 and as Malawi upon its eventual independence in 1964.

Having paused briefly in London, Johnnie wrote to his mother assuring her that he would have 'an awfully good time' in Africa and promising to write regularly while en route there. He enclosed some photographs of the 2nd and 4th Battalions of the Rifle Brigade, which Harriette had requested so that she could picture his friends. He related that he had visited the taxidermist, Rowland Ward, who would mount some of the heads of game Johnnie expected to send back for no charge, provided that others were offered Ward for sale. Johnnie also gathered his 'outfit for Africa'. In all, he spent a total of £44.10s.11d on such items as four pairs of tennis shoes and big waterproof boots (£2), three African tin boxes (£4.5s.6d), camp furniture from the Army and Navy Stores (£10.4s.10d), a revolver and 100 cartridges (£5.11s.0d), a 60lb spring balance (1s.8d), and a pair of khaki knicker breeches (£2.2s.0d). If nothing else, it demonstrated the need for an officer to possess private means. It also presaged a life style rather less luxurious than that enjoyed in India. Indeed, while Johnnie was to find it difficult to obtain the services of more than two or three indifferent native boys in BCA, Hubert in India was required to keep no less than seventeen servants as an unmarried subaltern.[1]

Johnnie was to travel with a fellow officer on secondment to BCA, Lieutenant (later Lieutenant Colonel) Randal Skeffington-Smyth of the

Coldstream Guards. 'Skeff', as he was soon to figure in Johnnie's correspondence and diary, had been left to book *wagons-lits* across the continent and, as
far as Modane on the Franco-Italian frontier, all went well. There, however, a
'beastly crowd' filled the railway carriage and proved tiresome enough for
Johnnie and Skeff to seek out a Cook's agent to secure a sleeping car from
Genoa to Rome. In Naples, which they reached on 26 August, they found
their ship still coaling and sought out an hotel for a bath and shave after two
and a half days without recourse to either.

At Naples Johnnie saw a number of Italian soldiers bound for the ill-fated
campaign in Abyssinia, a 'wretched looking lot altogether' with 'their noses
on the ground and not a smile among them'. His own discouragement was of
another kind for the ship that would take them to Africa was the SS *General*.
A German vessel, it was comfortable enough but it had little speed and it was
not expected that they would arrive at Chinde, the mouth of the Zambezi
river on the Mozambique coast, until early October. It was to prove a
desperately slow voyage with Johnnie chaffing from the fact that he could
draw no pay until he reached BCA. Through the heat of the Red Sea, for
example, with a temperature of between 85 and 90 degrees on deck and
worse below, the ship moved at barely 10½ knots with fearful vibrations that
made it hard to write legibly. Past Cape Gardafui and the Horn of Africa on 9
September, the ship encountered the monsoon to the considerable discomfort
of Johnnie and Skeff, who were both violently ill.

At least the bad weather kept Johnnie's fellow passengers quiet, his attitude
towards them passing from amusement to contempt. He got on well enough
with the crew, despite drifting into Hindustani rather than French on a
number of occasions, but not with the majority of the passengers, who were
Germans and Portuguese bound for their respective colonies of German East
Africa and Mozambique. The Germans appeared to begin drinking before
sunrise and 'simply kept on pouring liquid down their throats' while the
Portuguese were all 'very low caste'. Johnnie found it hard to sleep because of
the noise made by the German contingent at night and his opinion of the
quality of the European colonists was hardly enhanced when one of the
Germans was knifed by a Portuguese soldier. Johnnie resolved firmly to travel
back from Africa in a British vessel around the Cape, although a compensation was that so few of the others bathed that he and Skeff never had to queue
in the way common on P&O vessels.[2]

Judging by the passengers encountered on the boat, Johnnie was not
surprised that the German and Portuguese colonies were regarded as failures
and he evinced further evidence from his arrival in their East African
possessions. The *General* docked first at Tanga in German East Africa where
the houses were 'tumble down affairs' of plaster and wood, although a short
rail journey to up-country coffee plantations laid on for the passengers
suggested to Johnnie that the colony was at least good for game. On 16
September they put in at Zanzibar, which had passed within Britain's sphere

of influence as *quid pro quo* for Imperial Germany's acquisition of Heligo-
land under the Anglo-German Treaty of 1890. Rather than waste four or five
days while the *General* made a detour to Dar-es-Salaam and back, Johnnie
and Skeff remained at Zanzibar to inspect the palace, reduced to rubble on 27
August by two British gunboats during an attempted coup following the
death of the Sultan. The two young British officers lunched in the British Club
with the Consul-General and the local military and naval commanders, but
Johnnie was somewhat taken aback when a man to whom he was talking was
threatened by a drunken American Vice-Consul brandishing a revolver.[3]

On 21 September the voyage resumed, the next port of call being the
Portuguese port of Moçambique. Johnnie could scarcely believe that the
Portuguese had been there for 400 years. Such trade as existed was in the
hands of Indians and nothing had been done to improve the harbour. When
the tide was out, boats could not get within fifty yards of the shore and
passengers had to be carried ashore on native shoulders. As it happened, a
Portuguese military expedition was being prepared for the interior but Johnnie discovered that,

They set off amidst great excitement and the blessings of the priests, but in about a
week they begin to come back by twos and threes, and this goes on till they have all
come back. A devil of a telegram is then sent home, and crosses and stars are handed
round.

The port of Beira, which the *General* reached on 28 September, proved no
better, being 'a town of tin shanties, stores and sand'.[4]

In Beira Johnnie and Skeff left the *General*, which had passed their
intended destination of Chinde between Moçambique and Beira, and they
embarked in a small and smelly steamer called the *Peters*. Following its own
roundabout itinerary, the *Peters* also passed Chinde and ran aground at
Quelimane, from where Johnnie and Skeff were able to send a telegram
ahead to warn the British Vice-Consul of their impending arrival. They finally
reached Chinde on 8 October. It was a Portuguese possession but one with a
tiny British concession of just 200 yards by 400 yards surrounded by a nine-
foot timber stockade. The Vice-Consul had booked Johnnie and Skeff on the
Cameron, one of the latest Zambezi stern-wheelers, which they shared with a
missionary couple. Some sport was had by shooting at crocodiles and hippos
and the party also visited a riverside sugar factory. At Chiromo Johnnie and
Skeff had two days shooting with Captain Nicholas of the Royal Navy
gunboat *Mosquito*, and then proceeded for another three days seventy miles
up the river Shiré to Chikwawa in a grass 'house boat' called the *Scot*, which
towed a barge for accommodation. At this point rapids made the river
unnavigable.

Suddenly, the whole tempo of the journey quickened for while at
Chikwawa they heard that the BCA Armed Forces had gone out on an
expedition. Johnnie and Skeff hurried forward to Blantyre, twenty-eight

miles distant, in less than eight hours carried by *machilla*:

a hammock slung on a pole with a cloth roof to keep sun off, which is carried by 4 men while 8 others run along behind to relieve the others, they go at a tremendous rate and do as much as 30 to 40 miles in a day.

At Blantyre they were held up for two days awaiting instructions, which ordered them to the administrative headquarters of the protectorate at Zomba. After a final jolting journey in a 'Cape cart' drawn by mules along one of the few roads yet constructed, they arrived at Zomba on 21 October 1896.[5] It had taken over eight weeks, including forty days at sea, to reach BCA.

BCA had become a British protectorate only in July 1891 when the first Commissioner, Harry Johnston, arrived at Chiromo. Johnston himself had been instrumental in preparing the ground when, as British Consul at Moçambique in 1889, he had been authorised to report on the extent of Portuguese penetration of the interior and to conclude provisional treaties with tribes who might be prepared to accept British protection. The political manoeuvring between Imperial Germany, Portugal and Britain in East Africa was thus a prime factor in the creation of BCA and its northern and eastern boundaries with German and Portuguese territories were fixed by international agreement in 1890 and 1891. However, rival international claims were not the sole determinants of the protectorate's origins. Johnston's original treaty-making expeditions had been financed by Cecil Rhodes, who was seeking to extend the operations of his British South Africa Company north to the Zambezi. Although not entirely happy with the southern boundary for BCA as fixed in negotiations with Johnston, Rhodes continued to subsidise the protectorate until 1895.

Growing pressure for the commercial exploitation of BCA through the development of cash crops such as tea, tobacco, cotton and especially coffee also derived from the influence of Scottish missionaries, who had been active in the area since the mid-1870s. The precursor of the missionary efforts of such organisations as the Church of Scotland and the United Free Church of Scotland had been David Livingstone, who had explored Lake Nyasa and its vicinity between 1859 and 1863: Blantyre was so named because it was Livingstone's Scottish birthplace. Livingstone believed that the slave trade which flourished in the region could be undermined by the development of commerce which, hand in hand with Christianity, would ultimately civilise the African population. It was a philosophy emulated not only by the later missionaries but also by a group of Glasgow businessmen who established the African Lakes Company to work closely with the missions; it was bought up by Rhodes in 1893. Political, economic and evangelical pressures had all therefore combined to forge BCA.

However, if the protectorate's frontiers were a reality on maps in Lisbon or London, this was not so on the ground and Johnston was required to

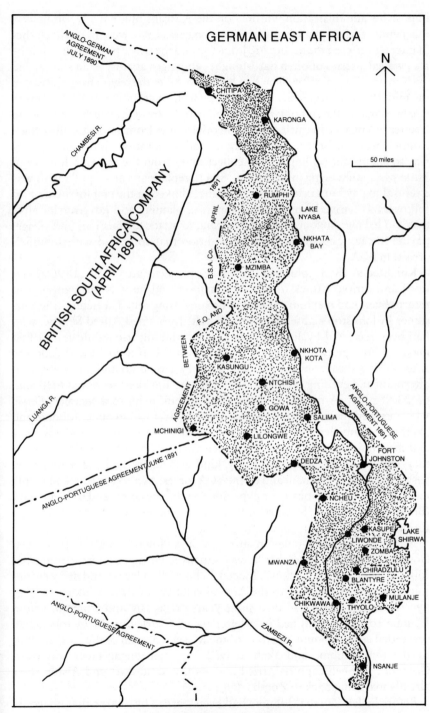

GERMAN EAST AFRICA

N

50 miles

ANGLO-GERMAN
AGREEMENT
JULY 1890

CHAMBESI R.

BRITISH SOUTH AFRICA COMPANY
(APRIL 1891)

CHITIPA

KARONGA

1891
APRIL

B.S.A. Co.

RUMPHI

LAKE
NYASA

NKHATA
BAY

MZIMBA

F.O. AND

BETWEEN

AGREEMENT

NKHOTA
KOTA

KASUNGU

NTCHISI

ANGLO-PORTUGUESE
AGREEMENT 1891

GOWA

SALIMA

LUANGA R.

MCHINIGI

LILONGWE

FORT
JOHNSTON

DEDZA

ANGLO-PORTUGUESE AGREEMENT JUNE 1891

NCHEU

KASUPE
LIWONDE

LAKE
SHIRWA

ZOMBA

MWANZA

CHIRADZULU

BLANTYRE

ANGLO-PORTUGUESE AGREEMENT

CHIKWAWA

THYOLO

MULANJE

ZAMBEZI R.

NSANJE

BRITISH CENTRAL AFRICA

impose his administration not only on the Africans but, equally, on fiercely independent white planters and the missionaries. There were frequent clashes of interest between the autocratic Johnston and the white population while he also waged a series of often hard-fought campaigns against Arab slavers and the Yao and Angoni tribes. The Yao had moved into the region from the east in the mid-19th century, while another large scale migration at the same period had been that of the Angoni (now Ngoni) peoples from the south. The Angoni frequently engaged in cattle raids upon other tribes from across the ill-defined frontier between British and Portuguese administration. Johnston's policy was to stamp out raiding and to collect taxes from the tribes, a hut tax of 3s.0d per annum being instituted in 1894 to replace an earlier poll tax. It was a refusal to pay hut tax as well as grievances linked to the employment of his followers as native labour by missionaries, planters and government alike that had led one Angoni chieftain, Gomani, to attack the missions and villages paying hut tax and spark off the expedition that coincided with Johnnie's arrival in BCA.

Knighted in 1895, Johnston had left the protectorate in May 1896 after a third and serious attack of blackwater fever and he was not expected to return: Skeff had met him in London before setting out. The acting Commissioner in Johnston's absence, a former solicitor named Alfred Sharpe, who had been recruited by Johnston while on a hunting trip, could not at first make up his mind whether to send Johnnie and Skeff to join the expedition. After a day's delay, Sharpe decided that they should go and, after a rushed afternoon and evening of preparation, Johnnie and Skeff set out at 6.30 a.m. on 23 October. A march of eighteen miles took them to a steamer, *Dove*, which carried them a further twenty miles up river to Liwonde. Johnnie and Skeff had compelled their carriers and *machilla* bearers to accompany them and they pushed on for two days to reach the mission station at Chiola. Here they could find no supplies of any kind as villages and grain had been destroyed both by Gomani and by the BCA forces. As a result, they could only move on and try and locate the expedition under the command of Lieutenant (Brevet Captain) F. T. Stewart and one of the administrators or Collectors, a former Guards officer named Edward Alston.

After covering 105 miles in just 4½ days, Johnnie and Skeff reached Gomani's kraal on 27 October. It was actually in Portuguese territory at what Johnnie described as 'Chekusi'. Indeed, in his earliest letters and diary entries Johnnie erred in referring to the Angoni chief variously as Chikusi or Chekusi. In fact, Chikusi had died some years previously and Gomani, whom Johnnie correctly identified in a letter to Sir Charles on 29 October, had succeeded as paramount chieftain of the Maseko branch of the Angoni. But, by the time Johnnie and Skeff arrived, the main engagement was over. Gomani had been captured, tried and shot, and Stewart and Alston were already marching back to Zomba.[6]

Before he left Zomba, Johnnie had been warned by Sharpe that he would probably be left behind to construct a fort to pacify the Angoni country and this proved the case. With a Sergeant Major Devoy, Johnnie selected a site at Dedza, some eleven miles east of Gomani's kraal, and established a camp there on 2 November. Another officer left behind from the main column, Lieutenant (Brevet Captain) W. H. Manning did the same fifty miles away at Gowa (now Dowa) on 9 November. A week later, Manning, Devoy and a Collector, Robert Codrington, departed for Zomba and Johnnie assumed command of both sites. Basing himself at Gowa, Johnnie was to remain there alone until 22 January 1897, when he was ordered back to Zomba to help train raw levies for the BCA Armed Forces.

Johnnie had been extremely disappointed to miss the chance of 'winning my spurs at last' in action against Gomani and, as his 25th birthday passed while on the march to kraal, mused that his own father had seen his first action at the age of only sixteen in the Sikh War. A further blow was Manning's reluctance to go after another chief, described by Johnnie both as Mpezeni and Chiweri, without instructions from Sharpe. Sharpe, however, was a far more cautious man than Johnston and let it be known that he was 'not going to be jostled into war by anybody'. Thus, the proposed expedition fell through and Johnnie could only pin his hopes on the expectation that there would be 'some good hard fighting up the west coast of Nyasa' in the new year. His discomfort was increased when Skeff, stationed by the lake, drew first blood and 'mopped up a native chief'. Yet, in reality, there was much for Johnnie to take pride in as, with that marvellous certainty of those engaged in the great Imperial adventure, he settled down to build his forts or *boma* and to administer personally an area he calculated at 60 or 70 miles by 25 miles.[7]

To assist him, Johnnie commanded a small force of Sikhs and Atonga (now Tonga) and Yao tribesmen of the BCA forces, or British Central African Rifles as they became in the course of 1896. Under the command of four or five seconded British and Indian officers contracted to the Foreign Office, there were some 200 Sikh volunteers from the Indian Army. The Sikhs served for two years in BCA, for which they received a bounty of 100 rupees and double pay. It was intended that the native contingent should number 1,000 men in eight companies, with the Atonga and Yao serving for three years for between 5s.0d and 10s.0d a month and free *posho* (food). At the time of Johnnie's arrival, the native levies were still in the process of being raised. Johnnie gave varying figures for the strength of his own force at Dedza and Gowa but, once Manning had left for Zomba, it appears to have amounted to 50 Sikhs and 120 natives as well as a 7-pounder gun, which the local Angoni looked on as a 'kind of devil'.[8]

Johnnie found his Atonga 'great men for loot and very good on the victorious side' but 'no great fighters till they see that their side is going to win'. Indeed, on 17 November, Johnnie heard that one of his Atonga had carried off a native woman while, in his temporary absence six days later, the

Atonga quarrelled with the Sikhs. Johnnie hoped that he could 'make something of them', but the complaints continued, and Johnnie despaired that his
work to gain the confidence of the local Angoni was ruined when a party of
Atonga he had sent to harry one of Gomani's followers turned to raiding
friendly villages. Sending back the fifty cattle and 200 goats seized by the
Atonga, Johnnie resolved 'to keep a real tight hand on them in future'. Yet,
despite his frequent recourse to the *chekoti* (hippo hide whip), the Atonga
still contrived to embarrass him, 'looting the people whenever I send them on
messages'. On 13 January 1897, therefore, he resorted to 1½ hours 'hard
drill' for them daily.[9]

Nevertheless, Johnnie was impressed by the way in which his Atonga could
manage to survive on so little food. Watching them erect themselves shelters
for the night before the quarters were completed at Dedza, he felt that 'it
would do a Company of English Infantry a world of good to look at them'.
For the main military muscle of his force, however, he naturally looked to the
Sikhs who assisted him in drilling the Atonga and directing labour on the
boma as he had no knowledge as yet of the local language. The Sikhs also
took a keen interest in the cattle customarily collected by way of fines on local
natives. In fact, in August 1897 when Johnnie was stationed at Zomba, he
returned from an expedition to find that the Sikhs there had stolen some of the
officers' milk cows and calves. They were thus 'capital men when on service
but in cantonments they are an abominable nuisance'.[10]

The *boma* at Dedza, which was completed with local native labour,
consisted of an earth embankment 4'3" high topped with a 10' timber
pallisade and fronted by a v-shaped ditch. Timber was hard to come by in the
immediate vicinity and entailed long trips to bring in, but it was readily
available at Gowa and here Johnnie constructed his own house of mud on a
timber frame. Both Johnnie and Manning had been 'rather proud of [them-
selves] and flattered [themselves] that no engineer could have done better' in
laying out the *boma*, while Johnnie was 'awfully proud' of designing and
building his own house. It also amused him, as he related to his mother on 13
November, to interview the local Angoni chiefs coming in to submit and
surrender their weapons.

you would laugh to see me sitting in a chair smoking a pipe, surrounded by natives,
who are all in a great funk of the white man at present, and say that he is most 'ukali'
which means 'fierce'.

Yet, Johnnie had a certain respect for the Angoni and reported that he was
compiling pedigrees for each of the native chiefs. The task was 'very interest-
ing', Johnnie's notes on the chiefs being entered at the back of his diary.[11]

Johnnie had actually received few instructions from Sharpe as to his duties
and his task was made the more difficult by the ill-defined nature of the
frontier with Portuguese territory, although little was ever seen of the Portuguese who rarely ventured out of Tete. One of the aims was 'to get all the

natives to come and settle our side of the boundary and leave a tract of uninhabited country on the border'. If necessary, Johnnie was prepared to force the tribes to come in once their crops were gathered, but 'I would treat them very liberally and give them every assistance'. In this way, he felt, 'they would take to the new country very quick' and he was anxious to reassure villagers who tended to 'fly directly they see anybody coming'. Certainly, Johnnie did his best to win over the local people. On 13 December, for example, he received seventeen headmen and, although he 'gave them a regular harangue and told them to pay their taxes', he also told them 'to look upon me as a friend'. As early as 27 October some 2,000 'friendlies' had appeared at Chekusi 'to ask for food which we gave them' and Johnnie and Skeff had been treated to a spectacular 'Zulu' war dance.

Johnnie found it desirable to detain Gomani's sister on 6 November to ensure that the Angoni continued to come in, but he released her once her brother, Mandala, appeared on 28 November. The sister received some beads and Mandala got twenty-four yards of calico. Clearly, calico was of some account in Johnnie's dealings with the Angoni since he complained in his diary on 4 January 1897 that he had spent all day on his accounts as 'one has to account for every yard of calico and have a receipt for it'. In a letter to Sir Charles four days later, Johnnie also related how he had become the local doctor 'and everyone comes to me who has a pain in the stomach' as well as how he had returned a slave girl to her mother and taken on a boy who had fled from his master after having his ear cut off. While at Gowa, he was also imposing controls on the movement of cattle to prevent the spread of rinderpest from Portuguese territory. At other times he was called upon to deal with man-eating lions, although with scant success.[12]

Contributing to the unsettled state of the country was the continued raiding and Johnnie was determined to 'sit on them tremendously'. In November a headman, who had been robbing travellers and interfering with the mails, was surprised at his village by Johnnie with two of his Sikhs. The man was arrested and sent down to Liwonde where he received six months' imprisonment from the Collector, Whicker. In December one Angoni chief, Chikunda, managed to evade pursuit by Johnnie and 45 of his men after firing at tax collectors, but one of Johnnie's Yao captured a member of a raiding gang and Johnnie had the man lashed to the 7-pounder for the night before being sent off to Whicker. On 8 January 1897 yet another Angoni headman, Chinsu Quedi, who had set upon some of Whicker's newly established native constabulary, was fined 20 goats by Johnnie. On the very same day that Johnnie fined Chinsu Quedi, he had to dispatch three men to detain another headman who had struck a tax collector with an assegai.

So Johnnie, still only 25 years old, continued to dispense justice in his domain, levying fines on pain of burning down the native villages. Indeed, by 2 December he had amassed such a herd of livestock – 370 cattle and 400 sheep and goats – that he had to sell some to missionaries and send off the remainder to Zomba. Some represented his own share of 'loot' from the Gomani expedition and he kept 47 cattle and 50 sheep and goats to provide his command with milk. He also obtained 20 chickens and a dozen pigeons which gave a 'homely look' to his house at Gowa outside which he began a small flower and vegetable garden. The garden was an experiment he was to repeat successfully at Zomba.[13]

In January Sharpe wrote to Johnnie to say 'he was very pleased to see the stringent measures I was taking to keep down raiding'. Such an accomplishment, however, was far from easy given some of the added complications with which Johnnie was faced. One problem was the activities of his own Atonga troops but, equally, when Chinsu Quedi complained to Johnnie that his village had been raided by a chief called Kambiwa, Johnnie was disturbed to find that the raiders had been accompanied by soldiers from Fort Johnston:

I called it a d--d shame and will write straight to Sharpe about it. There was Chinsu Quedi sitting on my verdandah being promised protection, etc while some grocer's assistant is raiding him in the name of the Govt. I will do my best to make it hot for him.[14]

Nor did Johnnie always appreciate the presence of the missionaries in his area.

The local missionary, Ross, a former 'cutter of uppers' at a Birmingham boot factory, was 'not at all a bad little fellow'. Ross cut Johnnie's hair for him but not his 'ripping' new torpedo beard, which Johnnie was delighted to find made people think he was at least five years older than he actually was. In turn, Johnnie nursed Ross through a bout of fever, but a group of missionaries some fifteen miles from Gowa simply got on Johnnie's nerves. On occasions, they would write for protection then write to say that they were in no danger. They complained about the conduct of Johnnie's Atonga and appeared to regard Johnnie in the same light in which the Angoni viewed Johnnie's 7-pounder. Johnnie clearly disliked their proximity and, referring to the London headquarters of the evangelical missionary societies, remarked in one letter to Hubert that 'they are always looking out for something and all our proceedings would not look well in Exeter Hall'.

Another irritation was an English planter named Diffey who had crossed into Portuguese territory in late November 1896 and begun to burn and loot villages there. He turned up at Gowa and promised to desist but more complaints followed in December and, in January, Johnnie caused a stir by referring the matter to Sharpe for, 'I think if a white man goes and sets himself up as a native chief, he should be treated as such'. Primarily, Johnnie regarded the Angoni inside Portuguese territory as much under his personal protection as if they had been on the British side of the frontier and he feared that it would encourage a resumption of raiding if they were provoked by Diffey. Diffey was then ordered by Sharpe to report to Zomba or face arrest and being handed over to the Portuguese authorities.[15]

Johnnie kept himself busy at both Dedza and Gowa with such duties. Indeed, in a letter to Sir Charles on 2 December he described his daily routine:

I begin the day by *chota-harzari* [light breakfast] at 6 a.m. and start work from 7 till 11 a.m. Then have breakfast. Start work again at 2 till 5. I have a cup of tea about 3 – and either go out shooting or watch the Atonga being drilled by the Sikhs. Dinner at 7 and turn in about 9.30 or so.

The life had its compensations, Johnnie noting in his diary that he had no need to worry about dress, 'my morning attire being pyjamas, a uniform great coat and Gum Boots'. But, it was also a lonely existence 'as one never sees another white man'. Johnnie spent his Christmas entirely alone. Not surprisingly, he was always anxious for news of home and the outside world. He was concerned for the health of Harriette – the 'Old Lady' as he called her – and for the somewhat uneven course of Hubert's engagement with Nora 'Daisy' Lewes, which his parents appear to have opposed. He was interested in Sir Charles' stud at Innislonagh and enquired frequently after his dog, Duchess, which he had arranged to be sent to Ireland from Aldershot. In terms of wider events, he had expressed his interest during the voyage out to Africa in the course of the Greek rebellion against the Turks on the island of Crete and did so on a number of occasions once he had arrived. Similarly, he was interested in finding out what was happening in Matabeleland and Mashonaland, where revolt had erupted between March and June 1896. Later, he expressed interest in the appearance of Cecil Rhodes before the Parliamentary enquiry in London into the circumstances of the Jameson Raid, and the outbreak of rebellion on the North West Frontier of India in July 1897 in which Hubert was to see service.[16]

As early as 29 August Johnnie had written to his mother from the *General* to remind her to send him regularly the weekly edition of *The Times* and this request was repeated in almost every letter from Gowa. It was supplemented by requests for copies of one of the illustrated periodicals such as the *Graphic* and of the *Field*. Johnnie had taken a selection of Dickens with him, including *David Copperfield* and the *Pickwick Papers*, and wrote that he preferred Dickens to any modern writer. He managed to obtain some books from the small library at Zomba, again mostly Dickens, including *Bleak House*, but literature was scarce and could not be bought. From time to time, therefore, he asked for additional volumes to be sent out such as Sir Walter Scott's *Marmion* and the 'Badmingdon (sic) Book on Big Game Shooting'.

The difficulty was that anything sent from Ireland took weeks or even months to arrive. The projected Cape to Cairo telegraph line was being pushed up the western side of Lake Nyasa and was due to reach Zomba by August 1897 but Johnnie expected it to be cut frequently, especially with the outbreak of hostilities in Matabeleland. He understood that a railway might

also soon be constructed from Chiromo to Blantyre but, in reality, construction was not to begin until 1903. Moreover, as Johnnie remarked in a letter to
Sir Charles in April 1897, the native mail carriers 'have to sleep in the trees
about 20 miles from here [Zomba], as the lions are so bad'. He did not receive
his first letter – from Hubert – until 12 November although it was dated 29
August, and his first letter from his parents arrived only on 19 November.
Similarly, Hubert wrote home from India to cousin Laura on 25 November to
say that he had 'not heard a word' from Johnnie. Johnnie's first copy of the
Graphic appeared only on 27 May 1897, although it was followed shortly by
a copy of Sir Charles' new book, *The Sikhs and the Sikh War*.[17]

Nor was it just letters and newspapers that took time to arrive. On 28
September 1896 Johnnie had written from Beira to ask for a pair of flannel
trousers after losing a pair in a ship-board accident: he was still vainly
enquiring after them the following June. Since the local brew was 'poison',
he had also asked in September for a case of 'Powers 10 years old whiskey', but
this only turned up on the coast, some five bottles short, in August 1897.
Rinderpest and tsetse ruled out the possession of horses in the interior and
Johnnie sent for a bicycle once he returned to Zomba from Gowa. Despairing
of ever seeing the one being sent from Innislonagh, Johnnie bought one for
£21 in July 1897 only for the bicycle from Ireland to arrive a month later.
When he broke the glass of his watch in May, Johnnie lamented that the
nearest watch repairer was in Durban.[18]

Life at Dedza and Gowa was also made difficult by the ever present threat
of disease. One of Johnnie's Sikhs died from blackwater fever on 12 November. A Royal Naval officer on one of the gunboats had died from the same
disease ten days earlier and, by the end of the month, a third man had died.
Johnnie himself felt 'seedy' from the heat at the end of November and found
the sharp drop in temperature at Gowa from 80 to 90 degrees in the day to 60
degrees at night most trying. Suffering from periodic attacks of neuralgia, he
had a bout of fever for three days in January when he returned briefly to
Dedza from Gowa although his universal remedy, Warburg's Mixture, invariably worked for him. There was also a risk from the variety of game,
especially lion and leopard, which Johnnie pursued determinedly by way of
recreation. But there were even further dangers. On 14 December he was
sitting on his verandah,

when there was a blind flash of lightning which knocked me quite silly – and I found
that a big tree about 50 yards off had been struck, the splinters fell within 20 yards of
me. I went to look at the tree but simply ran for my life as a swarm of bees were flying
about everywhere in great excitement.

On 19 January, when Johnnie was ordered back to Zomba, it was the height
of the rainy season that lasted from December through to March. In short, it
was 'a beastly time of the year to go marching'. Forced to cross several
swollen streams, Johnnie was less than amused to find Whicker drunk at

Liwonde and confusion as to whether or not his orders had been counter-manded. When he did arrive at Zomba on 27 January, Sharpe was away and Johnnie succumbed to fever for four days 'which I quite expected as I had been soaked with rain every day on the way'. Much to his disgust, some painful boils appearing at the same time proved to be 'from a certain fly laying eggs in one – which turned into maggots!!'.[19]

There were a few weeks of uncertainty as to whether Johnnie would remain at Zomba or return to Gowa. In the event, he remained to train his own company of raw levies in the BCA Rifles, an early request to his parents being for a copy of the new infantry drill manual published after his departure from England. There was no lack of company, however, for Zomba accommo-dated not only Sharpe but eighteen other white civilians, 'most of them Government clerks, etc', and a number of other seconded officers. When Johnnie arrived the latter comprised Manning, Lieutenant J. S. Brogden of the Royal Marines, Lieutenant L. L. Harper of the Royal Artillery, and Lieuten-ant (Brevet Lieutenant Colonel) Charles Edwards of the Indian Staff Corps. By virtue of his brevet Edwards, who commanded the BCA Rifles, was at 33 the youngest Lieutenant Colonel in the army.

Zomba was also comparatively comfortable. Johnnie expected to move into a brick house by August and Edwards was already living in a new house furnished with £300 worth of furniture brought out from England. How-ever, until the house was completed Johnnie had to make do with a wattle and daub affair plagued with rats until he acquired a cat. Johnnie was instru-mental in establishing a cricket club at Zomba, making 21 and 44 in the first 7-a-side match and he and Manning practised every evening for a couple of hours. There was cricket and football almost daily and Johnnie also took to taking long walks with Manning and Sharpe. To celebrate the Queen's birthday in May there was a 'gymkhana' against the residents of Blantyre with cricket, football, tennis and billiards. Johnnie did not entirely appreciate the Blantyre contingent, whom he described to Hubert as 'a drunken lot of swabs' who had been 'mostly behind plough or counter before they came out here'. However, it was not so much snobbery or class distinction on Johnnie's part but a dislike of those who failed to measure up to his own high standards of conduct.

Nevertheless, 'Zomba week' was a success. Although Johnnie was almost alone in not participating in a smoking concert, he did 'almost more' than his share in helping Zomba to victory in cricket and sprained his wrist playing football. There was a birthday parade with 350 native troops, 80 Sikhs and a battery of three 7-pounders, and races and sports were organised for the natives followed by pots of *pombe* or native beer. The troops then staged a native dance, which continued until 7 the following morning. The entire force of BCA Rifles from Zomba then went to Blantyre 'to give them a military show' for the Queen's Diamond Jubilee. There was also some horse racing, Johnnie winning all three races on a planter's horse, to the dismay of the employees of the British South Africa Company who had brought up racehorses from Rhodesia 'especially to win'.[20]

At Gowa Johnnie had thrown himself into his work as a way of fighting loneliness, but at Zomba constant exercise was a necessity in Johnnie's view as a means of preventing disease. There was no doubt that disease was more prevalent at Zomba. Following his earlier bout of fever upon his arrival, Johnnie succumbed to another four days' illness in mid-February in which his temperature touched 104 degrees. In early March Lieutenant Harper, whose company Johnnie took over in addition to his own, died of dysentery. Another subaltern, Lieutenant H. R. Beddoes of the Royal Dublin Fusiliers, became so weakened by fever that it appeared almost certain he must return home. Johnnie again had a touch of fever in early April as a result of another soaking – this on one of his regular weekend shooting expeditions to the top of the Zomba plateau. Ironically, Johnnie regarded the plateau as a particu-larly healthly environment and the white population later established a 'convalescent camp' on top of Mount Zomba.

In April, too, Alston died of blackwater fever and Edwards fell ill with the same disease. Johnnie helped nurse Edwards, but after twenty days' illness he died on 10 May 1897. For Johnnie it was a particularly chastening experience:

It rather knocks any ambition out of one, when one sees the youngest Lt. Col. in the Army dying – and one wonders where the good of getting on in this world comes in. It surely can't be any consolation on one's deathbed.

Generally, however, Johnnie expressed himself a firm believer in 'kismet', although the onset of fever tended to depress him temporarily. Despite the end of the rainy season and the arrival of colder weather at the end of May, Johnnie remained a prey to illness. He had dysentery in June and went for a few days' recuperation with a missionary couple at Domasi. In August fever struck again followed by diarrhoea in early September although, on this occasion,

It was completely my own fault as I wounded a lovely sable early in the morning and followed it till 1 in the blazing sun and then biked back about 22 miles and was so thirsty that I drunk out of a stream, of which the water was probably filthy although it looked all right.

It was all a contrast to India where he had always been so well, and concern for his health was one reason why he decided in July to terminate his secondment by the end of the year before another rainy season. He was to have one more bout of fever in October and was also ill in November from the shock of riding a horse into a iron telegraph post while racing for a planter at Blantyre.[21]

But ill health was not his only reason for wishing to leave BCA for the protectorate did not seem to offer as much opportunity as he had hoped for advancement. He often reminded his parents to send him copies of the Army

List so that he could check his progress towards the rank of Captain, and his letters to Hubert in particular displayed a belief that the Foreign Office was little interested in BCA and that greater opportunities lay in the East African Protectorate. Johnnie liked Sharpe immensely but he was clearly irritated by the latter's propensity to avoid trouble for, as he wrote to Sir Charles on 8 February,

There are a very nice lot of fellows out here now and we ought to make things 'hum' but the civil Government gives us no assistance whatsoever which is rather a mistake. Edwards tells me that one idea the Foreign Office had in sending us out was to 'check' the Germans who are pretty strong on the north end of the Lake.

A month earlier Johnnie had calculated that he would be able to save £340 from his pay in his first year in BCA, as there were few expenses to meet, and possibly £600 in two years. He hoped to buy a good hunter when he returned home. This was somewhat set back in March by an attempt by the Foreign Office 'to jump' Johnnie with a new contract in which he would be compelled to forsake any leave for three years unless he paid for someone else's passage out to BCA and refunded his own passage money. At least Johnnie was glad to note that both Manning and Edwards received some recognition for their past services in BCA.

For the most part, therefore, Zomba represented a series of disappointments. Nothing came of a rumoured expedition against a Yao chief, Mataka, with an estimated 30,000 warriors in February nor of Johnnie's hope of accompanying Sharpe on a boundary commission between British and German territory scheduled for June. By March Johnnie was treating rumours of an expedition against the Angoni around June as another 'castle in the air'. He had some hopes that Rhodes' affairs might lead to a 'row' in the Transvaal, in which case Sir Charles might be able to get him an appointment as an orderly officer. In May Johnnie began to hear rumours that the 2nd Battalion of the Rifle Brigade might be sent on the final advance towards Khartoum and Omdurman in the Sudan. Then, in early July, he received a letter from Colonel Howard to announce that the 2nd Battalion would indeed be included on the expedition if it took place. At once Johnnie wrote back to Howard to try to ensure that he could get back to the battalion. He also asked Sir Charles to raise the matter with yet another Gough cousin, although a more distant one – Colonel the Honourable George Gough, second son of the 2nd Viscount Gough, who was now private secretary to the Commander-in-Chief, Lord Wolseley.[22]

By this time Johnnie's two native companies – his 'junglies' as he called them – had improved immensely under his careful supervision. By July he considered them the equal of militia at home, even if they still called drill 'playing with the rifle'. Later, in October, they won the BCA Rifles' bayonet competition. By that time, too, they had been blooded for an expedition had taken place at long last in August 1897. Manning, who replaced Edwards as commanding officer of the BCA Rifles and also assumed the position of Deputy Commissioner to Sharpe, took four native companies comprising 400 men with 70 Sikhs and one 7-pounder against a (presumably Yao) chief, Kanyeri, who was raiding villages to the east of Lake Shirwa (now Chilwa). With him went Brogden, Lieutenant F. G. Poole of the East Yorkshire Regiment, who commanded at Fort Lister, and Johnnie who acted as staff officer until another Indian Army officer could be sent to BCA. After covering 200 miles in 9 days along jungle paths in single file, the last 52 miles in just 35 hours, Johnnie described his experiences in a letter to Hubert on 16 August:

The first day we were in Kanyeri's country I was advance guard and about 40 to 50 men came down to a stream we had to cross with the idea, I suppose, of stopping us, but I gave them a volley at 200 yards which 'made them leave that', as Uncle John used to say. We then deployed and went straight on Kanyeri's village clearing them out of the villages en route, with shrapnel and volleys.

Johnnie then took his company off separately, burning twelve villages and getting quite close to one native group without being spotted:

I then ran like a hare dropping one section to fire volleys at 300 yards and rushed the village with fixed bayonets with the remainder. They fired a few shots inside the village but the chief managed to clear. I chivied him for four miles as hard as I could run but was so done by then that I had to sit down. Altogether they lost about 40 men, but if they had really stood we would have killed a lot more.

Johnnie had been in little danger since the natives were poor shots and he found the most trying part of the entire expedition 'the long marches and filthy water'. He also suffered agonies from 'jiggers' in his toes. Nevertheless, he was pleased with the performance of his native troops and with the expedition, which had netted between 5,000 and 8,000 chickens and forty goats.[23]

The expedition over, Sharpe resumed a 'peace at all price' policy, refusing either to enforce taxation rigorously or to put down all raiding. Johnnie was relieved to be freed from the staff duties when a new Indian Army officer arrived and, in October, he went on a nine-day shooting expedition as his first leave since reaching BCA. The trip brought him 27 assorted head and, in all, he recorded 60 head of game as being his bag throughout his stay in the protectorate, each kill being entered at the back of his diary.[24]

The end was now in sight and Johnnie wrote to Sir Charles on 4 November 1897 to say that he expected to leave Chinde about 7 December and reach London about 14 January 1898. In some respects, his period in BCA had been worthwhile. He had gained some experience, was bringing back a fine collection of trophies and expected to return to the 2nd Battalion of the Rifle Brigade. He had also made a jump of six places in the Army List and could look forward to his Captaincy in the next year. But, at the same time, Johnnie felt frustrated. Soon after his 26th birthday, he wrote,

I am now rising 27!! it seems a desperate age and so far I seem to have done nothing. It is too disgusting reading the papers now, they are simply chok full of wars and fighting.[25]

By the same age, of course, Sir Charles had already won the Victoria Cross. It was hardly easy to match his father's record, although Sir Charles never showed anything but quiet interest and encouragement in his sons' careers.

Nevertheless, Johnnie found that his services had not gone unrecognised. Besides the award of the Central African Medal, which was not handed out liberally, Johnnie heard soon after his return home that Sharpe had sent a despatch to the Foreign Secretary testifying to the value of his services. It was forwarded to Johnnie in February 1898, together with a testimonial from Manning dated 29 November 1897, which had formed the basis of Sharpe's report:

The present efficient state of the two companies at Zomba is entirely due to the great interest taken by Lieutenant Gough in his work and also to his energy and tact in dealing with men who were made subject to discipline for the first time.[26]

If Johnnie could not yet match Sir Charles, he had done well in his first taste of active service. Johnnie had never expected his services would be noticed and it was gratifying to have this mention in despatches.

3

The Sudan and Crete, 1898–1899

JOHNNIE'S later letters from BCA had shown clearly his desire to get back to the 2nd Battalion of the Rifle Brigade and participate in the long-awaited final advance upon Khartoum and Omdurman. After a spell of leave he was able to do so. The battalion had moved from Aldershot to Verdala Barracks, Malta in the autumn of 1897 and Johnnie rejoined there on 14 May 1898 to a warm reception from friends he had not seen for almost two years. He penned a light-hearted account of his experiences in BCA for the *Rifle Brigade Chronicle* but, almost at once, the battalion received the anticipated warning orders on 10 June 1898 to join the British 2nd Brigade assembling for service in the Sudan.

For ten years after the death of Gordon at the hands of the Mahdi's Dervish army in January 1885, the prospect of reconquering the Sudan appeared distant. The Dervish advance upon Egypt had been halted at Ginnis in December 1885 and, thereafter, the Khalifa Abdullah el-Taaishi, who succeeded to the leadership of the Mahdist movement when the Mahdi died in June 1885, preferred to pursue territorial ambitions in Abyssinia. There was occasional skirmishing along the Egyptian frontier, as in August 1889 when another Dervish advance was turned back at Toski, and outside the Red Sea port of Suakin which represented the one remaining Imperial garrison in the Sudan. The comparative tranquility enabled the British Agent and Consul-General in Egypt, Sir Evelyn Baring (later Lord Cromer), to concentrate on the financial recovery which was deemed a prerequisite for reform and stability in Egypt. In turn, stability offered the hope of eventual evacuation, to which both Liberal and Conservative administrations subscribed, and of better relations with the French, who viewed the British presence with the utmost suspicion.

However, in his second administration between 1886 and 1892, Lord Salisbury had come gradually to accept the need for Britain to remain in Egypt indefinitely and, indeed, to extend her control to the Sudan to offset Italian ambitions in Abyssinia and the southern Sudan and French interest in the Upper Nile and Equatoria. Returning to office for a third time in 1895, Salisbury still regarded reconquest of the Sudan only as a long-term option and not one to be contemplated before the completion of a railway line through Uganda enabled the main thrust to be made from the south. Events were precipitated by the catastrophic defeat of an Italian army at Adowa in Abyssinia in March 1896 – Johnnie had seen the wretched Italian troops bound for Abyssinia when en route to BCA. The defeat threatened to encourage co-operation between the Abyssinians and the Khalifa against the European presence in the region and thus to strengthen the power of the Khalifa, which had been assumed to be weakening steadily.

A number of factors had conspired to delay the completion of the Uganda railway so the British advance into the Sudan would now have to proceed by way of Egypt. This began in June 1896, ostensibly as a diversion to take Dervish pressure off the Italian garrison at Kassala on the Atbara tributary of the Nile in the southern Sudan. In reality, Salisbury had seized the opportunity presented to recover lost territory, while at the same time serving British interests in international power politics. By demonstrating support for Italy, Salisbury was shoring up the Triple Alliance, in which Italy was a partner with Imperial Germany and Austria-Hungary, so that the political power of France and Imperial Russia should not be enhanced and the balance of power in Europe be tilted in their favour.

The successful occupation of Dongola by Anglo-Egyptian forces in September 1896 was followed by that of Berber in August 1897, the latter abandoned unexpectedly by the Dervishes after a limited Anglo-Egyptian advance on Abu Hamed. In many respects, the campaign then took on its own momentum as the Sirdar of the Egyptian Army, Major-General Herbert Kitchener, called for more British troops in December 1897 to repel an anticipated Dervish counter-attack on Berber. By this time, too, it was apparent that a French expedition commanded by Captain Jean-Baptiste Marchand, who had been sent out from France in June 1896, was attempting to establish a line of outposts between Brazzaville and Djibouti in order to gain control of the headwaters of the Upper Nile and, at the very least, to compel the British to concede a conference on the future of the entire Nile valley. In January 1898, therefore, Kitchener was promised the troops he required.

The first British contingent arrived in the Sudan to join the Anglo-Egyptian army in late January 1898, forming the 1st Brigade under Major-General William Gatacre. The Dervish advance on Berber all but ground to a halt through indecisive leadership in February and March 1898 and their army was put to flight at Nakheila on the Atbara river on 8 April. In order to complete the task begun so hesitantly two years previously, further reinforcements were then authorised including a second British brigade. Under the command of Brigadier-General the Hon. N. G. Lyttelton, who had commanded Johnnie's battalion in India, it would comprise a maxim detachment of the Royal Irish Fusiliers; a detachment of Royal Engineers; the 1st Battalion, Grenadier Guards from Gibraltar; the 1st Battalion, Northumberland Fusiliers and 2nd Battalion, Lancashire Fusiliers, both already in Egypt; and Johnnie's battalion from Malta.

Following the warning order to Johnnie's battalion, a number of officers and men failed the medical inspections held on Malta on 16 and 17 June and it was arranged to make up the vacancies from drafts from the 1st Battalion, Rifle Brigade in England. In fact, the 2nd Battalion had arrived in Malta seriously deficient in numbers and over 500 men had already been detached from the 1st Battalion when it passed through Malta on its return from service in Singapore in the previous February. In all, eight officers arrived on the SS *Nubia* on 11 July, one of whom had been allegedly offered £600 by another subaltern's wife to exchange with her husband in Malta. Some of the new arrivals, such as Lieutenant George Paley, were old friends of Johnnie, but others were young and inexperienced. Indeed, Johnnie felt that the battalion now had many officers 'too inexperienced to be put in responsible positions'. Several would probably 'knock up' with hard work and Johnnie blamed the War Office for 'posting them to us when they must have known we were going on service'.[1]

That Johnnie should evince such concern befitted his own experience of action in BCA and his new-found status as the only subaltern to command a company – A Company. Johnnie took one man from the new draft of other ranks as two of his company were boys, who must be left behind in Cairo once the battalion reached Egypt, making his command some 114 strong for active service. He worked hard to prepare them, for he had found, on issuing the men with overseas equipment such as helmet shades and spine pads earlier in July, that 'they always want everything done for them'. By the time they sailed from Malta on the *Nubia* on 12 July, Johnnie felt the battalion as a whole had improved its readiness. Colonel Howard had instituted a series of daily practices in advancing and volley firing and they had worked out a flexible means of organising fire and movement for the eight companies of the battalion. Johnnie hoped that 'a little roughing it' would benefit his men still further but he also took along footballs, handballs and fishing tackle for their amusement.[2]

The journey from Malta was comfortable and the battalion disembarked at Alexandria on 15 July 1898. Entraining for Cairo at 5.30 the following morning, they encamped on the dusty parade ground of the Lancashire Fusiliers at Kasr-en-Nil Barracks. As the next day was a Sunday, Johnnie visited the Cairo zoo and, on 18 July, the battalion paraded early at 4.45 a.m. to avoid the heat of the sun and marched off towards the pyramids. Johnnie's apprehensions of officers 'knocking up' were being fulfilled only too accurately. One subaltern was left in hospital at Alexandria before the battalion even left for Cairo and another who fell ill on the same day had to be sent back to Malta a week later. Hugh Dawnay succumbed to fever on 18 July and, ironically, Johnnie himself felt off colour and was found to have a temperature of 104°. Dust and flies in the tents on the barrack square were hardly conducive to recovery and Johnnie moved to hospital on 20 July to be tended by a 'motherly old nurse'.

The regimental doctor diagnosed flu but Johnnie himself suspected 'Maltese fever' and, although he left hospital after three days, he was not fit enough to play in a cricket match between the battalion officers and those of the Lancashire Fusiliers. He was able to visit the zoo again – evidently a Sunday entertainment – on 24 July in the company of George Paley and George Thesiger but, on the following day, neither Johnnie nor Hugh Dawnay was strong enough to go up the pyramids to which they had been taken by Howard. As Johnnie noted in his diary on 26 July, it was generally a 'bad sign' if he did not enjoy smoking and he later confessed to Hubert that he had been is a 'funk' that he would be left behind. He was determined to go and, accordingly, he marched with the first half of the battalion to proceed to the Sudan to Cairo station on 27 July. The amount of equipment carried in 'Xmas-tree order' made him sweat 'freely' over the relatively short distance covered on foot to the station but he had made it.[3]

The train reached Luxor at noon on 28 July. There was sufficient time for the officers to ride off on donkeys to find baths at the local hotel before the men were embarked in a narrow-gauge train at 4 p.m. A staff conference blocked the gangway so that Johnnie and half the battalion officers failed to secure dinner that evening and it was another staff officer who woke Johnnie at 3 the next morning as the train approached Shilal. During the four hours spent transferring to a Nile steamer there, Johnnie took the opportunity to acquire a new Egyptian servant as one he had hired in Cairo had disappeared at Luxor. For the officers, the steamer *Ibis* offered a 'ripping' deck with plenty of space since it was fitted to accommodate thirty, and the half battalion mustered but fourteen officers. Nevertheless, George Paley still contrived 'to keep on sticking his enormous feet' into Johnnie's face all night. By contrast, the men were accommodated in two-decker barges towed alongside and Johnnie felt sorry for 'the poor devils' confined there and loaded down with 'greatcoats and two haversacks full of kit for the campaign and water bottles'. The two-day journey up the Nile to Wadi Halfa was also unbearably hot, Johnnie noting in his diary for 30 July that it was 'much the same as yesterday – heat, heat, heat!'. To make matters worse, they ran out of both milk and lime and Johnnie suffered a stomach upset which he put down to drinking Nile water. The latter was a filthy 'thick pea soup colour' although they did have filters. Later, they also put alum into it, which caused the mud to sink to the bottom after about three hours and made the liquid more palatable.

At least the nights were reasonably cool with the temperature dropping to a mere 80° from the 115° during the day and Johnnie took to sleeping on the top deck despite being covered in smuts and cinders from the engines. Nevertheless, it was, as Johnnie wrote to both Hubert and his mother, a 'very jolly

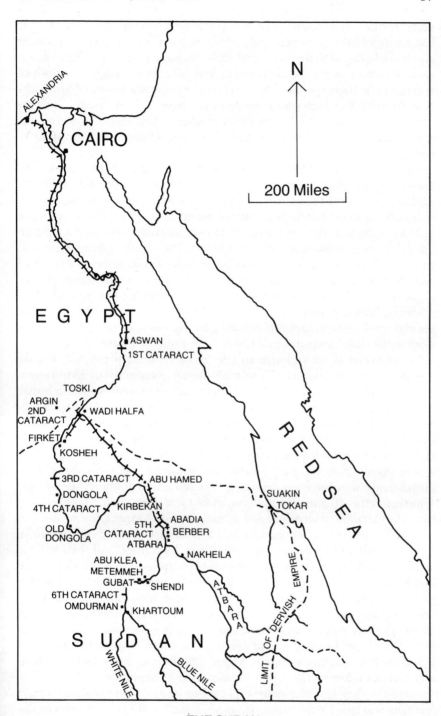

THE SUDAN

party' and he was 'as happy as I ever hoped to be in this life'. Just as in BCA, he had arranged for newspapers and periodicals to be forwarded to him and he also had editions of Shakespeare and the Bible, both 'capital reading'. Johnnie amused himself by playing chess and by watching the passing scenery, which was not as he had expected. For the most part, it was a matter of low rocky hills 50 to 60 feet high on each side of the river, a bank fringed with the ubiquitous date palms and frequent water wheels. Abu Simbel, however, was a particularly impressive sight with its 'wonderful figure carvings' up to 70 feet high.[4]

The *Ibis* reached Wadi Halfa at 1.30 a.m. on 1 August. Someone sounded the rouse to Johnnie's great annoyance since nothing could be unloaded until daylight and it only served to wake the men, who 'made a most abominable noise talking, in spite of the free abuse of the officers'. Finally disembarking at 4.30 a.m., the baggage was transferred to yet another train. After a frustrating delay, the men were marched off to breakfast washed down with Nile water while the officers fared rather better in an Egyptian army mess. At 4 p.m. the half battalion entrained once more, but the accommodation proved to be no more than cattle trucks, 33 men or eight officers to each. Surprisingly, Johnnie found the truck reasonably comfortable despite the cool of the night and the dust, each officer having an *angareb* or camp bed in which to sleep as the train bumped slowly towards the camp at Atbara.

By now early starts and arrivals had become standard practice, but the disembarkation at Atbara at 3 a.m. on 3 August in the midst of a sand storm was 'altogether very nasty'. Gatacre, now promoted to command both British brigades, came down to meet the train and, soon afterwards, Kitchener himself. Johnnie missed the latter, having been sent ahead to pitch camp outside the fort at the confluence of the Atbara and the Nile. It was no easy task with tents to which the men were unused; the men were still unwashed and unshaven from the train journey and everyone was soon coated with dust. Johnnie was simply too busy to get himself a meal although he managed some tea about 10 a.m. That afternoon Gatacre demanded a fatigue party from the battalion of an officer and 50 men to build a zareba around his goat house. The divisional commander had a poor reputation with the British troops, to whom he was known variously as 'Backacher' and 'Fatacre'. He could rarely delegate and it was not perhaps surprising that Johnnie should find him on first acquaintance inclined 'to hustle people too much'. As for the goat house, Johnnie quite expected that Gatacre 'will want a fatigue party under an officer to catch his chickens for him'. Nor was Johnnie impressed by Gatacre's ideas for forming brigade square, which took some eleven minutes if everyone 'ran like hares' and Johnnie put more faith in the ability of Lyttelton and Lyttelton's Brigade-Major, Charles à Court – the future military correspondent of *The Times* Charles à Court Repington.[5]

Although they had originally expected to hasten towards Khartoum, a fortnight was spent in the Atbara camp while the 2nd Brigade assembled. The second half of the Rifle Brigade arrived on 4 August in much the same state as Johnnie's party. The following day, Johnnie was detailed to lay out a camp for the 1st Battalion, Grenadier Guards. The Guards' arrival caused Johnnie no little amusement, but also resentment:

The Guardees were very funny when they saw the camp; every officer seemed to want a tent to himself. Their Colonel wanted to put the men's kitchen right in front of Lyttelton's tent but was told he had better put them elsewhere. Really the way they are pampered is disgraceful: they have been given four more tents a company than us, although they are the same strength. Their officers were given a saloon carriage up from Wadi Halfa, all other officers being stuck into cattle trucks.[6]

But, if there were rivalries in the 2nd Brigade, there was also a degree of hostility towards all the newcomers from the 1st Brigade, which was recipro-cated in kind until the latter began its move further up the Nile on 12 August under the command of Brigadier-General A. G. Wauchope.

Meanwhile, preparations continued at the Atbara camp. For Johnnie there was a fatigue duty of preparing a ramp beside the railway so that artillery could be offloaded. Similarly, he worked with his company on putting a telegraph line across the Atbara river. Hard training also took place both at battalion and brigade level although the Northumberland Fusiliers only arrived on 10 August and the Lancashire Fusiliers six days after that. Various manoeuvres were practised, some 'quite impossible', while Kitchener's only comment upon seeing Gatacre's forming square movement was that 'it was undoubtedly very good protection for the Brigade staff'. On 12 August field firing was practised, requiring a slow advance, firing on the move, and strict control. Johnnie found that the Northumberland Fusiliers next to his own company kept rushing forward and masking the fire of his men so that many would have been shot in a 'real show'. But Johnnie was pleased with his own company's progress both in musketry and fending for themselves as indivi-duals, although they were still inclined to charge too soon in attack without his closest supervision. Johnnie was also still worried that the battalion had 'too many children amongst the officers', even if he was confident that no other battalion in the Sudan was as efficient. Of one young subaltern in the battalion, Second Lieutenant Alex Harman, he wrote to Hubert that the other officers would say, 'he eats well and drinks well and sleeps well, but any work is too much for him'.

Life at the Atbara was made unpleasant by frequent sand storms which necessitated wearing goggles by day. Nor did the storms subside by night. On one occasion Johnnie's own belongings were blown away in the night and, on another, when he was sleeping at the end of the officers' tent line, he found his colleagues' possessions flying over his head. He also misplaced the 'machine' he was using to cut his friends' hair. A number of his fellow officers had succumbed to fever and Johnnie himself was again weak for several days. However, he found time to go shooting for dove and pigeon with George Thesiger and to go riding or walking with Thesiger and Reginald Stephens.

He dined with Gatacre and also with the assembled war correspondents and artists covering the campaign. Regular evening entertainment included 'sing songs' and there was the compensation that there were no insects or mosquitoes.[7]

Rumours were rife as to the likely conduct of the final advance upon Khartoum with some 23,000 Anglo-Egyptian troops expected to concentrate at Shablucka by 22 August and the 'big fight' anticipated around 10 September. Again, the battalion would move forward in two parties, the first leaving on 19 August. On this occasion, however, Johnnie found himself in the second rather than the leading party. There was a delay to their departure, but the steamer *Abu Klea* eventually arrived on 22 August to convey the battalion's second half. There were no cabins for the twenty officers on the steamer and Johnnie suffered an attack of neuralgia as the *Abu Klea* progressed with painful slowness up the Nile. By day the heat was stifling and, on the second night, there was a violent storm in which much equipment was lost overboard including a good many helmets. Everyone was a 'bit jumpy' that they would miss Kitchener's advance and, to their chagrin, they were overtaken by another steamer conveying the 21st Lancers. Johnnie resolved that there was little point 'distressing oneself over the inevitable' – that same belief in 'kismet' he had displayed in BCA – and he found some consolation in seeing the pyramids of Meroe and reflecting upon a lost civilisation. It was not the way of all his fellow passengers and the battalion's second-in-command, Major George Cockburn, eventually vented his anger at the slow voyage upon the steamer's hapless engineer. When the *Abu Klea* did finally reach Wadi Hamid on 26 August, it was to find that the main force had indeed left but without the Sirdar himself. Catching his first glimpse of Kitchener, Johnnie found him 'not at all an imposing looking man, but smart, with curious light blue eyes which strike one at once, as his face is so sunburnt'.

One company – C Company – was ordered to board another steamer at once to follow the main army, but Kitchener stopped half of it because he judged the barges carrying the men overloaded. The remainder of the battalion pitched shelters for the night and were then set to work on the morning of 27 August loading more barges with ammunition and stores. They worked solidly from 5 a.m. to 6 p.m., companies embarking one at a time as the barges were prepared. Captain H. M. Biddulph, commanding D Company, found himself with Kitchener aboard his barge and was so 'hustled' by the Sirdar's presence that he actually left 41 men behind. Even Johnnie began to wonder if they would ever manage to get away, with the advance guard of the army reputedly only 40 miles from Khartoum.

Three companies had gone by the end of 27 August including half of Johnnie's A Company under the command of Lieutenant John Harington, who had originally 'ploughed' a medical in London but then somehow contrived to get out to Cairo and rejoin the battalion. It was said that one of the Khalifa's gunboats had been blown up on a mine intended for the British, while news was received of the British gunboat *Zafir* capsizing through overloading. No lives were lost but valuable guns and ammunition ended up at the bottom of the Nile. Finally, the steamer *Akasheh* arrived for Johnnie's half company to be embarked. Passing the Shablucka cataract, they disembarked at Rojan island after dark on 28 August. Rising at dawn on the following day, they unloaded the barges and crossed the river to find no transport available for them. A seven-mile march took Johnnie's men to the main army in its zareba, where a particularly wet and stormy night was endured lying on the ground.

Reveille was sounded at 4 a.m. on 30 August and the entire Anglo-Egyptian force then marched for thirteen miles in hollow square towards Sayol. After the exertions of the last few days, Johnnie's men were 'very beat' scrambling through thorns and over stones and Johnnie dosed himself with quinine to ward off a slight fever. Fortunately, there was no night alarm although Johnnie had to take his turn at a one-hour stand-by duty between 1 and 2 a.m. The army moved off again at 5.30 a.m. with the cavalry actually coming up against Dervish mounted troops. The British division was formed up and the opportunity taken to refill water bottles, but the Dervish cavalry melted away and there was no action. Camp was pitched on a ridge known as Sururab just six miles short of the Kerreri hills, which looked down upon the Mahdist capital of Omdurman and the old city of Khartoum beyond. However, no sooner had the men begun to construct the zareba for the night than staff officers ordered it sited 200 yards further back. Johnnie was far from amused: 'Staff officers should be very particular in the first place so as to get everything shipshape ones (sic) and for all.'[8]

The very next morning more poor staff work came to light when the battalion found itself being led into a long nullah full of water. They had to march around it in a detour of some seven miles which took a great deal out of Johnnie's men. But, as they emerged from the Kerreri hills, they all heard the sound of the British gunboats bombarding Omdurman, Johnnie writing later to Harriette that 'it was worth seeing everyone chuck up their heads and quicken the pace'. They halted a mile beyond the hills and were just completing a defensive zareba when the order came to stand to as the Dervishes were advancing. However, the Khalifa stopped about four miles short of Kitchener's position and a new zareba was then constructed at the point to which the Anglo-Egyptian army had advanced to meet the challenge.

The zareba thus formed bulged outwards from the Nile around the village of El Egeiga, the river protecting the rear of the Anglo-Egyptian army. The 2nd Brigade was posted to the left or south and Johnnie's battalion, in turn, parked at the furthest point of the zareba towards Omdurman, where its field of fire was actually obstructed by a small village about 250 yards to its front. The great danger was a night attack, which might panic the Egyptian and Sudanese battalions in the army. The searchlights of the gunboats were thus constantly sweeping the plain in front of the Anglo-Egyptian positions throughout the night and all sentries were doubled. There was sporadic firing from Dervishes and, at 11 p.m., just as Johnnie was finishing an hour's duty, there was a sudden alarm. Johnnie fell in his company, who achieved it so quietly that many of those behind his position never knew it had been effected. Indeed, when Johnnie toured the lines with Howard and Lyttelton, they found the commanding officer of the 32nd Battery, Royal Artillery soundly asleep: Johnnie noted in his diary that Lyttelton had been 'annoyed'. There was a further alarm at 3.15 a.m., but again nothing materialised.

At 5.45 a.m. on 2 September 1898, the Anglo-Egyptian army was paraded while the cavalry went out on reconnaissance. Johnnie was late for breakfast and managed only a cup of cocoa before the cavalry began retiring before a force Johnnie estimated at between 45,000 and 50,000 Dervishes. The army had begun to march out of the zareba but now manned the position anew with little expectation that the Dervishes would actually press home an attack against such a well-defended position; but, as Johnnie remarked in his diary, 'By Jove, they did!' It was a remarkable sight:

We first saw Banners topping the low hills to our right and then the whole line came into view. It looked about 3 miles long and as thick as peas. As we were watching these men on the right, we saw some more flags on their left (about 2,000 yards off). They came over the rise in great style.

Johnnie could not help being struck by the 'plucky' Dervish advance, the enemy cheering wildly with their banners flying under the 'tremendous fire of guns, maxims and rifles'. The Dervishes opened fire at about 8,000 yards, sending bullets 'singing over one's head', but the Anglo-Egyptian force did not do so until the massed ranks of the Dervishes were within 2,000 yards of the zareba.

The intense fire from the Anglo-Egyptian positions forced the Dervishes to the right of the zareba and, to Johnnie's later disappointment, the Rifle Brigade was ordered to double across to their right to support the 1st Cameron Highlanders and 1st Seaforth Highlanders of the 1st Brigade. Johnnie's company lay down some 50 yards behind the Highlanders:

A man in my Company was hit at once just to my left, and the men had a very poor time doing nothing, just watching the bullets hitting the sand and seeing the Camerons getting hit just in front of us, altogether as nasty a kind of work as ever I want to do – no excitement by firing ourselves, simply standing still. 9 of our men got hit, 1 killed by a bullet through the head. We were really very lucky to get off so light; some of the bullets went uncommon close, the only thing I did not like was turning round to speak to my men, as I thought I might take it behind! which would never have done!

Concentrated fire broke the Dervish advance by about 9 a.m. and the 2nd Brigade was ordered to execute a wide turning movement on the left flank as Kitchener ordered an advance from the zareba.

The Rifle Brigade was once more on the extreme left and had some difficulty keeping up over the sand and rocks under a 'burning' sun and with

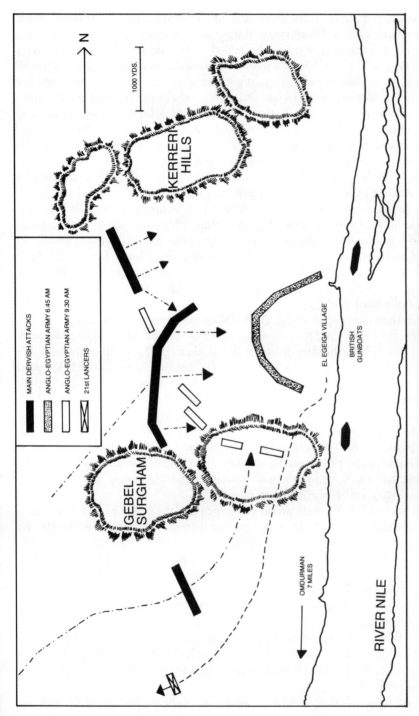

THE BATTLE OF OMDURMAN, 2 September 1898

KERRERI HILLS

GEBEL SURGHAM

EL EGEIGA VILLAGE

BRITISH GUNBOATS

RIVER NILE

OMDURMAN 7 MILES

1000 YDS.

N

MAIN DERVISH ATTACKS

ANGLO-EGYPTIAN ARMY 6.45 AM

ANGLO-EGYPTIAN ARMY 9.30 AM

21st LANCERS

sporadic sniping from the thousands of Dervishes attempting to flee across their front back to Omdurman. Rather than halt his advance to fire on the snipers, Johnnie sent twenty of his best shots out ahead of his company to try and deal with them. Many wounded Dervishes, who attempted to keep on firing, were also dispatched, Johnnie remarking that it was 'necessary but nasty'. Few of his men had had much to eat that morning and water bottles began to empty so that the company was 'most fearfully done up' by the time the advance was halted at about 1.30 p.m. At each halt two or three men had fainted and, when water was eventually brought up, Johnnie had to revive his Colour Sergeant by pouring it over his head.[9]

Most of the fighting during the advance had taken place far to the right of the Anglo-Egyptian line including the reckless charge of the 21st Lancers and the defeat of a second Dervish advance by Hector MacDonald's Sudanese Brigade. When the general Anglo-Egyptian advance was resumed at about 4.30 p.m., the line of the 2nd Brigade was straightened and it marched direct for Omdurman. Despite the stench of countless dead donkeys, the lack of any water and occasional sniping and firing, some the result of Sudanese troops looting, Johnnie's men 'lay down on their arms and slept like logs' after a 'fearfully hard day'.

On the following morning, the battalion marched back towards the zareba in search of water and Johnnie saw some of the estimated 7,000 Dervish dead. By comparison, the British had suffered about 500 casualties in Johnnie's estimation. In fact, the Dervish loss was conceivably in excess of 11,000 dead while the Anglo-Egyptian force had just 48 dead and 434 wounded, the majority in the 21st Lancers and the Sudanese Brigade. Johnnie visited the ruins of Gordon's palace and attended the moving memorial service on 4 September. Having penned a very hasty note to Sir Charles on the day after the battle, Johnnie set down to write a fuller account for his mother for he was conscious, as he had remarked to Hubert in an earlier letter, that he had been altogether 'too hot and too busy' to write to the 'old people' as often as they would have wished during the campaign.[10]

Johnnie felt immensely proud of his men and the way they had stood up to the physical strains of the campaign, but he regretted that the battalion 'did not get more of a chance'. Some of the army was already going back down the Nile while the Camel Corps had taken up the pursuit of the Khalifa, who had slipped out of Omdurman in the closing stages of the Anglo-Egyptian advance. Johnnie had to perform police duty in the Dervish capital – in reality, 'a lot of low mud houses 15 to 20 feet high, dotted about anyhow' – but he also explored the old city of Khartoum with Thesiger and rode over the battlefield again: Dervish wounded still lay out untended. On 5 September he had a touch of fever and four days later he had to leave a champagne lunch with the officers of the Grenadiers and Lancashire Fusiliers as he was feeling 'a bit seedy'.[11]

Two days before the onset of 'seediness', Johnnie had heard the rumour that a French force – that of Marchand – had reached Fashoda on the Upper Nile. Kitchener left the following day to confront the French, who were compelled to withdraw and, in March 1899, forced to accept a new division of spheres of influence in Central Africa. In the case of the Rifle Brigade, however, which had anticipated a leisurely voyage back down the Nile, another international crisis required their services: on 10 September they were ordered to Crete. By steamer and train the battalion retraced its route of July and August and arrived at Alexandria on 19 September. They sailed that same night aboard HMS *Tyne* and the SS *Augustine* to arrive off Candia (now Iraklion) on 23 September 1898.

The hurried departure from the Sudan for the Rifle Brigade, and also for the 1st Northumberland Fusiliers, had been occasioned by an attack on a detachment of the Highland Light Infantry and the murder of the British Vice-Consul and 600 Greek Cretan Christians on 6 September by Turkish Cretan Muslims known as Bashi-Bazouks. The presence of the Highlanders on Crete as part of an international peace-keeping force was itself a product of the Greek revolt against Turkish rule on the island that had aroused Johnnie's interest when he was en route for and serving in BCA. The desire of the Greek Christian majority – 270,000 compared to 70,000 Muslims – for freedom from Turkish rule had accorded well with ardent nationalism on the Greek mainland. There had been an earlier revolt on Crete between 1866 and 1868 when the Greek government had appealed unsuccessfully for European intervention against the Turks. When revolt erupted again on Crete in 1896, the Greeks appear to have expected support from the Great Powers and they began themselves to send troops to the island.

In fact, the European powers wished to maintain the status quo in an area of precarious stability and they agreed upon a naval blockade to restrain the Greek government. Indeed, Allied warships did fire on Greek forces on occasions. However, they did also suggest that Crete should become autonomous and put together a joint expeditionary force to occupy the island in March 1897. Unwilling to accept such a solution, the Greeks launched a disastrous war against Ottoman Turkey in April to seize both Crete and Macedonia, but when the Turks speedily overran Thessaly, the Greeks were compelled to accept European mediation. A compromise peace was imposed by the Great Powers by which the Turks withdrew from Thessaly in return for a sizeable Greek indemnity. Crete, meanwhile, was judged to be an autonomous province under Turkish suzerainty with the Allied contingents remaining in occupation to ensure a smooth transition to an indigenous Cretan administration. Britain, France, Italy, Austria–Hungary, Imperial Russia and Imperial Germany all participated in the occupation, although the German and Austrians withdrew in May 1898 in protest at what they judged to be the pro-Greek proclivities of their partners.

Ironically, the archaeologist Arthur Evans regarded the British Military Commissioner, Colonel (later Major-General) Sir Herbert Chermside – an officer with considerable experience of Turkish affairs – as being hopelessly biased in favour of the Turks. In particular, the archaeologist's anger was aroused by Chermside's inability to secure the release of Evans' Greek guide falsely imprisoned by the Turks in Candia when supposedly protected by Chermside's authority. Consequently, in articles published in the *Manchester Guardian* and later issued as a separate pamphlet in October 1898, Evans alleged that Chermside showed too much deference to the Turks and allowed their garrison to remain in effective control of the British zone around Candia. The Bashi-Bazouks were thus left free to terrorise the Christian population whereas, by contrast, the French had exerted full control over their zone around Sitia. However, Evans did recognise that there had been atrocities on both sides in what had resembled almost internecine conflict between rival town and village communities and that the British forces were just too small to restore order.

Initially, the 2nd Battalion, Seaforth Highlanders, half of the 2nd Battalion, Royal Welsh Fusiliers and No. 4 Mountain Battery, Royal Field Artillery had been sent to Crete in April 1897, contributing to a total Allied force of some 5,000 men. The Turks had a garrison in excess of 10,000 and the civilian population as a whole was itself heavily armed. Nevertheless, the Seaforths and the artillery were withdrawn to Malta in November 1897 when peace was signed between Greece and Turkey leaving just the Welshmen, who had been brought up to full battalion strength in July. In August 1898 the single British battalion was relieved by the 1st Battalion, Highland Light Infantry which took over the duties at both Candia and Canea (now Khania) where the 'International Board of Admirals' presided over the island administration.

The attack on the HLI, which cost them 35 casualties, resulted from the decision of the Allied admirals to take over the Tax Office in Candia and relieve the Turkish authorities of tax collection so that the proceeds could be devoted to raising a Christian gendarmerie to supplement the peace-keeping force. It was a decision much criticised by Francis Howard when the Rifle Brigade arrived on Crete, since the Highlanders had had to manage a number of outlying picquets and had barely 250 men available in Candia in the midst of a heavy local concentration of an estimated 20,000 Bashi-Bazouks. Moreover, since the Turks remained nominally associated with the Allied contingents in keeping law and order – the Turks had frequently complained that the Allied presence prevented them from protecting Muslim communities against Christian attack – nothing had been done to establish entrenchments or other fortifications around the British quarters inside the city walls for fear of hurting Turkish susceptibilities.[12]

The immediate necessity after restoring order was to provide for the rapid repatriation of the 4,000 Turkish troops still on Crete since there was a justifiable suspicion that the attack on the Highlanders had been encouraged by some Turkish officers and officials. There was also an urgent need to disarm both Christian and Muslim communities. Seventeen Bashi-Bazouks were apprehended for the murder of the British Vice-Consul with Howard presiding over their trial. Accounts vary, but it would appear that between five and twelve of the accused were hanged for the crime while others implicated in the rising were shot by Allied firing squads. The duty of hanging the ringleaders fell to volunteers from the Rifle Brigade under the supervision of George Cockburn, who was grabbed by one of the condemned men and nearly thrown into a ditch when he asked them for any last requests or messages.

With both the Highlanders and the Northumberland Fusiliers, the battalion was now quartered on top of the broad walls of old Candia, sharing accommodation with the Turkish garrison. Howard kept careful watch on the Turks and, as the day set for their repatriation on 5 November approached, the battalion and the Fusiliers surrounded the Turkish quarters. Escorted down to the dockside, the Turkish officers refused to embark, so Howard had a company of riflemen marched between the Turkish officers and their men. On the pretext of a conference, he got the Turkish officers to board the waiting ship where Chermside visited them with parting gifts: their troops were then embarked without incident.

The battalion's attention was then devoted to disarming the population. Over 1,000, mostly elderly, rifles were surrendered by Bashi-Bazouks alone and Howard persuaded the Christians to do likewise, although he suspected that both communities concealed as many weapons as they handed over. It was a process hampered by the onset of enteric fever in the battalion, a 'privilege of having been in the Soudan', according to the *Rifle Brigade Chronicle*, as it seemed the source of infection was probably contaminated water drunk from a stream on the night after the battle of Omdurman. Three officers and 35 other ranks were to die of the disease with many others, including George Thesiger and Hugh Dawney, evacuated to Malta to recuperate. The water at Candia was also suspect, with an investigation of the well used by the battalion revealing the bodies of five Christians that had been missed during the clean up of the September massacre.

The Christian community showed no inclination to assume the responsibility for the administration of the island and Howard was requested to second some of his officers for the purpose. Thus George Paley assumed control of the Temenos district while Johnnie, who like Paley had escaped enteric, was appointed District Commissioner of the Malevesi district, one of several locations popularly supposed to be the original source of Malmsey wine. Johnnie had previously been on outpost duty with his company at Yfferakia (now Yiofirakia), but was now to administer his new district, disarm the population and raise a local Cretan constabulary. He was also to dispense justice much as he had done in BCA: George Cockburn did the same in Candia in a court invariably peopled with cattle, sheep and produce as well as claimants. Another archaeologist, D. G. Hogarth – later head of the Arab

Bureau in Cairo during the Great War and a patron of T. E. Lawrence – has left an account of the activities of one British subaltern on Crete at this time who may serve as representative of them all:

He knew no word of Greek, and it was told of him that when he arrived on a polo pony to be a father to some twenty villages, the local Bishop called in state, bringing, as the ingratiating custom is, a turkey or two and a clutch of eggs. Our young law-giver, nosing a bribe, put him into the street, eggs, turkey and all.

Hogarth also sat in the subaltern's court, the 'judge' presiding in cricket shirt and knickerbockers, smoking 'his best loved briar' and hearing a case on sheep stealing and another in which a local woman falsely accused a man of assault. The man was fined a few piatres and the woman sent to hoe the Bishop's potato field for 14 days. ' "Ah! this is Justice," ' one headman remarked to Hogarth ' "We have not known it before on Crete!" '

Of Johnnie's own precise role little remains although his signature has survived on two deeds transferring the property of a Muslim to two Greeks in the village of Agios Myron and dated 25 May and 8 June 1899; while identification of some of the Cretan constabulary shown surrounding Johnnie in a photograph apparently taken at the same village at this time indicates that they were mostly prominent members of the local community. Among them was the local physician, Dr Zoudianos; an elected representative of the Canea assembly, Georgios Ioannidis; a future Greek M.P. and the owner of a wine business, Ioannis (Yangos) G. Macrakis; and a local man, Michael Hatzakis, whose statue still adorns the village square in Agios Myron. There was little relaxation as such with the battalion so widely dispersed, but Johnnie did manage a major though unsuccessful shooting expedition for ibex on Mount Ida.

Promoted to Captain on 5 December 1898, Johnnie also contrived to acquire another signalling certificate in the course of the year. On 12 May 1899 he appeared back in Candia briefly to command one of the battalion guards of honour for the state entry of Prince George of Greece, to whom the Allied powers had resolved to hand over the administration at a suitable time. In fact, Prince George had been on the island since November 1898 when, much to Howard's amusement, Johnnie had been mortified to discover that one of the Cretan constables he had allocated as the prince's bodyguard was a convicted murderer: Howard calmed Johnnie's fears by remarking that most of the Cretans were probably murderers anyway.[13] Howard had then left the battalion on the expiry of his period of command to be succeeded by Lieutenant Colonel C. T. E. Metcalfe.

Chermside left Crete in June 1899 and turned his duties over to Metcalfe. In July it was decided that Prince George should now assume all responsibility for civil administration and, on 24 July, Johnnie returned to the battalion from the Malevesi district. Just before relinquishing his command, Chermside wrote a most friendly letter to Johnnie in which he thanked him for his 'very prompt, intelligent, and accurate administrative work' and for the 'zeal, energy and ability' he had displayed. Subsequently, as Chermside had promised, Johnnie found that he was one of fourteen out of twenty-seven British officers engaged in the civil administration to be specially mentioned in Chermside's report for their 'ability, energy and judgement':

In little over a fortnight, these gentlemen successfully conducted the disarmament of a Province of some 100,000 inhabitants and organised local Governments and Gendarmeries, opened the district to the free circulation of Christians and Mahomedans and gained the confidence of the inhabitants.[14]

Chermside also expressed his regret that Johnnie was not going in for the Staff College entrance examination that year, because his duties on Crete had prevented him from undertaking the necessary preparation.

Once he had returned to London, Chermside generously raised the matter of the Staff College with the Commander-in-Chief, Wolseley, who promised a place for Johnnie in the following year since George Thesiger was the battalion's nominee for the current year. However, since Wolseley's guarantee was only verbal, Chermside had also spoken to Major-General Sir Neville Lyttelton, now back at the War Office as Assistant Military Secretary, and to George Gough, who was still Wolseley's private secretary. Lyttelton suggested that Johnnie write to him the following year even though Lyttelton would probably have moved on to a command at Aldershot.[15]

Back on Crete, Johnnie quashed a suggested anti-marriage club among the subalterns and captains by arguing that the projected fines ranging from £100 for a Captain to £300 for Second Lieutenants wishing to marry come 'at a most inappropriate moment'.[16] He also produced two ibex for the menagerie race at the annual regimental sports on 25 August, these animals probably being those that accompanied the battalion to South Africa later in the year and one of which survived as a battalion pet for some years.

By September 1899, the Rifle Brigade was the sole British battalion left on Crete and it was anticipated that they would soon be off to Bermuda. However, the growing crisis in South Africa intervened and, as soon as the Lancashire Fusiliers arrived on 1 October to relieve them, the battalion was embarked for Cape Town via Suez. The P&O vessel, which Johnnie recalled as the SS *Jelunga* and other accounts as the SS *Britannia*, broke down no less than four times en route through faulty feed pumps to its boilers. When the ship reached Aden, the battalion heard of an ultimatum presented to the British government by the Boer republics on 9 October: by the time they had reached Zanzibar on 19 October, a war had begun.

4

The Siege of Ladysmith, 1899–1900

A S an avid recipient of newspapers from home when on active service, Johnnie had shown himself keenly aware of the possibilities of professional employment in emerging international crises. In BCA, the Sudan had beckoned. Rather more fortuitously, Johnnie had also become involved in the affairs of Crete, in which he had expressed a continuing interest while in BCA. Another of his speculations there had been the prospect of some final conflict in South Africa to settle the issue of supremacy between Briton and Boer which, by 1899, many Englishmen believed to be long overdue. Indeed, writing to his parents from Crete on 30 September 1899, before the transport arrived, Johnnie declared, 'I hope that the Boers will not exist as a state by next Christmas, and then the Englishman will be able to go about in the Transvaal without being insulted.'[1]

Johnnie's reaction to the *casus belli* provided by the status of the so-called Uitlanders – British and other foreign immigrants – in the Boer republic of the Transvaal was understandable in view of the attention devoted to it in the British press. But the Uitlanders, who had arrived in the Transvaal with the discovery of gold on the Witwatersrand in 1886, were far from being the real issue at stake in southern Africa. The Boer descendants of the Dutch settlers, who first colonised the Cape of Good Hope in 1652, had passed under British rule in 1806. Their reaction to British policies, not least the intention to abolish slavery throughout Britain's imperial possessions, had led to the Boer 'Great Trek' of the 1830s. Away from British influence beyond the Orange and Vaal rivers, they had created their own states of Natal, the Transvaal and the Orange Free State. Concern for the security of the Cape route to India led to Britain annexing Natal in 1843 and the Orange Free State in 1847, while the attempt of the Transvaalers to intervene brought their defeat in a sharp action at Boomplaatz in 1848. However, there was then a reaction in Britain itself against imperial expansion and Britain abandoned its interests in the Transvaal and the Orange Free State in 1852 and 1854 respectively.

The imperial tide quickened in the 1870s and the British annexed the newly discovered diamond fields around Kimberley on the edge of the Orange Free State. The two Boer republics still appeared to pose a serious threat to the stability of British interests and, in search of some kind of federal solution to the problems of southern Africa as a whole, Britain moved in to annex a bankrupt Transvaal in 1877 and, not without difficulties, to crush Zulu military power two years later. But, in 1880, the Transvaal Boers rose in revolt and inflicted a series of humiliating defeats on British forces, culminating in that at Majuba on 27 February 1881. The result of this first Boer war was a conditional independence for the Transvaal in which Britain remained nominally responsible for the republic's foreign affairs.

It appeared that the Transvaal would again slide into bankruptcy, but the situation was transformed by the discovery of gold, which threatened to confer political supremacy upon the Boers by virtue of sheer wealth. Nevertheless, the influx of the Uitlanders drawn by the goldfields challenged that supremacy since they soon constituted a majority of the Transvaal population. Epitomised by their president, Paul Kruger, the Transvaal Boers clung determinedly to political power with the Uitlanders contributing five-sixths of the republic's tax income and being denied participation in the franchise. However, the Uitlander cause found powerful support from the 'Rand lords' such as Cecil Rhodes, Julius Wernher and Alfred Beit – men who had made their fortunes in the Kimberley diamond fields and were intent on securing full control of the goldfields as well.

In fact, Britain's interests appeared to be best served by expansion in the midst of the 'scramble for Africa' among the great powers of Europe. In southern Africa, Pondoland had been annexed in 1884, Bechuanaland in 1885 and Zululand in 1887, all thwarting Kruger's own attempts to widen Boer influence. Further afield, of course, Johnnie himself had witnessed the rivalry of the great powers in central Africa and had participated in the final conquest of the Sudan and the Upper Nile. Rhodes, too, had a dream of a Cape to Cairo railway running entirely through British possessions. The British South Africa Company (BSAC), with which Johnnie had come into contact in BCA, had been chartered to create what became Rhodesia – Mashonaland and Matabeleland had both been pacified by 1893, although there was the subsequent revolt three years later. Rhodes now cast covetous eyes on the Transvaal and a Uitlander revolt was planned with his support and with the knowledge of the British Colonial Secretary, Joseph Chamberlain. In the event, the uprising failed to materialise through the cosmopolitan composition of the Uitlander community, but Rhodes' administrator in Rhodesia, Dr. L. S. Jameson, then gambled by launching an invasion of the Transvaal with BSAC police. It was a foolhardy venture with the collapse of the Uitlander plot and Jameson was surrounded and forced to surrender on 2 January 1896, just three days after crossing the frontier.

The repercussions of the Jameson Raid were serious. Rhodes was compelled to resign as premier of the Cape Colony and to appear at the inquiry in London, which Johnnie had followed with such interest. Throughout southern Africa, Boer opinion was mobilised against what was regarded as a plot by the British government. The support of the Cape Dutch was lost and the Orange Free State concluded a defensive agreement with the Transvaal, which itself moved to modernise its armed forces. Chamberlain now wished to tread carefully but his choice as new High Commissioner to restore the Imperial position in South Africa was an ardent imperialist, Sir Alfred Milner, who was resolved to manoeuvre Kruger into direct conflict. In December 1898 an English Uitlander was shot dead by a Boer policeman after a brawl and, orchestrated by a leading employee of the firm owned by Wernher and Beit, over 21,000 Uitlanders petitioned Queen Victoria for aid.

Grasping this opportunity, Milner persuaded the British government that, if it now neglected to support the Uitlanders' grievances, it risked forfeiting British supremacy in South Africa and increasing German influence through the Transvaal. Reluctantly, the British Cabinet acknowledged that it must act although it hoped for compromise. Milner entered negotiations with the Boer leaders at Bloemfontein, capital of the Orange Free State, in May 1899, but all attempts at a compromise foundered on the hard-line attitudes displayed on both sides. Having waited for the grass to grow fully on the veldt to support his mounted commandos and convinced of the inevitability of war, Kruger issued an ultimatum on 9 October demanding the withdrawal of all British reinforcements landed in South Africa since June, the withdrawal of all British forces from the frontier, and the recall of any troops en route to South Africa. Two days later, Boer commandos invaded Natal and Cape Colony.

Despite Milner's machinations and skilled manipulation of the press on behalf of the Uitlanders, the British Cabinet had made singularly few preparations for the conflict in the hopes of compromise or of a relatively small show of military force being sufficient to nudge Kruger into concessions. As a result, the Cabinet had delayed taking the advice of its military advisers and it was only on 8 September 1899 that it was agreed to reinforce the existing 5,000 strong British garrison in Natal. Two additional battalions had been sent to Natal in August and it was now proposed to bring the total of reinforcement to 10,000 men. The majority were sought from British garrisons in India, but three battalions, including the 2nd Rifle Brigade, were found from the Mediterranean. If war broke out an army corps would be sent to the Cape from England under the command of General Sir Redvers Buller – its mobilisation was finally ordered on 7 October – but, in the interval, the Quartermaster-General at the War Office, Lieutenant-General Sir George White, was sent out to take command of the reinforcements in Natal.

White landed at Durban in Natal on the day that mobilisation was finally agreed in London, but it would be some time before his command would be assembled. Johnnie's battalion, for example, was still at sea. The actual preparation of the Rifle Brigade for the voyage had proved arduous for

Johnnie in particular since Hugh Dawnay had gone down with fever and Johnnie had taken over his duties as adjutant with little idea of what had been arranged. In all, 26 officers and 864 other ranks embarked on 2 October, but, incredibly to Johnnie, 160 of the battalion's best men had been withdrawn by the War Office at the very time it had warned the battalion for service. All boys and invalids also had to be left behind and the battalion was still suffering the effects of fever, which had struck in its last month on Crete. Johnnie had some doubts concerning Metcalfe's abilities as compared to such an outstanding Colonel as Francis Howard, but he had the same two subalterns – Harington and Fergusson – and 85 of the men who had served with A Company in the Sudan so 'we are pretty handy at anything from cooking down to picking up any loose articles that may be wanted (looting!)'.

Personally, Johnnie was anxious to see action again: 'I hope we go up with the main body, as although with such a large force a company commander would probably never get a chance still one would learn an awful lot.' At the same time he hoped that Hubert, who was attending the Staff College in England, and other Gough relatives in the army would get their chance. He anticipated that Hubert would do well although he confessed to Sir Charles in a letter on 18 October that 'I only wish I felt as certain of myself, but I mean to have a real good bid if I get the chance'. As the troopship made its slow progress towards the Cape, Johnnie and his colleagues studied the likely course of the campaign.

Expecting to go to the Cape, it was concluded that the battalion would become part of the main army under Buller advancing through Bloemfontein to the capital of the Transvaal at Pretoria – a 'long walk but perfectly safe' by Johnnie's reckoning. He remarked in his diary that intelligence on the available routes was surprisingly good and he also showed a good appreciation of the strength of White's force in Natal, which must hold any initial Boer advance, and the subsequent flank support that White must give to Buller once the main army had arrived. Johnnie expected the exposed British garrison at Mafeking on the frontier between Bechuanaland and the Transvaal to fall, but anticipated that the one at Kimberley would be able to hold out until relieved.[2]

Arriving off Durban at last in a heavy sea on 26 October, the battalion learned that its orders for the Cape had been countermanded. When White reached Natal, he had discovered that the General Officer Commanding in the colony, Major-General Sir Penn Symons, had pushed a brigade forward to Dundee and split his meagre forces in the face of an unexpectedly high concentration of between 15,000 and 20,000 Boers. Persuaded that withdrawal from such an exposed position as Dundee might induce a rising among the Afrikaner population in Natal or conceivably result in even more serious disturbances among the Zulu, White allowed Symons to remain – it was a decision that Johnnie roundly condemned when he reached South Africa.

In fact, Symons' brigade secured two early victories over small Boer forces at Talana Hill on 20 October and at Elandslaagte on the following day, but Symons himself was mortally wounded and, in face of superior Boer numbers, the brigade had to pull back to Ladysmith, ironically without any of the dire consequences predicted. White was well aware that Ladysmith, which had been the army's principal station in Natal since 1887, was equally exposed and that the most sensible line of defence would be on the river Tugela some fifteen miles further south. Withdrawal from Dundee and concentration at Ladysmith also stripped troops from Durban and the colony's administrative capital at Pietermaritzburg. But White decided to attempt to strike a decisive blow at the Boers from Ladysmith. It was in such circumstances that Johnnie's battalion was disembarked at Durban rather than allowed to proceed to the Cape.

Three companies, including A Company, were taken off the ship immediately, the men being lowered into lighters and tugs by basket since the ship could not cross the harbour bar. Soaked by spray and driving rain, they were pushed into a train for Pietermaritzburg. Although there were already reports of fighting at Greytown to the north east and at Ladysmith itself, the companies were ordered to prepare a camp for the rest of the battalion by the local commander, Brigadier-General (later General Sir James) Wolfe Murray, who struck Johnnie as both fussy and incompetent. Pietermaritzburg was unpromising as a potential garrison since it was dominated by surrounding hills and Johnnie felt that the battalion, the remainder of which arrived on the evening of 27 October, and the 300 or so other details and volunteers available would achieve little by trying to defend the town. He recognised that the Boers were skilled fighting men, but the early reports of British success suggested that they had deteriorated since 1881 and Johnnie believed that it would be only a matter of time before the Boers were forced to retreat. He assumed that White would await a Boer attack at Ladysmith and wanted desperately to get there for the six weeks or so 'useful fighting' he expected. On 28 October he got his wish: orders were received to move seven companies to Ladysmith in haste with two days' rations and two blankets, a waterproof and 200 rounds of ammunition per man.[3]

Detraining at 2.30 a.m. on Monday 30 October, Johnnie found that, contrary to his own tactical appreciation, White had not waited for the Boers but was trying to force the issue himself. Marched out at once to support Colonel (later General Sir) Ian Hamilton's brigade at Limit Hill, the battalion arrived in time to cover the retreat of White's beaten army. Johnnie saw the 1st and 2nd battalions of the 60th (King's Royal Rifle Corps) and the 2nd Gordon Highlanders retiring 'in the most awful confusion' while, elsewhere on the field, the 1st Royal Irish Fusiliers, the 1st Gloucesters and a battery of mountain guns were cut off and forced to capitulate when White failed to extract them. Johnnie considered the surrenders a 'most disgraceful affair', but thought White's conduct in abandoning them verging on the criminal. The battalion fell back into Ladysmith and spent the night of what became known as 'Black Monday' at Tin Houses Camp. It had been a chastening experience for Johnnie and he hoped he would 'never see another like it'.[4]

For White, too, it had been a shattering day and he subsided into indecision. On 2 November the Boers cut the railway and telegraph lines to the south and the garrison was trapped. When leaving Pietermaritzburg for Ladysmith, Johnnie had written to his mother that she 'must not mind if you do not hear very often, but you can be certain I will write as often as possible and as fully'. He had anticipated that there might be some temporary interruption of communication with Ladysmith but no more; a letter started to his parents on 10 November was not to be completed and posted until 2 March 1900!

Rather like Pietermaritzburg, Ladysmith was unsuited to defence. Situated at the edge of a plain, it was surrounded by commanding ridges and hills. Only those to the south, known to the British as Wagon Hill and Caesar's Camp and to the Boers as the Platrand, lay within the British perimeter, which extended for eleven miles around the town. The Rifle Brigade were allocated to the north western corner of the defences, manning Leicester Post and King's Post. Three companies were at King's Post, including Johnnie's, and it was also the brigade headquarters of none other than Francis Howard, who had come out to South Africa to take command of 8th Brigade with the local rank of Major-General.

Content to contain the garrison, the Boers pushed on to the Tugela to await any attempt at relief by Buller, who had arrived at Cape Town on 31 October. For Johnnie and his men, the siege rapidly became monotonous in those first few weeks. There was outpost duty but it was largely a matter of digging deeper shelters against Boer shells – Johnnie likened them all to rabbits seeking their burrows when a shell was fired. By 10 November, however, he had already got so used to shelling that 'one hardly looks to see where they go' and there was general amusement when young Fergusson was hit on the bottom by a spent shell. But Johnnie recognised that there would be losses in time. With that same fatalism that had marked his attitude to danger in both BCA and the Sudan, he wrote in the letter he was keeping up for his parents that 'if one is bowled over one's self (sic), I can only say that it is the death I would choose, and my real anxiety is not for myself but for the Old People at home'.[5]

Shells often came very close to Johnnie during the siege. On 22 November, for example, he and Hugh Dawnay, with whom he shared a 'dog-hole', got 'seven shots all to ourselves' from a Boer pom-pom. Ironically, the pom-pom was a one-pounder Maxim gun, not yet in service with the British army, which the Transvaalers had purchased from a British firm after the Jameson Raid. Then a larger gun on Thornhill's Kopje had joined in the bombardment and put a shell on top of a wall, behind which Johnnie was situated with a working party. On 1 December Johnnie was covered in dust when another shell burst on the same wall and that day his company seemed to be 'pursued'

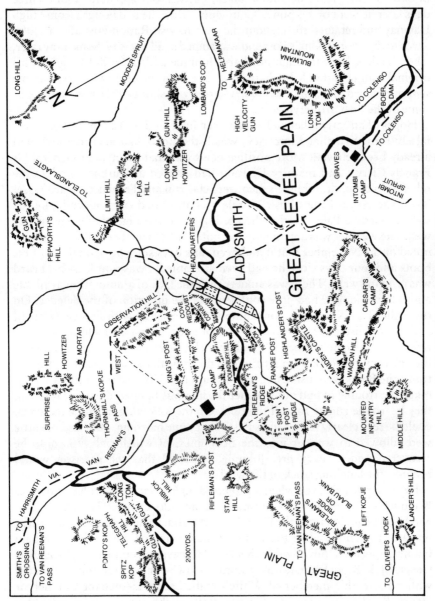

THE SIEGE OF LADYSMITH

by shells. There was also the danger from Boer snipers. Johnnie spotted one through his telescope on 17 November and fired three shots of his own when he saw the Boer leave his hiding place, but without apparent result. Three days later he went on his pony, 'Chin-chin', which he had bought from Hugh Dawnay and retained throughout the war, to visit Ration Post about 1,000 yards to the west of King's Post and was sniped at all the way. Some time later, when reading back through his diary, Johnnie added 'So did I' against his original comment that 'Chin hated it'. Indeed, for the next two days, Johnnie sent out picked men from his company to try to shoot either Boer snipers or some of the Boer artillerymen.[6]

Hopes of an early relief had at first been high, and on 12 November it was falsely rumoured that Kimberley, which the Boers had also invested, had already been relieved. More positive news was that Lieutenant-General Sir Francis Clery's 2nd Infantry Division had arrived at Durban to effect the relief of Ladysmith. Johnnie's men were cheerful and Francis Howard was a 'great success' at King's Post. Morale was also lifted every morning by the sight of George Paley's red nightcap. But there were inevitable tensions as well. The weather was appallingly wet until mid-November and Johnnie also noted on 12 November that it had been nine days since he had taken off his boots and four days since he had even attempted a wash; at least his beard was growing well.[7] There was anxiety over the lack of ammunition available and Johnnie for one had little confidence in the direction of the defence. On the night of 23 November, for example, he had sat up with Francis Howard and Paley to listen for sounds of a 'hare-brained scheme', which Johnnie also referred to as no better than a 'monkey trick', to let loose a railway engine on the line running north from the town in the hope that it would crash into any trains the Boers were using to bring up supplies. None of the staff had 'even taken the trouble to find out whether the line was tampered with or not' and they heard the engine run off the rails. On the following morning its wreck could be seen clearly from King's Post. That same morning, 200 head of cattle were allowed to wander into the Boer lines, of which only 70 could be recovered under heavy fire. Johnnie despaired that the garrison would become 'the laughing stock of the world'.

He was much relieved when a projected night attack on a ridge known as Blaauw Bank to the west of Ladysmith was abandoned on 29 November, as it had become obvious that the Boers knew the attack was coming. Johnnie had no faith in White, while the Chief of Staff, Major-General Sir Archibald Hunter, appeared 'full of wild schemes'. The cavalry commander, Brigadier-General J. F. Brocklehurst, was 'painfully slow' – an opinion Johnnie shared with a more able member of White's staff, Brevet Lieutenant Colonel Sir Henry Rawlinson.[8] The intelligence staff in the town was simply 'disgraceful'. To add to the disappointment, it was also now clear that Clery would not be attempting to advance until he had some supporting artillery.

Thus, days passed 'very much like one another'. Johnnie was convinced that the garrison needed a success and that, while it was too seriously stretched to take and hold positions beyond its existing perimeter, there was no reason why they should not attempt to seize a Boer gun or stage some lightning raid. On the night of 4/5 December, he got his chance to put into effect a scheme of his own. Johnnie's plan was to raid Thornhill's Farm, close to the railway and about 1½ miles beyond the British lines at King's Post, where, it was believed, Boers slept at night. Johnnie took his own company and that of George Paley, amounting to six officers and 177 men. They slipped out at 1.30 a.m. in heavy rain and pitch darkness. A great deal of Boer wire entanglements had to be negotiated before they surrounded a group of houses by a railway crossing and the farmhouse beyond. Sadly for all concerned – Johnnie called it 'cruel hard luck' – there were no Boers there although, if there had been, Johnnie was convinced none could have escaped. At least they had the consolation of looting armfuls of fresh vegetables and, when they got back to the British lines at about 4.45 a.m., were greeted with the news that Lieutenant-General Lord Methuen was advancing on Kimberley and that Buller had reached Pietermaritzburg to direct operations for the relief of Ladysmith.[9]

Three days later, Hunter, who had praised Johnnie for a 'good bit of work' at Thornhill's Farm, led a larger raid by 600 of the Imperial Light Horse – mostly Uitlander refugees from the Transvaal – and National Carbineers to capture a Boer 155mm 'Long Tom' and 4.5″ howitzer on Gun Hill. A revived spirit had gripped the defenders and, on the night of 10 December, Johnnie together with Colonel Metcalfe, Hugh Dawnay, an NCO, two men and an artillery officer named Wing, crept out to make a preliminary reconnaissance of Surprise Hill, where the Boers had another 4.5″ howitzer and a searchlight.[10] Despite the renewed activity by the garrison, the Boers appeared to post few if any picquets at night and Johnnie was delighted to be selected to lead an attack on Surprise Hill with five companies of the battalion on the night of 11 December. In his on-going letter to his parents, he wrote that he did not expect the Boers to stand and fight, but if anything did happen,

I want you both to know that my thoughts out here were constantly of the old people at home, and that my constant wish is to be a credit to them, and also a credit to my regiment.

The companies told off for the raid went out of the British lines at 11.30 p.m., the start being delayed for 1½ hours because of a bright moon. Half of E Company under Lieutenant G. B. Byrne was left at the railway line close to the perimeter defences and, after covering some 2,000 yards of difficult terrain, the remainder of Byrne's men were left in a donga at the foot of Surprise Hill. Reginald Stephens' B Company and George Paley's G Company were left halfway up the steep ascent, leaving Johnnie's company to attack with the support of George Thesiger and H Company. Both A and H Companies had been reinforced with an additional section from C Company and Johnnie deployed his men with two sections of H Company to his left and one to the right. The rest of Thesiger's men remained in immediate reserve together with some engineers sent up to destroy the gun.

Just fifteen yards from the summit, they were challenged by a sentry in English who fired on them. Metcalfe, leading with Johnnie, responded with a shout of 'Fix swords and charge', and Johnnie's men swept over the gun position, Johnnie loosing off a shot at a Boer in the gun emplacement as he rushed past. Halting his men some fifty yards beyond the gun, Johnnie kept them firing volleys for half an hour while Lieutenant Digby Jones of the Royal Engineers endeavoured to destroy the howitzer. The fuse failed at the first attempt and by the time the gun was blown up almost 2,000 Boers were swarming around the hill. The Boers were also dropping shells on to the hill top, one grazing Johnnie in three places. Johnnie remained to the end, recording that he 'never was in such a hot place in my life'. The companies had to cut their way back with the bayonet. Johnnie had to prevent some of his men from charging back up the hill at the Boers and ordered them only to fire if they could see the enemy distinctly and to rely on the bayonet to fight through any who had slipped around the flanks of the hill. At some point he had given his carbine to a pioneer and, becoming separated from his men, helped to bring in the wounded and to collect stragglers until daylight. Apart from the shrapnel grazes, he had been cut on the chin by a bullet and tipped on the finger by another. He also arrived back covered in blood from a wounded man he had carried.[11]

Johnnie had been delighted by the compliment paid to him in his selection to lead the attack and was well pleased with the battalion's efforts even if the cost had been relatively heavy. His own company had suffered the worst. Fergusson had been killed leading back part of the company and there were another five dead and fifteen wounded with two missing. From the 438 men of all ranks who had participated, twelve were dead, seven missing and 35 wounded. Some were seriously hit including Second Lieutenant A. Bond, whose leg had been smashed, and George Paley shot through the chest and hip.* It was estimated, however, that between 30 and 40 Boers had been killed and perhaps 60 or 70 wounded and it had done much for battalion and garrison morale. Unfortunately, the effect was much diluted by a blow that dashed the garrison's hopes and reduced them to near apathy. On 8 December they had heard that Methuen had been repulsed along the Modder river, but on 19 December came news that Buller, too, had been defeated at Colenso:

---

* Paley had been shot by Deneys Reitz, the son of the Transvaal State Secretary, whose account of the South African War, published in 1929, gives an alternative Boer view of the siege.

Buller has got the knock, it is too awful for words, 12 guns lost and over 1,200 casualties. How on earth it happened we have no idea; the accepted idea is that his guns got too far in front, and got knocked out by infantry fire. I must say the Boers teach our generals a lesson about the value of infantry fire, in my humble opinion it is the most deadly, and shakes troops more than artillery fire if it is only given a chance.[12]

To echo Johnnie's words, Buller had indeed got the 'knock'.

Having reached the Cape, Buller had recognised that he must relieve Ladysmith as well as securing Cape Colony before there could be any general advance on Bloemfontein or Pretoria. At the same time, something must be done to rescue Cecil Rhodes, who was trapped in Kimberley and addressing ever more urgent appeals for relief. Buller therefore split up his army corps with Clery's division being sent to Natal, Methuen's 1st Infantry Division sent towards Kimberley, and Lieutenant-General Gatacre's 3rd Infantry Division defending the Cape. Disaster befell all three. Gatacre blundered in attempting a night attack on Boer positions at Stormberg on 10 December and he lost almost 700 men as prisoners of war. Methuen had already been jolted at the Modder on 28 November and was thrown back at Magersfontein on 11 December. To complete 'Black Week', Buller attempted a frontal assault across the Tugela at Colenso on 15 December. As Johnnie heard four days later, such an attack against well-entrenched and concealed Boer riflemen was suicidal. Marching his army back to Frere, Buller sent two badly worded cipher messages that were to cost him his position as Commander-in-Chief. To the War Office in London, he appeared to suggest that Ladysmith should be abandoned to its fate while the second message, sent to White in Ladysmith by heliograph, appeared to counsel the town's surrender if he could not hold out for another month.

Johnnie learned confidentially of Buller's message from Francis Howard although the gist of what Buller had suggested became well enough known throughout Ladysmith in due course. Forage for horses was short, but Johnnie calculated that there were still rations for two months. However, 'if we are left here and have to surrender for want of food, I mean to leave the Army, as I never could hold my head up again'. Bond and Paley were both still in danger of losing their legs, and Johnnie's mood was not improved when the battalion was pulled into temporary garrison reserve; the wagons they were given to take them to any threatened point seemed likely to present the Boers with an inviting target for their artillery. Back at King's Post on 22 December, Johnnie found that the Boer howitzers were improving their aim and that the 'brilliant staff here' would not allow any more of Ladysmith's tin houses to be pulled down to provide more material for bomb-proof shelters. Moreover, there had been an outbreak of enteric, which had so badly hit the battalion on Crete.[13]

Nevertheless, there were still some grounds for optimism with rumours of further reinforcements reaching Buller and news of the appointment of Field Marshal Lord Roberts as Commander-in-Chief to supercede Buller, who was left commanding only the Natal Field Force. The latter news arrived on Christmas Eve and, on the same day, Johnnie received a message by helio-graph from his cousin, Alan Gough, at Estcourt, who reported that Hubert was also with Buller's forces. Hubert had been released from the Staff College on special service and had arrived at Cape Town on 15 November. After serving briefly with some Natal volunteers, he was appointed to the staff of Colonel the Earl of Dundonald and was soon commanding a composite squadron in Dundonald's mounted brigade. Hubert had been anxious for news of Johnnie from the moment he arrived and learned from Major Douglas Haig, who had been on the last train out of Ladysmith, that Johnnie had still been safe at that time. On 1 December, a war correspondent managed to get out of Ladysmith and Hubert discovered to his great relief that Johnnie was still alive and well. Hubert passed the news at once to Sir Charles and Harriette back home at Innislonagh. On the day Johnnie was preparing for the attack on Surprise Hill, Hubert was attempting to send his brother a heliograph message and tried again on 26 December, but there was no reply to either as 'I am afraid a great many don't get through'.[14]

At Ladysmith Christmas and the New Year proved relatively quiet, although the Boers lobbed over a few shells on Christmas Day and enlivened the New Year with firing their guns and rifles in the air. Johnnie managed a 'desperate big dinner, plum pudding espccially' on Christmas Day, but generally, life under siege had become very trying. It was impossible to find time to leave King's Post, except occasionally on a Sunday, and Johnnie was unable to visit Bond and Paley in the hospital established by mutual agreement at Intombi some miles outside the British lines. The guns of Buller's army could be heard most mornings, but Buller failed to send any news of his intentions and Johnnie was amused at a new name someone had coined, 'Sir Reverse Buller'. Depressing news continued. Lord Roberts' son, Freddie, had been killed at Colenso in an attempt to save the guns. A fellow officer out with a flag of truce on a burial party brought dack some details of Gatacre's defeat at Stormberg: Johnnie had seen enough of Gatacre in the Sudan to have no faith in him, but the surrender of so many British soldiers suggested to Johnnie that 'we don't get hold of the right class of men in the army nowadays'. Johnnie feared that too many generals and staff officers simply lacked common sense, a comment reinforced by the unexpected arrival of Hunter, who was rarely seen, at King's Post on 3 January. Hunter seemed full of 'impossible plans' and 'weird ideas' and 'if it wasn't for the possibility that we may be asked to carry them out, would make one roar with laughter'. At least Johnnie had managed to get a heliograph message to Hubert with New Year wishes, Hubert conveying this in turn to Innislonagh on 5 January 1900.[15]

Since early November the Boers had made little effort to penetrate the defences of Ladysmith, but Kruger, who was anxious to secure strategic victories rather than tactical successes in order to force the British into negotiations, persuaded his generals to launch a new offensive. The chosen point for attack was the inadequately fortified Wagon Hill and Caesar's Camp. There was considerable confusion among the defenders when the Boers attacked in the early hours of Saturday 6 January. By early morning they had fought their way on to the top of Caesar's Camp and its south eastern slopes, held by the Gordons and the 1st Manchesters. Five companies of the Rifle Brigade were sent to support the Manchesters at about 8 a.m.

Johnnie found absolute chaos on Caesar's Camp:

When we got there, we could not find anyone in command and no one knew in the least what was meant to be going on. The only man there was a Major Simpson who had been hit by a spent bullet and had hardly recovered himself.

F Company under Captain Sydney Mills was sent forward to reinforce No 5 Picquet, although no one was clear where the position was supposed to be and whether or not the Boers were on the top of the hill. There was little cover beyond some small bushes and a few cacti scattered through the grass and Mills' men came under heavy fire at close range. Mills was hit and his company pinned down for the next ten hours. As each successive company was brought up on the left of its predecessor to try and work around the flank of the hill and isolate the Boers on top, much the same thing occurred. In D Company all the officers were hit within minutes; Reginald Stephens was struck bringing up B Company and George Thesiger shot through the neck when he tried to lead H Company to help Stephens. In the unexplained absence of Metcalfe, who failed to materialise in the firing line at all, Johnnie soon found himself the most senior officer still in action. He got his own men to ground and, 'by dint of creeping on my tummy and taking every bit of cover', managed to locate the other companies. He had no orders of any kind and could not find out what was happening to the right of the battalion positions. It was clear, however, that there were too many men in the firing line and, when Captain Nevil Macready of the Gordons brought up his own company, Johnnie told him that he had tried to send back messages to this effect and Macready moved off to try to locate his battalion over to the right.

It had been unbearably hot all morning, but at about 4 p.m. there was a violent thunderstorm. Johnnie noticed that the Boers were trying to push reinforcements of their own up on to the hill and sensed that it was the moment for decisive action. Communication between the companies was difficult, but fortunately it seemed that Johnnie's intentions were felt almost telepathically among the men crouching behind what cover they could find:

We shoved in all our supports and the Boers went; we then opened a most tremendous fire at them as they went down the slope, but the bush was very thick so that one had to fire at random, except at the river [Klip] which they had to cross (900 yards away). We knocked over a good few at this place, and the ones that got away will remember that place to their dying day.

At sunset Johnnie gathered the remnants of his command together on the hill.

It was cold as the rain was still pouring down and Johnnie huddled together for warmth with Second Lieutenant Charles Donald Wood amid the bodies of both Boers and British. Indeed, when the CO and Adjutant of the Manchesters passed during the night, they were so struck by Wood's youthful appearance that they gave him and Johnnie a mackintosh under which to shelter.[16]

There had also been bitter fighting on Wagon Hill in which Digby Jones, who had blown up the gun on Surprise Hill, lost his life and Hamilton had himself become involved in hand-to-hand combat. At Wagon Hill, too, the coming of the storm had seen a British counter-attack and the Boers had been driven off. On the following morning, Johnnie counted 52 dead Boers around his own position and calculated the overall Boer loss at this point at about 90 as he could see many more bodies further down the slopes. He was later to recount to Hubert his rather macabre amusement when the regimental sergeant major arranged the Boer bodies in a neat line, but was most concerned as to whether Johnnie wanted the heads or the feet aligned since the Boers were of varying heights. The battalion itself had suffered 53 casualties including six out of the ten officers engaged. But there was little time to seek recuperation for the battalion was ordered to stay and take over the defence of Wagon Hill and Wagon Point.

Johnnie, who was given command of both A and G Companies, now had the task of fortifying Wagon Point. There were no defences of any kind and, for the next three days and nights, Johnnie had his men hard at work until, in Francis Howard's estimation, the position was 'impregnable'. Unfortunately, it rained solidly and the exposed position laid it open to Boer artillery fire from three sides so the work could only be carried out safely between 7 p.m. and midnight. Even then, there was no rest as the men had to stand to at dawn in case of any renewed attack. Nor did Johnnie derive much comfort from being transferred from Howard's overall command to that of Ian Hamilton, whom he considered as full of childish ideas as Hunter. Johnnie and his colour sergeant were also 'horribly frightened' when a huge 100lb shell landed between them. All in all, he was getting 'thoroughly tired' of the siege. Wagon Hill had taught him 'what an awful toss up it is whether one will ever get through a fight', and, although he had heard from Hubert again by heliograph, relief seemed no closer. After 3½ years of almost continuous service, with the exception of three months at home recovering from BCA, when he had felt far from well, he was feeling 'very old' and could 'not imagine myself say larking or doing anything so foolish'. Some days later on 21 January, filthy dirty and soaked through when his tarpaulin blew away, he noted, 'the longer this siege goes on the more I wonder where is the fun or glory in soldiering'.[17]

When he finally completed his letter to his parents, Johnnie was to apologise for some of its more depressing entries, but in reality there was much to be depressed about. Johnnie found it galling to see staff officers 'come up most beautifully dressed, polished boots, white collars, etc, and to hear them buck about their hardships'. Equally annoying, White appeared to be pampering his old regiment – the Gordons – with only one of their companies compelled to do duty at night and the remainder able to sleep under canvas. Johnnie's men had now been on constant duty for twelve weeks and, since arriving at Wagon Point, they had got soaked through on three nights in every four. Vegetables had all but disappeared, there was no water for washing, and dysentery was common, Johnnie's own stomach giving him 'bother and pain'. The men were 'painfully weak' and looked 'pinched and worn'. A final blow was to hear on 30 January that Buller, whom Johnnie now considered a 'myth', had once more failed to break through to Ladysmith and suffered a defeat at Spion Kop six days earlier.[18] Johnnie had already stopped writing the letter to his parents on 26 January and, with the news of Spion Kop, he left off writing his diary as well.

On 14 February, bolstered by ten days of 'splendid weather', Johnnie resumed his diary although he was not to add to the letter to Sir Charles and Harriette until after the siege had ended. In the interval, he had received a letter from Hubert by means of an African runner and they had also been able to exchange heliograph messages. But Buller had again suffered a reverse at Vaal Krantz and Johnnie was convinced that he would never get to Ladysmith. Rations in the besieged town were now running low with ½lb of bread a day or two to two-and-a-half biscuits. On 20 February Johnnie noted that it was now ¼lb of bread and, occasionally, two ounces of mealie porridge. They were still getting a pound of meat each day although it was now horse meat or trek oxen, the latter including bone in the weight. Johnnie found horse meat 'steaks' to be 'capital', while Hugh Dawnay described mule as a luxury and biscuit fried in wagon grease as a welcome change: Francis Howard also recalled the 'chevril' – bovril made from horse flesh.

Real luxury items were now fetching high prices. On 14 February, Johnnie recorded that eggs were 45s.0d a dozen, a ¼lb tin of Capstan tobacco was £3 and 150 cigars fetched £6.10s.0d. By 20 February, when eggs were reserved for the wounded – they were also receiving mule-foot jelly as a substitute for milk – the price had reached 4s.0d each and 150 cigars had soared to £19. Tea and sugar were available in small quantities, as was coffee. Johnnie was particularly pleased when a young naval officer, who had been stationed at Wagon Point for a month, was sent off elsewhere as he had had too good an appetite in 'these hard times'. Johnnie and Harington were dosing themselves with cod-liver oil, but Johnnie was now finding it difficult to keep down food, his clothes were in an awful state, and the least exertion was absolutely exhausting. Then, on 27 February, the ration was reduced to only 1¼ biscuits a day with, it was rumoured, but four day's food supplies left in Ladysmith.[19]

With the exception of the attack on 6 January, the Boers had never seriously tested the defences and it was always starvation and disease that was more likely to force White's surrender. Almost certainly, the rations could have been made to strech into April, but medical arrangements were far from ideal and the toll from dysentery and typhoid as well as enteric grew steadily. However, at what seemed the eleventh hour to many of the defenders, news arrived on 27 February that Roberts, advancing on Bloemfontein, had forced the surrender of the main Boer army under Cronje at Paardeburg; Kimberley had already been relieved by Roberts' cavalry. It was also the day – ironically, the anniversary of Majuba – upon which Buller finally succeeded in outflanking the Boer positions covering Ladysmith. On the following morning, which was the 118th day of the siege, Johnnie and the other defenders saw streams of Boers, which Johnnie estimated at 15,000, making their way to the north. Johnnie together with ten other officers and about 100 men volunteered to try to harass them but they knew, in reality, that they were incapable of doing so.

Just before dusk, Johnnie heard cheering and saw distant horsemen. Then, at midnight, he received a signal-lamp message from Hubert to meet him at the Iron Bridge at 5 a.m., for unknown to Johnnie, it had been Hubert's squadron that had led the advance into Ladysmith. The two brothers had not seen each other for more than three years. Approaching the bridge at the appointed hour, Hubert saw an unfamiliar officer with a carefully trimmed 'naval' beard riding towards him on a grey pony:

I had not expected to see him with a beard. He recognised me, however, and said: 'Hallo Hubert' . . . and opened our reunion by simply remarking, 'How fat you have got!'

To Johnnie, Hubert indeed looked 'most thundering fit with a double chin', while to Hubert, Johnnie seemed 'fitter and browner than any man of the garrison I had seen'. Johnnie borrowed some cigarettes and a pot of jam from some of Hubert's men and the brothers rode off together to visit Bond and Paley in hospital, Johnnie giving them the jam. It was the longest distance he had ridden in four months.[20]

There was an embarrassing scene on 1 March when the garrison struggled out to meet Buller and his army only to find that the march past had been postponed for another two days. Johnnie was impressed by the troops of the relieving force but not by Buller. More important, there was an abundance of food, Johnnie writing in the final instalment of his Siege letter to his parents on 2 March that 'jam and milk nearly bring tears into our eyes'. He felt reasonably fit, but 'decent grub' upset his stomach and he had to stick to bread and milk for the time being. Walking was still difficult and he borrowed a fitter pony from Hubert. Between 70 and 80 letters also arrived with the resumption of communications and Johnnie took the opportunity to send a belated siege Christmas card to Innislonagh.

In all, the Rifle Brigade had lost five officers and 61 men dead from all causes during the siege while eight other officers had been wounded and three invalided. By 5 March some 230 reservists had arrived to fill vacancies caused by battle and disease and Johnnie was delighted by the news that they would be returned to Francis Howard's brigade when Hamilton went off to join Roberts' main army. For the time being they remained at Wagon Hill, although there were now tents instead of tarpaulins and there was the prospect of between three and four weeks in which to recuperate in a rear area. Hubert wrote home that he hoped that Johnnie would show him some of the sights of Ladysmith when he felt stronger and, in turn, Johnnie accompanied Hubert to the battlefields of Spion Kop and Colenso on 20 and 29 March in a party which also included the cavalry commander, Brocklehurst, and, on the latter occasion, Captain Guy Wyndham of the 16th Lancers.

Both brothers were characteristically generous to each other in correspondence home, Johnnie reporting that Hubert had made a great name for himself during the relief operation, 'which I always knew he would when he got the chance'. In turn, Hubert recorded that 'on all sides I heard how well Johnnie had done'. Indeed, Hunter had told Hubert that Johnnie 'made a name which would never be forgotten in Ladysmith or the Rifle Brigade'. There seems little reason to doubt Hubert's statement for Johnnie had done very well during the siege. In fact, it does seem that Johnnie had become the effective commander of his battalion when so many other officers had been hit on 6 January and others had become ill. Certainly Hubert claimed this to be so in his autobiography.[21] Johnnie makes no mention of Metcalfe after commenting on his unexplained absence from the firing line on Caesar's Camp, but it is possible that the Colonel became ill subsequently. In any case, Metcalfe was most appreciative of Johnnie's conduct during the siege and Johnnie was duly mentioned in Sir George White's despatch of 2 March 1900 along with Thesiger, Paley, Hugh Dawnay and Captain H. Biddulph. Indeed, it seems that Metcalfe may even have contemplated recommending Johnnie for the Victoria Cross for the action at Surprise Hill, but felt he could not do so as it had been too dark to see who reached the top of the hill first. Johnnie was flattered but most insistent that he deserved no such honour:

I wrote to him and told him not to take my breath away, as to begin with nobody could say who was first up and also that it was no V.C. act, to be up first and that such a thing had never entered my head – and that I thought I had been done uncommon well as it was. I hope he will never refer to the subject again; one would naturally like to earn a V.C. but as I know jolly well I have never done anything approaching a V.C. act in my life, I hate to have people talking such rot.

As it was, Metcalfe gave Johnnie a good report and placed him 'first among Field Officers' when he eventually compiled the battalion's confidential reports for his period of command in December 1901.[22] Undoubtedly, it had been a formative, if uncomfortable chapter in Johnnie's career.

Although he had seen the capabilities of the Boers at close hand, Johnnie could still not quite bring himself to believe that they were capable of defeating British troops. At the time he had heard of Buller's disaster on Spion Kop, he had written, 'how on earth men who call themselves Englishmen could allow themselves to be turned off a hill by a pack of Dutch Peasants I am damned if I know!' And, now, with Ladysmith relieved and Roberts marching on Bloemfontein, it seemed that victory could not be long post-poned. On 10 March he wrote to his mother that he expected the war to be over by the first or second week in May. Johnnie was far from being the only one to make such a miscalculation.

5

South Africa, 1900–1902

O N 6 April 1900, Hubert, who was due to leave with his command for outpost duty to the north, rode over to Ladysmith to see Johnnie, but the Rifle Brigade had departed for two days' exercise around the former battlefield of Spion Kop.[1] By the time the brothers met again in late July, the defeat of the Boers seemed even more complete. Roberts' main army had taken Bloemfontein on 13 March, Johannesburg on 31 May and Pretoria on 5 June, forcing Kruger to flee his capital. The last of the three towns besieged by the Boers at the opening of the war – Mafeking – had been relieved in May. By July, Buller's Natal army had crossed the Drakensbergs and was poised for an advance into the south eastern Transvaal, where a substantial number of Boers were still in the field under the command of Christiaan Botha.

Johnnie's battalion had moved to Arcadia near Ladysmith on 16 March to complete its recuperation from the siege. The officers enjoyed themselves with duck, pigeon and quail shooting but Johnnie also organised a signalling course for the subalterns, which continued until they left Arcadia on 13 April. Within Lyttelton's 4th Division, chosen by Buller to spearhead the advance, the battalion was now included in Major-General Walter Kitchener's 7th Brigade. Walter Kitchener was the brother of Herbert, who had been raised to the peerage for his victory in the Sudan and had come to South Africa himself as Roberts' Chief of Staff. On 4 June the advance reached Newcastle on the approach to the major pass through the Drakensbergs at Laing's Nek and Johnnie participated in the three days of turning operations between 6 and 9 June which enabled Buller to seize the latter, dubbed the 'Gibraltar' of Natal. As Buller paused to consolidate, the Rifle Brigade manned some fourteen posts around Newcastle but, from time to time, companies were detached on reconnaissance missions as on 1 July when Johnnie and George Thesiger went on a two-day jaunt. However, these were fewer than in the case of other battalions in the brigade because, as Johnnie reported to his father on 4 July, Walter Kitchener did not get on with Colonel Metcalfe and 'took precious good care' that Metcalfe was left behind as often as possible.

Nevertheless, Johnnie managed to get out on another reconnaissance with two companies of the Rifle Brigade in a small force led by Wolfe Murray, whom Johnnie had last encountered at Pietermaritzburg before the siege of Ladysmith. No Boers were seen, but it had made a change to be on the move and, a week later, Johnnie was complaining that they were 'reduced to having Field Days'. As at certain times during the siege, Johnnie was obviously depressed. Somewhat gloomily, he listed the sieges of the European legations at Peking and of the British resident at Kumasi in the west African protectorate of Ashanti, both of which had started in June 1900, and his own belief that more Sudanese regiments in Egypt would mutiny – one had done so in January 1900 – as evidence of the likelihood that wars would never cease. He was anxious to return home once the Boers were defeated – 'as I should like to do a bit of quiet before I am sent on another campaign'. There had been a time 'when I thought that I would never get tired of wars', but as a friend of Sir Charles had said during the Sikh wars, 'I now think that "a little is good but too much is enough" '.[2]

Yet, whatever his own mood, Johnnie kept such thoughts for his correspondence home. As always, he was concerned for the welfare of his men and was eagerly awaiting some tobacco Sir Charles had promised to send out for distribution to his company. Moreover, among the officers, Johnnie continued to display a strength combined with a 'ready wit and keen sense of humour' that clearly played an important part in maintaining the battalion's confidence. Of this, there is the testimony of a young London stockbroker, Lieutenant (later Major) E. T. Aspinall, who joined the Rifle Brigade on a year's attachment from the militia – he was an officer of the 7th Battalion, Rifle Brigade (1st Tower Hamlets Militia). Labelled the 'City man' by Johnnie, Thesiger and Reginald Stephens, Aspinall was able to make a detached assessment of each of these three close friends and leading personalities in the battalion.

While Thesiger struck Aspinall as the most methodical and Stephens as the best regimental officer, Johnnie was 'the masterful personality'. More autocratic than either Thesiger or Stephens, Johnnie dominated all:

His was the strong will, which combined sound judgement with a quick decision, and he possessed an iron nerve. Never did he 'suffer fools gladly', and was critical, even of his friends, though his criticisms were very humourous, even if his wit was a trifle caustic.

One story related by Aspinall well illustrates the light-hearted spirit among the battalion's officers in which Johnnie was such a central character. Aspinall had had some success in beating his fellow subalterns at draughts, whereupon Johnnie proclaimed, 'This will never do, we must take this young blighter on and down him.' There followed endless games in which Stephens took on Aspinall while Johnnie sat between them, offering constant advice to both.[3]

Aspinall also recalled much 'good-humoured badinage' when Johnnie was chosen on 15 July to go out to the Boers around Utrecht with a flag of truce. The Boers had sent in a messenger to Newcastle and, fearing a ruse to gain intelligence, Wolfe Murray resolved to send the Boer envoy back via Durban and Delagoa Bay. Johnnie had to inform the local Boer commander of what had occurred, quite expecting that he, too, would be sent back the same way. Indeed, two days later, another young subaltern in the battalion, Second Lieutenant Ralph Verney, noted in his diary that, as Johnnie had not returned, 'we are afraid that the Boers will keep him until they get their other messengers back, just to pay us out'. In fact, Johnnie was able to return direct to Newcastle on 18 July, having been delayed only by the need to wait for a reply from the Boer commander and then until the next period of darkness in order to avoid British and Boer patrols. On the following day, Johnnie received a telegraph message from Francis Howard requesting his services while Howard's ADC recovered from sickness. Johnnie wrote that he was 'delighted at the idea of doing a bit of soldiering on horseback as "footslog-ging" is a poor game and I dislike it more everyday'. By contrast, Metcalfe later wrote to Sir Charles that he had released Johnnie with the utmost reluctance, 'for a better regimental officer than Johnnie I never wish to see'. Johnnie was not to return to the 2nd Battalion, Rifle Brigade, his regimental service ending at the age of twenty-nine and in the rank of Captain. Just over two weeks later, George Thesiger also left to became ADC to Lyttelton.[4]

Francis Howard now led one of three 'flying columns' under the overall command of Major-General H. T. Hildyard. The concept itself had been borrowed from the Boers. In March 1900 the new Commandant-General of the Orange Free State, Christiaan de Wet, had urged the Boer leadership to resort to guerrilla tactics as a means of continuing the war after the defeat of the field armies. De Wet himself, his brother Piet, and the Transvaaler, Koos De La Rey, had soon proved the worth of their highly mobile flying columns in hitting hard at the British and seemingly vanishing as quickly as they had appeared. Hildyard's intention, when Johnnie joined his command at Laing's Nek and marched with it to Sandspruit, was to keep the Boer commandos away from the main railway line from Newcastle to Johannesburg.

Almost inevitably, the operations were desultory affairs and Johnnie was constantly on the move. On 22 July the columns converged on a small hill known as Gras Kop, driving off a Boer artillery piece, while on 24 July the object was to 'knock the Boers off the Rooi kopjes position'. Five days later, it was a case of sending out patrols to exchange shots with the Boers and, on 30 July, Hildyard's force took part in a strong reconnaissance for Buller's planned advance. However, Johnnie was enjoying the duties of an ADC. At Rooi kopjes he was responsible for seeing Howard's mixed column of Gordon Highlanders, Manchesters and Leicesters off the hills after nightfall while, by complete contrast, he was breaking in a new horse for Howard a week later. Soldiering on horseback was altogether 'more attractive' than doing so on foot, especially as Johnnie heard that Metcalfe wanted him back as battalion adjutant, Johnnie feared that he might be stuck with the adjutancy on a long-term basis and was relieved that Howard's ADC would be absent for some weeks to come. It was at Sandspruit, too, that Johnnie met up with Hubert again when Hubert's mounted infantry were attached briefly to Hildyard, before being detached to guard lines of communication once Buller's advance began.[5]

The immediate object of that advance, which began on 7 August, was to secure the towns of Ermelo and Carolina, Howard's force being reconstituted as the 8th Brigade and coming once more under the command of Lyttelton's 4th Divison. Johnnie regretted that Hildyard would not play a part in the advance as he had found him a 'very good man' with a thorough knowledge of the country. Johnnie was also concerned that Lyttelton 'was a little inclined to be casual about what happens to people who may be detached from his immediate command'. Nor did he have confidence in Brocklehurst and Dundonald, who were deputed to command the cavalry and mounted troops in the advance, a view he shared with Hubert. In the event, there was no resistance at Ermelo and Johnnie was amused by Buller's glowing despatch on a minor affair at Amersfoot on 25 August, which hardly compared with Hildyard's success in turning a similar number of Boers off the Rooi kopjes with far fewer men. It merely demonstrated that there was 'an awful lot of hanky panky' in the army with regard to the attribution of reward.

But, while Johnnie was still critical of commanders and their staffs, he was beginning to discover himself just how difficult it could be to command larger numbers of troops than a company. On 23 August, for example, the Boers had begun to shell a camp being laid out at Golak Farm. Three battalions of Howard's brigade were sent to hold a picquet line, but Major E. H. Molyneux-Seel, acting commanding officer of the 1st (King's) Liverpools pushed on three miles ahead of the others without letting Howard know. Twice Johnnie went to tell Molyneux-Seel to stop, but on both occasions the latter insisted that he was not advancing at all. Towards dusk, Howard withdrew his troops, but the Liverpools had gone so close to the Boer positions that they could only be extricated with difficulty. Johnnie, who had already had his bridle cut by shrapnel while taking a message to an artillery battery, again went out to find Molyneux-Seel. He asked the Liverpools' commander to point out his forward position on a map 'but as a matter of fact his firing line was a mile beyond it'. By the time the Liverpools had been pulled back, they had lost 92 casualties, including some 30 men taken prisoner. Not surprisingly, Johnnie was highly critical of Molyneux-Seel in his letters home and found him and another of Howard's subordinates 'quite hopeless', although he appreciated that 'now-a-days even a Colonel of regiment has very little control once the fight has begun and it mostly depends on the Company Commanders'.[6]

By this time, Howard's ADC had returned to duty but Howard persuaded

Metcalfe to allow Johnnie to remain for the time being as an orderly officer. Although not anxious to return to the battalion, Johnnie was still very concerned for its welfare. On many occasions during the advance, Howard and Johnnie visited the Rifle Brigade lines and Aspinall noted that Johnnie was 'always anxious that the general should have a good impression of his old battalion; for he never failed to point out anything he thought perhaps had been missed, that would rebound to our credit'. If Howard became noticeably bored or impatient, Johnnie would tactfully suggest a visit to the magazine or some similar device to divert Howard's attention. Naturally, therefore, Johnnie was distressed by the heavy casualties suffered by the battalion when it led the assault on the Boer position at Bergendal near Belfast on 27 August while Howard's own brigade was acting as rearguard. Roberts' army had now linked with that of Buller to eliminate Botha's forces but the action to turn the Boers off the Bergendal kopje, dominating the route into the eastern Transvaal, was entrusted to Lyttelton's divison. The Rifle Brigade had seven officers and 79 other ranks killed or wounded, including Metcalfe who was hit in the stomach and arm. One rifleman won the Victoria Cross. Johnnie went over to see Metcalfe in hospital and, while he was there, Roberts asked to meet him as the son of a former Indian army subordinate. In fact, Roberts was anxious that Johnnie should pass on his regards to Sir Charles. Metcalfe later wrote to Sir Charles that the encounter had been most amusing as Johnnie 'absolutely refuses to unbend with him at all'.

Bergendal proved the last major set-piece battle of the war. Botha's army collapsed and the British moved steadily through the Transvaal. Johnnie, who was again put in Orders as Howard's ADC on 3 September, moved through Machadodorp, Elandspruit and Helvetia to arrive at Lydenburg on 7 September. Both at Elandspruit and Lydenburg, Buller seemed somewhat *kuchpurwani* ('careless' in Hindustani) to Johnnie in siting the British camp under direct fire from neighbouring Boer-held kopjes. Invariably Howard's brigade was given the task of clearing the Boer positions. Howard was then placed in command of lines of communication around Lydenburg. The Rifle Brigade was told off as one of the garrison battalions in the town and Johnnie, who became Howard's Brigade Signalling Officer on 10 September, stayed as well.[7]

Lydenburg proved a comfortable town, Johnnie and Howard occupying a well-furnished house. Sleeping in a 'huge double bed with sheets(!)' was Johnnie's ideal for 'making war in an enemy's country' but he was also busy in assisting Howard to safeguard communications and establish British administration over a troublesome population consisting almost entirely of Boer women and children. With an estimated 400 Boers in the vicinity of the town, even an inspection of the British outposts required a large escort to guard against snipers. Johnnie wanted Howard to try and surround the local Boer commando, but the maps available were too inadequate for accurate planning of operations and the British cavalry patrolling the area too inept to guarantee success. Generally, Johnnie believed the cavalry should rely more on dismounted use of their carbines instead of making 'a point of rushing to their horses' all the time.[8]

Boers were now coming into Lydenburg to surrender in large numbers and Johnnie had definite views on how the war might be concluded quickly. He approved of detaining such Boers 'so that they won't be able to break their oaths and take up arms against us when they get a good opportunity'. He also hoped that the Boer women and children in Lydenburg and its vicinity would be sent to Cape Town and interned. Not only would this solve the problem of feeding the civilian population when it was proving difficult to maintain the garrison's own supplies but it would also prevent food distributed by the British being given to Boer commandos in the field. Aspinall recalled that Johnnie had been critical of expeditions to 'pick crops' as it mixed farming with fighting but, as early as 29 July, Johnnie had expressed satisfaction in a letter to Sir Charles that 'we are at last beginning to drive in all horses and livestock that we find, and also that we commandeer foodstuffs from the farms'. Moreover, like Hubert, Johnnie fully agreed with the policy of burning down Boer farms, a practice which had originated in Roberts' army rather than that of Buller, who had been loath to do so at first. On 11 July Johnnie had noted his support for the burning down of a farm of a Boer who had taken up arms again after surrender; and after a patrol of the 19th Hussars had been fired at from a farm flying a white flag on 15 August, Johnnie wrote that it should be burned down: in the event, five farms were destroyed in retaliation for the incident.[9] It was a brutal policy but one that did ultimately deprive the Boers of the food and support they required to remain in the field.

Another practice, which also contributed to eventual victory, was evident in the spread of British outposts around Lydenburg. Later in the war, blockhouses linked by barbed wire fences became commonplace as a means of depriving the Boers of mobility and protecting British communications. It was with similar intentions that Howard maintained a number of strong-points every eight or nine miles on the roads into Lydenburg, each garrisoned by four companies of infantry, a squadron of cavalry and two guns. Convoys would also be accompanied by a squadron of cavalry, two infantry companies and two guns. Nevertheless, communications were frequently cut since Lydenburg was not served by railway. Johnnie had been unable to buy anything in the way of cigarettes or other luxuries since leaving Newcastle in July and, as on his other campaigns, he was vainly awaiting items he had asked to be sent from Ireland weeks and even months before, such as gloves, coloured silk handkerchiefs, cigarettes and books.

The garrison as a whole was short of equipment to such an extent that the Rifle Brigade could find boots for only 550 out of 900 men. Cavalry horses had been fed on nothing but oats since July and hay was desperately needed to fill them out for campaigning. There was also a shortage of grazing for the

10,000 head of cattle and sheep confiscated from Boer farms: they simply could not be allowed to wander beyond the limits of the town outpost lines with so many Boers ready to swoop down on them. Yet, despite the problems, Johnnie was sure that Lydenburg and similar garrisons must be maintained. It was rumoured that they might be withdrawn but Johnnie felt this would only enable the Boers to reoccupy towns and take up arms again on a large scale. On the other hand, since it was intended to string Lyttelton's division out from Middelburg to Lydenburg, he also rather feared that the garrison might be besieged in Lydenburg.[10]

Change was in the air as the rumours indicated. Buller was due to leave for home by the end of October and Roberts would also return to England in December to succeed Wolseley as the army's Commander-in-Chief. Kruger had already left Africa for Europe. At Lydenburg, Howard became seriously ill in early October and Johnnie was unsure of his own position since he had been seconded to Howard's staff and, in theory, no longer belonged to his old battalion. Johnnie discovered that it was not intended to evacuate Lydenburg after all and that Walter Kitchener would remain in command of a garrison consisting of the Rifle Brigade and the 1st Devons with some supporting artillery. However, he had no desire to go back to the battalion because he found increasingly that he could not get on with George Cockburn, who had taken over command when Metcalfe was wounded. After a few days, it was decided that Johnnie should remain on the brigade staff of Howard's successor in case Howard recovered but it soon became clear that Howard would be invalided home. Consequently, Johnnie decided to apply for civil or constabulary employment.

In the meantime, he accompanied the brigade on a major foray to Middelburg between 9 and 16 October, a distance of 83 miles. There was constant sniping and the brigade suffered 15 casualties while taking five Boers prisoner and seizing 3,000 head of sheep. Johnnie then travelled on to Pretoria to see Howard and accompanied him to Durban. While in Pretoria, Roberts offered Johnnie the appointment of District Commissioner at Lydenburg. Having seen Howard safely off to England at the end of October, Johnnie then returned to take up this new post. Gazetted as District Commissioner on 31 October 1900, he actually arrived back at the town on 9 November. It was also the date of the last official despatch by Buller, in which Johnnie was mentioned for his services as ADC and Brigade Signalling Officer on the recommendation of Howard.[11]

As District Commissioner, Johnnie was now responsible for all the fortified posts on the roads through the mountainous terrain between Lydenburg and the railway line. On 14 December, for example, he wrote to Sir Charles that one of his posts had been attacked and that he had gone out to conduct its defence. In fact, there were only 30 or 40 Boers involved and they soon retired. Earlier, in November, he had been up at 3 one morning with a small force to protect a party of native Kaffirs expected to bring in cattle to the

British lines although they did not materialise. Similarly, in January 1901 he was out with some mounted infantry to gather in 300 head of Kaffir cattle so the Boers could not seize them. His duties also included assisting Walter Kitchener in the general defence of the Lydenburg area as required. Boer commandos were still extremely active and, when they cut the telegraph lines just before Christmas, Kitchener asked Johnnie to lead a cattle catching raid in retaliation on Christmas Day, 'so that I will spend my Xmas day despoiling my neighbour'.

When the British garrison at Helvetia – mostly comprising the Liverpools – was surprised by Boers under Ben Wiljoen and lost 235 men captured and a 4.7″ gun, Johnnie accompanied Walter Kitchener with a small relief column. However, the Boers were so strong that Johnnie and others persuaded Kitchener to return to Lydenburg at once for fear of leaving it unprotected. Johnnie found Kitchener reasonably 'easy'. Certainly, Kitchener had a warmer personality than his brother, who had succeeded Roberts as Commander-in-Chief in South Africa. But Walter Kitchener still displayed a 'childish delight in doing almost stupid things' such as building roads to so-called 'sanitary camps' in impossible locations devoid of any water supplies. Kitchener also indulged in 'jollies' – night marches – which rarely achieved any results. Moreover, Johnnie was exasperated 'that after he has told one to run a show that he goes off and issues orders on his own account, without even letting one know'. Inevitably, confusion resulted.

But, for the most part, Johnnie's work was one of civil administration similar to that experienced in BCA and on Crete; indeed, Chermside had been instrumental in recommending Johnnie to Roberts for such employment. It involved 'mostly making enquiries into the whereabouts of different people in the district, and as to their treatment'. In early December, when Boers were raiding the farms of erstwhile colleagues who had surrendered, Johnnie wrote to the local Boer commandant to inform him 'that I have got the [raiders'] names and that at the end of the war they will have to pay for this even if we have to sell up their farms'. Later in the same month, he was annoyed to discover that his fellow commissioner at Barberton had been accepting the parole of Boers and sending them to live in Johnnie's district. Having 'no intention of having a lot of these double-dealing gentry loafing about', Johnnie promptly re-arrested the Boers and sent them away to prison camps.[12]

When not working, Johnnie had his own house in Lydenburg. Later Reginald Stephens moved in with him and, once Stephens left in November 1901, Johnnie's assistant commissioner, a man named Knight, took his place. Johnnie messed with the Rifle Brigade, which remained at Lydenburg until July 1901, although it is apparent from his letters that Johnnie's relationship with George Cockburn continued to deteriorate. Johnnie employed a Rifle Brigade sergeant as his clerk and he was pleased to hear that the men in his old company missed him greatly. It was rumoured in the battalion that Johnnie was earning £1,000 per annum as District Commissioner whereas his pay was £30 a month in addition to the usual regimental pay and allowances. However, this still amounted to 'quite a small fortune' and Johnnie looked forward to investing some in South Africa after the war.

The garrison was also soon ensuring that there was adequate entertainment. Johnnie took part in a paperchase on 16 November and, despite never having jumped before, his horse brought him in second. At the start of December, a polo ground was laid out although, again, the Boer ponies available were untrained and the fun was somewhat dangerous. The tobacco expected from Innislonagh never arrived – Johnnie had some for his old company brought up from Durban – but other requirements did eventually find him in December including the silk handkerchiefs, cigarettes and some books.

In January 1901 he was delighted to receive a plum pudding, though now he also wanted some Bedford cord riding breeches. By the end of the war, over a year later, they had still not arrived, but Johnnie did receive a copy of *Kim* in January 1902 and an electric torch sent by Hubert three months later. At the same time, Sir Charles was at last able to report that some of the items Johnnie was endeavouring to send home had reached Innislonagh, including a kaross made from silver jackal skins and a pencil made from a cartridge case picked up at Caesar's Camp in January 1900. There was also a suit of Dervish chain mail recovered from the battlefield at Omdurman though Johnnie was concerned that Sir Charles had not mentioned receiving a top of a railing spike from the Mahdi's tomb.[13]

On occasions, Johnnie was troubled with a stomach upset and found the wet and stormy weather at Lydenburg in November and December 1900 unpleasant, although hail storms did enable the officers in the mess to ice their butter! Intriguingly, Johnnie also appears to have become involved briefly with his Catholic cousin, Elinor de la Poer, although there is but one reference in a letter to Sir Charles on 3 January 1901, in which Johnnie remarked,

I was much amused at your distress about what you call my entanglement or engagement with Elinor. You may be relieved to hear that Elinor is now afraid that the Pope won't sanction a mixed marriage (it sounds as though it was a marriage between a black and a white).

In any case, Johnnie's link with Elinor, who eventually became a nun after the death of her future husband, was entirely by correspondence. But there was another girl at Lydenburg with whom Johnnie became a firm favourite. He was befriended by a family called McIntyre living next door whose youngest daughter – the ten-year-old Effie – was soon 'ruling me with a rod of iron'. When Effie caught fever, Johnnie spent his spare time reading to her. In May 1903, when it was wrongly reported in Lydenburg that he had been killed in Somaliland, Mr McIntyre wrote to Sir Charles at Innislonagh to try to discover the truth since Effie was 'quite inconsolable'. More crucially, however, Johnnie was now thinking seriously of what steps he should take in his military career, even if he was also keen to get home.[14]

His thoughts returned to the Staff College, which appeared to be the best way forward. Established at Camberley in 1858, after a previous existence as the senior department of the Royal Military College, the Staff College had gradually won acceptance within the army as providing the most appropriate professional training for staff officers. Under the direction of Hildyard, who had been commandant from 1893 to 1898, the course had become far more practical and it was now widely recognised that passing through the college was an important foundation for progress towards the army's highest ranks. Staff appointments on campaign were given increasingly to Staff College graduates.

Johnnie, however, had missed entering for the qualifying examination through service on Crete, and although both Chermside and Lyttelton had promised to do something for him in June 1899, the war in South Africa had then again intervened. Johnnie lamented that 'one seems to be always on active service and leave is quite out of the question'. It was also irksome that officers with less service experience, who did not happen to be in South Africa, were available to take up places at the college.

Accordingly, while in Durban to see off Howard, Johnnie had applied to go to the Staff College, but without taking the examination by virtue of being unable to do so on active service. He did not expect to be able to gain entry in this way, but at least it made the War Office authorities aware of his desire to attend. At the same time, Sir Charles was also pressing the War Office on Johnnie's behalf. Back in July 1899 Sir Charles had contacted Wolseley and had done so again in June 1900. Francis Howard, who believed Johnnie 'quite one of the best officers I have ever come across in whatever position he is placed', was also endeavouring to obtain a Staff College nomination for Johnnie. But, on 10 October 1900, Wolseley had replied that passing the entrance examination was a *sine qua non* of admission. Had Johnnie taken the examination, Wolseley would have gladly used his powers to nominate two officers to ensure Johnnie got one of the limited places available, since qualification in the examination alone did not necessarily guarantee it. The most Wolseley could do was to write to Roberts to indicate that he would have nominated Johnnie if able to do so. Sir Charles was never one to give up the attempt to obtain what he regarded as proper recognition for his sons' abilities. In November 1899 he had also written to the Governor of Natal, Sir Walter Hely-Hutchinson, to look out for Johnnie. Thus, when Wolseley could do nothing, Sir Charles wrote both to Roberts and the influential former professor of Military History at the Staff College, Colonel G. F. R. Henderson.[15]

There was some compensation for Johnnie when he was gazetted Brevet Major on 19 April 1901 with the appointment back-dated to 29 November 1900, brevet rank yielding seniority in the army but not in the regiment and conferring no pay increase. But Johnnie himself recognised that he must sit the Staff College entrance examination. In August 1901, therefore, he travelled down to Pretoria to sit it although he had been unable to do any preparation:

So that as you may imagine there is little or no chance of my even qualifying, as after 13 years away from Algebra, Euclid, etc, one naturally does not remember much.

There were fourteen papers totalling 42 hours' work covering Mathematics (three papers); Military Engineering (two): Military History (two), which included a paper on the closing stages of the Peninsular War; Tactics (two); Military Topography; Military Law; Military Administration; Geography and a language. From the options available – French, German, Hindustani, Russian and Arabic – Johnnie chose French. It took a full week to sit all the papers in the company of five other candidates, all of whom had experienced similar difficulties in working for the examination. There were virtually no textbooks available in South Africa. Johnnie managed to borrow a book on military law in Pretoria but could find none of the set texts on fortification. Nevertheless, he felt he had done enough to qualify in all but mathematics.

Sir Charles promptly wrote to the Adjutant General at the War Office, Sir Evelyn Wood, to request that Johnnie be considered for nomination if he did not receive the necessary marks to qualify. On 20 October, Roberts himself replied to inform Sir Charles that he would nominate Johnnie. He also took the opportunity of assuring Sir Charles that Hubert, who had been given a brevet lieutenant colonelcy at the same time as Johnnie's brevet majority, would not suffer from being captured with most of his command at Blood River Poort on 17 September 1901 – Hubert had escaped from the Boers the next day. Johnnie, however, did not learn of his nomination until nine days after Sir Charles when Hugh Dawnay's brother, Peter, wired him the news from London. The actual marks did not reach Johnnie until late November: he scored 2,046, just 46 above the minimum pass. He had failed mathematics, his 179 marks falling some 156 short of the pass mark, but his failure had been waived with the nomination. He also wrote that he was pleased to have qualified in all the other subjects, his best mark being 414 out of 600 for tactics.

In reality, Johnnie's performance was worse than he either knew or cared to admit. It is possible to identify him as candidate number 86 in the report on the examination printed in November 1901. While he had indeed scored 2,046 marks, he was actually credited with only 889. The mark accumulated in the three mathematics papers not only fell 271 rather than 156 marks short of the minimum, but was so low that it was discounted altogether. Similarly, he had failed to attain a minimum qualifying mark in military engineering, military administration, geography, military history and French with the result that a further 968 marks were discounted. Out of 39 candidates, he had been placed 38th. In all, 18 candidates had failed, while two of those who did

qualify could not be recommended for admission – even though 24 competitive places were available – because of the artificial quota placed on the
various arms of the service.[16]

In effect, then, the authorities were waiving far more than just a failure in
mathematics and it was fortunate indeed that Johnnie had secured Roberts'
support. Ironically for a soldier who would become widely known as one of
the luminaries of the Staff College, Johnnie had achieved entrance to both the
Royal Military College and to Camberley on nomination rather than by
examination results. The next course at the Staff College was due to begin in
January 1902 but it was by no means certain that Johnnie would be able to
attend. On the one hand, he wanted to remain to see the war finished and,
while not entirely convinced as yet of the value of Staff College training,
'every day one goes out one learns something of one's profession and some
day it may be of the greatest importance, and actual experience gives one such
a lot of confidence'. In fact, in October 1901 Major-General Bruce Hamilton,
whom Johnnie had never met, had tried to acquire his services as staff officer,
apparently on the recommendation of Hubert. Although Johnnie could not
be spared from Lydenburg, he considered that such an experience would have
been far more practically rewarding than attendance at Camberley. On the
other hand, he regretted ever becoming District Commissioner, particularly
when he was being constantly reminded of the necessity of his remaining at
Lydenburg.[17]

To some extent, the nature of Johnnie's services had remained precisely as
before, but the authorities in Pretoria did not learn that, in addition to routine
administration, Johnnie was gaining considerable experience of staff work.
From August to September 1901 onwards, some 2,000 Boers were operating
around Lydenburg as they had been driven from other parts of the country.
Consequently, the policing of the area was of particular importance to the
garrison commander, now Lieutenant Colonel C. W. Park of the 1st Devons.
Johnnie had become well acquainted with Park when they had travelled up to
the town together in November 1900. He had a high opinion of Park's
abilities and expected him to go far in the army – Park was to become a
Major-General, but died at the early age of 57 in March 1913. Finding
co-operation with Park easy, Johnnie accompanied him on column in
October 1901, scouting ahead with a 50-strong party of 'Burgher Volunteers'
– Boers prepared to fight for the British against erstwhile colleagues.

Johnnie arrived at Krugerspost in the Orighstad valley to join Park, having
taken seven prisoners and 60 head of cattle along the way. But Park, who had
been in action with the Boers himself, was late to arrive at the rendezvous,
leaving Johnnie 'rather nervous' that his own small group would be isolated.
On the following day, Johnnie's volunteers got above 200 Boers: 'we let them
have it as hard as we could and 4 were seen to fall, so that we fairly scared
them off'. The expedition then retired on Lydenburg, burning some Boer
farms and rounding up 200 women and children. On 3 November a scheme

Johnnie proposed to Park resulted in the garrison netting ten Boers, 200 head of cattle and 800 sheep. There was another 'trek' with Park on 17 December.

Then, when Park's own staff officer was wounded, Johnnie was invited to take over the duties. He was still acting in this unofficial capacity in February 1902, but was doubtful if he ought to be. He was 'certain to get hauled over the coals' but, had resolved to 'say I am visting my district if any nasty questions are asked'. Working with Park was certainly a rewarding experience since his command eventually amounted to more than 1,500 mounted men, almost 1,000 infantry and six guns when two other columns were combined with it in February. Johnnie was careful to ensure that the column's camping grounds were picked properly and adequately defended with outlying picquets to guard against surprise, as he believed this a major reason for continuing Boer success in the guerrilla conflict still raging. He would also have preferred to dispense with at least three-quarters of the column's transport:

I am firmly convinced that we would be much more successful if columns only carried blankets and ammunition, and got their food from depots established off the line [of march], the enormous string of supply wagons is enough to break one's heart.

However, whatever the difficulties with the ox-drawn supply train, Park's column enjoyed much success while Johnnie was acting as its staff officer. Ben Wiljoen was captured and, in four days between 21 and 25 February 1902, they took 196 other Boers prisoner and accumulated 107 rifles, 72 horses, 7 mules, 629 head of cattle, 35 sheep and goats, 4 wagons, a trolley, 2 cape carts, 40 bags of meal and 10 bags of mealies. A further 10 bags of meal, 2,000 lbs of mealies, 100 saddles and all the blankets and clothing in three laagers were destroyed.[18]

When not out on column, or when Park halted for a few days on the march, Johnnie caught up with his administration. In November 1901, for example, he was required to administer the oath of allegiance to Boers in his district and, in January and February 1902, he had to undertake the inoculation of cattle in his area against rinderpest. He also mounted raids of his own independent of Park, using his Burgher volunteers or 'looters' as he preferred to call them. Johnnie was proud of the 'best fort in South Africa' which he had built for his small command and, on 6 February 1902 it beat off a Boer attack. Johnnie wrote to Sir Charles that he had conducted the defence and 'had the pleasure of getting a good many bullets over my head'. Once Park's official staff officer returned to his duties on 3 March, Johnnie's expeditions with his own volunteers increased. For greater mobility they usually operated without supply wagons. On 19 March Johnnie reported gleefully to his father that the volunteers, now incorporated into the so-called National Scouts, were having 'many enjoyable outings' and that he had made himself 'generally unpleasant to my local Boers, who are a poor lot'. He was out again in early May to try to trap a troublesome Boer leader called Muller by closing the Steenkampsberg passes, but was then compelled to return to Lydenburg when Muller was named as a peace delegate by the Boers for the forthcoming conference at Vereeniging on 15 May.[19]

Rumours of an end to the war had been circulating freely in recent months. At times, Johnnie was optimistic that the Boers were truly beaten, only for some sudden Boer success to lift the spirits of the commandos still at large. Indeed, as late as 7 March, Lord Methuen's column in the western Transvaal was worsted by De La Rey at Tweebosch and Methuen captured – Johnnie immediately noticed the increase in Boer activity in his own area. For himself, he was ambivalent about the negotiations that had begun at Pretoria on 11 April and which were to be reconvened at Vereeniging:

The betting about Peace is even money, and curiously enough I feel quite indifferent as to whether it is peace or war. I should hate to see a kind of half-hearted surrender, it is much better to go on until we get them right on their knees, which by August they certainly ought to be in any case.

Whatever the outcome, it seemed unlikely Johnnie would escape Lydenburg quickly for Lord Kitchener had made it known that the town would not be handed back to civil administration for some time. Johnnie was also well aware that he had missed the start of the Staff College course by the time he had been officially seconded to it from the Rifle Brigade on 26 March 1902. He hoped he might be able simply to start late; if he was put back a full year, he was minded to refuse to go altogether. Nevertheless, Johnnie felt well and contented. He had got over periodic neuralgia by wearing smoked glasses in the glare of the day. His teeth needed some attention, he thought, but, at 10 stone 6 lbs, he 'never felt so fit in my life'.[20]

The Boers had been forced to the negotiating table through the relentless pressure of the steady extension of blockhouses and wire – there were 8,000 blockhouses in South Africa by May 1902 – on their mobility, the destruction of farms and livestock, and the incarceration of almost 94,000 of their women and children in 'concentration camps'. The Boer leadership was also concerned by growing signs of native unrest, which Johnnie also noted, and the fact that the British had armed Africans, Coloureds and collaborationist Boers. Yet, the terms accepted by the Boers on 31 May 1902 were far more generous than Milner for one would have liked. There had been some earlier abortive talks at Middelburg in February 1901, which had foundered on the then British insistence on an extension of the franchise in the former Boer republics to the native population. At Vereeniging it was agreed that consideration of enfranchising Africans and Coloureds should be postponed until after the Boer republics regained self-government. The British also agreed to a total amnesty for all Boers and to provide substantial financial compensation for war losses. In return, the Boer republics became incorporated into the British Empire and they surrendered control of Swaziland and part of the Rand. The promise of self-government in particular was a blow to

Milner's hopes of securing a total victory and, in effect, Milner and his post-war administration would have only a limited period in which to attempt an anglicisation of the Boer republics to prevent future Afrikaner domination. In fact, the Transvaal and the Orange River Colony, as the Free State had become, gained that self-government in 1907.

Johnnie was offered a part in Milner's post-war civil administration, Milner offering him the magistracy of Lydenburg at £1,000 per annum to settle Boer families back on the land and to handle compensation claims. However, the job would mean no leave for another year and Johnnie turned it down. He expected to be asked to bring home a party of reservists in a few months time, but in the event Lydenburg was handed back to the civil administration earlier than anticipated and Johnnie was released on 7 July. A week later, Sir Charles had a wire to say that Johnnie would be sailing home on the *Kildonan Castle*, due to leave Cape Town on 23 July 1902.

If the outcome of the war had been less than might have been expected, Johnnie was personally satisfied with the Vereeniging terms. The Boers still had close to 20,000 men in the field at the end and, assuming they had begun the war with over 100,000 men against the small British garrison, then the country had been saved 'by the grand fighting of our men'. Johnnie considered himself fortunate to have secured his majority and to have come through unscathed. He had received the thanks of Milner's colonial secretary, W. E. Davidson, for his services at Lydenburg, a gold watch from the town's local intelligence staff, and an embarrassing valedictory address from the inhabitants. At various times both Hubert and Alan Gough had reported to Sir Charles on Johnnie's growing reputation and, certainly, the letters Sir Charles preserved from Wolseley, Roberts, Chermside, Howard and others indicate the high regard in which Johnnie was held. By contrast, Hubert had had the misfortune to get captured at Blood River Poort and had also been invalided home in January 1902 after losing a finger to a Boer bullet in November 1901.

Characteristically, Sir Charles was less satisfied and he continued to seek both complete exoneration for Hubert and proper official recognition for the services of both sons. On Hubert's behalf he wrote to Roberts, the Adjutant General and the Military Secretary at the War Office. Disappointment that neither Hubert nor Johnnie were mentioned in Kitchener's final despatch brought further broadsides from Innislonagh. In the case of Johnnie, Sir Charles enlisted the help of Park, who agreed to raise the matter with Lieutenant-General Sir Ian Hamilton, formerly Kitchener's chief of staff and soon to become Quartermaster-General at the War Office, and Kitchener's military secretary, Colonel Hubert Hamilton. However, Kitchener was insistent on keeping his list as short as possible.[21]

Now 31, Johnnie had been on active service, with but a short break between BCA and the Sudan, for seven years. He was looking forward to at least three months' 'quiet' at Innislonagh where he hoped Sir Charles had a good new horse awaiting him. Then he could join the Staff College in January 1903, although a year later than intended. It was not to be, for on 27 October 1902, while staying with cousin Laura in London, Johnnie received a telegram from the War Office informing him that he had been selected for special service in Somaliland. A second telegram that afternoon ordered him to leave on 31 October to join the SS *Caledonia* at Marseilles.

It was a 'great surprise'. Johnnie would have no time to see his parents before leaving. He knew that Harriette in particular would be distraught and he received a 'pathetic telegram' from her. Sir Charles, who would look after Johnnie's horses and his financial affairs in his absence, comforted himself with knowing that at least Laura was able to see Johnnie off and that such short notice indicated the authorities might 'have a special billet' in mind for Johnnie. On 28 October Johnnie hastened to the War Office to see Colonel F. W. Benson, the AAG responsible for the Staff College, who promised to do whatever he could to get Johnnie straight to Camberley whenever he returned. He also saw officials at the Foreign Office who gave him to understand that the posting would be for about six months. There was little time for anything else. His shooting boots were still at Innislonagh and much else at Portsmouth awaiting shipment to Ireland.[22] He had to leave a list of requirements with Hubert's wife, Nora (familiarly known as Daisy), since much of his laundry was still in the wash. The Commander-in-Chief, Roberts, had also wanted to see Johnnie, to wish him luck, but Johnnie did not receive the telegram until the day he was due to leave, since it had been sent to Ireland, and he was unable to keep the appointment. His next letter to Sir Charles, dated 2 November 1902, came from the *Caledonia* bound for Aden.

6

Somaliland, 1902–1904

AS the *Caledonia* sailed eastwards, Johnnie was comforted by the thought
that, while he would not be going to the Staff College, at least he would
be spared the kind of 'petty fogging soldiering' which he had experienced in
his all-too-brief service at home: the precise nature of what Johnnie had been
required to do between returning from South Africa and being ordered to
Somaliland is unclear. Walter Kitchener was also on board the vessel as well
as a 'tremendous crowd . . . mostly ladies'. Johnnie had no particular wish to
mix socially with Kitchener, but he enjoyed the company of the remaining
passengers. Of far more importance was some degree of preparation for the
campaign ahead, Johnnie reading and then recommending to Sir Charles the
official blue books on Somaliland and *Seventeen Trips in Somaliland* by E. J.
E. Swayne.[1]

In fact, Brevet Lieutenant Colonel (local Colonel) Swayne had commanded
the operations in Somaliland in both 1901 and 1902, before being recalled to
the War Office for consultations after suffering defeat at the hands of the
forces of Mohammed-bin-Abdullah Hassan at Erigo on 6 October 1902.
Better known to the British as the 'Mad Mullah', Hassan had emerged at the
head of a fanatical quasi-religious movement in the Ogaden in the 1890s,
raiding into British territory in 1899 and 1900. That territory itself had been
established gradually as a British protectorate since 1885, when troops from
Aden had occupied Berbera after its earlier abandonment by the Egyptian
authorities, who had maintained a presence on the Red Sea coast since 1866.
At the time of the British occupation of Berbera, the Italians were occupying
Massawa, also formerly under Egyptian control, and had extended their
influence southwards from Eritrea.

The French, too, secured a stake in the area by purchasing the Ghubbet
Kharab from the Sultan of Tajura in 1885 and, three years later, obtained
control of Djibouti in the settlement of a boundary between a British and a
French Somaliland. The boundaries between British Somaliland and the
further protectorates established by the Italians on the eastern coast between

1889 and 1892 were then agreed in 1894. The largely waterless desert and thorn scrub of the Haud, comprising much of the interior, thus parcelled up between the European powers had little importance in itself. However, the Horn of Africa did have strategic importance, especially for the British route to India, and British Somaliland was administered by the Government of India until 1898. Indeed, Somaliland's real significance was as a necessary ancillary to the garrison of Aden which was dependent upon supplies of meat brought down by caravans to Berbera.

The emergence of the Mullah, who was able to unite many of the warring nomadic Somali tribes, posed a threat not only to all the European powers but also to the authority of Emperor Menelek of Abyssinia. Accordingly, the Abyssinians participated in a joint operation with the British in 1901. But, since the control of British Somaliland had been passed to the Foreign Office in 1898, Indian troops had been withdrawn and the campaign was undertaken with locally raised native levies under Swayne's command. Neither the operations in 1901 nor those in the following year succeeded in eliminating the Mullah's 15,000 strong army and, at Erigo, Swayne's levies broke in panic and lost a maxim gun. Although the Mullah had also suffered a large number of casualties, the unreliability of the levies forced the withdrawal of the whole expedition.

At the time of the action at Erigo, Swayne's forces had consisted of some 2,360 men, of whom 1,500 were levies. His only regular troops consisted of 60 Sikhs of the 1st Battalion, King's African Rifles; 300 Yaos from British Central Africa in the 2nd Battalion, KAR (formerly the BCA Rifles); and 500 Somalis in a newly raised 6th Battalion, KAR. Now, more than 1,000 reinforcements were ordered hurriedly to Berbera from Aden, India and East, Central and South Africa. Six additional special service officers, of whom Johnnie was one, were also sought from England. Negotiations were begun at the same time with both the Italian and Abyssinian authorities, the intention being to co-operate with an Abyssinian army and to land the reinforcements from India at Obbia in Italian Somaliland in order to strike at the Mullah from the east, north and west. The operations would be directed by none other than Johnnie's erstwhile colleague in BCA, W. H. Manning. Manning was still only a captain in his regiment but had the brevet rank of Lieutenant Colonel and the additional local rank of Brigadier-General in his capacity as Inspector-General of the KAR. The latter was an appointment that Johnnie had welcomed when he first heard of it in South Africa in December 1901.

Manning arrived at Berbera on 22 October 1902, the 1st Bombay Grenadiers disembarking from Aden the same day. Elements of the 3rd and 5th Battalions, KAR reached the Somali port on 9 November, the date upon which the *Caledonia* docked at Aden. Sir Charles had speculated that Johnnie might be employed as Manning's chief staff officer, but in fact the appointment was already held by Major (local Lieutenant Colonel) G. T. Forestier-Walker. Johnnie himself would have preferred either another staff appointment or command of the levies. On reaching Berbera on 11 November, after transferring to a small boat at Aden, Johnnie discovered that Manning had selected him to be staff officer of a flying column being formed at Bohotle under the command of Captain (local Lieutenant Colonel) A. S. Cobbe, who had won the Victoria Cross for gallantry at Erigo.

Johnnie had already been required to bring over three months' supply of food for himself from Aden at some considerable expense as well as two small ponies allocated to him. He had every expectation that the expedition would cost him more than his £500 per annum pay. Indeed, Johnnie's accounts with Cowasjee Dinshaw and Brothers of Aden indicate that he spent £1,610 7s 0d between October and November 1903 although some of this was recovered from the Treasury. Now, he faced a journey of some 170 miles south to Garrero in the company of Brevet Colonel Charles Melliss of the Bombay Grenadiers, who had won the Victoria Cross in the third Ashanti war of 1900, and another special service officer, Brevet Major Tom Bridges. Each was allowed five camels to carry their three months' supplies and another to carry a water tank. Thus, less than three weeks after receiving his orders in London, Johnnie was accustoming himself to the motions of a camel in Somaliland.

There had hardly been time to take much in, although Johnnie had been delighted to find that the regimental pet of the 2nd KAR was his old dog 'Goa' from his days in BCA; sadly, Goa was to be carried off by a leopard four months later. Despite the scarcity of water, Johnnie liked the country, the plateau which they reached before passing into the Haud having a 'ripping climate' at this time of year. The Somali servant taken on at Aden was 'cheery and hardworking' and both Melliss and Bridges proved agreeable companions. However, it became clear that the Mullah was not going to be easy to track down since 'he has no village or any definite objective for us to attack and as he apparently does not expose himself much in a fight he is a difficult man to catch'. Even more of a problem was the Mullah's ability simply to withdraw 400 or 500 miles deeper into the Ogaden beyond the effective reach of Manning's command, which would be forced to rely on long and tenuous supply lines in the waterless country.

The difficulties were compounded still further by the previous incompetence of Swayne, one of whose miscalculations had been to fail to keep a rash promise made to Somali camel owners that they would receive one camel for every two lent to the government at the end of a campaign. As a result, they were now reluctant to part with their animals again and Manning was having the utmost difficulty in securing sufficient baggage camels. As the dry season had begun and would last at least until April, the wells in the Haud were drying up, making camel-borne water supplies even more vital. Indeed, when Johnnie arrived at Garrero on 21 November there was talk of the possibility of having to pull back on Berbera if the wells gave out. But, in any case, nothing could be attempted against the Mullah for six to eight weeks.[2]

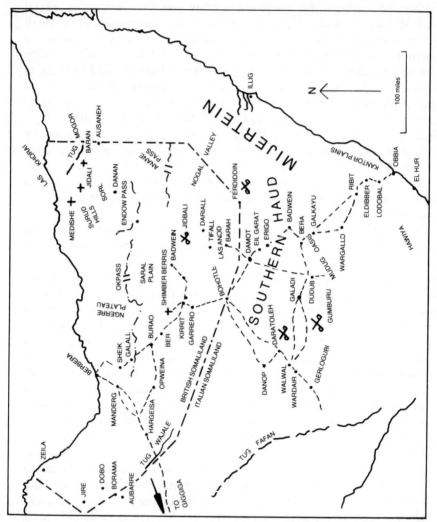

It was not a happy note on which to start the campaign and, writing to Hubert, Johnnie suggested that, 'As far as you getting out here goes, I don't think it would be worth your while unless it turns into something bigger.' For himself, Johnnie now suspected that he would not be at home for at least a year and, if this again delayed his attendance at Staff College, then he would try to get on another expedition in Africa, perhaps one against the Nandi in Uganda. In the meantime, he was living in a grass hut and messing with Bridges on good fresh mutton and camels' milk. Work was under way to disband most of Swayne's levies and to keep vital wells clear while supplies were moved up from Garrero to Bohotle, some 50 miles further south. The Mullah was reported at Mudug and the column would eventually make for this location in the hope of catching him. Johnnie would have liked to have got away to hunt some of the lions in the vicinity but was too busy. However, Melliss was unfortunate enough to be badly mauled by a lion on 4 December and it would be almost a year before he was able to return to his duties.

Ten days after Melliss' accident, the column moved to Bohotle with the first supplies to establish a forward base. The move gave Johnnie his first experience of handling larger numbers of camels, which the Somali drivers allowed to scatter unless closely supervised. It also introduced Johnnie to the Haud, the 20' high thorn scrub being so thick that visibility was often less than 30 yards, though the camels proved good observation platforms. Water was far more plentiful at Bohotle than at Garrero but moving the column beyond the former would be a minor problem. Johnnie calculated that a force of 1,200 men would need 720 camels to carry water alone for just ten days' subsistence. Yet, there were only 241 camels available at Garrero where 2,300 camel loads were piled for movement to Bohotle. By contrast, the Mullah's forces could exist largely on camels' milk.[3]

All in all, Johnnie was not finding it easy to get the flying column organised. The officers were 'inclined to be a bit casual' in obeying his orders and unnecessarily brutal to the Somalis, upon whom the transport system was utterly dependent. The peculiarity of local rank was also creating difficulties. Cobbe, who had been expected to command at Bohotle, was now ordered to Obbia to join Manning. This left command in the hands of Captain A. W. V. Plunkett of the 2nd KAR who, though actually junior to Johnnie, held the local rank of Lieutenant Colonel. Plunkett was pompous and did not strike Johnnie as 'a fellow who would do well on his own'. It was to prove a tragically prescient judgment. Johnnie also had to cope with a bout of fever and his mood was not tempered by reading De Wet's partisan account of the South African War which someone had lent him.

By early January 1903, Johnnie's illness had passed although the mass of mosquitoes at Bohotle meant that fever was still rife there. Stores were still being laboriously collected for the proposed advance on Mudug in co-operation with Manning's column from Obbia, which had disembarked on

26 December. Johnnie now anticipated the advance taking place around the middle of February and, besides fulfilling his staff duties, he was also running the intelligence network at Bohotle with 80 Somalis to try to determine the Mullah's precise whereabouts. It appeared that the Mullah was still at Mudug with some 1,200 riflemen and 7,000 spearmen, the lack of water forcing him to dispense with most of the 30,000 or 40,000 spearmen he could have mustered. The problem would be if the Mullah retreated before the columns from Obbia and Bohotle combined against him, for Obbia would be cut off by the return of the monsoon in April and the entire expedition would then have to depend upon supplies collected at Bohotle.

In mid-January, Johnnie received a letter from Cobbe at Obbia, which indicated that Manning was personally sorry it had not been possible to employ Johnnie with the Obbia column which would provide the main thrust on Mudug. Johnnie was not too disappointed at first since he had some hopes that 'we may have all the best of the show after all', but on 24 January he reported to his mother that 'we have received a great blow by being ordered to send all our transport back to Berbera to be transhipped (sic) to Obbia, as Manning's force seems to be completely hung up for want of camels and we are sacrificed'. Making the best of it, Johnnie proposed raiding the Mullah for camels and got the provisional agreement of Lieutenant Colonel J. C. Swann, who had replaced Plunkett in command of the Berbera-Bohotle column. Spies were sent out and Johnnie hoped to 'get a show up in about ten days'. A week later, Johnnie was still moving up supplies while awaiting reports from his agents but, he had been able to get in a three-day shoot and had also read the autobiography of Sir Harry Smith, which he recommended to Sir Charles as 'a real good book'.[4]

Unfortunately for Johnnie, the proposed raid fell through when the spies reported that the Mullah had removed his animals out of effective reach. Indeed, the Mullah had moved to Galadi, some 100 miles west of Mudug, and appeared to be ready to go south, conceivably as a result of learning of the landing at Obbia. Johnnie found time to send home for a suit of grey flannels; to ask Sir Charles to check on his accountants; and to send the skin of a leopard he had shot on his short expedition to Elinor de la Poer. He was fit and well though still troubled by his teeth and by the neuralgia that so often afflicted him on overseas campaigns. He was quite appalled to learn that Hubert had suffered an attack of gout, which he hoped to be spared himself, but was glad that Sir Charles was recovering well from a badly swollen ankle.

At least the column was beginning to take shape at Bohotle with 1,000 men, five maxim guns and three 7-pounder artillery pieces. There were only 80 camels, however, when 500 would be needed and an acute shortage of water tanks to be carried on the camels. While the authorities appeared to have failed badly in the provision of water tanks, they had sent out a 'marconigraph', as a proposed means of communication with the Obbia column. Johnnie showed some interest in this 'contraption', operated with a balloon by a naval party to supplement the telegraph lines being erected between Berbera and Bohotle. As he told Hubert in a letter on 16 February, the juxtaposition of wireless telegraphy and old 7-pounder muzzle-loaders side by side 'gives one an idea of the curious way this show is run'. In the event, the marconigraph was to prove a failure and was withdrawn altogether in May 1903, Johnnie being amused by the discovery that the seamen (or the 'handy-men') were 'no better than anyone else'. Although not now responsible for the intelligence network, Johnnie took obvious pride in the accuracy of the spies and scouts' reports now reaching Bohotle which suggested that a party of 60 to 100 of the Mullah's spearmen were at Damot. Damot was 45 miles to the south east of Bohotle and on the route to Mudug. The spearmen thus might prove an easy and convenient prey for a dash from Bohotle.[5]

On 3 March, Johnnie at last got his wish. With orders to if possible force an engagement, he took out a party of two companies of the 7th Bombay Pioneers, a detachment of Bombay Sappers and Miners with the marconigraph party, 100 Somali mounted infantry and 50 Somali Camel Corps troopers with two maxims. Before light on the following morning, Johnnie went ahead with the mounted infantry and Camel Corps. They halted a few hundred yards from the site of what the Somali guides had claimed was the Damot Wells. At dawn, however, it became apparent that the force was four miles from the wells and the tribesmen bolted as Johnnie galloped for them. Only nine were taken prisoner:

I was awfully disgusted at not getting the lot, but after all at the outside there could not have been 50 of the enemy there, not a very glorious victory – the pity was in my not bagging the lot, which I think I would have done if the guides had not sworn that we were so close to the wells, and thus made me waste three quarters of an hour waiting for it to get light.

At least Damot seemed to have good and plentiful water, though Johnnie was not quite sure whether it was permanent water or simply temporary storm water, the early rains having now fallen before the main monsoon. Accordingly, he left a small party in a strong zareba to secure the wells and returned to Bohotle.

After another quick raid on another party of the Mullah's followers at Lasante, 30 miles south of Bohotle, the main column moved off to Damot on 14 March 1903. Due to the failure of the marconigraph, no news had been received from Manning's column, but it was anticipated that they would also have advanced from Obbia to reach Mudug on 4 March and Galadi on 9 March. It now seemed likely that the Mullah himself was not at Galadi and, therefore, that the tribesmen would not put up much of a fight. Certainly, it seemed that the Bohotle force would have little to do and Johnnie's mind returned to the matter of the Staff College. As usual, Sir Charles had been active on his son's behalf and had written to the commandant at Camberley, Colonel H.S.G. Miles, to enquire whether Johnnie might be allowed to attend only a year's course of lectures from January 1904 to become staff qualified. Indeed, as the operations in Somaliland might descend to mere punitive action against Somali tribes, Johnnie hoped he might be out of the country altogether by June. It was also becoming unbearably hot – far worse than in the Sudan five years before – and water was being rationed to one gallon a day for officers, horses and camels and half a gallon a day for other ranks.

Once the column reached Damot, there seemed a chance that Johnnie might yet be able to join Manning, who had managed to make contact on 17 March and had requested 300 men of the 2nd KAR and some of the Somali mounted infantry to rendezvous with him at Galkayu, as he now did not intend to advance on Mudug until 28 March. Swann, who had earlier quarrelled with Plunkett and was beginning to get on Johnnie's nerves, initially refused to allow Johnnie to take the detachment to Galkayu and Plunkett was detailed to do so instead. But, on 23 March, Johnnie received a personal order to join Manning's staff. Taking 20 men of the Somali Camel Corps for escort, Johnnie completed the 108 miles from Damot to Galkayu without incident. With hardly time to wash or change, Johnnie then journeyed another 80 miles with Manning's column to Galadi, which was deserted. He was then sent back to Damot to take command of the Bohotle flying colum on 1 April, Swann having been ordered to command the lines of communications between Bohotle and Berbera. Manning intended to pursue the Mullah, who had moved further to the west in the vicinity of Wardair and Walwal, and Johnnie's orders were to prevent the Mullah escaping to the north and to 'raid and loot and generally punish' those tribes around Bohotle that had supported the Mullah.[6]

With his Somali cook as a guide and the company of W. T. Maud, the war correspondent of the *Daily Graphic*, Johnnie rode back across the Haud to Damot, meeting a party bringing up his kit which he was able to direct back. His command would consist of a mixed force of 6 officers and 80 Somali mounted infantry; 50 Somali Camel Corps and 50 of the (Indian) Bikanir Camel Corps; 8 officers and 260 men in three Yao companies of the 2nd KAR; and one officer and 85 men of a Sikh company of the BCA Indian contingent with three maxim guns. Supporting the fighting men would be 192 drivers and followers with 406 baggage animals capable of carrying 5 days' water and 12 days' rations. Captain C. M. Bruce, RFA would act as Johnnie's staff officer and Captain G. M. Rolland, 1st Bombay Grenadiers, as intelligence officer. There was also a medical officer with an NCO and 130 bearers, making a grand total of 543 combatants and 324 non-combatants.

Johnnie conferred with Swann when he arrived at Damot and it was decided that he should move in a south and south westerly direction to co-operate with Manning's operations from Galadi. Swann wanted Johnnie to advance 109 miles to Hodayuwein in one bound, but Johnnie decided that he could not risk doing so without firm information on water supplies, some being reported at Danop. Instead, Johnnie pushed out 40 and 50 miles with his infantry on 13 April. The mounted contingent started a day later and, after watering with the infantry from the water tins Johnnie had carried with him, moved on under Johnnie's personal command to find sufficient water to sustain the force as a whole. It was quite a gamble and Johnnie 'had never been so anxious' in his life but, on 17 April, they located water at Danop to the east of Hodayuwein and some 90 miles from Bohotle.

The position at Danop, which was a commanding one, was held by a few tribesmen but Johnnie's mounted men quickly drove them off. Johnnie had intended to withdraw if there had been no water at Danop and to make a raid south with the mounted men to catch some of the Mullah's stock. Therefore, he had already ordered the infantry, commanded by Captain (local Major) H. B. Rowlands of the 2nd KAR, to turn back to Bohotle when scouts had first reported that the water at Danop was insufficient to last more than three days. An inspection after the capture of the wells showed far more water than this, but not enough for his entire force, so Johnnie cancelled his previous orders and directed Rowlands to bring up 50 Sikhs, 100 Yaos and two maxims, while allowing the remainder of the infantry to return to Bohotle as planned.

In fact, Rowlands did not receive the order to move up to Danop, no less than six messengers losing their way, and more messages had to be sent back to him on 18 April. In the meantime, Johnnie put out patrols towards Wardair, where the Mullah was reported to have gathered 1,500 riflemen and 4,000 or 6,000 spearmen. Johnnie did not intend to risk attacking the Mullah with only 300 men, but he had expectations of being able to beat off any attempt to dislodge him from Danop. In any case, the last message from Manning on 8 April indicated that a strong advance guard under Cobbe would probably reach Wardair on about 16 April to be followed by Manning. However, water governed all and Johnnie might be forced to retire from Danop before he could co-operate with Manning and Cobbe.[7]

A few enemy horsemen appeared at Danop during the course of 18 and 19 April, but nothing transpired and, on the morning of 20 April, Rowlands arrived with the infantry. Further patrols were sent towards Wardair on 21 April, one of which returned with two prisoners who said that the Mullah had fought an action at Gumburu and had suffered heavily. They also said that there were perhaps 60 riflemen and 300 spearmen at Daratoleh, some 28 or 30 miles from Danop. The report was confirmed by a Somali boy called Ibrahim whom Johnnie had sent out three days earlier. Johnnie believed that Manning would now have united with Cobbe at Gumburu and would push on to Wardair. By moving to Daratoleh he himself would either be able to co-operate fully with Manning, or, if as reported, the British forces had halted at Gumburu, he could 'draw off some of the enemy and divert his attention from the Galadi force'.

In consequence, Johnnie resolved to move to Daratoleh on 22 April with his mounted troops and some of the infantry mounted on ponies or riding double behind the camel sowars. In all, he would take out 2 officers and 45 men of the Bikanir Camel Corps; 4 officers and 104 men of the Somali Mounted Infantry and Somali Camel Corps; 2 officers and 30 men of the 2nd KAR riding with the Bikanirs; and one officer and 12 Sikhs of the BCA Contingent riding ponies. The medical officer, Horton, would also accompany the force, as would Bruce and Rolland and Maud of the *Daily Graphic*. For good measure, he would also take Armourer Sergeant A. Gibb of the Army Ordnance Corps, attached to the 6th KAR, with his maxim gun. The total number of men including Johnnie was 206. The rest of his force remained at Danop.

Unknown to Johnnie, while the Mullah had indeed suffered casualties at Gumburu on 17 April, the action had more than merely temporarily halted Cobbe's advance. On 10 April, Cobbe had left Galadi to carry out a reconnaissance towards Wardair with 508 officers and men, 167 drivers and followers and 380 baggage camels. After some desultory skirmishing over the next few days, during which the column traversed about 50 miles, Cobbe decided that the thorn scrub was becoming too thick and the tracks through it too indistinct to proceed any further and he proposed to retire towards Gumburu, which he had passed on 12 April.

Cobbe had been instructed not to attack the Mullah's main body without Manning's support and he intended to leave an outpost at Gumburu before returning to Galadi. However, rainfall delayed his departure from Gumburu and increased enemy activity on 16 April persuaded Cobbe that it would be better to stay at Gumburu and await Manning. Patrols were sent out on both 16 and 17 April, and on the morning of the 17th half a company of the 1st KAR, commanded by Captain H. E. Olivey, ran into a large body of enemy tribesmen. Plunkett, who was accompanying Cobbe, felt that Olivey was being an alarmist in calling for support but Cobbe was less sanguine. Cobbe therefore ordered Plunkett to take a company of the 2nd KAR, 50 men of the 2nd Sikhs and two maxims to bring in Olivey's party. As both Cobbe and Tom Bridges, who was also present, later wrote to Johnnie, Plunkett was told firmly that his orders were only to extricate Olivey. The order was made definite because Plunkett seemed 'spoiling for a fight'. Foolishly, once he had reached Olivey, Plunkett ignored his instructions and advanced on the enemy.

After two or three miles Plunkett was faced with 'numbers like the sand' and, although he formed his command into square, it was totally overwhelmed when ammunition ran low 'in a stabbing, bayonetting melee'. Of the combined force of Plunkett and Olivey, only 40 native troops struggled back to Gumburu: all nine white officers and 187 other ranks perished. Cobbe was powerless to effect relief with almost 40 per cent of his fighting strength lost. Manning relieved Cobbe on 19 April and decided to withdraw the entire force to Galadi to reorganise and to replenish the supplies and transport lost in the abortive advance. Thus it was that Johnnie's own column was moving towards an enemy that was far greater in numbers than he expected, far better armed through the capture of modern rifles from Plunkett – the maxims had been destroyed by the troops before they could be taken – and flushed with success.[8]

Johnnie was to describe the movements and action of his command at Daratoleh on a number of occasions. Brief accounts were penned to Harriette on 23 April and to Hubert on 3 May. He was also required to write an official report, dated 28 April, which was eventually published in the *London Gazette* with other official despatches on 7 August 1903. In fact, Johnnie had also written a long account to Sir Charles as well as another to Hubert longer than that in his letter of 3 May, but both were lost in a camp fire at Bohotle on 2 May, together with all Johnnie's official papers and most of his belongings. The fact that it was Johnnie's first effort destined for official publication may explain why the original version was judged by Manning's staff officer, Forestier-Walker, to be an 'inchoate document' requiring further details of the initial movements of Johnnie's force from Danop and the strength of the force at various stages.

The fire could only have made revision more difficult, a draft in Johnnie's papers showing additions on 12, 14 and 17 May before Swann forwarded the final document to Forestier-Walker on 22 May. In any case, these additions did not alter the somewhat terse description of the action at Daratoleh. Fortunately, Johnnie wrote one further frank personal account on 12 September, which may have been purely for his own use since the actions of individuals are revealed in a way scrupulously avoided in all the other accounts he compiled. A further account also appeared anonymously in the section of the official history of the campaign, published by the War Office in 1907, dealing with strategy and tactics. Manning contributed some general points on the use of squares and 'notes and sketches' were 'furnished by an officer who commanded a column'. Since these notes and sketches all refer to the officer's experience at Daratoleh, there is no doubt that the author was Johnnie. The affair was also reported by Maud for the *Daily Graphic* but it is Johnnie's personal account of 12 September that will be most closely followed.[9]

Johnnie moved out of Danop at 4.50 a.m. on 22 April, riding with Bruce and Rolland just behind the advance guard of the Somali Mounted Infantry. Progress was slow due to the dense bush and indistinct tracks, the column managing only four or five miles an hour. At about 7.30 a.m. they were fired on by three enemy scouts, who immediately fled. The mounted infantry gave chase, killing one and wounding another while the third escaped on foot. Ominously, the scouts had all been carrying modern rifles although it did not occur to anyone that they had come from British forces. Johnnie decided he must get to Daratoleh before the surviving fugitive could warn his fellows and the column pressed on. Two hours later, where the bush was getting progressively thicker, the advance guard again made contact with enemy scouts.

Johnnie dismounted his force and formed square with the camels and ponies in the centre. In his personal account, he remarked: 'I had some difficulty in getting this done as quickly as I wished, and I was glad that no attack was made on us at this moment.' Yet, the notes Johnnie contributed to the official history three years later indicate just how carefully he had planned his tactics. The Bikanirs in the centre of the line of march actually formed the front face of the square, the Yaos the left, the Somali Camel Corps the right face, and the Sikhs a reserve in the centre. The mounted infantry, who had been the advance guard making contact, moved swiftly to the rear past the already formed Bikanirs to enable the latter to bring fire to bear immediately on any enemy, who would not expect 'to run their noses on to the proper front face'. Equally, Johnnie had had a plan worked out should he have been caught strung out on the line of march, though he intended to have sufficient scouts out himself to ensure that he could not be surprised. Nor did he intend to form square in a clearing and let the enemy pour fire on his troops from cover as Plunkett had done: instead Johnnie would form square on the edge of any clearing so that it would be the enemy who must cross open ground.

In the event, the enemy scouts melted into the bush, although one mounted enemy tribesman earned Johnnie's admiration by galloping suddenly right up to the square to carry out 'one of the most daring bits of scouting' Johnnie had ever seen. Johnnie's command then advanced slowly on foot for another half mile before he mounted them again in their original formation. However, at 10.20 a.m. the advance guard reported that a very large enemy force was moving towards them. Johnnie variously estimated it at between 300 and 600 riflemen and between 400 and 1,000 spearmen, the larger figures reflecting information subsequently collected from other sources by the time he wrote his personal account. Square was formed once more, one man in every four being detailed to stay with the ponies and horses, which were tied down, and the camels, which were hobbled. Johnnie was amused to see Maud calmly 'pulling out his sketch book and picking out a comfortable spot in the shade of a Bikanir camel'.

Almost at once, Captain (later Major-General) L. H. R. Pope-Hennessy, who was to become one of Johnnie's closest friends, opened volley fire with his Somali Camel Corps. The ground was flat but thickly covered with 15 to 20′ high thorn bush interspersed with 3½′ high grass and the ensuing fire fight took place at between only 20 and 50 yards distance. To Johnnie's horror the Bikanirs, whom he had judged totally reliable, started to throw themselves on the ground when they came under fire and to discharge their own rifles high in the air. Fortunately, the situation was restored by Sergeant Gibb with his maxim and the other native troops were all shooting steadily, if with some excitement, as Johnnie walked around the square.

As Johnnie walked up to talk to Captain (local Major) A. G. G. Sharp of the Somali Mounted Infantry, who had earlier annoyed him by fussing over the placing of the maxim, Sharp was shot through the thigh. Johnnie moved up the Sikhs to keep down the enemy fire, which seemed particularly heavy at this part of the square, and went to find Horton, the medical officer. Horton was shooting away at the enemy himself, but Johnnie ordered him to attend Sharp and set up a hospital under cover of the camels. In the meantime, Gibb had sufficiently dampened the ardour of the enemy attacking the front face to enable Johnnie to move the maxim to the rear face:

I went over with him [Gibb] and saw him comfortably started, it was just wonderful how the enemy seemed to wither up when they got a maxim playing on them. I never saw anyone work a maxim like Sergeant Gibb, he was grinning all over and as pleased as a school boy.

Johnnie moved on and, noting the rapidity with which ammunition was being expended, ordered all the reserve ammunition collected from the camels. In order that additional infantrymen could ride behind his camel sowars, Johnnie had set off with a reduced amount of reserve ammunition; it would appear, nevertheless, that more than 17,000 rounds were fired in the course of the action as a whole. C. E. Callwell, the author of the War Office's standard manual on colonial campaigning, *Small Wars: Their Principles and Practice*, in referring to both Gumburu and Daratoleh, later commented that it would have been preferable to fire volleys as a means of conserving ammunition. In the case of Daratoleh, volleys were fired at least initially, but it is unclear from the various accounts whether the troops were subsequently allowed to fire independently.

It is clear, however, that Johnnie was concerned with the ammunition supply throughout for, when the reserves were collected, 'I must say it gave me rather a shock when I saw how little there was of it'. It is also apparent from a letter Johnnie sent to Sir Charles on 30 May that 'nearly all' Johnnie's command were using expanding ('dum-dum') bullets. This was contrary to official orders, but Johnnie was convinced that their stopping power saved his square from being overrun. Johnnie believed strongly in 'nothing except expanding bullets being used against savages' and, when asked to report on the service bullet from his experience at Daratoleh, Johnnie got round his embarrassment by the non-committal answer that 'from my experience in my fight I thought expanding bullets should be used against fanatics'.

Another of Johnnie's concerns was that casualties were mounting. He later noted in his contribution to the official history:

As in most fights of this kind, our troops suffered most from the enemy's fire going over the heads of one face of the square and hitting the men of the opposite face in the back, so much so that complaints were received 'that our own people were shooting from the centre of the square', which impression was, naturally, apt to upset the steadiness of the men.

The war correspondent of the *Daily Telegraph*, Bennet Burleigh, was not present at Daratoleh but interviewed the participants soon after and recorded it had been a 'weird struggle for the most part against an unseen enemy' since the Mullah's men were largely concealed by the bush. Indeed, the tribesmen's presence could only be detected by the noise they were making and the incoming fire from black powder cartridges in the old Austrian Gras rifles that many of them carried. Those armed with modern smokeless Lee Metfords taken from Plunkett's force did not give themselves away in the same fashion. Captain C. Godfrey, commanding the Sikhs, had his leg broken by one bullet and Rowlands of the KAR was also hit, a bullet passing through his arm into his back while he conferred with Johnnie. In striking contrast to Sharp, who kept demanding Johnnie's personal attention and bewailing the fate of himself and the force as a whole, both Godfrey and Rowlands bore their injuries stoically.

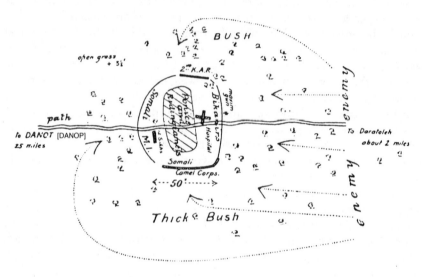

DARATOLEH, 22 APRIL 1903, FROM A SKETCH BY
JOHNNIE

At about 1.30 p.m., Johnnie ordered Captain R. E. Townsend, who had taken over command of the Yaos from Rowlands, to charge out for 100 yards to ease the pressure on the square. Johnnie went with the Yaos and they scattered the tribesmen. Johnnie then ordered Pope-Hennessy to do the same with his Somalis. The enemy fire slackened after these successful charges and Johnnie considered whether or not he should use the opportunity to retire on Danop. As he did so, one of the enemy ran towards the square and Johnnie himself shot the man through the arm. The tribesmen was dragged into the square by some of Pope-Hennessy's men and questioned. The man claimed that the Mullah himself was present in person and this convinced Johnnie that he must withdraw while he could since it seemed unlikely that Manning or Cobbe could be anywhere near. Some of the Mullah's men had taunted

Johnnie's Somalis by calling out that they had destroyed the Galadi force and, although Johnnie could not believe it, it was undeniable that some of the enemy were wearing items of KAR uniform. Johnnie later remarked that he was also 'rudely surprised' by the number of modern rifles in the tribesmen's hands. Thus, it was resolved to retreat.

Horton began to get the wounded up on to the camels with the help of Maud, a task completed by about 2.30 p.m., by which time enemy fire was again increasing. Johnnie had arranged for Captain W. G. Walker of the Bikanirs to charge out for 100 yards with his own men, reinforced by the Sikhs, to drive back the enemy from the front face of the square. On the return of Walker, who had been accompanied by the ubiquitous Maud, the mounted infantry of the rear face charged out in turn to begin the withdrawal since, of course, they were closest to the direction of Danop. The camels in the centre were quickly closed up behind the mounted infantry and the other faces retired in an elastic square formation.

Johnnie had been relieved to see Walker's men follow their officer readily enough but, as Johnnie fell back with them in the first stage of the retirement, he suddenly found that the 35 effectives of the Bikanirs had become but five or six:

It was a terrible blow to me and I honestly thought that this was the beginning of the end, but my old friends the Yaos saw us out of it, being as steady as rocks and splendidly led by young Townsend who had been slightly wounded in the hip, his helmet having a great bullet hole and his sleeve cut open by another bullet, but all the same smiling away and as cool as a cucumber.

One of the Yao NCOs pulled at Johnnie's sleeves crying 'Hi maxim, maxim, mzanga' (Hi, the maxim, the maxim, quickly). Seeing the need, Johnnie got Gibb down from his camel and into action. He also sent four of the mounted infantry off at 'full tilt' to Danop to ask for as many men as possible to come out to meet him with as much ammunition as they could carry.

The retirement continued with 20 Yaos and some Somalis supplementing the remaining Bikanirs in the rearguard. The others, whom Johnnie was to describe as 'the rottenest fighters I have ever met', took refuge with the camels, 'and no one had the time to try and kick them out of it'. Whenever the square crossed a clearing, Johnnie halted at the far end 'and got some pretty shooting at the most venturesome' of the pursuers. The square was not again subjected to the same pressure as in the first few minutes of the action, but because of the thickness of the bush enemy tribesmen were able to get very close 'and we lost a good many men'. Johnnie, who had seen a number of men shot down by his side, was feeling 'awfully tired' by this time and mounted his pony so that he could move around the square more easily. Then, while he was with the right face of the retreating square, he heard much heavier firing at the rear. One of the Bikanirs, 'who was sitting up on his camel with evidently no intention of doing any fighting himself', remarked to Johnnie that one of the officers with the rearguard had been wounded. Johnnie dismounted and ran back where he met Rolland who told him that Bruce had been badly hit and 'he wanted a camel to bring him away on'.

Ordering the square to halt, Johnnie went to find what was happening while Rolland secured a camel. Turning a corner on a path through the scrub, Johnnie saw Bruce lying on his back and Walker kneeling beside him and firing at the enemy:

It was as fine a sight as ever man wants to see and it gave me quite a lump in my throat. When I got to Bruce it was quite obvious that he could not live: I remember I put my finger in his eye and his eyelid never moved, which meant that he was practically gone then.

A letter written by Rolland to a relative and later published in *The Times* on 10 August and other provincial newspapers in the same month described how Bruce had been shot through the right side at close range some 400 yards away from the main rearguard. Bruce was a heavy man at 14 stone compared to Rolland, who weighed only 9½ stone, and neither Walker nor Rolland could lift him. Rolland had therefore gone for a camel while Walker stayed to defend Bruce. With Walker were two Yaos, Sergeant Nderamani and Corporal Surmoni; Lance Naik Maieya Singh of the Sikhs; and Sowar Umar Ismail of the Somali Camel Corps. Although the enemy fire was not heavy, they were closing to within barely ten yards and Johnnie found 'every bullet came horribly close'. Rolland now returned and said he had a camel ready. In Johnnie's words:

We then tried to carry Bruce and found it most difficult, but eventually we got him along in a blanket between us and put him down beside the camel. As we were trying to lift him a bullet came among us with a great smack; just missing my hand it went through Bruce's thigh but he was too far gone to feel anything and only looked up for a second and I think he actually died then. The Sikh just then got a bullet through his arm, and we just managed to get Bruce's body on the saddle and immediately moved off and rejoined the square. It was a very near thing indeed.

The rescue of Bruce's body at about 5.30 was almost the last act of the fight at Daratoleh for enemy firing died down considerably as the square reached more open country.

Johnnie got the Somali Mounted Infantry on horseback to clear the way, then mounted the remainder of his command. Pope-Hennessy's men covering the retirement. Sharp, who had earlier demanded a personal escort of Sikhs when the retreat began, then issued an order to trot which Johnnie countermanded quickly for fear that it might result in a disorganised gallop. Sharp tried again and Johnnie 'eventually got tried a bit too high and told him "to go on with his Somali Mounted Infantry and to go to hell for all I cared" '. Indeed, Sharp did then move ahead, upsetting the formation, and Johnnie had to sort it out: the resourceful Pope-Hennessy restored Johnnie's temper with a welcome bottle of beer. At 1.30 a.m. on 23 April, the column reached Danop, being met about six miles out by a party alerted by Johnnie's messengers. Rolland, whose account was judged, rather unjustly, by Johnnie to be 'most hysterical', recalled the last phase of the retirement as a 'terrible march' with the smell of the dead being carried on the camels and with no time for snatching food, water or respite. Indeed, few of the men had managed more than a handful of rice or a few biscuits since the early hours of 22 April and they had covered some 54 miles in less than 21 hours while being in continuous contact with the enemy for over seven hours.

Godfrey had died of his wounds during the retirement and he and Bruce were buried at Danop with Johnnie conducting the service. Sharp, Townsend and Captain E. M. Hughes of the Bikanirs had been wounded as well as Rowlands, who had to have his arm amputated and who subsequently died of fever. A total of 13 native troops had been killed and 25 wounded. Some 26 camels and ponies had been lost and, all in all, it represented a casualty rate of 22 per cent in Johnnie's force. The enemy loss was estimated at between 150 and 200 and, while losing none of their own weapons, Johnnie's men had brought away 11 enemy rifles.

It was not until the following day – 24 April – that Johnnie received a message from Swann that Plunkett had met with disaster and that he should withdraw. Having already decided to pull back unless he heard news of the Galadi column, Johnnie left Danop that afternoon. Swann had sent a force of 150 men under Captain H. F. Byrne with 12 days' rations and 140 water tins to Johnnie's assistance and Johnnie met Byrne 20 miles out of Bohotle, which was reached on the morning of 28 April. It had been a most memorable few days for Johnnie. Although Tom Bridges referred to Johnnie's action at Daratoleh, somewhat playfully, as a 'successful side show', *The Times* was moved to describe it as 'the only bright spot in this tiresome campaign'. According to Captain Hubert Lenox-Conyngham, a veterinary inspector at Bohotle, Johnnie received 'the greatest credit from everyone' and Rolland's letter referred to him as 'a splendid soldier, so cool and calm – he is a good fellow'. Moreover, two years later, a former interpreter with the Somali Mounted Infantry wrote to Johnnie to say that Daratoleh and Johnnie's name were widely spoken of among the Mullah's army.

As his immediate superior, Swann was the first to comment officially on Johnnie's 'care, foresight and dash' in proving himself a 'most capable commander', while Manning, who sent his personal congratulations, praised Johnnie in his despatch of 28 June for 'skilful handling of a small force in difficult bush country, when surrounded by superior numbers of a brave and fanatical enemy' as 'worthy of high commendation'. When the news reached England, Lord Roberts also sent his personal congratualtions, while Sir Charles, who proudly wrote to Laura that Johnnie was 'really one of the bravest and best officers of his age in the army', was also to receive a succession of congratulatory telegrams on Johnnie's conduct from the Gough clan.

Johnnie himself concluded,

Taking it all round I think my first independent command was full of incident and difficulties to be overcome – good practice for the future.

However, at the same time, he was distressed at the death of Bruce, a 'real good fellow' who had shared his quarters at Bohotle. One of Johnnie's first tasks was to write to Sir Charles Bruce, the Governor of Mauritius, with news of his son's death. He also recommended Rolland and Walker for the Victoria Cross, the two Yaos and the Somali for the African Distinguished Conduct Medal, and the Sikh for the Order of Merit for their roles in the attempt to save Bruce. But, he suppressed any official mention of Sharp's conduct or that of the Bikanirs as well as his own part in Bruce's rescue. He therefore cut out any reference to the latter in Maud's first account of the action for the *Daily Graphic* and it was not until Maud reached Bohotle that an additional telegram was despatched to the newspaper's London office:

My despatch from Danop, dated April 23rd, describing Daratoleh was censored by Major Gough who passed everything therein except mention of himself in connection with the rescue of Captain Bruce.

This revelation reached England, of course, well in advance of the official despatches and was to have major repercussions for Johnnie later.[10]
    Meanwhile, Johnnie had cause to be dispirited. After the camp fire at Bohotle, he had no clothes left and was managing with a coat made from a blanket and a shirt made from a Sikh's puggaree until he could get new supplies from Aden. Worse, he was disgusted at the inaction following the affairs at Gumburu and Daratoleh. Believing that the Mullah had suffered heavily, Johnnie felt a new advance was urgently necessary for 'every week we wait will add to the Mullah's power and prestige'. Unfortunately, the transport was in utter chaos. Johnnie was reluctant to criticise Manning and blamed an 'inefficient and objectionable' staff, the prospect of having to join them, if his own column was broken up, being quite appalling.
    Adding to his frustration, Johnnie was forced to confine 40 of the Somali Camel Corps who had served him so well at Daratoleh in the guardroom after they refused to obey Pope-Hennessy's orders. Although he had listened to the men's grievances, Johnnie had no intention of emulating Swayne who 'used to turn out British officers if the Somalis came and complained'. Then, in mid-May, came the news that Maud had died of fever at Aden while on the way home to his pregnant wife. Johnnie was 'most awfully distressed' when he had come to like Maud so much, and he asked Sir Charles to write to the editor of the *Daily Graphic* to suggest a public subscription to which he would gladly contribute anonymously. All in all, therefore, the euphoria of Daratoleh faded quickly, and Sir Charles was greatly concerned when Johnnie began to suggest that he might leave the army to take up pig farming since 'I must say my thoughts are more inclined that way than to rising to

become a general in the army'.[11]

The situation in late May was still unclear with the onus on the British government either to order a complete withdrawal from the interior or to send yet more reinforcements. Johnnie felt that withdrawal would result in the need for an even larger expedition in the future and thought it best 'to go on until the Mullah is absolutely crushed'. While the decision was awaited, the expeditionary force sat it out, although it was resolved to bring Manning's column from Galkayu and Galadi to Bohotle. Once again, Johnnie lost all his transport animals to enable this to be done. He was now convinced that his own command would be broken up once Manning arrived and he hoped to be able to go home. As he wrote to his mother on 30 May, he had 'no shame about going, as I honestly think I have done my share of battle fighting'. A day later, he also wrote to Sir Charles that he was not ambitious,

but there is one thing I have always looked upon as the duty of a soldier, i.e. to study his profession earnestly so that if one day he is put to the test and has the lives and honour of his men put in his keeping that he should be able to give a good account of his trust. It often struck me, especially in South Africa, that it would be an awful feeling for a commander to feel he had thrown his command away and lost valuable lives through incompetence, which could have been rectified by the study of his profession. I can only say God was very good to me in my first command and to Him be all the praise.

The news that Sir Charles' ankle was still causing trouble and that Harriette was also in poor health were additional reasons for going home, even if Johnnie expected he had lost any chance of getting to the Staff College.

It did not appear that Manning's column could be transferred to Bohotle until the end of June and it was a possibility that the Mullah's army might try to intercept the movement since the Abyssinian army was reputedly retiring from the campaign for want of water and grain. In such circumstances, Johnnie would have to do his best to help Manning across the Haud and he sent out a patrol to locate sufficient water to maintain his own column for a week or ten days to the south west of Bohotle. He found time to win the 'Somaliland Grand National' in the Bohotle gymkhana on a new Somali pony, but in early June the Mullah's horsemen tore down the telegraph lines north and south of Bohotle and it was reported that the Mullah himself with 5,000 horsemen was advancing on Damot, where there was a small garrison of 120 men. Manning, too, was due to reach Damot by 21 June and it looked increasingly that there would be a renewed struggle.

Unfortunately, Swann and Johnnie could reach no agreement on what the role of the Bohotle column should be. Swann was an ideal commander on lines of communication, but was far more interested in building roads than military operations and he had little or no grasp of the needs of the situation. Initially, Johnnie wanted to take out as large a force as possible – about 600 men – on 12 June but he saw the logic of the more cautious Swann's argument that this risked exposing both the column and the garrisons of Bohotle and

Damot to defeat in detail. Moreover, when Johnnie did send out a patrol of 45 Somali Mounted Infantry, all of whom had fought well at Daratoleh, no less than 16 promptly deserted to the Mullah. Then, to Johnnie's surprise, Swann changed his mind on 13 June and ordered him to take out 600 men to ensure that Damot was safe. In fact, a messenger arrived from Damot just before Johnnie was due to leave saying all was well. Secure in the knowledge that Damot was safe, Johnnie felt it better to wait for further information on the Mullah's movements, but it took sometime to convince Swann that the sortie should be postponed.[12]

Further confusion followed with this reversal of roles between Johnnie, who was now cautious, and Swann, who was now seemingly intent on launching Johnnie into the Haud. On 20 June, Swann again ordered Johnnie to move to Damot, this time taking 550 men with the object of pushing the remaining 35 effectives of the Somali Mounted Infantry and 30 British mounted infantrymen into Damot as a reinforcement. But Swann insisted that Johnnie should avoid any fighting. Feeling that 550 men was too small a force, Johnnie pointed out that 'it does not rest with me whether there is a fight or not as the enemy has some 4,000 horsemen besides any number of spearmen and consequently he can fight or not as it suits him'. Swann refused to allow Johnnie to see the parade states of the Bohotle garrison, but Johnnie reckoned the effective total at 1,000 fighting men. He felt, therefore, that Swann must make up his mind either to send enough men – 750 to 800 – to take care of themselves to Damot and make it the centre of operations, with a small garrison at Bohotle, or to leave the larger force at Bohotle. Since Manning had only 1,400 men and over 1,800 baggage animals, Johnnie's preference was for taking at least 750 men to Damot to help out. Adding to Johnnie's resolve was a letter addressed to the Bohotle garrison by the Mullah which made it appear that he intended to fight.

On 22 June, Swann, who appeared to have been drinking heavily during the evening, summoned Johnnie at 11 p.m. 'and told me (in a most offensive manner) that I was to march to Damot and connect with the GOC [Manning], who at that time had not been heard from and we had no idea where he was'. Swann then 'proceeded to say I was to go right through the enemy however strong they were'. Johnnie was incensed to be told that he could take only 525 men – 'while [Swann] sat here with some 500 to 600 men behind earthworks and in a masonry fort'. Moreover, Johnnie was also ordered to take 280 baggage animals because Manning was short of rations, even though Swann knew this to be wrong. As Johnnie wrote to Sir Charles,

I thought the whole thing so serious that I wrote everything down and left it behind to be sent to you in case we were mopped up, which I think would have happened, at any rate I felt certain I was in for a 'regrettable incident' and meant to have my opinion on the situation before I started down in writing.

Thus, while his small command was hastily preparing for a 5.30 a.m. start,

Johnnie set down his disagreement with Swann's instructions 'as I fully realise that my column may be absolutely swamped by numbers'. If a fight could not be avoided, Johnnie believed that a minimum of 800 men should be sent since Bohotle's fortifications could be held easily by only 200 or 250 men. Swann was dividing the force unnecessarily and Johnnie believed, although he confined it to a private letter to Sir Charles, that Swann's orders 'were greatly prompted by a desire to look after his own skin'. In the event, all was well, for Johnnie had hardly gone 12½ miles with his column before he met a messenger from Manning announcing that the Galadi column had reached Damot and the Mullah's army had retired.[13]

Manning reached Bohotle without further incident on 23 June and reprimanded Swann for his error of judgment. Johnnie was offered command of the 2nd KAR in place of the dead Plunkett. It meant local rank of Lieutenant Colonel and £900 per annum at the age of 31, but Johnnie did not wish to be 'isolated in lonely parts of Africa'. Manning had not actually expected Johnnie to accept, but presumably made the gesture in appreciation of Johnnie's services while he still had the gift of such appointments. A telegram had been received by Manning while on the march between Damot and Bohotle announcing his supercession by Major-General Sir Charles Egerton from India. Egerton would bring further reinforcements from both India and Aden and Manning was to concentrate purely on the protection of posts between Bohotle and Berbera until Egerton had the opportunity of assessing the situation at first hand.

Manning seemed to Johnnie to be relieved that he could hand over the responsibility for the campaign to another man but he was 'very down about everything' and uncertain of his future. Johnnie, too, did not know what the future might hold, but was occupied with bringing in the Damot garrison before being ordered to report himself to Sheikh in mid-July, Egerton having reached Berbera on 3 July 1903. Johnnie had no desire to stay any longer, especially as it was clear that the Indian army was now going to dominate the campaign. Johnnie did not trust Indian troops, except the Sikhs, after his experiences and he expected that Egerton, like Manning, would fail through transport problems. More to the point, 'the Indian Army is a jealous one and I should probably have some rotten job to do'. Of course, there had long been rivalry between the Indian and home establishments, the struggle for influence over Imperial military policy being personified by the animosity between Wolseley, as representative of the home army, and Roberts' as representative of the Indian army. Both men had been equally determined to secure personal advancement for themselves and their adherents. Ultimately, the 'Indians' had triumphed with Roberts' succession to Wolseley as Commander-in-Chief in the War Office. Although Johnnie's father had been an officer of the Indian army and Johnnie himself clearly enjoyed Roberts' favour, a British officer *per se* could still expect little advancement in 'a regular Indian campaign'.

Upon arriving at Sheikh, Johnnie found himself posted to command the Indian Mounted Infantry and the Bikanir Camel Corps, for which he had so little regard. It 'knocked on the head' any idea of a swift return home since he was ordered to concentrate the 500 men of his combined command at the hot and dusty Bihendula, 20 miles out of Berbera on the main route to Bohotle. Egerton had formed two infantry brigades from the existing force and the reinforcements which seemed to Johnnie of little use in 'this waterless and barren country'. Indeed, the ponderous Indian establishment seemed entirely wrong for the campaign against the Mullah, and Indian troops appeared to Johnnie 'the worst possible for this country because of their caste prejudices'. Manning was placed in command of one of the brigades, but he told Johnnie privately that he was considering the offer of being High Commissioner in southern Nigeria. Having seen something of the Indian contingent under his command, half of whom were drawn from the Bombay presidency, Johnnie could 'not imagine any very glorious deeds being done with my commando' and he was less than amused to find that his opposite number in the British Mounted Infantry, Major Paul Kenna, V.C., who had come out to Somaliland at the same time as Johnnie, had been given local rank of Lieutenant Colonel. Bihendula proved to have a bathing pool and pleasant fig trees, under which Johnnie pitched his tent, but he did not relish the prospect of staying there for several months. As a result, he wrote to Sir Charles on 3 August asking his father to use his influence and that of Major-General Hugh Gough, still on the active list, to get Johnnie ordered home in time to join the Staff College in January 1904.[14]

Johnnie himself wrote to Francis Howard, soon to become Inspector of Recruiting at the War Office, and 'a good many others' who might be able to help. He also wrote privately to Egerton's chief of staff, Major H. E. Stanton, 'asking how I stood with reference to the Staff College', and he managed to extract a promise that Egerton would write to the Military Secretary at the War Office on Johnnie's behalf. In the immediate future, however, there was little prospect of any kind of advance before October or November, since the transport situation remained unchanged and the Mullah would almost certainly retire into the interior. At least Johnnie was fit and now intended to have his long-troubled teeth seen to by a dentist expected to join the expeditionary force. He also received the welcome news that both Walker and Rolland had been awarded the Victoria Cross in the *London Gazette* of 7 August 1903. However, he was increasingly concerned by the way 'the press keep on digging up my affair at Daratoleh'.

Originally, Johnnie thought that Maud's version, written with the best of intentions but looking 'at the show from the point of view of "copy" for his paper', would harm the chances of Rolland and Walker in getting their reward. Subsequently, Johnnie feared press stories would reflect badly on himself, writing – when it was wrongly reported he had been given a camel by Lord Cromer –

besides this kind of thing does one a lot of harm and one will be put down as one of the advertising gang, which is rather hard on me as I don't think anyone has a greater horror of that kind of thing than myself.

He simply did not want his name in the newspapers and was distressed when Rolland's letter appeared in *The Times* on 10 August. It later transpired that Bruce's aunt, Margaret Helen Macmillan, had also determined to get Johnnie's part in the rescue acknowledged.[15]

In Somaliland, Johnnie had a touch of fever at the end of August; the suggestion by a native hospital orderly, however, that the end of Johnnie's uvula should be removed had an immediate effect in reducing the size of the swelling. Johnnie also got in some shooting before his command was ordered down to Berbera to await the eventual advance. Although he found it very hot, Johnnie had an agreeable room in a house formerly occupied by Swayne and he was able to enjoy luxuries such as eggs, fish and soda-water unknown in the interior. Better still, was the news that reached him from the War Office in mid-September, that arrangements were being made to get him to the Staff College in January. Well pleased, Johnnie went off for a week's rest in the hills.

However, on his return to Berbera, Johnnie was furious to discover that Egerton had decided to replace him with an Indian Army officer in command of the mounted infantry. As Aspinall's account of Johnnie in South Africa had demonstrated, Johnnie always spoke his mind and was not slow to criticise those who did not measure up to his own high standards. Egerton may possibly have had it in mind that an officer who was going home in December, when the next advance would have barely begun, ought to be replaced sooner rather than later. Johnnie may therefore have over-reacted by calling it 'downright wicked for such a slur to be thrown on me' and blaming the jealousies of older Indian army officers 'at what they think the indecent push and dash of youngsters'.

A letter Johnnie wrote to Hubert on 4 October suggests that he had Swann and Lieutenant Colonel C. G. M. Fasken of the 2nd Sikhs, who had been made a local Brigadier-General, in mind: 'Both rotten soldiers but Indian'. Nevertheless, Egerton's protestations that he thoroughly appreciated Johnnie's efforts sounded hollow and the alternative employment offered Johnnie – buying ponies in Abyssinia, working with tribesmen in the north east, or acting as staff officer to Kenna – unconvincing. Consequently, Johnnie wrote to Egerton to say that he himself had pointed out the difficulties of putting a British officer in command of Indian troops at the very beginning and that to replace him now 'was a great blow on me as a soldier'. Johnnie was also concerned that his replacement might prejudice opinion of him in the War Office.[16]

Egerton replied by asking Johnnie again to consider becoming staff officer to Kenna. If Johnnie had been offered the appointment in the first place, rather than superceded and given it as one of three options, he might have accepted, but 'with the evidence of some very underhand work going on', he was not keen to do so. When Egerton then appointed one of his protégés, Major R. G. Brooke of the 7th Hussars, who was not an Indian army officer, to command the mounted infantry, it seemed even more to Johnnie that his removal was 'as obvious a job as could be imagined'. Meeting Egerton at Burao on 15 October, Johnnie 'asked him plainly to tell me if he had any reason for putting another officer into the Indian M.I. beyond what he had said in his letter'. Egerton assured Johnnie that it was merely because Brooke had passed in Hindustani and Johnnie had not, but Johnnie still got the distinct impression that the general was 'a bit ashamed of the job that had been done'. As it happened, all ended well for Johnnie when Manning asked him to take temporary command of the 2nd KAR and a 'movable column' at Eil Dub, some 25 miles east of Garrero. It would not be a long appointment for orders had now arrived for Johnnie to join the Staff College in January.

Johnnie stayed with Manning and Cobbe for a few days then travelled to his new command, bringing them up to Wadamago on 2 November and to Bohotle on the following day as Manning's brigade was concentrated to support Egerton's intended advance from Garrero. Precisely what Egerton intended to achieve was not clear. The transport situation had not much improved and the unexpectedly low rainfall in the Haud threatened the advance, although it also had the effect of forcing the Mullah to remain in the Haud rather than retiring south. Egerton's intention was evidently to entrust most of the fighting to his Indian troops with much of Manning's column being left at Bohotle without transport. Once more Johnnie was disgusted by 'jobbery', especially when he had such a low opinion of Fasken, Kenna and Brooke. However, there was the real prospect of going home. Johnnie made arrangements with Hubert to buy him a new hunter and for Sir Charles to settle his bills at Rowland Ward's, cancel his newspapers and cigarettes and to ask cousin Laura to stop sending parcels. His last letter from Bohotle, dated 10 December, also requested Sir Charles to order him a completely new wardrobe since he possessed but one flannel suit.[17]

As he prepared to leave Somaliland, Johnnie still had little expectation that Egerton would manage to trap the Mullah. It was again hoped that the Abyssinians would be able to advance into the Haud, this time as far as Galadi, Badwein and Galkayu. The British would then attempt to engage the Mullah in the open as he fell back from the Abyssinian advance. The Mullah's whereabouts were not known, however, and, with nothing to do, Johnnie spent his last few days 'working at my French' and confessed himself 'utterly indifferent' to the outcome of the campaign. Final orders arrived on 18 December, Johnnie expecting to reach London on about 10 January. This would be only 12 days before the start of the Staff College term and Johnnie was uncertain whether he could get over to Ireland. He proposed to stay with Laura as he had before embarking for Somaliland 14 months previously.

On 30 December Johnnie wired Sir Charles from Aden that he was sailing on the SS *Mongolia*. To his delight, when he reached London, the commandant of the Staff College, now Brigadier-General Sir Henry Rawlinson, immediately agreed that Johnnie should delay starting at Camberley until 1 February so he could get to Innislonagh for a short leave. Fitting in tea with Lord Roberts, lunch with Francis Howard and two trips to the theatre, Johnnie left London for Ireland on 13 January and reached Innislonagh on the following day.[18]

Writing a hasty note to his parents on 12 January to announce his imminent arrival at Innislonagh, Johnnie was perhaps a little ruefully jealous at the news that Egerton had got his fight after all. On 10 January the Mullah, contrary to Johnnie's estimate, had come out to do battle in the open within two days' march of Eil Dub. Egerton had been able to concentrate 3,200 men and had mauled the Mullah badly at Jidbali. Subsequently, the Mullah's army of 6,000 to 8,000 men was driven as far south as transport would allow. The final act of the campaign would come on 21 April 1904 with a British landing at Illig in Italian Somaliland, which the Mullah had fortified. The Mullah had thus been forced out of British territory and the campaign was declared at an end although it was by no means the last of Mohammed-bin-Abdullah Hassan. Indeed, his power would not be destroyed finally until the British deployed air power against him in 1920.

Still, Johnnie's return home was very much an occasion for celebration, Sir Charles noting that Johnnie was 'looking very fit and well and very cheery'. It had been Sir Charles' hope that Johnnie would get some reward out of his services in Somaliland when he had not received sufficient recognition for his role in South Africa. Having not received a mention in the *London Gazette* of 7 August, Johnnie himself did not expect any honours, although Manning had hinted in November that he might receive the brevet of Lieutenant Colonel.* However, two days after his return to Innislonagh, on Saturday 16 January 1904, news reached Innislonagh that, in the previous day's *Gazette*, Johnnie had been awarded the Victoria Cross for Daratoleh:

During the action at Daratoleh, on April 22nd last, Major Gough assisted Captains Walker and Rolland in carrying back the late Captain Bruce (who had been mortally wounded) and preventing that officer from falling into the hands of the enemy. Captains Walker and Rolland have already been awarded the Victoria Cross for their gallantry on this occasion, but Major Gough (who was in command of the column) made no mention of his own conduct, which has only recently been brought to notice.

Thus, uniquely, three Goughs – father, son and uncle – would hold the highest award for gallantry simultaneously. In addition, Johnnie would also become the third serving member of the Rifle Brigade to hold the award, Walter Congreve having won the Victoria Cross at Colenso and Rifleman

---

* The eventual publication of Manning's last official despatch in the *London Gazette* on 2 September 1904 displayed his high regard for Johnnie as a 'very capable and resourceful officer'.

Durrant at Bergendal. At the same time, Johnnie was given a Brevet Lieutenant Colonelcy with the almost unprecedented compliment of having this
ante-dated to 22 April 1903, the day of the action at Daratoleh.[19] Although
there had been the representations in the press, the official recognition was
due to Walker, who had written to Manning on 25 November 1903 to point
out Johnnie's role in Bruce's rescue and that he was equally deserving of a
Victoria Cross. Manning wrote to the Secretary of State for War the next day
and, at the War Office, where Johnnie was already under consideration for
the brevet and a DSO, his cause was warmly supported by Roberts. The
Secretary of State, Brodrick, agreed to the award on 1 January 1904 and the
King was contacted twelve days later.[20]

Congratulations flowed in to Innislonagh, not least from Margaret Helen
Macmillan, and, after spending several days hunting with Hubert, Johnnie
travelled back to start at the Staff College. On 29 February, Johnnie and Sir
Charles, who had come over especially for the occasion, went to Buckingham
Palace for the investiture, after the Lord Chamberlain had determined Johnnie's availability. Joined by Hugh Gough and also by Sir Charles Bruce,
whose presence was 'very touching', they were escorted into the throne room.
Sir Charles captured the scene for Harriette, who was not strong enough to
travel in the bitter winter weather:

The Lord Chamberlain then read *through his spectacles* the card, on which was 'Lt.
Colonel J. E. Gough – to whom Your Majesty will present the V.C.'. Instantly
someone stepped forward from the King's left and placed a stool before the King and
then someone handed him the V.C. and Johnnie, who after bowing remained standing
before the throne, now came forward and knelt on his right knee; the King then took
the V.C., pinned it on his breast, then *shoved out his right hand*!! wh[ich] Johnnie took
up *most gracefully* and tenderly touched with his lips! – the King was *beaming* over
with smiles! Johnnie then rose, and moved *gracefully* backwards and passed on.

A short round of visits followed, Sir Charles and Johnnie lunching with
Roberts. Sir Charles also took the opportunity of reading the report of the
recent War Office (Reconstitution) Committee chaired by Lord Esher, which
suggested the establishment of a General Staff. This 'most rising line' in the
army would include Hubert among its number, Sir Charles wrote to Harriette. As for Johnnie, 'they all have their eyes on him'.[21]

1. Johnnie as a schoolboy at Eton

2. Subaltern in the Rifle Brigade, c.1892

3. Johnnie with his mother Harriette, father Sir Charles and brother Hubert
   at Innislonagh, 1896

4. In British Central Africa, 1897

5. With his Company of BCA rifles at Blantyre, June 1897

6. Sudan 1898: 2nd Bn. Rifle Brigade rum issue

7. Battle of Omdurman: 2nd Bn. Rifle Brigade behind the firing line

8. Crete 1899: Johnnie and his Cretan Constabulary at Agios Myron

9. South Africa: Johnnie and his Boer 'looters' at Lydenburg, 1902

10. W. T. Maud's sketch of Johnnie at Daratoleh, 22 April 1903

11. Johnnie in Somaliland, May 1903

12. Dorothea Gough (née Keyes), 1908

13. Diana Gough on the beach at Brighton, 1914

14. In a relaxed mood at Rockingham with [?] Jack Bagwell, October 1906

15. Johnnie and officers of the King's African Rifles, during tour as Inspector
General, 1908

16. Men of the KAR at firing practise during Johnnie's tour, 1908

17. Henry Wilson and his directing staff at the Staff College, 1910

18. Brigadier-General Johnnie Gough V.C. (left) and Brigadier-General Hubert Gough arriving at the War Office, Monday 23 March 1914

19. The Retreat from Mons, August 1914: Haig, Major-General Monro,
Lt. Col. A. J. B. Percival and Johnnie (right) confer in a French village
street

20. Johnnie on his last leave, November 1914

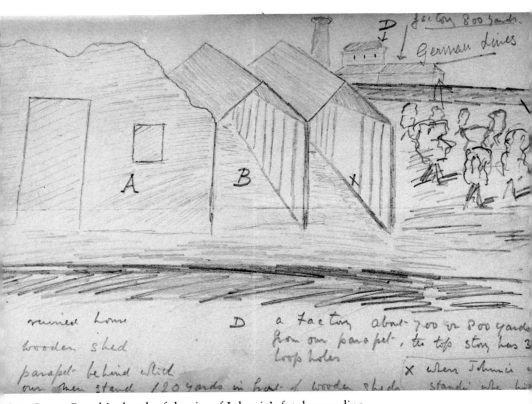

21. Owen Gough's sketch of the site of Johnnie's fatal wounding

22. Johnnie's funeral at Estaires, 22 February 1915

23. Johnnie's grave in Estaires Communal Cemetery

7

Building a Reputation, 1904–1914

JOHNNIE arrived at the Staff College at a moment when its importance
was being more widely recognised. The lessons of the war in South Africa
were being absorbed and reform was in the air. Generally, Staff College
graduates had performed well in South Africa when untrained regimental
officers, who filled well over half the staff appointments, had often failed.
Even witnesses without Staff College experience who appeared before the
Royal Commission on the War in South Africa were appreciative of Staff
College training. There was still some seeming reluctance to employ Staff
College graduates within the War Office – only seven of the 52 headquarters
staff between January 1901 and November 1903 possessed a *psc* qualifi-
cation* – but the army was entering a period of significant change.

Under the direction of St John Brodrick as Secretary of State for War, an
Army Board created in 1899 had become a War Office Council in the
following year, although the simultaneous existence of such a body of collective responsibility and a forceful Commander-in-Chief such as Roberts
was a somewhat unsatisfactory arrangement. In 1901 Brodrick had supported the establishment of the post of Director General of Mobilisation and
Military Intelligence and, out of his proposal for a new Cabinet Defence
Committee in 1902, evolved the Committee of Imperial Defence of February
1903 as a special forum for the discussion of defence questions. A month
earlier, the former Commandant at Camberley, Hildyard, had become the
first Director of Military Education and Training and strenuous efforts were
being made to overcome Treasury opposition to an increase in the number of
officers attached to the War Office Intelligence Division.

The Royal Commission on the War in South Africa, which had been
chaired by Lord Elgin, had adhered to its relatively limited terms of reference,
but it had become apparent during its deliberations between September 1902

---

* The letters meaning Passed Staff College appended to an officer's Army List entry
after successful completion of the course at Camberley.

and July 1903 that even more fundamental issues on the army's command structure and administration required to be addressed. As a result, the War Office (Reconstitution) Committee was inaugurated in November 1903 under the chairmanship of Lord Esher. Working with great speed and conducting its proceedings without reference to Brodrick's successor, H. O. Arnold-Forster, the committee issued three reports between January and March 1904. The first recommended a permanent secretariat for the Committee of Imperial Defence and the creation of an Army Council within the War Office. The second, which was that mentioned by Sir Charles in his letter to Harriette at the time of Johnnie's investiture, recommended the creation of a General Staff with a Chief of the General Staff replacing the Commander-in-Chief and becoming first military member of the Army Council. The committee enjoyed the executive authority not only to suggest a new organisation but also to appoint the first military incumbents of the Army Council, a clean sweep of the existing War Office high command being made on 'Black Monday', February 1904. Even Roberts was informed by letter on the Sunday afternoon that the new Army Council would begin work on the following day and that he was dismissed. The choice as first Chief of the General Staff was General Sir Neville Lyttelton, who had been serving as Commander-in-Chief in South Africa since the war's end.

The army now had a Chief of the General Staff, but no actual staff as such – the General Staff not being formally established until more than two and a half years later. One reason for procrastination was the difficulty of determining the precise qualifications required for service on the staff. Some elements argued for a 'Blue Ribbon' staff drawn entirely from Staff College graduates and others for the inclusion of officers who had not gone through Camberley but who were deemed to be suitably experienced in administration. It was certainly the intention of the Esher Committee that General Staff officers should be taken 'mainly' from Staff College graduates and a War Office Committee on General Staff Appointments in November 1904 was also to conclude that a *psc* was an essential qualification for staff employment. In the end, the Army Order establishing the staff in September 1906 laid down that, apart from exceptional cases, the qualification required would be a *psc* and eight years' experience in the service. It also stipulated a maximum four years' tenure in any appointment and resolved another issue of some controversy by giving the Army Council, through a Selection Board, rather than the Chief of the General Staff alone, responsibility for maintaining a confidential General Staff List of suitably qualified officers for staff employment.[1]

Thus, while few aspects of the organisation of the General Staff had been completely settled when Johnnie went to Camberley, it was obvious that Staff College graduates must play a central role in the army's future. Consequently, there was keen competition and more than 100 candidates had sought the 24 competitive places available for 1904: Johnnie, of course, took one of the eight nominated places. The majority of the successful candidates had seen service in South Africa and, like Johnnie, had held brevet or local rank which had given them far more command experience than might otherwise have been the case in officers of junior field rank. They were also remarkable in other ways. Those entering their second and last year when Johnnie arrived included Johnnie's old friend George Paley, and future distinguished officers such as Captain (later Lieutenant-General Sir) Sidney Clive; Captain (later Major) Adrian Grant-Duff, who was to be killed in September 1914; Captain (later General Sir) John Burnett-Stuart; and Major (later Colonel) Raymond Marker, who was to be killed in November 1914. Johnnie's own intake included Major (later Major-General) H. L. Reed, V.C.; Captain (later Major-General) Hugo DePree; Brevet Major (later Major-General) Arthur Daly; Brevet Major (later Lieutenant-General Sir) Richard Butler, who was to succeed as Haig's Chief of Staff when Johnnie was killed; and Captain (later Brigadier) Charles French, who was the son of Johnnie's first cousin, Frances Maria French (*née* Gough). Charles French in particular considered that none of his other friends at Camberley was as 'real' as Johnnie who treated him more like a brother than a cousin. Johnnie let French choose him as a working partner whenever possible, French later writing that 'there wasn't one single fellow of our year who wouldn't have been proud & glad to work with him, for we all knew him to be easily the first of our batch as he was the most popular'.

The 1905 intake, when Johnnie entered his second year at Camberley, was similiarly distinguished by the inclusion of future noted soldiers such as Brevet Major (later Major-General Sir) Charles Gwynn and Brevet Major (later Major-General) Hubert Isacke. It also included some old friends of Johnnie in the persons of Captain the Honourable Hugh Dawnay; Brevet Major Tom Bridges; Brevet Major Reginald Stephens; and Alexander Cobbe, V.C., now reduced to his army rank of Captain from the lofty heights of local rank in Somaliland. Two other holders of the Victoria Cross also arrived in 1905, Brevet Major (later Colonel) Frank Maxwell, killed in 1917, and Brevet Major (later General Sir) Lewis Halliday. Indeed, when the King visited the Staff College on 26 June 1905 he remarked on the fact that five students including Johnnie wore the Victoria Cross and another 20 the DSO. The six directing staff were similarly notable including Brevet Colonel (later General Sir) Richard Haking; Brevet Colonel (later Major-General Sir) Thompson Capper, who was to die of wounds at Loos in September 1915; Brevet Colonel (later Lieutenant-General Sir) Launcelot Kiggell; Brevet Lieutenant Colonel (later General Sir) John DuCane; and, to the amusement of both brothers, Hubert, who had been appointed in January 1904. In the words of the sixth member of the directing staff, Colonel (later Major-General Sir) George Aston, there was a 'new spirit' at Camberley compared with that before the South African War.

Before the war, the first-year syllabus had comprised military history, geography, fortification, artillery, applied field fortification, minor tactics, staff duties, military topography, reconnaissance, law, languages and natural sciences. Those passing an examination at the end of the first year went on to the second year of more practical 'schemes' and the composition of essays or 'memoirs'. There was also one war game annually between the senior and junior divisions and a period of attachment to other arms of the service. While Miles had begun to make some changes in the light of the war, by introducing more attention to staff duties and administration and extended outdoor exercises and continental tours, Henry Rawlinson had an even greater impact on what was taught at Camberley.

Rawlinson was appointed Commandant in December 1903 and under his energetic direction 30-mile bicycle exercises become common; these often began with rail journeys to distant destinations, although places nearer the college were also used – Frimley, Chobham, Bagshot and Wellington. Isacke, for example, noted in his diary for 19 May 1905, 'Biked to Wellington and sat in the ditch discussing a scheme with Kiggell.' The syllabus was also oriented more towards the practical study of the art of command and the operations of war. In Johnnie's very first term, for example, the outbreak of the Russo-Japanese War in February 1904 brought close study at Camberley with weekly assessment by staff and students. The particular demands of warfare on the North West Frontier, simulated in North Wales, had been included towards the end of Miles' period as Commandant. To this, Rawlinson added careful study of the military problems associated with operations on the French and Belgian frontiers with Germany, itself a reflection of the steady reorientation of British military strategy away from the defence of India to the possibility of resisting German aggression in Europe. In August 1904, Aston, a Royal Marine, joined the directing staff: this resulted in a closer under-standing of naval matters – which Rawlinson encouraged – and from 1906 the annual enrollment on the course of two naval students. The examination at the end of the first year was also reduced in importance in favour of grading by personal assessment of the directing staff, although the potential problems in deciding whether weaker candidates should be granted the *psc* notwith-standing an assessment of their unsuitability for staff appointment remained to be resolved.[2]

At the same time as raising the standard of professional study, Rawlinson was concerned to encourage social and recreational pursuits. Hubert recalled in his memoirs the importance to the Staff College of the winter Drag Hunt, of which he had been Master in 1899, and of cricket in summer. Johnnie together with Charles French was a Whip for the Drag in the 1904/5 season, meetings taking place regularly on Tuesday and Friday afternoons. Johnnie again appeared regularly at the start of the 1905/6 season, often riding out with Hubert Isacke. In the summer of 1905 Johnnie appeared in two matches for the Staff College 1st XI cricket team: against the Garth Hunt on 21 July and against the Free Foresters on 29 July. Earlier, on 17 and 20 May, he had played for the seniors in their annual match against the juniors, scoring 26 and taking a wicket. He ended the season with a rather modest batting average of 8.6 but topped the bowling with 6 wickets at 11.0 runs. There was also the annual Staff College point-to-point, in which Johnnie certainly participated in 1905, Sir Charles writing to Laura on 23 March that year, after Johnnie had already ridden in the Rifle Brigade meeting, to ask her to remind him to have his horse well saddled and bridled as Johnnie was proving a bad correspondent.[3]

It was often the practice for students to spend their leave between Staff College terms in visits to foreign manoeuvres or battlefields. Tom Bridges, for example, did both and journeyed as far as the United States to view the battlefields of the American Civil War. It is uncertain whether Johnnie travelled in this way and it seems that most of his leaves were spent at Innislonagh together with Hubert and Daisy. In season, the brothers rode with the Tipperary Foxhounds as they had both done during Johnnie's short leave between Somaliland and Camberley: at that time, Sir Charles had lamented to Laura how quiet it was once the brothers had returned to England for 'my stables were quite full – seven horses and four stablemen'.

Another of Johnnie's pursuits at the Staff College was fishing, in which he found a boon companion in George Aston. Aston, who later wrote that he could not help 'giving the palm' to Johnnie among all the students he taught at Camberley, also recalled in his *Mostly About Trout*, published in 1921, one hot and idyllic July day on the Itchen between Tichbourne and Avington Park. The fishing itself was disappointing but,

There was one compensation, companionship of the best, that of a fine soldier, late of the Rifle Brigade whom many would place at the very top amongst those who put the soul into the little old British Army of 1914.[4]

Thus passed two years.

Completing his course at Camberley on 22 December 1905, Johnnie's next appointment with effect from the following day was to the headquarters of the Irish Command at the Kilmainham Royal Hospital, Dublin. Initially, his appointment was as Deputy Assistant Adjutant General (DAAG) to the chief staff officer, Colonel (temporary Brigadier-General) F. Hammersley. In turn, Hammersley's superior was the General Officer Commanding in Ireland, General Lord Grenfell. Later, once the regrading of staff appointments had been completed, Johnnie's post was designated as General Staff Officer Grade 2 (GSO2).

It was an agreeable posting for Johnnie, notwithstanding his apparent dislike of chair-bound soldiering after his return from South Africa. The Irish Command was a popular one for officers for it offered light duties and the varied amusements of hunting, racing and weekending in the homes of the Anglo-Irish ascendancy. As Johnnie well knew from his previous service there with the Rifle Brigade, the 'season' comprised a period of general furlough between December and March, then training from March until the autumn manoeuvres in September. Hunting took place from October to March and coincided latterly with the post-Christmas Dublin social season. Duties in aid of the civil power were by now infrequent since the para-military Royal Irish Constabulary and Dublin Metropolitan Police were usually capable of meeting most emergencies without recourse to military assistance in these years before the escalation of the Home Rule crisis.

With the exception of the short period between March and December 1905, when Walter Long was Chief Secretary, policies pursued by the Conservative and (from December 1905) Liberal administrations were generally conciliatory towards Irish grievances. The one occasion on which the army acted in a constabulary role at one remove during Johnnie's period in Dublin was during the riots of August 1907 accompanying a labour dispute in the Belfast docks, when troops were required to assist the police. Ordinarily, there was little contact between army and police nor, indeed, much between the Royal Hospital and the seat of administration in Dublin Castle. It was a division accentuated by the election of the Liberal government in Britain which led to Dublin society boycotting social functions at the Castle in favour of the army's alternative calendar of events.

Thus, there was little real work for the staff beyond the formal ceremonial, such as the departure from Dublin of the 2nd Earl of Dudley as Lord Lieutenant of Ireland on 13 December 1905 and the state entry of his successor Lord Aberdeen, on 3 February 1906, which was virtually Johnnie's first official duty. Many officers with Irish staff appointments in the past had actually contrived to spend long periods with their regiments. General Sir Neville Lyttelton had managed to complete five or six months regimental duty each year with the Rifle Brigade when serving on the Irish staff early in his military career. Grenfell himself as GOC was frequently absent in London in his capacity as Gold Stick to the King and as a member of the War Office Selection Board. In any case, with only the best part of two infantry divisions and a single cavalry brigade stationed in Ireland, his duties were primarily social. Johnnie, too, commanded the annual summer camp of the 2,600-strong Public Schools Volunteer Brigade, made up of public-school cadets, at Aldershot in July and August 1907, with George Paley acting as his chief of staff and Hugh Dawnay as one of the battalion commanders. The Rifle Brigade had a long association with the camp and Johnnie's obituary in the *Eton College Chronicle* as well as others in 1915 suggest that he had taken a keen interest in the camps. He had attended the 1906 camp and certainly regarded the schoolboy corps as ideal reserves of officers.[5]

Not unexpectedly perhaps, in professional terms Johnnie's period in Dublin passed unremarkably although, on 14 August 1907, he was simultaneously promoted to the brevet rank of Colonel and appointed an Aide de Camp to the King in succession to Colonel Sir Henry Dixon. According to the *Army and Navy Gazette*, it was a 'well deserved compliment'. But by far the most important development of the two years in Dublin was Johnnie's meeting with Dorothea Keyes, secretary to the Lord Lieutenant's wife, Lady Dudley. While in Somaliland, in July 1903, Johnnie had written to Sir Charles how one of Harriette's letters 'was full of plans for my marriage, but as long as they keep me out here, I am afraid I can't oblige and I rather doubt my being able to do so even when I do get home'. Of course, there had been the brief allusion to a relationship with Elinor de la Poer and there is also a family tradition of Johnnie having been close to his first cousin, Lucy Gough, the daughter of Bloomfield Gough. However, until his return from Somaliland, Johnnie had had precious little time in which to satisfy his mother's desire that he should marry. In fact, he met Dorothea almost as soon as he arrived at Irish Command, Dorothea writing to her mother, Lady Keyes, on 16 January 1906, after staying the weekend with Lady Chamberlain at Oatlands, Castleknock in County Dublin, 'Sir Charles Gough's second son – Colonel Johnny Gough – had been here for the weekend – such a nice person. He has just got a staff appointment in Dublin and has taken a house near here. He has just left the Staff College'.[6]

The daughter of a distinguished Anglo-Irish family, Dorothea Agnes Keyes had a background not dissimilar to that of Johnnie. The Keyes family could trace its lineage back to at least the fourteenth century and was associated with the counties of Derbyshire, Devon and Kent before being granted lands in County Donegal under the Ulster Plantation of 1611. Thomas Keyes had become an assistant surgeon in the Madras Army of the Honourable East India Company in 1820 but died five years later while trying to help stem a cholera epidemic in Kamptee. His wife, Mary Anne Keyes (*née* Patton), then made an epic journey by ox-cart across India to Madras with her three young sons – all under five years of age – to return home to Donegal. One son died in Ireland but the other two both entered the Madras Army. The second, Charles Patton Keyes (1823–1896), was to take part in fifteen major expeditions on the North West Frontier and to be recommended for the Victoria Cross for gallantry against the Mahsud Waziris in 1860 and on the Ambeyla expedition three years later. In 1870 Charles Keyes married Katherine Norman, the young sister of the future Field Marshal Sir Henry Norman. In all, they were to have five sons and four daughters. Dorothea, the eldest daughter, was born on the frontier in 1874. It later transpired that Dorothea and Johnnie had been born within 20 miles of each other.

Like Johnnie, Dorothea was an 'orphan of the Raj' and suffered early tragedy. Charles and Katherine Keyes had returned to England in 1878 with their then five children. Charles had been commanding the Punjab Frontier Force but had suffered ill health after the Jowaki expedition of 1877. He was sufficiently recovered to return to India with Katherine in 1882, but the five eldest children, two more – Katherine and Phyllis – having been born in England, remained in the care of a country parson in England. Norman, the eldest, was eleven; Roger was ten; Dorothea, eight; Charles Valentine, six; and Terence, five years old. The children do not appear to have been happy at the parsonage. Within a year, Norman was dead of appendicitis, an occurrence which brought Roger and Dorothea particularly close in the absence of their parents. A year later, General Sir Charles Keyes, as he now was, retired to live at Sandgate in Kent, but he was not a wealthy man and when he died, on 5 February 1896, Katherine Keyes was left in considerable financial difficulties. Roger had embarked on a naval career (destined to make him Admiral of the Fleet Lord Keyes) in 1885; Charles Valentine ('Charlie') had been commissioned into the India Staff Corps in January 1895; and Terence was at Sandhurst, from which he was also commissioned into the Indian Staff Corps in January 1897. However, all of them would still have expected some kind of allowance, although Roger in particular had been careful to avoid debt for his father's sake. Dorothea, Katherine and Phyllis remained at home while Adrian, born in 1882, and Madeleine, born in 1885, were still at school.

In effect, Dorothea became a second mother to the family and took the courageous decision for its time of enrolling in a secretarial course and seeking employment. Possibly through the good offices of an old school friend, Hilda Chamberlain, daughter of Joseph Chamberlain, she obtained an appointment as private secretary to Frederick Oliver at the London store of Debenham & Freebody. Trained for the legal profession, Oliver had been persuaded by Ernest Debenham, a fellow student at Cambridge, to help save the firm from financial ruin. However, Oliver, who was to become a notable journalist, political polemicist and historian, was not enamoured of the world of business and seems at an early stage to have recognised Dorothea as something of an intellectual soulmate. Certainly, Dorothea became a firm friend of Oliver and his wife Katie. However, she chose to leave Debenhams in 1901, the catalyst appearing to be the murder of her brother Charlie in West Africa. Charlie was perpetually in debt during his army career and when serving in India had turned frequently to Dorothea for help. In fact, as soon as she began earning, Dorothea had started to send small sums of money to her brothers and sisters and they all tended to turn to her when in financial or other difficulties even though somewhat in awe of her. Charlie's need to reduce living expenses led in the end to his transfer to the West African Frontier Force. He distinguished himself in the third Ashanti war in 1900 and on the Kontagora expedition, going on to capture a rebel stronghold at Rabah in northern Nigeria. Within days of the Rabah success, however, Charlie was murdered – shot twice through the body while himself unarmed – on 21 June 1901 at Argungu by one of three French traders suspected of cattle theft. He had gone to arrest them and was killed while trying to disarm their native followers; two of his small escort were also killed. When the news reached Dorothea, she wrote to Katie Oliver that she would return to work after a few days but by 15 July she had determined to leave altogether.[7]

Oliver regretted Dorothea's departure, writing to her from Debenhams in September 1901:

Doesn't a soft sigh heave when you see this quaint well known, old-world heading? Don't memories of happy, useful days crowd in upon you? Thoughts of how you bested dishonest clergymen, rapacious widows, and American millionaires?

He went on to wax lyrically on the 'gentle humming of the electric fan', the 'sharp cheery rattle' of the typewriters and the 'fresh and hungry air' of the office. But he could not persuade her to return. Dorothea, however, had maintained her contact with Hilda Chamberlain. Indeed, a year earlier, when Hilda's brother, Austen, had been Civil Lord of the Admiralty, Dorothea had sent him copies of Roger's letters describing the capture of the Taku Forts at the mouth of the Peiho river by the force attempting to relieve the European legations at Peking. Oliver certainly approached Austen Chamberlain on Dorothea's behalf to try to discover if Charlie's murderers, who had fled into French territory, could be brought to account. Chamberlain offered to raise the issue in the House of Commons but Dorothea and the family decided that no useful purpose would be served by doing so since the murder was a criminal and not a political offence. Moreover, the French authorities appeared to be willing to apprehend the traders if possible. Similarly, it may well have been the Chamberlain connection which secured Dorothea an appointment in the following year as secretary to Rachel, Lady Dudley, whose husband became Lord Lieutenant of Ireland in August 1902.

Arriving in Dublin to take up her new position in November 1902, Dorothea plunged into the social duties of her employment. She attended bazaars, command performances, horse shows and balls and was involved in the Royal visits of July 1903 and May 1904. But her considerable organisational skills honed at Debenhams were also put to use in Lady Dudley's Nurses' Scheme, through which district nurses were recruited and installed in the depressed west of Ireland to alleviate the appallingly high mortality rate of Irish peasant women in child bearing. Thus, Dorothea's letters to her mother describing her duties at Vice Regal Lodge or Dublin Castle could be interrupted suddenly by the need to visit a nurse at some distant location by jaunting car. Dorothea also helped Lady Dudley, who was in poor health, to write the first annual report on the scheme in July 1904, and she usually attended meetings of the organising committee. But, of course, there was also the diversions of the Dublin season, be it yacht racing on Lord Dudley's own craft, dining with Lord Grenfell or twice meeting, in November 1902 and January 1904, 'a very old young man', Winston Churchill. And, it was at a weekend party that Dorothea met Johnnie in January 1906.[8]

Johnnie was not a sparkling wit in the manner of the more extrovert Hubert and was always well controlled. Nevertheless, as Aspinall's comments in South Africa had indicated, Johnnie was far from lacking in humour and was an extremely lively conversationalist. By contrast, Dorothea – 'Dorrie' as she became known to him – was reserved and even severe in manner if not intent. Oliver fondly recalled her 'stern eyes' in one of his letters to her, while the Keyes brothers and sisters often referred to Dorothea as the 'stern daughter of the voice of God'. But the couple were undoubtedly well matched and Adrian Keyes later recalled that Johnnie was the first to laugh at Dorothea and was responsible for 'humanising' her. Oliver's daughter Beatrix also considered that Dorothea became 'less critical' and 'less frightening' after meeting Johnnie. Through the match, too, Johnnie became acquainted with Oliver and in future years enjoyed being drawn into the periphery of the political world through Oliver's contacts with such men as Sir Edward Carson, Leo Amery, Arthur Lee and Lord Milner.

The marriage of Johnnie and Dorothea took place on 29 June 1907 at the Chapel Royal, Hampton Court Palace, where Lady Keyes had a grace-and-favour apartment in the Clock Tower. The service was conducted by the Sub-Dean of the Chapel Royal, Dublin, and the Chaplain to the King. Both Sir Charles and Harriette attended, as did Hubert; Lady Keyes; the younger Keyes sisters; Katherine Keyes' husband, Charles Wintour; and Roger and his wife, Eva. Roger, then the youngest captain in the Royal Navy, gave Dorothea away. The best man was Johnnie's old company subordinate from the Rifle Brigade, Captain John Harington. After a honeymoon spent in South Wales, Johnnie and Dorothea moved into Quarryvale house at Capelizod, County Dublin. It was not long, however, before the Goughs were on the move. On 1 October 1907, Johnnie took up a new appointment as Inspector-General of the King's African Rifles and the couple moved to temporary accommodation in Grille's Hotel, Belgravia.[9] Johnnie was appointed in succession to Manning, who had soldiered on as Inspector-General since the end of the Somaliland campaign but was now taking over as Acting Governor and Commander-in-Chief in Nyasaland.

The task of appointing Manning's successor was that of the Colonial Office which had been responsible for the KAR since 1905 when it assumed responsibility for the administration of Nyasaland, Somaliland, Uganda and the East African Protectorate (later, in 1920, Kenya Colony). The process began in June 1907 when fifteen officers were marked for possible appointment. At 35 years of age, Johnnie was by far the youngest candidate, but he had recent experience in Somaliland and the warm support of Manning. As a result, he was one of four officers shortlisted, and on 17 July the Colonial Secretary, Lord Elgin, concluded that Johnnie was the right choice. However, although the Army Council had a high opinion of Johnnie and proposed 'to put him into an important post, when he is a little more senior', they did not think he was old enough and suggested four entirely new candidates. Elgin's officials in the East Africa Department of the Colonial Office, headed by the Assistant Under Secretary, H. L. Antrobus, suspected that they were being palmed off with less able officers whom the War Office could not or would not place elsewhere. Accordingly, Elgin pressed strongly for Johnnie as 'an officer who will, it may firmly be expected, be selected for further and higher employment in the army'. Elgin also suggested that Johnnie could be given a local rank if the War Office objected to promoting him Brigadier-General which hitherto had been the normal rank associated with the appointment. On 10 September the Army Council acceded to Elgin's wishes and Johnnie was seconded to the Colonial Office. He remained a Brevet Colonel without any additional local rank in East Africa and the opportunity was also taken to reduce the Inspector-General's salary from £1,200 to £1,000 per annum. Johnnie was still entitled, though, to a daily allowance of 3 guineas when on the overseas tours necessitated by his office.

There were many matters already awaiting his decision when he arrived at the Colonial Office in Downing Street such as the most appropriate rank for commanding officers of KAR battalions, the best bandolier equipment for the 2nd and 6th KAR, and the various vacancies to be filled on secondment: one of Johnnie's first decisions was to recommend his best man, John Harington for colonial employment. Later a Brigadier-General, Harington was himself Inspector-General of the KAR from 1923 to 1927. But, in many respects, as the reduction in salary indicated, a predominant theme of Johnnie's period as adviser to the Colonial Office was that of economy. Manning had overspent the travelling budget for the year by £107.12s.8d and Johnnie even had difficulty securing a £30 outfit allowance for his first overseas tour.[10] More important, he was faced immediately with a demand emanating from white settlers and colonial administrations in East Africa for a reduction in the strength of the KAR. There were now five battalions, of which the 1st and 3rd were stationed currently in the East African Protectorate, the 2nd in Nyasaland, the 4th in Uganda and the 6th in Somaliland. The five Indian and 24 African companies, totalling some 3,290 men, were paid for by the local colonial administrations, but it was a burden resented since they did not perceive any security threat in East Africa. In fact, after the suppression of the last major rising – that of the Nandi tribe in the East African Protectorate between September 1905 and February 1906 – the Colonial Office had agreed to a reduction of six companies by June 1908. However, the Governor, Sir James Hayes Sadler, and Legislative Council in Nairobi now proposed the complete disbanding of the 1st KAR, a battalion raised in Nyasaland which served as a kind of general reserve for East Africa. They proposed to substitute armed police for troops and to rely on assistance in emergencies from the other protectorates.

The Governor and Council found some support for reduction from Elgin's Under Secretary of State, Winston Churchill, who was visiting East Africa between October and December 1907. Churchill telegraphed his support for Hayes Sadler to the Colonial Office on 17 November and, in a second telegram , also suggested withdrawing much of the garrison of Somaliland to the coast and placing it under the same administration as that of Aden. In common with others in the Colonial Office, Johnnie opposed Churchill's Somaliland scheme and was equally wary of any reduction in the KAR. In a note of 25 November 1907 to H. J. Read, the Principal Clerk of the East African Department, Johnnie voiced his distrust of the police as a substitute for the military. He suggested not only that the War Office be asked to comment before any decision was taken but also that nothing should be done until he had had the opportunity of visiting East Africa himself. Elgin concurred in Johnnie's judgment and it was left for him to inspect the police as well as the KAR and to consult with Hayes Sadler and the Governor of Uganda, H. Hesketh Bell.[11]

Inadvertently, Johnnie also became embroiled in a controversy over the use of armed native levies in support of military or police operations in East Africa. Johnnie was questioned closely on his views as early as 22 October by another departmental official, R. Popham Lobb. Lobb was highly critical of the often savage conduct of such levies and the high native death toll in recent expeditions. Johnnie was reluctant to dispense with levies altogether, as Lobb advocated, but he did agree that they should be severely limited in number and kept under strict military control. His views were interpreted by Lobb as support for a wider critique of military policy in East Africa when this was hardly the case. Similarly, when Johnnie noted on 7 November that the use of 2,000 levies on the Bamiro expedition of July 1907 had been excessive, this was also taken up by Lobb when, in fact, Johnnie was making a criticism of the effectiveness of the police for requiring such support. Lobb managed to effect clearer rules on the employment of levies, but this development was delayed by his transfer to Bermuda whence he continued to launch broadsides against the native death toll. Eventually, the Colonial Office took the issue to the Colonial Defence Committee which, in turn, referred the matter to the Committee of Imperial Defence in June 1909. The latter committee, however, confined its deliberations to the use of levies in a general war and failed to make any recommendations as to their employment on punitive expeditions.[12]

It was, therefore, with important issues to consider that Johnnie prepared for his first inspection tour. It was planned to sail from Marseilles on 10 December 1907, reaching Mombasa on 27 December. After inspecting troops and police in the East African Protectorate, the tour would proceed through Uganda and Nyasaland and terminate in Somaliland on 14 June 1908. Johnnie could expect to be back in London by 26 June. The itinerary was the work of Johnnie's staff officer, who had drawn it up before Johnnie's actual appointment. The staff officer was none other than Pope-Hennessy who had himself been appointed in August 1907 after coming home from East Africa a few months earlier to recuperate from enteritis. In theory, Pope-Hennessy was due to return to his British regiment, the Oxfordshire Light Infantry, by February 1908 at the end of ten years' secondment to the KAR. Johnnie was anxious to retain Pope-Hennessy's services and argued that he could not be deprived of his staff officer halfway through an overseas tour. As a result, Pope-Hennessy got a six months' extension and was able to accompany Johnnie. To the surprise and alarm of the Keyes family, Dorothea also announced her intention of going with Johnnie. On occasions, she had 'pigged' it when visiting nurses in Ireland but, at the same time, had regularly sent her washing and mending to the Keyes family nanny in England. Therefore, there were family predictions of impending disaster once Dorothea experienced conditions in East Africa. In a small notebook, Johnny listed his luggage and that of Dorothea. His own comprised three tin boxes, a leather portmanteau, a dressing case, clothes bag, .303" rifle, .450" rifle, a box of cartridges, a helmet case, a luncheon basket, two deck chairs and a sword; while Dorothea took a bed, a holdhall, a dressing case, a green canvas portmanteau, a 'big box', a small leather portmanteau, an umbrella, a Kodak and a thermos flask. Thus equipped they would be ready for most emergencies.[13]

The somewhat traumatic journey out to Mombasa appeared to suggest that the family fears might well be realised. The Channel crossing was bad, the railway journey to Marseilles tedious, and the voyage across the Mediterranean in the SS *Oxus* extremely rough. Dorothea found the *Oxus* a 'horrid old ship, very dirty and without any modern conveniences or appliances and absolutely no ventilation but the port holes'. Johnnie passed the time by reading Parkman's *Montcalm and Wolfe* and revising on the infantry drill manual. He also asked Sir Charles to purchase and send on the latest volumes of Sir John Fortescue's *History of the British Army*. Poor Dorothea, however, spent much of the voyage ill in the cabin and even Pope-Hennessy succumbed. Nevertheless, Dorothea was able to take some pleasure in the arrangements Johnnie was making to have her presented at Court as the wife of one of the monarch's ADCs. The company on board was also agreeable, including Captain (temporary Lieutenant Colonel) B. R. Graham, going out to command 4th KAR; an American lady named Macmillan, whose millionaire husband – a close friend of Theodore Roosevelt – farmed near Nairobi; and two young women, Ruth Seymour and Nonie Sherston, who were going out to visit and to marry respectively. More bad weather was met in the Red Sea which undid a partial recovery Dorothea had made at Suez and, when the *Oxus* docked at Djibouti on 21 December, she found it a 'god-forsaken broiling spot in absolutely arid surroundings'. While agreeing that Djibouti was even worse than Berbera, Johnnie and Pope-Hennessy had the consolation of finding some old soldiers who had served with them in Somaliland.

Yet more bad weather was encountered out from Djibouti but, despite the journey, Dorothea was entranced by the view entering Mombasa on 27 December. After staying the night in the house of the Lieutenant-Governor, Frederick Jackson, who was reputedly the model for Rider Haggard's Allan Quatermain, Johnnie and Dorothea discovered that the Inspector-General was entitled to 'a very comfortable arrangement called an inspection carriage, with a kitchen attached'. The railway journey up to Nairobi was therefore undertaken in some style, Pope-Hennessy, Graham and Ruth Seymour sharing the facilities. The train climbed some 4,000 feet during the night and the party was woken by 'delicious fresh mountain air coming in through our open windows'. Subsequently, both Johnnie and Dorothea marvelled at the teeming game across the great plain leading to Nairobi. There they were met by Captain (temporary Lieutenant Colonel) J. D. Mackay of the 3rd KAR and Major H. A. Walker of the 1st KAR and their wives. Dorothea found Nairobi unattractive and the church at which she and Johnnie attended Nonie Sherston's wedding on 30 December proved 'an ugly little tin building'. It was also far too hot to venture out sightseeing.[14]

Dorothea wrote to Sir Charles on 3 January 1908 that Johnnie was 'enjoying his work immensely and looks and seems extremely fit'. Indeed, Johnnie had begun sizing up the KAR officers as soon as he stepped off the train at Nairobi. Mackay struck him as a 'good solid fellow', but he was displeased to find a seconded Rifle Brigade subaltern, Lieutenant (temporary Captain) G. C. Sladen, had left Zanzibar without permission to lay complaints before him about the drunken and 'generally rowdy' behaviour of another officer, Captain H. S. Lloyd. Johnnie had already inspected the headquarters and three companies of the 1st KAR in Nairobi by 13 January and, finding the organisation of a local white volunteer corps in a 'hopeless muddle', was 'trying to devise a good simple working scheme'. But the pressing issue was the question of reducing the 1st KAR. Hayes Sadler had been on safari when Johnnie reached Nairobi but returned on 4 January and broached the subject in his very first meeting with Johnnie on the following day.

Johnnie said that he would report on the matter as soon as he had had a chance to review the situation in the protectorate, but three days later Hayes Sadler said that the matter was urgent and that no provision had been made for the battalion's upkeep in the protectorate estimates. Neither Dorothea nor Johnnie had been impressed by their first sight of Hayes Sadler, whom they felt 'weak', and Johnnie believed that, under settler pressure, the Governor was trying to 'jump' him. Nonetheless, he complied with Hayes Sadler's request and prepared a memorandum for the Executive Council. This argued that the 1st KAR was composed of good fighting men who were not only more efficient than armed police but had the great advantage of being recruited largely from Nyasaland rather than the EAP. Summarising possible threats that might arise, Johnnie put the requirement for troops at anything from the two companies that would suffice to deal with unrest in the Kisii tribe to the 1,500 he felt might be needed for operations against an estimated 11,000 Somali tribesmen in the northern province of Jubaland. With the 1906 reductions still under way, Johnnie felt any further decrease in strength would be an unjustifiable risk. He then attended a meeting of the Council 'at which the members showed their extraordinary ignorance of the subject' and was delighted when the members decided there should be no further reductions.

Determining that the need to inspect the police as well as the KAR would take two months longer than originally anticipated, Johnnie struck Nyasaland off his itinerary before setting out on 13 January from Nairobi. The first stage was a 25-mile trek by mule cart, a 'weird' four-wheeled vehicle being provided for Dorothea and Johnnie by Ali Khan, across an arid plain to Juja Farm to enable Dorothea to stay a few days with Mrs Macmillan, while Johnnie and Pope-Hennessy used the farm as a base for forays to two outposts conducting a cattle quarantine on the Athi river. The farm was a 'charming little bungalow' with all possible modern conveniences including electric light, but in 'the least attractive spot in Africa'. Two days later, a messenger arrived to inform Johnnie that the Kisii of the south west had risen after wounding the local political officer and that Mackay was going out after them with three companies. Johnnie found it somewhat ironic that only days before Hayes Sadler 'had assured me that there was no earthly possibility of trouble in the country', and he was concerned that it would take five days to concentrate Mackay's force at Nairobi. In fact, the affair turned out to be far from serious, but the 200 casualties inflicted on the Kisii and the 7,000 cattle and 5,000 sheep and goats seized for the loss of one native levy wounded in Mackay's command was to arouse Churchill's anger at the Colonial Office and provide Lobb with further ammunition for his personal campaign.

The actual conduct of such operations was the responsibility of Hayes Sadler and not Johnnie. In both South Africa and Somaliland, Johnnie had certainly believed in the vigorous prosecution of war but 'savagery' for its own sake had earned his condemnation in the debate on levies. Moreover, there is some indication that both Johnnie and Dorothea disliked the attitude of some settlers. Later, when they visited Uganda, the discovery that one of the district commissioners, George Wilson, was a former Australian music-hall singer turned missionary led Dorothea to comment that 'the class of men who wield authority astonishes me more than anything else'. Similarly, while inspecting the KAR at Fort Hall, Johnnie was appalled to learn that the provincial commissioner, C. R. W. Lane, had demanded that the KAR present arms to him, and 'stopped it at once'. He was also rather amused at Hayes Sadler's discomfort over questions from the Colonial Office on the Kisii affair. When Lieutenant C. V. C. de Crespigny of the KAR was acquitted, of what was termed 'culparable neglect' in killing his native servant with a hog spear, by a white jury that 'knew its duty to a white man', Johnnie remarked that the EAP was indeed a 'curious country'. On his return to England, Johnnie resisted an attempt to have de Crespigny promoted to command a company and was more than pleased to have him returned to his British regiment.[15]

Completing business on the Athi river, Johnnie and his party left Juja Farm for Fort Hall on 17 January. Some 80 porters had been hired but they proved a 'wretched crowd' and Dorothea had either to walk or to ride, rather than be carried in the travelling chair which Mrs Macmillan had thoughtfully provided. In any case, the eight porters originally deputed to carry Dorothea ran away so she borrowed a pair of Johnnie's knickerbockers and his Burberry and took to riding a mule. She was pleased with her progress since it does not appear that Dorothea had even ridden a horse previously, 'I have ridden each day since and can now ride up and down the most precipitous banks and nullahs without blinking, and Johnnie says I have quite a good seat!' She was also now feeling 'extraordinary better and think camp life agrees with me very well'. This was despite some of the difficulties of the journey such as failing to find the Tana river until a day later than expected and the constant persistence of ticks. Johnnie reported that 'it really is most exciting having the daily tick hunt after one's evening bath' but Dorothea proved to have a 'wonderful eye' for the insects.

Each day they would rise at 5 or 5.30 a.m. and the march would begin an hour later in the hope of covering about 12 miles before halting in the midday heat. Game was plentiful and, while Dorothea rested and slept, Johnnie and Pope-Hennessy would go out shooting in the afternoon. Dorothea wrote to Harriette how Johnnie 'says that he now lives again, that an office is a miserable existence'. On 21 January, they encountered no less than 18 rhinos. Lieutenant (local Captain) R. S. Hart of the 1st KAR, who had come out to meet then on the Thikha river, had to shoot one of five that ringed the party at one point, and later the same afternoon Johnnie also had to shoot another that 'came at him at a steady jog trot'.

From Fort Hall, which was reached on 24 January, they moved on to Nyeri and to Naivasha where they met up again with Ruth Seymour whose brother owned a local hotel. The route from Fort Hall had traversed the Kikuyu Reserve where a chief Dorothea variously recorded as Wambingu and Wambugu staged a tribal war dance in their honour. They had then crossed the Aberdare mountains before emerging once more on the open plains where grass fires were so prevalent that a protective ring had to be burned around the camp site. Along the way they met Colonel the Hon. Sir William Colville, late of the Rifle Brigade, on safari, and at Nyeri found another official whose attitude both disliked. This individual, a Mr H. Silberrad, was the Acting District Commissioner. Dorothea thought he misused his authority and, ironically, a few months later in May 1908, he was suspended for interference with and keeping of native women.

Naivasha was reached on 2 February, and as it was on the railway line Johnnie took the opportunity to make a diversion to police posts at Nkuru. He also wrote to Elgin to suggest, on the basis of his observations so far, that the musketry requirements for the KAR should be improved by introducing a new scheme he had devised similar to that employed in the West African Frontier Force. On 6 February Johnnie, Dorothea, Pope-Hennessy and Miss Seymour journeyed on to Kisumu, lunching with Hayes Sadler and Mackay, who had just returned from the Kisii expedition. Four days later, Johnnie and his group boarded the steamer *Winifred* for a voyage across Lake Victoria to Entebbe in Uganda. The steamer was equally alive with passengers, fleas and cockroaches and Dorothea was again seasick. Since it remained foggy throughout, there was not even a view. They found the Governor, Hesketh

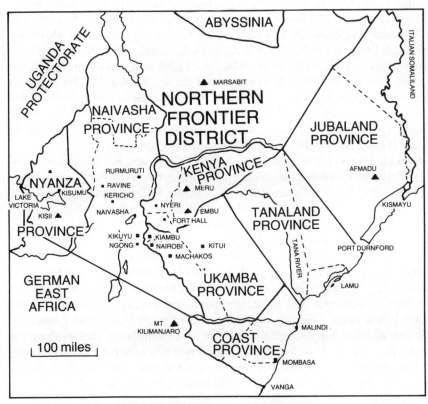

THE EAST AFRICAN PROTECTORATE

Bell, absent from Entebbe, but Graham was there to meet them, together with Captain W. H. Nicholson, a touchy and bad-tempered officer commanding the Indian contingent of 4th KAR. After four days in Entebbe, which Dorothea thought most attractive and picturesque, it was on to Kampala, which was sadly distinguished only by its ticks and fleas, and which was in the grips of spirillum fever.

It was here that Johnnie and Dorothea were to part for it had been agreed that she could not accompany Johnnie to Jubaland or to Somaliland and ought to return to England now rather than suffer 'a very hot journey home' in six weeks time. She would be accompanied by Ruth Seymour. Accordingly, Dorothea and Ruth left Kampala on 18 February to return to Mombasa through Entebbe and Naivasha to catch the SS *Natal*, with the expectation of being back in England by 19 or 20 March.[16] Johnnie remained in Uganda for a few days to take in the headquarters of the 4th KAR at Bomba and then returned to Mombasa himself to cross over to Zanzibar where the 1st KAR had two companies. It was his first visit since 1896 and he found the Agency building there far more comfortable than Government House in Nairobi since it had a bathroom 'with a real long English bath with taps!'

Johnnie was back in Nairobi by 9 April to complete his inspection of the 3rd KAR and on 18 April was able to take time off for a few days lion hunting. Then, with Hayes Sadler and Pope-Hennessy, he left for an inspection of Jubaland. To Johnnie's dismay, Hayes Sadler spent only four hours at Kismayu in Jubaland on what was supposedly an official inspection of the entire province bordering on Italian Somaliland. It also transpired that it was only the Governor's second visit since being appointed Commissioner in December 1905 and that trip had also been for a matter of a few hours. By contrast, Johnnie remained until 11 May. He believed that the province had 'a future in front of it' with the steady opening up and exploitation of the Juba river by the Boma Trading Company and the Empire Navigation Company. In consequence, Johnnie anticipated trouble with the Somali tribes along the indistinct frontier. Concluding that there might be a need for a 2,000 or 2,500 strong expedition – he had estimated only 1,500 men a few months before – to pacify the frontier in the event of hostilities, Johnnie 'gingered up everybody' to collect information useful for military purposes and was confident that 'if I am called upon to take action I have got a plot in my pocket which I will work up at home'.

Visiting the outposts at Gobwen and Yonti re-introduced Johnnie to the delights of riding a camel. By this time, however, Pope-Hennessy, whose health had caused Johnnie some disquiet in Uganda, was decidedly weak, so Johnnie left him at Yonti and went on with a small escort to Afmadu 'to give me some idea of what the country would be like for fighting'. Torrential rain checked this reconnaissance and Johnnie returned to Yonti. Pope-Hennessy had made a recovery and on 10 May they took the steamer *Rose* to pay a courtesy call on the Italian outpost on the Juba river opposite Gobwen. The

Italian guard of honour was 'a poor lot badly drilled and armed with rusty rifles', but Johnnie was impressed by the wireless station the Italians had erected. Next day, he and Pope-Hennessy returned to Kismayu and embarked for Aden on the SS *Madeira*. From Aden they crossed to Berbera on 19 May to inspect the 6th KAR. Concluding the work in Somaliland, Johnnie and Pope-Hennessy returned to Aden and caught a German ship, the *Gneisenau*, on 12 June. They reached Naples on 20 June and were back in London three days later, Johnnie finding that he had been promoted Major in his regiment on 6 May 1908.[17]

Johnnie had begun to compile his written official reports during the latter half of the tour of inspection. His small notebook indicates just how closely he had observed the performance of the KAR units he had seen with such detailed jottings as 'always keep reserve in hand', 'section too loose' and so on. His report on the 4th KAR was completed at Bomba on 21 February, that on 1st KAR in Zanzibar on 7 April, that on 3rd KAR at Yonti on 3 May, and that on 6th KAR on 6 June. There was also the report on the East African Protectorate police – '100 solid pages of typewritten material' – written at Nairobi on 16 April. Together, the reports formed a comprehensive review of the military position in East Africa and formed the basis for a further paper Johnnie was to write at the Colonial Office in August.

One problem was recruitment of native troops. Both the 3rd and 4th KAR were largely dependent upon Sudanese recruits, 432 out of 761 men of the 3rd KAR and 595 out of 774 men of the 4th KAR coming from the Sudan. But it was now proving difficult to maintain the supply and the British authorities in the Sudan were not being helpful. This particularly affected the 3rd KAR, which also drew upon 14 other tribal groups. Johnnie most admired the martial qualities of the Atonga, Angoni and Yao in the 1st KAR and most distrusted the Masai and Swahili in the 3rd battalion. He suggested an attempt to draw in recruits from the Nilotic Bakedi and Nandi and from Abyssinia. Almost as soon as he had taken up his appointment, Johnnie had approved a request from Hayes Sadler to send a recruiting party into Abyssinia: the result was a success with Captain G. R. Breading returning in September 1908 with 95 new recruits for the 3rd KAR.

Another problem addressed was that of the concentration of battalions for training. Neither the 3rd, nor 4th KAR had yet managed to do so and Johnnie suggested that the 3rd battalion at least could be brought together for six months a year if its two companies in Jubaland were relieved from time to time by the 1st KAR. This arrangement was introduced in July 1908. In turn, he was also concerned with maintaining adequate drafts for whichever of the two Nyasaland battalions – 1st and 2nd KAR – was serving in the EAP at any particular period. As Dorothea had written to Sir Charles on 5 February 1908, the whole question of the lack of adequate reserves or a white volunteer system exercised Johnnie greatly. The 3rd and 4th KAR both lacked any reserve at all, and in the case of the 6th KAR in Somaliland the only additional manpower available were former levies who had never proved reliable in the past.

Police were simply not a viable alternative. Johnnie had gone out with little expectation of finding much of value within the police, although he had favoured exposing their men to drill and musketry for use in emergencies. Nothing he saw in East Africa changed his views. After visiting the police at Nkuru, he had merely remarked that they were 'bad as usual'. Similarly, after completing his police report, he was invited to dine with police officers in Nairobi. Rather gleefully, he had written to Dorothea that 'If they knew what I have said about the Police, I daresay they would not ask me to dinner!' What Johnnie did have to say was comprehensively damning. The police were quite useless for field operations, their standard of musketry with old-fashioned Martini Henry rifles non-existent, their drill abysmal and they possessed no overall organised system of training. The white officers were of poor quality, since no care was taken to select good men, and the little training received from the Royal Irish Constabulary before posting was wholly inappropriate for East Africa. As in the case of the KAR, Johnnie found some fault with some of the 18 tribal groups recruited. He believed the Kavironde, Wakamba and Nubians unreliable, although he felt the Wanyamwezi could make reasonable police with training. He also felt Ugandans might be recruited. His recommendations included the urgent establishment of a central training depot and of a modern Criminal Investigation Department, arming with modern .303″ rifles and much greater care in officer selection. It should prove possible to reduce some 600 men from the 2,033 establishment while increasing pay for the remainder.

Other difficulties had also come to light during the tour. Both the 3rd and 4th KAR were short of medical assistance, the latter battalion having a high sick rate at Bomba, where there were many cases of guinea worm, and poor and insanitary barracks in Kampala. In the case of the 3rd KAR, Johnnie had been somewhat surprised and horrified to be asked to assist in an amputation at Kismayu in Jubaland and had only been spared the ordeal by the arrival of Captain R. S. Salkeld, the acting Provincial Commissioner, and the commander of the battalion's camel company, Lieutenant E. C. D. Gepp. Poor health also extended to battalion transport animals, the 3rd KAR's camels suffering from mange and the 6th KAR having serious problems with pony remounts.

However, despite the shortcomings, the state of the KAR in general was good, notably the 1st KAR, which Johnnie had watched conduct 'field days in savage warfare'. The 4th and 6th KAR also earned praise, the latter's Somalis now resembling regular troops far more than in the past, even if they could still only be used for protection duties rather than the pursuit of tribal raiding parties. The biggest problem was the 3rd KAR whose older soldiers, inherited from the Imperial British East Africa Company, had 'a glorious contempt for musketry' and whose officers Johnnie upset 'by asking them questions about their old soldiers – they could hardly answer one'. Yet, even the 3rd KAR was much improved from its last inspection by Manning. To try to improve the officers' professionalism, Johnnie also arranged for Hugh Rees Ltd to supply each of the battalion libraries with some 45 books which he believed consti- tuted necessary reading. Included were von der Goltz' *A Nation in Arms*, Douglas Haig's *Cavalry Studies*, Henderson's *The Science of War* and *Stone- wall Jackson*, the four published volumes of Fortescue, Churchill's *The River War*, Ian Hamilton's *Staff Officer's Scrapbook*, Sir Charles Oman's *History of the Peninsular War*, several volumes on the 1866 Austro-Prussian and 1870 Franco-Prussian wars, and the British official history of the South African war.[18]

Each report had been forwarded to the Colonial Office through the appro- priate local administration. Thus, both Hayes Sadler and Hesketh Bell had had the opportunity of commenting on Johnnie's conclusions. Hayes Sadler concurred in general terms although he doubted that the Nilotic tribes would come forward to join the 3rd KAR. He was less happy with the report on the police and convened his own committee to discuss Johnnie's recom- mendations, which delayed transmission of the original to the Colonial Office until June. Hayes Sadler complained, memorably, that his police force was 'not altogether so useless as would at first sight appear', but his mitigating plea of financial difficulties cut little ice at the Colonial Office. Hesketh Bell failed to make the detailed reply he had promised in April 1908. He had to be reminded to do so in July, at which point he ignored Johnnie's strictures on the barracks at Kampala to concentrate on the question of reserves. Indeed, one clear result of Johnnie's tour was progress towards a proper KAR reserve. Johnnie wanted a universal system in East Africa, but in fact separate schemes were forwarded by Walker, who had now taken over as commanding officer of the 1st KAR, and Captain (temporary Lieutenant Colonel) E. H. Llewellyn of the 2nd KAR in Nyasaland. By November 1908, however, Johnnie had devised a scheme for both Nyasaland and the EAP in which former soldiers would serve for three years, during which they would be liable to one month's annual training.

The second main result had been to dispose of any question of reducing the KAR at least for the time being. Johnnie devoted much of his official report of 17 August 1908 to a recapitulation of the case against reduction. He envis- aged the possibility of the Masai growing restless when their cattle herds increased beyond the grazing capacity of the tribal reserves. He also postu- lated the rather more remote likelihood of the Baganda causing difficulties in Uganda. In either case, over 1,000 men might be needed to suppress revolt, yet local officials would not take either contingency seriously. More intracta- ble problems could well arise in Jubaland despite Hayes Sadler's lack of concern with the province. While agreeing with Manning's previous policy of holding only Kismayu, Gobwen and Yonti, Johnnie believed that between 2,000 and 3,000 troops might be required to suppress Somali opposition to commercial exploitation of the interior.

The situation in Somaliland was still more worrying. It was true that the Mullah had been relatively docile in recent years but this could easily change and there would be little hope of preventing any determined incursion. Churchill, of course, had proposed a complete withdrawal to the coast, but Johnnie felt this would harm Britain's relationship with the other European powers in the region. It was also necessary to hold on to Burao in the interior for the sake of the 6th KAR's morale and in the hope that any attempt by the Mullah to besiege the post might enable reinforcements to trap him in open battle. In any case, relief of Burao would need 2,000 troops. Nor did Johnnie discount the possibility of future clashes between the KAR and generally better-equipped forces from German East Africa. In short, reduction was a high-risk policy and Johnnie felt the Colonial Office should assume financial responsibility for the battalions. It was a view that commanded respect in the Colonial Office and the new team of the Marquis of Crewe and J. E. B. Seely, who had replaced Elgin and Churchill in Asquith's new Cabinet of April 1908, agreed that there could be no reduction in the KAR.[19]

Following up the reports occupied much of Johnnie's time once he had returned to London, but now family matters also required his attention. On her return, Dorothea, who was now pregnant, busied herself with preparations for moving to a new home, the Old Rectory, at Stoke d'Abernon in Surrey. While the house was being altered, she had stayed with Hubert and Daisy at Aldershot, where Hubert was now commanding the 16th Lancers. In May, Dorothea moved to the Old Rectory, and on 18 October 1908 Johnnie and Dorothea's visitors' book recorded – 'Diana arrived at 5.5 p.m.' Johnnie, however, had little time to accustom himself to the new role of father.

A month earlier, Hugh Dawnay*, whom Johnnie had secured as his staff officer in succession to Pope-Hennessy, had arranged the inspection itinerary for 1908/9. After an excursion to Entebbe, Johnnie would again visit Zanzibar, and then make the trip to Nyasaland he had had to cancel on the last tour. He would return from Chinde on 27 May 1909.[20] But again circumstances were to prevent any visit to Nyasaland: this time the very crisis in Somaliland which Johnnie had feared might arise.

Following his defeat in the 1903/4 campaign, the Mullah had retired into Italian Somaliland. In March 1905 he had accepted limited autonomy under Italian protection in what became known as the Pestalozza agreement after the Italian consul at Aden who had first opened negotiations with him in the previous year. However, the Mullah did not cease either to intrigue with the tribes in British territory or to make periodic raids against tribes enjoying British protection. The almost inevitable financial retrenchment after the major expedition of 1903/4 had resulted, meanwhile, in a reduction in the

---

* Hugh Dawnay's wife, Lady Susan, was Diana's godmother, and Johnnie in turn was godfather to the Dawnay's son, (later Vice-Admiral Sir) Peter Dawnay. Johnnie's other godchildren were Pope-Hennessy's son John, the future art historian, and Neill and Angela Malcolm's daughter Helen.

British military presence. By 1907 the Indian Army element, initially two full battalions, had declined to two companies in the 6th KAR. The latter battalion's original Somali companies had been converted into a standing militia in 1905 in the expectation of finding all recruits from India, but from April 1908 four new Somali companies were raised for the 6th KAR and the militia discontinued. In addition, political officers had formed a tribal militia as a first 'line of observation' and there was a small force of 180 armed police. As Johnnie had noted, the 850 men of the 6th KAR were not sufficient to resist a major invasion and such an eventuality would be met by retiring all mounted troops to the coast, leaving outposts at Burao and Sheikh.

This had been the policy which had earned Churchill's opposition in October 1907 since he judged Burao and Sheikh too weak to be held and of no importance. Withdrawal hardly represented an heroic policy, but it was justified in Churchill's view as 'the only one which the utter poverty of this wilderness of stone and scrub, and the military strength of its fanatical inhabitants render it worth while for a British Government to pursue'. The British Commissioner in Somaliland, Captain H. E. S. Cordeaux, had argued in November 1907, just as Johnnie did in his report of August 1908, that withdrawal would have a detrimental effect upon the European powers and the tribes and might spread unrest into Jubaland. Cordeaux had also pointed out that a policy of ignoring the interior had resulted in the major expeditions of the recent past. Nevertheless, he was prepared to countenance some further financial economies in response to Churchill's demand for the withdrawal of the remaining Indian troops provided that Johnnie felt these commensurate with efficiency. Johnnie's initial comment that British forces should not be pulled back even one yard had drawn Churchill's criticism in a memorandum in January 1908 after Johnnie's own departure from East Africa. The fact that the Italians also appeared to be cutting adrift from their East African possessions suggested to Churchill that there would be little European reaction while either staying put, as Johnnie suggested, or leaving posts at Burao and Sheikh, as Cordeaux wanted, implied the need for large reinforcements should the Mullah attack in force.[21]

As already remarked, Johnnie had been encouraged by the progress of the 6th KAR when he saw them in May 1908, but the situation was far from satisfactory. As he wrote in a memorandum in June, tribes such as the Dulbahanta would expect British protection if the Mullah moved against them, but if they did not get it, they would join the Mullah in common cause. By August the exhausted state of grazing in the Mullah's enclave suggested that his followers were poised to move back into British territory, especially as the Mullah had begun to demand the withdrawal of the advanced line of observation maintained with the tribal militia. In late September, Johnnie urged that Cordeaux lay in supplies and transport in case of need and companies of mounted infantry at Aden were placed on alert as immediate reinforcements. Johnnie also favoured punitive action against the Warsangli,

who had been showing signs of restlessness since January and to whom the
Mullah had now extended his protection.

Both Uganda and the EAP were each requested to hold three KAR companies in readiness, but Johnnie wanted clear guidance on whether such
reinforcements should be used merely to extricate the garrisons at Burao and
Sheikh or as the basis for a major expedition against the Mullah. In the event
of an expedition being authorised, Johnnie had a plan worked out which he
submitted for consideration on 8 October. As a counter to the Mullah's
undoubted mobility, Johnnie proposed a striking force of mounted infantry
and camel corps totalling 2,259 combatants with only 230 non-combatants
in support, all of whom would be mounted on ponies or riding camels rather
than burden camels. This striking force would carry at least five days' supplies
and would be kept in the field by two infantry support columns, each
consisting of 647 combatants and 545 non-combatants, whose total of 1,543
burden camels would carry an additional eight days' supplies for the striking
force. Both striking force and support columns would be liberally equipped
with maxim guns and an additional infantry battalion would act as line of
communications troops between Berbera and an advanced base located at
Burao. Johnnie wanted three months' supplies accumulated at Burao in
advance and he drew up all the telegrams required to put the plan into
operation as soon as possible. Earlier, the Colonial Office had secured
Treasury agreement to an additional £5,000 for Somaliland and Johnnie
urged that it be spent at once on remounts and supplies.[22]

However, on the eve of his departure from London, Johnnie was still
uncertain as to the government's intentions. He now felt it highly likely that
the Mullah would move against Burao and he wanted 300 men of the 1st
KAR, now back in Nyasaland, sent for immediately. He was convinced that a
major expedition would be required, but as he noted on 17 November, 'I
would suggest that something definite should be settled . . . so that we are not
taken by surprise if action is suddenly forced upon the Government.' Colonial
Office officials agreed that Johnnie must receive guidance, and a copy of his
note of 17 November was sent to the Prime Minister with Crewe's endorsement for despatching the 1st KAR to Somaliland. Churchill reacted by
reissuing to the Cabinet the memorandum he had written on Somaliland a
year previously, Crewe doing likewise with Cordeaux's original response. As
a result, the Cabinet decided that it 'was not prepared to entertain the
question of sending an expedition' and everything must be done to avoid
hostilities, even to the extent of exploring the possibility of reaching some
accommodation with the Mullah. But, paradoxically, it was also resolved to
reinforce Somaliland with 1,500 men from Aden and East Africa if Cordeaux
deemed it essential.[23]

Johnnie and Hugh Dawnay had arrived at Berbera on 14 December to
inspect the 6th KAR and Johnnie was immediately asked by Cordeaux for his
view on whether reinforcements should be requested. Johnnie was beginning

to come to the conclusion that Churchill was right to the extent that there must either be a full expedition or a complete withdrawal since the forces available could not adequately protect tribes friendly to the British. However, either course would require careful preparation and Johnnie therefore favoured asking for the reinforcements and using them to occupy the Ain valley both as a 'palliative' measure and to teach the Warsangli a lesson. Cordeaux liked neither extreme but concurred in requesting the troops offered. In fact, the 300 men of the 1st KAR had been sent for in November and they arrived at Berbera as early as 6 January 1909, but the 3rd KAR, less two companies left in Jubaland, and the 4th KAR, who were to form the majority of the reinforcements, did not disembark until 12 February.

In view of the uncertain state of the country, Johnnie had decided to confine his official inspection to 6th KAR's ordinary company work and he disposed of his report on the battalion by 10 January. Once again, the Somalis were much improved but Johnnie was worried by their shortage of remounts and concerned at the fact that many of the officers were ignorant of the language of their men. He then turned to the more pressing matter of laying in four months' supplies at Burao and starting an animal register to provide transport for the 3rd and 4th KAR. Then, on 19 January, he received a telegram from the Colonial Office ordering him to abandon the rest of his planned tour and to remain in Somaliland as Officer Commanding, Troops. He was charged with keeping open communications between Berbera and Burao but was to undertake no action that might lead to the necessity of mounting a full-scale relief expedition. Any advance into the Ain valley must likewise not compromise government policy on avoiding entanglements.

For Dorothea, who had hoped to join Johnnie at a later stage in the tour, it was something of a blow and she was described by her sister-in-law, Eva Keyes, as 'rather fussed about J as they are sending out reinforcements'. However, Johnnie threw himself into the task with his customary vigour and moved forward to Burao to take personal command of the 1st and 6th KAR on 21 January. He then led four companies from each battalion on to occupy Wadamago in the Ain valley, which was reached on 5 February. Supply convoys were immediately instituted between Burao and Wadamago where the troops practised bush formations, zareba building and field firing. In between trips back to Burao, Johnnie conducted personal reconnaissances to inspect wells at Garrero, Dabba Dald and Eil Dab, where he left a company as garrison. He was particularly concerned about the lack of transport animals since the number of baggage camels available for daily hire was beginning to drop with the approach of the rains and the far from complete stores at Burao were already being drawn upon. The problem was made worse by the arrival of 3rd and 4th KAR, of which the former was brought forward to Wadamago while the latter came to Burao.

By 15 March, when Johnnie wrote to Cordeaux on the problems, it appeared that if more burden animals could not be found, the Ain valley would have to be abandoned by the end of April and Burao by the end of July. Only a full-scale expedition could ensure the complete security of British Somaliland although a possible alternative was to distribute weapons to friendly tribes. Later in the month, Johnnie also enthusiastically forwarded a suggestion by his Director of Supplies and Transport, Major G. E. Pigott (a Sandhurst contemporary), that an experimental mechanical vehicle be sent out to Somaliland for testing as a possible solution to the lack of animals. The general conditions were also extremely arduous with 45 per cent of the 6th KAR being declared anaemic in April and many of the British special service officers succumbing to various fevers. Few tents were available and the constant but necessary work of carrying water supplies, which had to be rationed strictly, was laborious in the debilitating heat of April and May.[24]

Although there had been no actual fighting other than desultory skirmishes between scouting parties, the concentration of troops in Somaliland was proving expensive, the estimates rising from £37,000 for 1906/7 to £89,000 for 1908/9 and projected to reach £190,500 for 1909/10. In March, 1909, therefore, the Cabinet had again emphasised the need to avoid hostilities with the feeling in favour of a complete withdrawal running strongly. Two months later, it was resolved to send the Governor-General of the Sudan, Lieutenant-General Sir Reginald Wingate, to report on the situation and make recommendations as to future policy. In the meantime, Johnnie had been very active dashing between Burao and Wadamago. He again made personal forays to Badwein and Gosawein in early April and led a company from the 3rd KAR from Wadamago through Eil Dab to Lassador between 16 and 24 April to try to catch reported raiders. Wingate arrived at Berbera on 26 April in the company of the legendary Baron Sir Rudolf Slatin, who had been a captive of the Mahdists in the Sudan from 1884 until successfully escaping from Khartoum in 1895. Wingate had the greatest praise for Johnnie's efforts:

I consider that you, your staff & the troops deserve the highest commendation for the excellent military arrangements in Somaliland & I consider it a privilege to be able to report on the thorough efficiency of all ranks under most difficult circumstances & very trying climatic conditions.

It was praise Wingate was to repeat in his official report in June but, by that time, the climate and conditions had taken their toll on Johnnie. It was not unusual for Johnnie to have fever on his overseas tours but this time it was more serious. Wingate had written to Johnnie upon hearing that he had been taken ill on 23 May and suggested that he leave Wadamago for the marginally healthier Sheikh. On 3 June, however, Johnnie was placed on the sick list at Sheikh with what appears to have been hepatitis and he was compelled to leave Somaliland on 14 June, crossing to Aden for a passage home on HMS *Philomel*.

Johnnie spent the summer recuperating at Stoke d'Abernon but he was never fully to recover from his last visit to Somaliland. Consequently, when his doctors advised him that he 'ought not to go out to a tropical climate for some time', he decided that he must quit as Inspector-General and sent in his resignation on 3 September 1909. It was accepted with genuine regret, Crewe thanking Johnnie for his 'ability and tact' and his service under 'exceptionally difficult and trying conditions' in Somaliland. Johnnie had offered to stay on as long as the Colonial Office had need of his services and it was agreed that he should do so until mid-November. Thus, he continued to advise on Somaliland in the light of Wingate's reports, which appeared on 12 and 17 June. While the Mullah threatened British territory, Wingate saw no possibility of withdrawal but, as the government had set its face firmly against a major expedition to push the Mullah south, the only realistic alternative was giving the tribes autonomy and arming them. Wingate also favoured abrogation of British recognition of the Pestalozza agreement in the hope of forcing the Italians to take action themselves against the Mullah.

Following a raid on a British advanced post in August, Johnnie agreed that withdrawal was becoming more difficult if the Mullah was not to gain considerably in prestige, but he still maintained that it must now be complete withdrawal or a major expedition. Certainly, he supported a 'home rule' policy for the tribes and arming them but he did not see this as viable unless the Mullah was pushed south. He also agreed that the Pestalozza agreement should be wound up and the Italians induced to act. But what he could not support was a suggestion by Cordeaux to stiffen the tribes by a temporary advance of mounted units to Yaguni since this would only deceive them into believing the British intended to stay. Another concern was the security implications for the other protectorates in the long absence of their KAR battalions and Johnnie advised that it was now time to replace them with troops from India. In September he wrote to Wingate commenting on the lack of decisions:

We are no nearer a policy than we were before – everything is left to chance and we look no further ahead than the immediate present, confining ourselves to taking measures for immediate security and refusing to recognise that these temporary measures may commit us to a line of policy that may be most inconvenient next week.[25]

Johnnie's views, as summarised in a memorandum of 4 October 1909, were then conveyed to a Cabinet committee established to review Somaliland policy following Wingate's report and Crewe's request to allow the friendly tribes to retaliate against the Mullah's raids.

The final decision, taken on 27 October, was for withdrawal to the coast as soon as feasible; and in January 1910 Manning was recalled to carry out the policy after Cordeaux's successor, Major-General de Brath, appeared unable or unwilling to achieve the task. The Ain valley had been evacuated as early as 17 December 1909 and Manning completed the withdrawal by March 1910. The 1st, 3rd and 4th KAR were returned to East Africa and the 6th KAR disbanded with Indian troops being introduced to hold a coastal enclave around Berbera. Johnnie was reasonably hopeful that 'our friendlies' could pull themselves sufficiently together to offer resistance to the Mullah, but in the event chaos reigned in the interior. As a result, a new Somali unit – the Camel Constabulary – was raised in 1912 and the interior was reoccupied two years later pending a full-scale expedition against the Mullah, which was launched after the end of the Great War.

While the last act of the Somaliland deployment was being played out, Johnnie was occupied with the kind of routine matters he had first experienced at the Colonial Office two years previously. He engaged in discussions with the India Office on the suitability of various Indian classes for services in the KAR Indian contingents, made recommendations on increased pay for the Indians and on changes in KAR seniority rules. He also devoted some attention to the use of experimental mechanised vehicles in East Africa. After his endorsement of experimentation in Somaliland in March 1909, the War Office Mechanised Transport Committee had sent out a Fowler steam tractor. Unfortunately, the trials in July had not been successful since the engine had required too much water, but Johnnie still believed that there was a possibility of success with a paraffin or petrol engine. In October, therefore, he went to Aldershot to view trials of possible contenders. He was also involved in the selection of his successor. He failed to get Hugh Dawnay, who had stayed in Somaliland, back to help the incoming Inspector-General, but his warm recommendation of George Thesiger as his successor was sufficient to have Thesiger selected over three other candidates.

In addition to Crewe and Wingate's good opinions, Johnnie also received the public thanks of Cordeaux when the latter's official despatch of 31 March 1910 was finally published in June 1910. Cordeaux put down the excellent behaviour of the troops in Somaliland to Johnnie's example of 'patience and cheerfulness . . . under all conditions and inspite of constant ill health which eventually necessitated his being invalided home'. Recognition accompanied the despatch with the award of the Companionship of St Michael and St George, an honour which delighted Sir Charles since it was specifically 'stated in recognition of your services in Somaliland'. Sir Charles was especially pleased as Johnnie was 'not one who seeks his own advancement – but is more thoughtful of his duty to his country'.[26] However, a more immediate recognition of Johnnie's qualities and Somaliland service had come with his appointment from 23 December 1909 as GSO1 at the Staff College with the rank of full substantive Colonel – he had jumped that of Lieutenant Colonel altogether.

Rawlinson's successor as Commandant at Camberley in January 1907 had been Brigadier-General Henry Wilson. Wilson had the reputation of acquiring the services of the directing staff he wanted and this was certainly the case with Johnnie's appointment. Wilson learned of Johnnie's resignation as Inspector-General at an early stage, for his diary records that he raised the matter at the War Office on 28 September 1909. Wilson wanted to retain the services of Major (temporary Lieutenant Colonel) the Hon. George Morris and to replace the departing Major (temporary Lieutenant Colonel) George Barrow with Johnnie. However, Wilson's nominal superior, the Director of Staff Duties, Major-General Douglas Haig, preferred Colonel T. D. Foster to Johnnie. Undismayed and confident in the knowledge that Haig was shortly to depart to India as Chief of the General Staff there, Wilson buttonholed the Chief of the Imperial General Staff, General Sir William Nicholson, as well as Haig's designated successor as DSD, Launcelot Kiggell. Having Kiggell to lunch on 9 October, Wilson was able to herald Nicholson's agreement to Johnnie's appointment in his diary as 'a good business'. Both Johnnie and Dorothea stayed with Wilson and his wife at the Staff College on the weekend of 22 to 24 October and Dorothea came back to continue house hunting on her own in early November. Johnnie also came back to stay with Wilson between 24 and 26 November and attended Wilson's luncheon for the directing staff on 18 December. Dorothea and Johnnie were again guests of the Wilsons for tea on Boxing Day. They moved into their new house, Thornhurst in Camberley in early January 1910 for the start of the new Staff College term.

Since Johnnie's departure as a student, the college had continued to grow in stature. Wilson lent more emphasis than Rawlinson to staff duties and was insistent on grounding the students in what he termed the principles of administration. Wilson also made Camberley the agency through which to try to create a genuine 'school of thought' wedded to the recognition that Britain must be ready to meet continental obligations. Continental tours, notably those of the battlefields of the Franco-Prussian War became an even more significant feature at the end of the first term of the students' second year. Implicit in his interest in guiding thought towards a European war was Wilson's willingess to introduce political considerations into the tuition. A fervent advocate of conscription, Wilson did not shrink from discussing the subject with students, his first lecture on the subject being delivered in November 1909. Wilson had similarly progressive views on the need to transform the cavalry into mounted infantry and, in fact, discussed Erskine Childers' critique of the traditional cavalry role in *War and the Arme Blanche* with Johnnie upon its publication in February 1910. Unfortunately, Wilson's diary does not reveal Johnnie's response but, from his ideas on military subjects generally, it is more than likely that Johnnie shared Wilson's views.[27]

Wilson's tenure at Camberley was of the utmost significance and, before he left to become an even more influential Director of Military Operations at the War Office in July 1910, he had twice secured increases in the numbers of directing staff and students to a total of 15 and 98 a year respectively. On leaving, Wilson warmly praised Johnnie's role at Camberley: 'You know how much I think of you, & how much I have valued your help, & now how much we look to you in the time to come'. Wilson's successor, Major-General

William Robertson, was very different in personality but equally successful in shaping the nature of the syllabus and of those students who undertook it. Wary of any mention of politics, Robertson still concentrated on the likelihood of the army's employment on the Franco-Belgian frontiers, but he also directed study to the practical difficulties of war. Problems were sprung upon students at unexpected moments and elaborate outdoor exercises evolved to test previously neglected subjects such as conducting retreats. The course as a whole, however, still bore some similarity to that followed by Johnnie as a student. Military history, geography, tactics and Imperial defence were all covered in the first year, although the study of military history and the lessons that could be derived from it was a constant element throughout both years. Attachment to other arms was still undertaken as were visits to engineering and artillery establishments. During the second year, there was not only the European tour but the staff tour in Wales and, a new departure since Johnnie's time, a joint exercise with the Royal Naval College. Students also participated in the annual autumn manoeuvres while the very last staff tour of the second year was now attended by the Chief of the Imperial General Staff.

Johnnie fitted well into the scheme of things at Camberley under both Wilson and Robertson. As one of two GSO1s, he was responsible for the first-year students of the Junior Division with six other members of the directing staff under him although it was customary to mix divisional directing staff whenever possible. One of Johnnie's particular tasks was the preparation of staff tours, the first tour of the second year being preceeded by a war game played out between the two GSO1s, who then acted as Commanders-in-Chief in the field with students as their staffs. Johnnie's experience of both independent command and the provision of professional advice to civil servants and politicians made him well qualified for his duties at Camberley. Of course, he was also widely read, especially in military history, and he had given much thought to his own profession. Consequently, his contribution to the Staff College was highly valued even amid that of other distinguished members of the directing staff during his time there such as George Morris; Brevet Colonel (later Major-General Sir) Edward Perceval; Lieutenant Colonel (later General Sir) George Harper; Temporary Lieutenant Colonel (later Lieutenant-General Sir) William Furse; Temporary Lieutenant Colonel (later Brigadier-General) C. R. Ballard; Lieutenant Colonel (later Lieutenant-General Sir) Louis Bols; Lieutenant Colonel (later Major-General Sir) Hugh Jeudwine; and Major (later Brigadier-General) Philip Howell, who was killed in 1916.

Although some thought George Morris, who was to be killed in September 1914, the most able instructor at Camberley, Robertson himself described Johnnie as 'brilliant and accomplished' and recommended him for accelerated promotion in his confidential report for 1912:

He is essentially practical in his views – has strong determination & plenty of commonsense. Under his guidance there has been a marked improvement in the standard reached by the students in work connected with minor tactics & staff duties in the field. He possesses in a high degree the qualifications for command, is equal to any amount of responsibility, active, a good horseman, & a keen soldier in all respects. He is very helpful to me.

Hubert claimed in his memoirs that it was from notes taken during Johnnie's lectures that the future Field Marshal Earl Wavell, who graduated from Camberley in 1910, wrote his 1939 Lees Knowles lectures, 'Generals and Generalship', although it is possible that George Morris was equally influential. There is also a letter, however, in Johnnie's papers from another student, Captain (later Major-General Sir) George Richardson of the New Zealand Staff Corps, who graduated in 1912. Richardson wrote on leaving Camberley to say,

how indebted I feel to you for the energy & time you have bestowed on us, and the good I have got out of your teaching. You have brought such a fascinating interest to me in the subjects you have given us, that will make History appear in a new light.

Richardson's only regret was that he felt himself a 'poor instrument' to convey what he had learned to others when he returned to New Zealand.[28]

Temporary Lieutenant Colonel (later Major-General Sir) Neill Malcolm, who joined the directing staff in January 1912 and was later both GSO1 when Johnnie was chief of staff to I Corps and also Hubert's chief of staff in 5th Army, was another who recorded his observation of Johnnie at Camberley:

There his strong personality had full scope, and the absolute genuiness of his character had a wonderful effect on his students. He was not very fluent, and his language was simple, but he gained a tremendous hold over his class, for he not only taught them, but he imbued them with something of his own vigorous spirit and high ideals. I do not think that any of those who were at the Staff College during the years 1910–11–12 can ever lose what he gave them.

Something of the flavour of Johnnie's delivery and of his ideas can be gauged, too, from his book, *Fredericksburg and Chancellorsville*, and his three published articles since all were essentially versions of his lectures.

One article, 'Local Counter-attacks', was actually delivered as a paper for the Military Education Committee of the University of London on 17 December 1913 in a series of lectures which also included contributions by Henry Wilson and George Morris, but it has every appearance of having been a Staff College paper as well. Like the other two articles, it was published in the *Army Review*, which had been established in 1911 as a means of disseminating General Staff opinion widely through the army. The other two articles, 'Peace Training for Command', which appeared in October 1911, and the anonymous, 'The General Reserve: A Letter to a Young Officer', which appeared in April 1914 but was actually a commentary on the *Field Service Regulations* (*FSR*) of 1912, were more clearly Staff College lectures. Pope-Hennessy, who graduated from Camberley in 1911, discussed the latter article with Johnnie some considerable time before its appearance in print, and when it was published complimented him on making his recollection of George Morris' lectures on the subject seem 'crude, one sided & prejudiced' by comparison. Johnnie's book, which was published by Hugh Rees Ltd as part of the Pall Mall Military Series in 1913, is clearly stated as being based upon a lecture course at the Staff College in the previous year. Moreover, its provenance is shown by phrases transferred direct into the text such as, 'The Commandant was only saying the other day. . .'.[29]

One theme that runs through each of Johnnie's publications is an emphasis upon the lessons to be learned from military history in the absence of any coherent doctrine in the British army or authorative literature other than the manuals and *FSR*. However, there was only value in reading military history if past campaigns were studied by officers 'with their minds intent upon how to apply what they read to modern conditions'. Thus, Johnnie illustrated his lecture on counter-attacks by reference to the French experience at Wörth in August 1870 and his own experience at Caesar's Camp in January 1900, and the article on reserves had examples taken from the Austro-Prussian War of 1866 and the Russo-Japanese War. *Fredericksburg and Chancellorsville*, of course, was devoted to the American Civil War but from the perspective of the defeated Union Army at these battles of December 1862 and May 1863 rather than that of the victorious Confederate Army.

Johnnie had a high regard for the *FSR* which he considered 'about the best in the world'. But he was careful to stress in all his writings that there were 'no hard and fast rules for fighting battles' and that, 'No regulations in the world could do more than outline general principles; it is for soldiers to apply them as best they can.' Consequently, he stressed the need for commanders to write clear directive orders and for these to be thoroughly explained to subordinates so that they could employ the best means available to them in any given situation in accordance with the general aim. The larger the manoeuvre intended, then the bolder and simpler the overall plan must be. In short, war was 'greatly a matter of commonsense'. However, at all times, commanders should be prepared to deal with the unexpected and to make up their minds to act decisively for 'battles have been lost over and over again because the commander has either waited too long . . . or, seeking to minimise his risks, has struck but a half-hearted blow'. For Johnnie, therefore, victory could only be gained by prompt and resolute action and this entailed employing the largest force available for any attack commensurate with the retention of a small but sufficient reserve to strike a surprise local counter-blow if required. Such a counter-blow, moreover, would only be directed at the flanks for there was no purpose to be gained in reinforcing failure. Thus, while Johnnie clearly subscribed to the prevalent 'offensive spirit' within the army, he was too much of a realist to expect the structured and predictable sequence of events on a battlefield envisaged by many of his contemporaries.

Interestingly, both Henry Wilson, who provided an introduction to *Fredericksburg and Chancellorsville*, and a reviewer of the book in the

Journal of the Royal United Services Institution chose to underline Johnnie drawing out the dangers of civilian interference in the conduct of military operations. Additionally, Wilson also interpreted the book as an attack on amateur citizen armies. In fact, neither point was overtly emphasised in the book but, in his anonymous article on reserves, Johnnie did include a footnote stating that 'An Army should be composed of men representative of the spirit of manhood of the nation and of a strength commensurate with the tasks that may be imposed on it.' Similarly, while at the Colonial Office, he had criticised the employment of members of the recently created Territorial Force in the East African Protectorate Police and on secondment to the KAR. Subsequently, Johnnie was consulted in March 1913 by Frederick Oliver, who had drafted a memorandum advocating the reintroduction of conscription. Oliver's principal collaborator was Hugh Dawnay but it is clear that Johnnie was also very much in favour of conscription provided that the period of training for conscripts was long enough to produce a confident soldier. In advocating this course, Johnnie shared the view of many soldiers, for the Army Council itself went as far as to recommend conscription in April 1913 amid the increasing support for some form of universal military service which would enable Britain to match the manpower of continental armies. There was rather less support for conscription among the public at large, and in fact the kind of short-service system suggested by the National Service League, of which Lord Roberts had become president, as a means of securing political acceptability would not even have provided an adequate army for home defence let alone the needs of a far-flung Empire: the League suggested a four-month period of initial training while Johnnie advocated two years.

Not unexpectedly, each of the five parliamentary bills introduced to implement conscription between 1908 and 1914 failed. However, the campaign by the National Service League ensured that considerable hostility was directed against the Territorials. When he came to office in December 1905, the Liberal Secretary of State for War, R. B. Haldane, was forced, through political necessity, to modify his original design of a 'real national army'. Thus, the Territorial Force, which replaced the former Yeomanry and Volunteers in 1908, reflected crucial compromises. It was intended that the Territorials would both support the regular army in the field and provide for wartime expansion with a period of six months' training upon mobilisation fitting the force for overseas service. It was not at first clear how sufficient drafts would be found for the regulars while the Territorials trained, although the transformation of the Militia into the Special Reserve partially solve the problem. Unfortunately, Haldane chose to advertise the Territorial Force as a 'practical test of the voluntary system' so that its very existence could be interpreted as an obstacle to conscription and it met great criticism from the likes of Roberts and his circle, which included both Wilson and Rawlinson. Johnnie was equally critical of Haldane's reforms, not only on the ground that we had chosen to rely upon training our national forces after war had actually broken out; but also because we had not taken care to provide ourselves against the very emergency which was contemplated, by having a reserve of officers competent to undertake the training of the new army in case of need.

In fact, according to Oliver, Johnnie was most concerned at the lack of officer reserves.[30]

In many respects, Johnnie was approaching the pinnacle of his career when at the Staff College and had firmly established his reputation within the army – he had been featured front page in the *United Service Gazette*'s 'Portrait Gallery' in December 1912. Both Johnnie and Dorothea also enjoyed entertaining old friends at Thornhurst such as Pope-Hennessy, Dawnay, Thesiger, Paley, Stephens, Raymond Marker, Harington, and Hilda Chamberlain. They also took a full part in the social life of the college, Johnnie turning out for the Staff College Past against the 1st XI cricket team in July 1911. In his capacity as an ADC to the King, Johnnie also attended the funeral of Edward VII in May 1910 and the coronation of George V in June 1911. But, sadly, two occurrences were to overshadow the overall happiness of life at Camberley. The first was the death of Sir Charles on 6 September 1912. Both Johnnie and Hubert were able to be with their father at the end, Hubert writing to Johnnie at the height of the Curragh Incident in March 1914 to enquire,

Do you remember the old man lying, dying & sending for us after dinner to say his last farewells, & how when we came into the room, he said with that extraordinary gallant smile of his – 'Two very smart young men'? I would have given anything to hear him say to us on Monday evening [23 March] – 'Two very gallant & honest young men'!

In practical terms, it gave both brothers considerable financial security since they received a substantial share of Sir Charles' railway and other stocks: they reinvested them in May 1913 in concerns ranging from Cuban, Canadian and Brazilian railways to the P&O, Japanese government stock and the City of Budapest Loan. But, of course, it robbed them of Sir Charles' unfailing love and effort to ensure recognition for his sons' achievements.

The second misfortune was Johnnie's continuing ill health, which Frederick Oliver firmly attributed to 'the after-effects of his last Somaliland campaign'. As a result, Johnnie was compelled to leave the Staff College, although he had already served there for over three years, on 21 January 1913 to go on half-pay. In fact, it was at St Jean de Luz in the Pyrenees where he discussed conscription with Oliver in March 1913 while endeavouring 'though not very successfully' to shake off his illness. Arriving there in January 1913, Johnnie did manage to get in some golf and visits to Wellington's battlefields in the vicinity. He also corrected the proofs of *Fredericksburg and Chancellorsville*, of which Hugh Rees were publishing 1,000 copies at a cost of £125, with Johnnie finding £80 himself. By the time of his death, just over 200 copies had been sold and, even if all had been sold, Johnnie would only have received about £95 in royalties. Nevertheless, the book was still required reading for Staff College entrance in 1933 and it was well received upon publication, Major the Honourable (later Lord) William Hore-Ruthven, the Brigade-Major of the Brigade of Guards, writing to Johnnie to congratulate him on producing 'an absolute model of what a book of that description should be like'.[31]

At the end of March 1913, Johnnie returned home and then went to Innislonagh. He had made something of a recovery and, on 31 July 1913, he received a letter from the War Office offering him the appointment of Brigadier-General, General Staff to the Aldershot Command from 1 October with a salary of £1,000 a year or £800 if quarters were provided. Johnnie's star was in the ascendant again. Ironically, he would be chief of staff to the man who had opposed his appointment to the Staff College four years before – Lieutenant-General Sir Douglas Haig.

8

The Curragh Incident, 1914

IN many respects Johnnie and Haig were an unlikely combination. Haig was not only dour and inarticulate but also usually surrounded himself with obsequious mediocrities who would offer no challenge to the authority he believed should rest solely with the commander. Significantly, two of his existing personal staff – John Charteris and Captain H. B. D. Baird – who had come to Aldershot with him from India in March 1912 were not Staff College graduates. A hypochondriac who dabbled in spiritualism, Haig was also a curious mixture of the progressive and the reactionary in military terms. Thus, while undoubtedly anxious to bring the Aldershot Command to a high state of modern military efficiency, Haig persisted in ignoring the way in which firepower had neutralised the battlefield utility of his beloved cavalry. By contrast, Johnnie had become at least associated with the Roberts circle which vehemently opposed the traditional cavalry role and favoured its conversion into mounted infantry. Johnnie also shared this group's advocacy of conscription and its distrust of the Territorials, while Haig, as Director of Military Training, had been primarily responsible for establishing the Territorial Force.

Something of the obvious contrast between the two men was reflected in Johnnie's apprehension towards the offer of appointment in the army's premier command, which would provide I Corps upon any wartime mobilisation of an expeditionary force. At the time he received the War Office letter, Johnnie was staying with Frederick Oliver at Dungevan Castle on the Isle of Skye. Writing to his own brother in September 1917, Oliver enquired:

Do you remember, by and by, how when we were at Dungevan Castle, Johnnie Gough got notice of his appointment to be Haig's chief staff officer at Aldershot, and how, mixed up with the pleasure of his appointment, he had doubts as to whether he would get on with him, owing to the unfavourable idea of Haig's overbearing character which Johnnie's gossips had stuffed him up with?

Johnnie's letter to Haig on 3 August 1913 expressing concern that he had no personal experience at Aldershot may also have had rather more to do with reservations about Haig than lack of confidence in his own abilities. However, three days later, Haig replied that Johnnie should put his mind at rest on this score for, 'I think it is a very good thing to have new blood here in order to help people get out of the groove along which there is a tendency for Aldershot tacticians to move.' Indeed, Haig said that he had especially asked the CIGS, Field Marshal Sir John French, for Johnnie's services and offered to put him up until he, Dorothea and Diana could move into the official quarters at Blandford House, Farnborough. It has been suggested by one of Haig's biographers that Haig wanted Kiggell for his chief of staff but this appears to be a misreading of a letter from Haig to Kiggell welcoming the latter as chief of staff for the autumn manoeuvres of 1913. In any case, Kiggell was too senior for appointment at Aldershot.[1]

Hubert, who was himself one of many wartime army commanders reluctant to contradict Haig, wrote in his memoirs that Johnnie did not hesitate to stand up to Haig or to the equally strong-minded Robertson. Another of Haig's biographers, Duff Cooper, almost certainly went too far in claiming that, at the time of his death, Johnnie was 'an old and dear friend' of Haig but there is little doubt that there was a friendship and a mutual respect wholly lacking in Haig's relationships with his other wartime chiefs of staff such as Kiggell and Lawrence. As Hubert claimed, it does appear that Johnnie was able to suggest or to criticise without creating friction. Even during the latter stages of the Great War Haig's subordinates were occasionally capable of changing his mind if they applied more subtle pressures and Johnnie obviously possessed this ability. According to Haig's wartime diary, Johnnie once remarked – as did others – that Haig needed no chief of staff, which suggests a certain frustration. Nonetheless, Johnnie was not in the same mould as Charteris or Kiggell, both of whom Hubert characterised as yes men. The War Office confirmed Johnnie's appointment on 18 August 1913 and he took it up officially on 9 October – a few weeks short of his 42nd birthday, following the return of the Aldershot Command from command exercises and the autumn manoeuvres which Johnnie attended as an observer. According to the *Daily Telegraph* Johnnie's appointment 'gave the greatest satisfaction in military circles'.[2]

Among Johnnie's earliest official duties was representing Haig at the annual conference of staff officers, held in 1914 at the Royal Military College. These gatherings had started in 1906 as a forum for staff officers to discuss matters of interest. Those attending varied from year to year and Johnnie had only once previously attended, in January 1910. On that occasion his contribution was limited to a brief comment, in a discussion on 'the necessity for an officer to collect and record war experience', testifying to the value of the official history of the Somaliland campaigns of 1901–4 for his own administrative preparations in 1909. However, four years later, his greater seniority and experience gave him the confidence to interject frequently in the discussions. Moreover, he actually opened the four-day conference on 12 January by presenting a paper on the subject, 'Can more be done to render Officers competent commanders in war'. He did so at the specific request of Robertson, now Director of Military Training at the War Office.

Johnnie considered the question in terms of character training, theoretical training and practical training. He wished to see officers relieved of unnecessary correspondence and administration and junior officers given far more responsibility, notably within the context of a properly constituted company system. Johnnie's thoughts on theoretical training returned to the themes of his publications with military history being used to set officers practical problems; and he lamented the inability to give opportunities of handling troops 'at something approaching war strength' rather than the skeleton formations usually under command. There was general agreement on the validity of Johnnie's comments, Robertson remarking that when they were both at the Staff College, 'we often discussed it, as we thought that something more ought to be done than is done to render officers competent commanders in war'. In summing up, Sir John French also supported Johnnie's views on company systems of training but, as time was 'getting on', he allowed Robertson's concluding remarks to stand as his own. During the remainder of the conference Johnnie faithfully reflected Haig's views on the need for the lines of communication to be under the direction of a Commander-in-Chief and how staff tours could be used to develop doctrine in a command. More personal opinions were expressed by Johnnie on the need for flexibility among staff officers so that any officer could take over the duties of another if required and also for artillerymen to be able to practise in divisions rather than brigades. He also wanted officers given the chance to command all-arms forces. Towards the end of the conference he also clashed with the Director-General of Military Aeronautics, Brigadier-General Henderson, in opposing the suggestion that the Royal Flying Corps should report to an intelligence staff rather than direct to a commander. Naturally, Johnnie took a full part in field days and other exercises at Aldershot, the little notebook he had used in East Africa now being used for comments on British units such as 'try to get the men to grasp realities of war'. An anonymous obituarist in the *Irish Times* who had been at Aldershot 'was amazed at the trouble' Johnnie took over officers' essays.[3]

However, as early as January 1914, Johnnie's attentions were being diverted increasingly to the growing crisis over Irish Home Rule, the Liberal government's Goverment of Ireland Bill having been rejected by the House of Lords for a second time in July 1913. There had been abortive bills before. In 1886 such a bill had split the old Liberal Party and propelled 'Liberal Unionists' into the Conservative Party, which had then adopted the title of Unionists. The bill was lost in the House of Commons. A second bill fell foul of the Unionist majority in the House of Lords in 1893 and when a Liberal administration was once more returned in 1906 it evinced little initial interest in reviving the issue. But, home rule was then resurrected as a consequence of the constitutional struggle over the powers of the House of Lords. Unionist use of the Lords' veto to block Liberal social reforms including David Lloyd George's 1909 'People's Budget' culminated in Asquith's calling of a general election in January 1910. The Liberals lost their large overall majority and were returned with a total of only 275 M.P.s to 273 Unionists, 40 Labour M.P.s and 82 Irish Nationalists. With Labour and Irish support a Parliament Bill was introduced which the Lords sought to amend out of all recognition. A second election was fought in November 1910, but while 57 seats changed hands the Liberals ended precisely matching the Unionists with 272 seats apiece: Labour now held 42 and the Nationalists 84. With the King agreeing to create sufficient Liberal peers to ensure passage if the Parliament Bill was again opposed, it passed in August 1911. The effect was to deprive the Lords of all power over finance bills and to restrict its suspensive veto to two successive parliamentary sessions.

Thus, when Asquith resolved to revive home rule as a personal policy in April 1912, the Lords could only delay the legislation. The second rejection of the bill – the first had been in January 1913 – was the last legally possible. If introduced a third time the bill would become law but the Unionist leader, Andrew Bonar Law, had clearly implied in his 'Blenheim Pledge' of July 1912 that Ulster Loyalists could go to any lengths to resist home rule and still receive the blessing of the Unionists at Westminster. In reality, Asquith's bill offered little more than local government powers to any administration in Dublin, but the Loyalists were well satisfied with the status quo and feared the consequences of Catholic domination from Dublin. While some Unionists were genuinely concerned with the possible fate of the Loyalists under home rule others were more apprehensive of the repercussions in the Empire if Ireland was allowed to go its own way. Indeed, even the exclusion of Ulster from the provisions of the legislation could not be accepted by way of compromise due to the existence and influence of southern-based Unionists who campaigned to remain in the union through the agency of the Irish Unionist Alliance. Undoubtedly there was also an understanding within the Unionist leadership that the issue could be used to break the government, which was adjudged to have no electoral mandate for home rule.

In Ulster itself Loyalists were prepared to use force against the imposition of home rule. The government had allowed the provisions of the Peace Preservation Act to lapse and sympathetic magistrates began granting licences for drilling during the course of 1912. The Ulster Unionist Council led by Sir Edward Carson organised the drilling associations into an Ulster Volunteer Force (UVF) in January 1913, a force mustering 41,000 volunteers by the following April. In response a 4,000 strong Irish Volunteers force appeared in nationalist areas in November 1913. As Ireland rapidly became an armed camp, however, Asquith's government showed characteristic lack of purpose. Members of the Cabinet had not seriously considered Ireland at all prior to February 1912 and soon become hopelessly divided on the best policy to pursue. The result was that matters were allowed to drift without resolution.

One crucial question left unanswered was what would happen if Ulster did indeed resort to force of arms and Carson declared a provisional government in Belfast. Here the attitude of the army became of supreme importance, for if required to enforce home rule on a recalcitrant Ulster it would clash with the UVF. The army was no longer dominated by the Irish. Only 9.1 per cent of the rank and file were Irishmen in 1913, and although there were many prominent Anglo-Irishmen in the officer corps such as Roberts, Wilson and Johnnie, this was also not predominantly Irish in its composition. Nevertheless, the instincts of the officers as a whole were primarily Unionist. The UVF was led by a former Indian Army officer, Lieutenant-General Sir George Richardson, who had been personally recommended for the appointment by Roberts. Other former British officers also served with the UVF, Captain Wilfred Spender's long struggle to leave the army to do so becoming a cause célèbre in 1912 before he was able to retire in August 1913. The perception, therefore, was that large numbers of officers would decline to serve against Ulster, and by the autumn of 1913 this was causing considerable disquiet in many quarters.

Just before taking up his appointment at Aldershot, Johnnie had been contacted by Robertson, who had been close to the King during the autumn manoeuvres in September. Concerned by what he heard of the army's attitudes, the King had directed his private secretary, Lord Stamfordham, 'to see an officer who could give him a sober opinion'. Robertson had suggested Johnnie and summoned him to the War Office to ask him to get in touch with Stamfordham. In a later account, written in June or July 1914, Johnnie recalled the meeting as having taken place 'around the middle of October'. In fact, Johnnie wrote to Stamfordham on 22 October, but it was not possible to arrange an interview until the Royal Family returned from Sandringham and it was not until 7 November 1913 that Johnnie finally appeared at Buckingham Palace.[4]

Although Johnnie had sometimes evinced an interest in political events during his career – primarily if they offered the prospects of military employment – he was hardly a deeply political animal. But his contacts with Oliver and his own personal involvement in the conscription debate had contributed to a degree of politicisation. Moreover, service at the Colonial Office had introduced him to the implications of government policy at first hand. Oliver, too, later wrote that Johnnie 'had strong prejudices as well as affections' and the Adjutant General, Lieutenant-General Sir John Spencer Ewart, certainly lumped Hubert, Johnnie and Wilson together as 'three bigoted Irish Protestants, all ready to make political capital' out of the crisis that developed. George MacMunn, then Deputy Assistant Director of Remounts at the War Office also later recorded Johnnie and Wilson as 'bitterly and enthusiastically for the North'. Yet, Johnnie's account of events in the autumn of 1913 actually showed that he had discussed Ulster with both Haig and Ewart during the autumn manoeuvres. While Haig had appeared 'anxious to avoid discussing the subject'. Ewart 'appeared to sympathise with my views'.

Johnnie, of course, was not an Ulsterman but of that southern Anglo-Irish hierarchy which considered itself English. In their boyhood, it will be recalled, both Hubert and Johnnie had been exposed to that 'solidly religious atmosphere' and anti-home rule background among the de la Poers and Goughs. There had been that especial concern on the part of Harriette and Sir Charles when Johnnie had been seemingly involved with a Catholic cousin during the South African War. Indeed, Harriette was described when she died in 1916 as strongly low church and both bigoted and prejudiced, seeing the Pope 'as everything evil mentioned in Revelation'. Thus, Johnnie's interview with Stamfordham revealed the genuine depth of his feelings, Stamfordham noting that Johnnie 'spoke with evident feeling but with reticence for he said it was so painful a subject that he tried to put it away from his mind'. Johnnie himself remembered that he had 'made no secret of his views' although he was careful to avoid 'saying anything in the Army which would tell against discipline'.

In fact, like other officers, Johnnie was not necessarily against home rule in principle. What did concern him was the complexion of the administration likely to emerge in Dublin after its implementation. As he told Stamfordham, he wanted an administration that would be 'loyal', 'clean' and not 'priest-ridden'. He suspected that Irish Nationalists were incapable of resisting corruption and graft and 'probably the country would be inundated with unscrupulous Irish American low class politicians'. Johnnie also believed, 'knowing the Irish priesthood as I do', that there was little chance of avoiding the intrustion of Catholicism into politics. But, above all, there was the attitude of the Nationalist towards monarchy, Empire and army and the real prospect of 'these disloyal men', who had jeered British troops during the South African War, becoming 'our rulers'. Significantly, the only Loyalist tract extant among Johnnie's papers is 'Nationalist Loyalty or Illustrations of Openly Avowed Hatred of the Soldiers of the King'. Johnnie's account also refers to this aspect of the consequences of home rule as 'an outrage to every decent feeling I possessed', while Stamfordham recorded Johnnie remarking on this point that it was 'simply intolerable to think of'. Johnnie repeated these arguments almost exactly in writing to Oliver in December 1913 after reading Oliver's *The Alternatives to Civil War*, which urged concessions on both sides and advocated a kind of federalism for Ireland (and other parts of the Empire) as a means of avoiding civil war.

Johnnie anticipated that the UVF would maintain 'a fairly correct attitude' on law and order and would avoid clashes with British troops. Consequently, many officers would refuse to act against Ulster. Many calculations were being made at this time as to the precise percentage who would resign.

Johnnie's own estimate as expressed to Stamfordham was between 40 and 60 per cent of a regular officer corps of just under 13,000. Stamfordham noted Johnnie's prediction slightly differently as 'at least 60 per cent of the officers ordered to Ulster would refuse to go and 30 per cent of those *not* ordered there would resign their commissions'. Johnnie made it clear he would resign even though it meant ruining his career:

I laid stress on the fact that my whole life & ambitions had practically been limited to thoughts for my family, my country & the army & it was a bitter blow to find myself forced into the present position, but I had thought out the question and had no doubt in my own mind that I had come to the correct & honourable position.

Johnnie also said to Stamfordham that he had been asked why he did not resign at once but his answer was that he saw 'no reason why I should throw up my career because an injustice *might* be done' and would wait until it had been perpetuated while making no secret of his intentions. Interestingly, when the Curragh crisis broke in March 1914, Francis Howard wrote to Hubert, and later to Johnnie expressing a fear that Johnnie might resign prematurely; indeed Johnnie's initial reaction to proceedings showed every sign of forgetting his earlier intention of waiting upon events.[5]

There were those who counselled such gestures. During his interview Johnnie had declined to name an individual who had urged him to resign. It was, in fact, Princess Alexander of Teck (later Princess Alice, Countess of Athlone) whom Johnnie presumably knew through his duties as ADC to the King. Prince Alexander (later the Earl of Athlone) apparently agreed and 'spoke bitterly' to Johnnie about Asquith's government. At a wider level, however, much rhetoric was being directed at the army by the Unionists. Johnnie had commented to Stamfordham that while he was quite prepared to be court-martialled 'they couldn't try 16 or 17 General officers', no doubt reflecting Carson's announcement in the autumn of pledges allegedly received from 'some of the greatest generals in the army' to assist Ulster. Bonar Law even gave serious consideration between December 1913 and March 1914 to amending the Army (Annual) Act so that the army could not be employed in coercing Ulster, while Carson and Lord Milner spoke of establishing a guarantee fund to reimburse any officers who forfeited their pensions by resigning.

Intimately involved in fuelling the anxieties and instincts of the officer corps on the Ulster issue was Roberts and his coterie, to the extent that Asquith and others believed the old Field Marshal personally responsible for the 'mutinous talk' in the army. Certainly, Roberts intended to use his influence to the full even if he was ultimately concerned by the probability that such strain would be put on the army's discipline that it might never recover. Thus Roberts was quite prepared to support Bonar Law's attempt to amend the Army (Annual) Act and to declare the Home Rule Bill illegal and unconstitutional if the King signed it. Nothing illustrated the cynicism of

Roberts and his circle better than the way in which they also attempted to press the Territorials they had spent six years denigrating into political service by encouraging them also to espouse Ulster's cause.

Not surprisingly in view of his opinions on Ulster, Johnnie was soon approached. On Boxing Day 1913 he had a round of golf on the Swinley links near Roberts' Ascot home, Engelmere. Johnnie's partners were Wilson and Rawlinson, now commanding the 3rd Division in Southern Command. According to Wilson's diary, he was able to report to Roberts in the afternoon that the two had had 'much talk in the morning with Johnnie Gough about Ulster, & that Johnnie had definitely made up his mind to join Ulster if the worst came'. As a result, possibly as early as the following day, Johnnie was asked by Rawlinson to meet Roberts. Johnnie told the old man 'practically what I had told Lord Stamfordham' while Roberts outlined his own intentions with regard to the Home Rule Bill. It appears from Johnnie's account that Roberts did not believe any resignations would be accepted and he 'ended by saying that we ought to act together but he trusted matters would be settled without coming to extremes'.[6] Unfortunately, events were to conspire to bring the question of the army and Ulster to crisis point.

One factor contributing to the crisis was that some senior officers including French seriously underestimated the real depth of feeling among officers. French did anticipate 'larger or smaller defections' but evidently believed that a strong stand against disaffection would have the desirable result of ending it once and for all. The GOC in Ireland, Lieutenant-General Sir Arthur Paget, estimated the possible loss of 15 per cent of officers serving in Ireland in a crisis but, again, could not bring himself to believe that he would ever be asked to coerce Ulster. Haig, of course, had simply declined to discuss Ulster with Johnnie. Nor did French's blustering threats of courts martial create an atmosphere conducive to mutual understanding within the officer corps. In this, however, he was supported by Haldane's successor as Secretary of State for War, J. E. B. Seely, whom Johnnie had known at the Colonial Office. Seely himself delivered a highly incoherent exhortation to discipline to the GOCs of the home commands in December 1913, but his statement was just as confused as the government's policy as a whole. Asquith and Haldane, now Lord Chancellor, appear to have favoured some kind of military measures in Ireland in the autumn of 1913, possibly approximating to the kind of deployment in aid of the civil power used during South Wales industrial disputes three years earlier. But others did not and all that was done was to issue a Royal Proclamation on 1 December banning the further importation of firearms into Ireland.

The same government confusion was also apparent in March 1914 when military movements were ordered which were totally unexpected, the situation in Ireland being not noticeably different from that in the previous autumn. The government had introduced the home rule bill for the third time on 4 March but it was still some months from becoming law. The catalyst of the March crisis appears, therefore, to have been the Unionist rejection on 9 March of a plan proposed by Lloyd George for the exclusion of Ulster from home rule coupled with the receipt in London of new reports from the Royal Irish Constabulary. Presented to the Cabinet on 11 March these estimated the strength of the UVF at 80,000 men with 17,000 firearms. There were also rumours of possible UVF raids on arms depots in Ulster to secure more weapons although these had been current since the autumn and were not apparently substantiated by the RIC reports. But whatever the information available it was evidently judged sufficient to justify the establishment of a special Cabinet sub-committee that same day. Much remains unclear since the government failed to produce the evidence in its own defence, but the UVF did plan to proclaim a provisional government if the bill reached the statute book.

The sub-committee was nominally chaired by the Lord Privy Seal, the Marquis of Crewe, who had also been at the Colonial Office in Johnnie's time. But Crewe fell ill and since the Chief Secretary for Ireland, Augustine Birrell, and the Attorney General, Sir John Simon, were usually absent, effective control devolved upon Seely and yet another of Johnnie's former political superiors at the Colonial Office, Churchill, who was now First Lord of the Admiralty. On the advice of the sub-committee, orders were issued to Paget in Ireland on 14 March to take precautions for the safety of arms depots at Omagh, Armagh, Enniskillen and Carrickfergus. But, in the belief that any troop movements might 'precipitate a crisis', Paget hesitated. He was summoned to London for a series of talks on 18 and 19 March. A total of fourteen individuals were involved but only Seely, Paget, French and Ewart were present throughout. Churchill, Crewe, Birrell, the First Sea Lord, Prince Louis of Battenberg, and the army's acknowledged expert on aid to the civil power, Major-General Sir Nevil Macready – last encountered by Johnnie at Caesar's Camp during the siege of Ladysmith – attended the majority of meetings. It was decided to add Dundalk and Newry to the list of threatened locations, primarily for the security of artillery batteries in their vicinities, and to move a battalion from the exposed Victoria Barracks in Belfast to Holywood. As Paget had complained of lack of intelligence, three officers were to be sent to perform this service and it was also decided to appoint Macready as Military Governor of Belfast in case hostilities developed. Asquith directed that all planned movements should take place by 21 March and the necessary orders were telegraphed to Dublin in Paget's name.

While the military advisers present during the discussions opposed the moves ordered, it is clear from surviving accounts that no participant interpreted them as other than precautionary. Moreover, whatever motivation the Unionists were later to attribute to the government, the measures were little enough in reality. But there was obviously a belief that even limited military movements might provoke the UVF or even the nationalists into military action. Larger military operations were therefore discussed and Seely,

French, Ewart and Paget together agreed that officers with a close connection to Ulster should be permitted to 'remain behind either on leave or with details'. Paget favoured removing others without such a family connection who refused to comply with orders in the event of 'serious trouble arising' and to this Ewart and French also agreed. Other preparations were also put in hand to some extent. Overall responsibility for wider operations was vested in the hands of Robertson as DMT after Wilson successfully persuaded French that Ireland counted as 'home defence' and did not fall within the sphere of the Director of Military Operations.

Paget was also explicit when he returned to Ireland that he could expect reinforcement by the 1st Division from Aldershot, the 11th Infantry Brigade from Colchester and the 18th Infantry Brigade from Lichfield as well as another cavalry brigade. The appointment of three intelligence officers and a soldier with the emotive title of 'Military Governor' was also suggestive of wider operations. However, Haig was to claim that he had not seen any plans for moving the 1st Division from Aldershot and Johnnie, who would have been a party to any such detailed planning, never claimed this either. When Macready fell ill he was hastily replaced as prospective Military Governor of Belfast by Paget's Major-General in charge of Administration, Major-General L. B. Friend. Yet neither Friend nor the RIC Commissioner in Belfast had any idea about what they were supposed to be doing. Paget's chief of staff, Brigadier-General G. T. Forestier-Walker – last seen by Johnnie in Somaliland – did draw up tentative plans for forming a field force, but again Robertson had effectively undermined them from the beginning by pointing out in unequivocal terms the practical military and political difficulties of undertaking any large-scale operations against Ulster.[7]

Yet there was one further factor in the equation which was to persuade the Unionists that there had been a 'plot' to coerce Ulster in March 1914 – Churchill. The First Lord had added to the prevailing tensions with a particularly inflammatory speech in Belfast on 14 March which conveyed his belief that home rule must be pressed now the Unionists had rejected Lloyd George's exclusion proposals. Three days later the Cabinet had noted Churchill's announcement of the forthcoming annual practice of the Royal Navy's 3rd Battle Squadron at Lamlash off Arran, where it would proceed from its present station in Arosa Bay near the Portuguese port of Vigo. In addition, during the talks on 18 and 19 March it was resolved to send two 'scouts' – HMS *Pathfinder* and HMS *Attentive* – to Carrickfergus and two cruisers, HMS *Royal Arthur* and HMS *Gibraltar*, to Kingstown near Dublin in case Ulster's Great Northern Railway Company refused to convey troops north. HMS *Firedrake* was also to be made available for Paget's personal use at Kingstown. The naval movements were not unduly provocative and the decision had been taken collectively. However, it appears highly likely that an additional decision to reinforce the 3rd Battle Squadron at Lamlash with elements of the 4th Destroyer Flotilla was that of Churchill alone. Asquith's cancellation of the orders of both the 3rd Battle Squadron and 4th Destroyer Flotilla on 21 March are circumstantial evidence of Churchill's possible intentions. Again, after Carson had made a dramatic departure from the House of Commons on the afternoon of 19 March during the debate on home rule amid rumours of his possible arrest and the probable declaration of a provisional government when he reached Belfast, Churchill had blustered that 'his fleet would have the town in ruins in twenty four hours'.[8]

The evidence concerning naval movements is not conclusive, and on balance it does not appear that there was any plot as such. Little thought had been given to the implications of any military operations and while it may have been intended to seize public buildings in Belfast no provision had been made for disarming the UVF. What Seely and Churchill's true intentions may or may not have been will never be fully and satisfactorily answered but all was thrown into utter confusion by Paget's understanding or misunderstanding of government policy. Carson's language on 19 March had prompted a final hurried meeting at 10 Downing Street on the evening of Paget's departure for Dublin. Earlier in the day he had talked of leading his army 'to the Boyne' and Churchill's obvious belligerence may have further destabilised the old soldier. Certainly, Paget was observed in a highly excitable condition at Euston Station that night as he prepared to catch the night mail.

When Paget arrived back in Dublin on the morning of Friday 20 March, the movements previously telegraphed from London had already been carried out. Guards had been posted at barrack gates with live ammunition. It had all been unexpected and on the evening of 19 March the commander of the 5th Division in Ireland, Major-General Sir Charles Fergusson, was compelled by events to cancel a dinner he had planned with the Inspector of Cavalry, Major-General Edmund Allenby, over for the start of the annual training season, and the commander of the 3rd Cavalry Brigade stationed at the Curragh camp near Dublin. The latter appointment had been held ever since January 1911 by none other than Hubert. Hubert had no idea what was happening, and alerted both by Fergusson's non-appearance and the orders issued wrote to Johnnie just after 11 p.m. Hubert, of course, was as implacably opposed to the imposition of home rule on Ulster as Johnnie, but at this stage it seemed that it was only proposed to 'dot squadrons about the country'. As it appeared 'there is no question of fighting at present', Hubert intended 'as far as I can foresee my action at all . . . to quietly receive orders & carry them out'. Indeed, none of the principal actors in the unfolding drama with the exception of the commanding officer of the 5th Lancers, Lieutenant Colonel Arthur Parker, ever indicated that they would refuse to obey any direct order throughout the entire affair.

Hubert also told Johnnie that he was summoned to meet Paget on the following morning, 20 March. It was a meeting attended also by Fergusson, Friend, Forestier-Walker, Colonel F. F. Hill commanding No 11 District and two of Fergusson's brigade commanders, Brigadier-Generals S. P. Rolt and

G. J. Cuthbert. The contemporary accounts penned by Hubert and Fergusson and the slightly later recollections of Friend and Rolt make clear Paget's astonishing error of judgment during the meeting in seeming not only to imply that active operations against Ulster were imminent – he spoke of Ulster being in a 'blaze' by Saturday – but also that he was putting an ultimatum before his officers. In line with the concession he believed he had obtained in London, Paget offered those domiciled in Ulster the option of 'disappearing' during active operations. Those unable to claim this exemption who refused to take part would be dismissed without pension. Essentially, Paget was offering a choice as to whether to obey or not in advance of operations being ordered in a way that appeared to give officers brutally short notice in which to consider the implications of their choices. Why he acted in this manner is uncertain, Paget subsequently claiming that he only intended to ascertain the reliability of his senior officers and never meant a formal ultimatum to be placed before junior officers.[9] The most charitable explanation is that Paget simply lost his head.

Hubert was particularly incensed by Paget's attitude and the enormity of the repercussions of moving against Ulster. As soon as the meeting was concluded he telegraphed Johnnie at Blandford House at 11.17 a.m.:

Have been offered dismissal service or undertake operations against Ulster. Two hours to decide. First means ruin of army as others will follow. This only consideration that counts. Am taking first contingency. Do you think if I am right?

Hubert then went to inform Arthur Parker whose regiment was stationed in Dublin's Marlborough Barracks before motoring to the Curragh to put the ultimatum in turn to his brigade's other regiments, Lieutenant Colonel Maurice MacEwen's 16th Lancers and Lieutenant Colonel Ian Hogg's 4th Hussars. Similarly, Fergusson put the ultimatum in writing for the benefit of outlying artillery, engineer and other supporting units in 5th Division while Rolt and Cuthbert carried it verbally to the infantry. All were under the firm impression that the ultimatum had been officially sanctioned by the War Office. Indeed, one of Fergusson's battalion commanders, Lieutenant Colonel C. A. H. Brett of the 2nd Suffolks, wrongly assumed that there was an actual War Office 'secret letter' setting out its terms. It was also Brett's understanding that the order had the King's sanction. Fergusson had given that impression and used it as an argument to hold his officers to their duty when he made an extensive tour of his units on the following day, Saturday 21 March. Before he did so it was clear that large numbers would have resigned rather than coerce Ulster including at least 42 infantry and at least 18 artillery officers.

The use of the King's name became a matter of some controversy when a letter from Brett to Rolt referring to the 'secret letter' and the King's sanction for both the operations and the ultimatum reached Buckingham Palace by way of Fergusson, Paget and French. However, it was not Fergusson who was responsible for the introduction of the King's name but Paget. Paget had implied the King's approval at a second meeting on 20 March attended by Fergusson and officers of Paget's staff and those of Major-General W. P. Pulteney's 6th Division based at Cork. Hubert had been excluded since Paget made it obvious in the morning that those declining to coerce Ulster need not attend. Some of those present at the second meeting were prevailed upon by Paget to suggest that Fergusson must have misunderstood what was said but this failed to convince Stamfordham and the King, especially when Hubert and his officers gained exactly the same impression from an address Paget made to the 3rd Cavalry Brigade on the morning of 21 March.[10]

The latter meeting was a disastrous attempt by Paget to 'put a little heart' into the cavalrymen for there had been an even more violent reaction to the ultimatum among them than among the infantry and artillery. In going round his regiments, Hubert had declined to give specific advice to individuals on the choice they should make, but he had made it clear that he would himself resign. One of his audience in the 16th Lancers' mess, Captain T. W. Pragnell of the 4th Hussars, was convinced that Hubert's parting remark, 'as for myself, I am damned if I am going', could not have been 'more calculated to influence us to follow his lead and back him up at whatever cost'. When someone as popular as Hubert took such a stand it was almost inevitable that others would follow. It is notable how most officers of the brigade on detached service invariably sent in their resignations automatically on receipt of the most sparse telegrams sent them. In all, 60 of the 72 officers 'doing duty' with the 3rd Cavalry Brigade offered their resignations including Lieutenant J. B. Gough – Bloomfield's son – who was attached to the Royal Horse Artillery in the brigade. A further five officers claimed the Ulster domicile exemption.

Some were uneasy, especially Ian Hogg, who could have claimed the exemption but chose not to do so, and his second in command, Major Philip Howell. At Howell's suggestion, Hubert was persuaded to write to Paget giving the numbers resigning but also calling for more clarification as to what precisely was meant by the phrase 'active operations' used in the ultimatum. It was in response that Paget duly appeared next morning. Unfortunately, his long and rambling discourse made a highly unfavourable impression on his hearers including those such as Lieutenant Colonel R. W. Breeks of the III Brigade, Royal Horse Artillery who had actually decided not to resign. Nevertheless, Hogg and Howell were able to convince all but six of their regiment's 17 officers to withdraw their resignations as they were now convinced there had been a misunderstanding and that Paget had given acceptable guarantees. Hubert and most of the others remained unimpressed and Parker in particular, who had had a number of separate interviews with Paget, was outspoken in his opposition to any compromise. Elsewhere, by now, Fergusson had been more successful in getting his officers to withdraw their resignations as already indicated.[11]

In London this sudden eruption of the crisis had caused equal confusion. Almost certainly the first news of what had occurred was Hubert's telegram to Johnnie. It had arrived at Blandford House at 12.40 p.m. on 20 March but Johnnie was out on a field exercise and the telegram lay on the hall table until he returned at about 2 p.m. Johnnie was horrified and hurriedly despatched a response at 3.40 p.m.:

I will not serve against Ulster and if you are dismissed my resignation goes in at once. Wire what happens to you.

Telling Major-General Lomax commanding the 1st Division that 'I was going to London to see if it was true that Hubert was to be dismissed & if a fact to resign my command', Johnnie drove up to London. A note he later appended to an album of his Curragh correspondence indicated that he took his 'Wolseley valise & war kit on the back of the car' and Johnnie also told Oliver that if, as he had thought at the time, civil war had already broken out in Ireland, he would have gone straight to Ulster. In London Johnnie first called briefly to see Dorothea, who was staying at Harriette's flat, 48C Sloane Square. He then went round to Wilson's house in Eaton Place at about 6 p.m. Wilson was still at the War Office but Johnnie got Wilson's wife to telephone for her husband to return home at once. Johnnie 'told him the story & he got on the telephone with Seely & Sir J. French'.

In fact, Wilson and Johnnie only managed to contact French who, according to Wilson, denied any knowledge of events '& talked windy platitudes till I was nearly sick'. Neither French nor Seely's private secretary, G. C. N. Nicholson, appears to have responded in any positive way to what Wilson and Johnnie were trying to convey and it was not until the first telegram was received from Paget that Seely had French and Churchill summoned from the theatre to Seely's house at about 9.30 p.m. Churchill was threatening to bring Hubert and his officers 'over in a battleship to be tried by court martial', but Ewart, who arrived at about 11 p.m. to find Lloyd George also present in Seely's house, instilled some sanity into the proceedings. With the receipt of further telegrams from Paget it was decided to bring Hubert, his three colonels and Hill, who had also resigned, to the War Office for interview and to refuse all other resignations. Ewart could not comprehend what had happened when there had been no question of moving the 3rd Cavalry Brigade and was eminently sensible in arguing that it was best to hear out Hubert and his companions before jumping to conclusions.

Wilson was also correct if, as recorded in his diary, he 'persuaded Johnnie not to send in his papers till tomorrow while we must find out if this is all true'. Certainly when Johnnie wrote to Haig that evening, Haig being on leave at Littlehampton, he said that 'there may have been a mistake'. However, he intended to visit the War Office on Saturday morning to 'find out for certain and then act according to my conscience'. By this time, too, Johnnie had also received a second telegram from Hubert indicating that his resignation had been held over and ending 'Don't do anything at present'.[12] Nevertheless, early next morning Johnnie sent a further message to Hubert, 'Well done, well done. I am with you heart and soul and so are many others.' Then he went to the War Office and presented the Military Secretary, Lieutenant-General Sir William Franklyn, with a letter of resignation:

In view of the military movements which have been ordered against Ulster, and the action of the GOC-in-Chief in Ireland in giving officers two hours to decide between dismissal from the service or an undertaking to act against Ulster, I have the honour to hand in the resignation of my commission as an officer in HM's Army.

At first Franklyn had refused to see Johnnie as it was 'a political matter' but he relented and, to his credit, asked Johnnie whether he would like him to hold the letter 'until I had been able to verify the news from Ireland'. Johnnie agreed but told Franklyn 'that I did not wish him to make any secret of my intention to resign & would be glad if he could tell both Seely & French'. Another who counselled caution was Haig who replied by telegram to Johnnie's letter of the previous evening:

Hope you will not act precipitately. I feel equally strongly on subject as you. There is no question of Army Fighting against Protestants or against Catholics. Our duty is to keep the peace between them.

But, even if he had now held back his resignation temporarily, Johnnie was still aiming to spread the news of the events at the Curragh as widely as possible in order to mobilise support for Hubert.

During Saturday afternoon Johnnie contacted Lady Lugard, who had wide associations among Unionist circles, and she at once got in touch with Bonar Law. As it happened, Bonar Law was already aware of events since he had received an anonymous telegram from the Curragh on the previous evening but Lady Lugard's information was additional confirmation. Johnnie or possibly Dorothea also made contact with Austen Chamberlain, Chancellor of the Exchequer in the last Unionist administration. It was a link Hubert reported to his wife, Daisy, from London on 22 March and Johnnie's contacts with Chamberlain continued throughout the crisis. Indeed, Chamberlain terminated a telephone conversation with Dorothea on 24 March because he feared the line was being tapped. Wilson had also been busy with his Unionist friends and had seen the editor of *The Times*, Geoffrey Robinson (later to assume the surname Dawson), on Saturday afternoon. Consequently, Johnnie received a telegram from the newspaper's military correspondent, Repington, just after 3 p.m. enquiring if his reported resignation was fact. Roberts had also become aware of what had occurred from a telegram from Hubert he had received that morning, and during Saturday Roberts not only made a gratuitously offensive telephone call to French but hastened to London to see Seely and the King. It must be emphasised that there was no premeditation between officers in Ireland, their military supporters in London and Unionist politicians since the crisis had arisen so abruptly. However, there is a distinct suggestion of something insidious in these contacts so quickly established once Paget's miscalculations had precipitated crisis, and in these contacts Johnnie played a full part.[13]

Early on Saturday evening Johnnie got another telegram from Hubert announcing his departure for London with his colonels and asking to meet Johnnie at Sloane Square in the morning before his appointment at the War Office set for 10 a.m. Later, Hubert sent another telegram saying that he would evacuate his children from Ireland and send them to a cousin in Hertfordshire. Johnnie returned to Aldershot overnight and travelled up to London once more on Sunday morning to arrive at his mother's flat at about 9 a.m. Hubert had arrived in the early hours after crossing on the night mail. Wilson also came for breakfast as did the King's assistant private secretary, Clive Wigram. In fact, throughout the crisis the Palace was fed with information through Wigram, as well as one of the King's equerries, Lieutenant Colonel Frank Dugdale. It must soon have become apparent over breakfast from Hubert's account how far Paget had blundered, Johnnie remarking to his brother that 'our case was unshakeable'. Johnnie had already discovered from his visit to the War Office that 'the line the W.O. meant to take up was that there was a complete misunderstanding, that the alternatives put before us by Paget should never have been put, and that we were to be reinstated'. This immeasurably strengthened Hubert's hand. He had also brought with him typed copies of relevant documents for distribution to sympathisers and it is clear from a letter sent by Howell to Wigram and from a later account by MacEwen that Hubert and his colonels had come with the express intention of securing a written guarantee that the army would not be used to coerce Ulster. Wilson also seems to have been thinking along the same lines and, according to his diary, he had presented French with a form of guarantee on the previous day while both he and Robertson urged the CIGS to force Asquith into concessions.[14]

Following the breakfast deliberations at Sloane Square which was to become a focus for constant activity – Harriette was apparently besieged by 'ladies coming for news' and delighted in the nickname given her in the press of the 'Mother of the Gracchi' as she presided over 'a sort of levée of all the Ulster adherents in her drawing room' – Hubert and Johnnie took a taxi to the War Office. There they met MacEwen and Parker at about 9.45 a.m., Hubert being handed a letter left for him with the doorkeeper by Roberts after the old Field Marshal's interview with Seely on the Saturday. This gave Hubert additional indications that Seely had never intended an ultimatum put before officers and that 'there was some hope for him if he could satisfy the AG that he would have replied to a question more properly put in a proper & subordinate manner'.[15] Hubert, MacEwen, Parker and Hogg, who had sent a telegram to Churchill as a former officer of the 4th Hussars pleading for 'sensible handling' of the affair, were then each interviewed in turn by Ewart accompanied by Macready. While there was evidently some personal animosity between Hubert and Macready over a now obscure quarrel concerning Macready's relations with Hubert in the former's capacity as Director of Personal Services at the War Office, the interviews were relatively free of tension. They more than confirmed Ewart's view that Paget was to blame and that, with the exception of Parker, all would have obeyed any direct orders to move north. Accordingly, Ewart decided to send for Paget, and during the afternoon Hubert and the others were asked to come back to the War Office at 11 a.m. on Monday, 23 March. Thus far, Ewart had been concerned only to establish the facts.[16]

From the account by Seely's private secretary, Nicholson, it is apparent that there were some kind of further negotiations during the Sunday afternoon intended to get Hubert and his colonels back to duty. However, Parker was not prepared to go back and the others felt unable to do so 'so long as he stood out'. This applied even to Hogg who had withdrawn his resignation but had still gone to the War Office lest Paget's assurances were repudiated. Also, of course, no written guarantee had yet been extracted and Hubert and the others had quickly realised the strength of their position with the tremendous support already being generated for them in the army. Johnnie was also unsatisfied, one correspondent of Hubert writing how he had gone to Sloane Square on Sunday afternoon and seen Johnnie:

Your brother stood in the hall of the flat. I asked him 'And what are you going to do?' Then the answer: 'There is only one thing to do.' Whereupon I seized his hand wildly.

Nonetheless, Johnnie had subtly changed his position. Either while still at the War Office on Sunday morning or immediately after returning to Harriette's flat he had sent a new communication to Franklyn asking him to destroy his original letter of resignation and substitute another:

In view of the action of the GOC-in-Chief in Ireland in giving officers a few hours to decide whether they would undertake operations against Ulster or be dismissed the service, I wish to place on record that I am in agreement with those officers who decided to accept dismissal. Further I think it is only right for me to make it clear that any action taken against these officers should equally apply to myself.

Franklyn was uncertain whether this second letter should have been directed through Haig as Johnnie's immediate superior or sent direct to him but he did as Johnnie requested and sent the new letter to Ewart. As far as Franklyn could judge, it 'does not seem a resignation but an invitation to discipline' which should be dealt with by Ewart. Johnnie never received any reply and Haig later told Johnnie that he had seen the letter lying on Ewart's desk on the Monday while French had remarked, 'Your Gough is as bad as any of them, what business is it of his that he should interfere?' Curiously, the letter together with Franklyn's note ended up among Seely's private papers while a partial copy has survived in the papers of the Admiral of Patrols, Rear Admiral John de Roebeck. Presumably, de Robeck received the copy from one of his own subordinates, Roger Keyes, now Commodore of Submarines and a key figure in generating support for Hubert in the Royal Navy.[17]

During the course of Sunday afternoon Johnnie also saw both Roberts and Haig. Having heard Johnnie's version of events and received copies from him of the relevant accounts of the events at the Curragh over tea, Roberts then telephoned to confer with Austen Chamberlain and wrote to Wilson. Rawlinson was also at Roberts' home for the weekend and recorded that Johnnie left at 5.30 p.m. to see Haig at Aldershot. Johnnie had previously made arrangements for a car to be sent to pick up Haig from his Littlehampton hotel while also telling Haig by telephone that he would be visiting the War Office. Haig's attitude was still an unknown quantity but as Johnnie wrote to Oliver he was pleasantly surprised to find Haig supportive:

I had at that time no idea what his attitude would be (so much for the Army plot!). Sir D. H. rose to the occasion & said that he for one would not shoot down the Northern Protestants, but that the Army's job was limited to keeping 'law & order'. He, Sir D. H., ended by saying he would go up with me on Monday morning & would use his influence with the War Office & also explain the attitude of the Army & Aldershot in particular.

However, it is worth noting that, in writing to Hubert's wife on 23 March, Dorothea expressed some reservations concerning Haig:

When we got home last night we found that Aldershot was fairly roused and prepared to resign en bloc if they got the lead, which Sir Douglas is not prepared to give.

Moreover, although Haig did indeed go to London with Johnnie on Monday morning and did inform French of the depth of feeling in the Aldershot Command, he also began to work closely with Haldane to find a solution to the crisis. Just as he had initially telegraphed Johnnie to be 'calm' he also advised Hubert to settle and return to the Curragh as soon as possible. Haig blamed French for placing the army in a difficult position by not standing up to the politicians but was entirely careful to keep a foot firmly in both camps.[18]

Of the strength of support for Hubert at Aldershot there was little doubt, a frequently stated rumour having it that only one officer in the entire command would have willingly gone to Ulster as a reinforcement to Paget's field force. Johnnie had assured MacEwan of Aldershot's solidarity on the Sunday afternoon and was clearly instrumental in establishing this support in the first place. Hubert praised Johnnie later for 'arousing the spirit of the Army' and much the same was said by MacEwen, Parker and Colonel Hill. Parker, for example, felt that without Johnnie's 'energy, determination, and foresight we could not have achieved the success we did'. Support was also being mobilised at the War Office where such pressure was applied to those with doubts as to the wisdom of the course Hubert and Johnnie were following that the atmosphere became 'unpleasant'. Both Major- General F. J. Davies, the Director of Staff Duties and Johnnie's predecessor as Haig's chief of staff, and Robertson were solidly behind Hubert. Robertson, indeed, was as relieved as Johnnie that Haig seemed 'solid' since, as he wrote to Johnnie, 'I half feared he might take another view. It has made the position so much cosier.' Ironically, while Wilson had done much to politicise the War Office staff he was wavering on whether or not to resign. Now he was being firmly pushed by the very men he had alerted to the crisis as well as by Johnnie, Hubert writing to Nora on Sunday evening that Wilson was acting 'entirely under pressure from J!'.[19]

Letters and telegrams of support were also pouring in from other parts of the country and from the army overseas. Johnnie received one letter from his old Somaliland friend, Tom Bridges, back in London from his position as military attaché in Brussels: Bridges had been telephoned by Wilson to hold his resignation until the Monday morning. There were also communications from Francis Howard, Peter Dawnay and Arthur Daly, who had been at the Staff College with Johnnie and was now at the Royal Military College. Another correspondent was the Rifle Brigade's chronicler, Colonel Willoughby Verner, whose obituary for Johnnie included praise for his 'magnificent moral courage and utter disregard of self and any personal consequences' in March 1914 in brushing aside the 'threats and cajolery of pitiful time servers'. Hubert, too, received messages from many of Johnnie's friends including A. S. Cobbe, Francis Howard, Arthur Daly, George Paley, George Thesiger, Reginald Stephens, Neill Malcolm and Hugh Dawnay. Other correspondents had known Johnnie at Staff College including Hugo De Pree, R. J. F. Hayter, Frank Maxwell, Charles Gwynn, H. L. Reed and Lewis Halliday. Hubert and Johnnie's cousin, Charles French, now a company commander at the Royal Military College, was another correspondent.[20]

Armed with so much evidence of support, Johnnie arrived at Sloane Square with Haig at 10 a.m. on Monday 23 March to meet Hubert. While Haig went on to meet Haldane at the House of Lords, the two brothers went to the War Office where a photographer captured their arrival. They met Parker and MacEwen, who had breakfasted with the Honorary Colonel of the 16th Lancers, Major-General J. M. Babington, and walked on to the War Office in Babington's company. Hogg also attended although his presence is ignored in accounts by the other participants. Those of both Hubert and Johnnie suggest that the group had sufficient time before Hubert was called into French's room at 11.15 a.m. to discuss 'the plan of campaign'. According to Johnnie, they decided,

We would not fight against Ulster, & if there were going to be operations against Ulster then we *wanted* to be dismissed as we would then be free agents to take whichever side we liked in the Civil War. We did not trust the Government; we felt we were dealing with unscrupulous lawyers, whose word was not worth a brass farthing. We felt uneasy that these above mentioned lawyers would try to entrap us with words, & that above all they would try & force the Army into a false position under the plea of maintaining law & order.

Thus, in his interviews with first French and Ewart and, subsequently, with Seely and Paget also in attendance, Hubert pressed for a definite assurance in writing that the army would not be used to coerce Ulster. Without such an undertaking he would not return to Dublin. To this written guarantee Seely eventually agreed as a means of clearing the 'misunderstanding' that had arisen. Ewart was charged with drawing up a suitable form of words and Parker, MacEwen and Hogg were brought into French's room just after midday to be told with Hubert that they could return for the document at 4 p.m. Outside in the waiting room the four then conferred with Johnnie and Babington. Wilson was not present and a careful reading of his diary shows that Hubert consulted him in his own room at 12.30 p.m. although Wilson also claims that he drafted the letter Hubert then sent to Ewart as a result of these deliberations.

This letter sought clarification of what might occur if the government later tried to use the army to coerce Ulster in the guise of keeping the peace:

On thinking over the points raised by the Secretary of State this morning, the question has arisen in my mind, and it will undoubtedly be one of the first questions asked me by my officers, when I see them, viz:
In the event of the present Home Rule Bill becoming law, can we be called upon to enforce it on Ulster under the expression of maintaining law & order?
This point should be made quite clear in your draft letter, otherwise there will be renewed misconceptions.

It was now about 1.30 p.m. and, while MacEwen and Babington went off to the Senior Club for lunch, Hubert and Johnnie met Haig and the Major-General in charge of Administration at Aldershot, Major-General F. S. Robb, at the Marlborough Club.

Meanwhile, Ewart had produced a document from drafts prepared by Seely's secretary, Nicholson, and a member of Macready's staff. Since Seely had gone on from a Cabinet meeting to an audience with the King, the document was sent over to the Cabinet room at 1.30 p.m. Hubert's letter to Ewart was sent over shortly afterwards, Nicholson telephoning 10 Downing Street to ask that Seely be shown it as soon as possible. In Cabinet Asquith had amended Ewart's draft and then handed it to Seely who returned from the palace just as the Cabinet adjourned. Glancing only briefly at Hubert's letter, Seely added two more paragraphs to the guarantee. He believed that the document as it stood would not satisfy Hubert and also that he had the discretion to amend it without further consultation. Lord Morley, with whom Seely was conversing at the time, apparently concurred although Margot Asquith was to claim that Morley was too deaf to hear what was going on and too vain to admit it. Returning to the War Office Seely gave the amended document to Ewart to be typed, telling him that he would sign it if possible, but if he was in the House of Commons that Ewart and French should go ahead and sign on behalf of the Army Council.

As now amended with the addition of Seely's final two 'peccant paragraphs', it was as Ewart recognised, 'an historic document':

You are authorized by the Army Council to inform the officers of the 3rd Cavalry Brigade that the Army Council are satisfied that the incident which has arisen in regard to their resignations has been due to a misunderstanding.
It is the duty of all soldiers to obey lawful commands given to them through the proper channel by the Army Council, either for the protection of public property and the support of the civil power in the event of disturbances, or for the protection of the lives and property of the inhabitants.
This is the only point it was intended to be put to the officers in the questions of the General Officer Commanding, and the Army Council have been glad to learn from you that there never had been and never will be in the Brigade any question of disobeying such lawful orders.
His Majesty's Government must retain their right to use all the forces of the Crown in Ireland, or elsewhere, to maintain law and order and to support the civil power in the ordinary execution of its duty.
But they have no intention whatever of taking advantage of this right to crush political opposition to the policy or principles of the Home Rule Bill.

Concerned that he and French could not alone signal the government's agreement to the terms, Ewart wanted it signed by Seely as well. Accordingly, he and French went to the Commons where Nicholson went into the chamber at about 4 p.m. and obtained Seely's initials on the document. They returned to the War Office where Hubert, Johnnie and the others had arrived during their absence. Hubert was again ushered into see French and Ewart, given the guarantee and directed to return to Dublin that night.

Hubert asked for fifteen minutes to consider and took the guarantee outside to Johnnie, Parker and MacEwen. It is unclear whether Hogg was present but Babington was and Wilson had now joined the group. Based on his own testimony it is usually suggested that Wilson now prompted a request for yet further clarification since the reference to crushing political oppositions in the last and crucial paragraph seemed ambiguous. All present felt this and, again, careful scrutiny of what Wilson actually wrote indicates that the short written statement Hubert then added to the document was a collective effort. All accounts including that of Wilson refer to 'we' in discussing the response. Again, correspondence or accounts by Hubert, MacEwan and Parker ascribe a particular role to Johnnie in all the deliberations at the War Office. By temperament he tended to shirk the limelight and to leave the centre stage to those like Hubert who enjoyed it – Oliver later wrote that Johnnie 'banished all meanness from his neighbourhood, all thoughts of self interest and personal advancement'. Johnnie was also reluctant to credit himself with greater courage or cooler judgment than his fellows, but there is little doubt that Johnnie should rightly replace Wilson as the key figure in the negotiations as a whole.

Hubert with MacEwen and Parker as witnesses then took the document back into French and Ewart where Hubert read out the statement:

We understand the reading of the last paragraph to be that the troops under our command will not be called upon to enforce the present Home Rule Bill on Ulster, and that we can so assure our officers.

In Hubert's oft-quoted account:

Sir J. French said 'That seems all right' and then on second thoughts he said 'Let me have a look at that paper'. I gave it to him – he walked up and down once or twice reading it and then – without further remark, sat down at the table and wrote under my signature 'That is how I read it – JF'.

Pausing to speak to a few friends in the War Office, Hubert and Johnnie then went back to Harriette's flat for tea. They had won a most significant political victory.[21]

Just how significant was not at first realised by the Cabinet. Speeches by government representatives that night, notably by Haldane, gave every indication that all was well. On the following day, too, Ewart felt confident enough to refuse Colonel Hill's request for a similar written guarantee on the grounds that government statements negated its necessity. But the nature of Seely's initiative soon became apparent. Hubert had spoken of the guarantee to the editor of the *Morning Post*, H. A. Gwynne, as he boarded the train to Dublin at Euston and Wilson had leaked details to all and sundry within minutes. Called to the room of Asquith's private secretary at the Commons during the afternoon of 24 March, Ewart was asked to produce all relevant documents. He was horrified to find that only Seely had seen Hubert's letter sent over to the Cabinet and that Seely had amended the document without consultation.

On the following day Asquith formally repudiated the guarantee given to Hubert. Efforts were also made to retrieve the actual document by both Asquith and Paget. However, Hubert had immediately and prudently put it in trust for his eldest daughter with the family solicitors in Dublin. Possibly as part of this attempt, Johnnie was invited to dine with Seely on the evening of 27 March. Both Hubert and, curiously, Haig wanted Johnnie to avoid the meeting and all were relieved when Seely cancelled on 26 March. Seely, of course, had been put in a difficult position, albeit of his own making. He offered to resign and the Army Council – French, Ewart, the Master General of the Ordnance, Colonel (temporary Major-General) Sir Stanley von Donop, and the Quartermaster General, Major-General Sir John Cowans – offered to follow suit. Seely's resignation was refused, but feeling they had been placed in an intolerable situation French and Ewart pressed their resignations on Asquith. Haig and Haldane, as already indicated, attempted to find a compromise, but there were others such as Wilson and Gwynne who tried to make the maximum political capital out of the government's discomfort by persuading French to stick to his decision. When Haldane's draft statements failed to satisfy French and Ewart on one hand and Asquith on the other, they did resign on 30 March. Seely had little choice but to go as well and Asquith himself became secretary of State for War on 31 March.[22]

Neither Asquith's assumption of the War Office appointment nor his later announcement in the Commons on 29 April that he would answer no more questions on the Curragh incident ended the affair. For one thing, there was the issue of whether there had been a government plot to coerce Ulster. Many officers were only too happy to supply details of all they knew to Unionist politicians to try and substantiate a plot. Among them was Johnnie and, in addition to his contacts with Chamberlain, he supplied some information to Repington and substantially more to Oliver. Among the papers he collected was a detailed analysis of railway movements ordered in Ulster which was forwarded by one 'Jack' – probably John Bagwell, general manager of the Great Northern Railway, whose family were old friends of the Goughs at Clonmel – to Johnnie on 22 April. Then again there was the continuing controversy over the use of the King's name which dragged on until July. Hubert was among many totally mystified by Paget's survival, which only gave more currency to the theory of a plot since the government seemed excessively concerned to shield Paget from his grievous errors.

Even more important were the continuing repercussions of the support generated for Hubert and Johnnie within the army. Indeed, one of the principal reasons for French and Ewart's relief at getting Hubert back to Dublin on 23 March was their fear that there might be 'a sympathetic strike and widespread resignations throughout the army'. Beyond the support at the War Office and at Aldershot, there had been all those letters and telegrams Hubert and Johnnie had received. Their supporters embraced soldiers as well known as Rawlinson; the GOC at Southern Command, Lieutenant-General Sir Horace Smith-Dorrien; Allenby; and the Inspector of Infantry, Major-General Thompson Capper. Support was overwhelming at institutions such as the Royal Military College and the Staff College, in other cavalry regiments and the army abroad. It extended, too, as noted to the Royal Navy.[23]

Yet not all soldiers did support Hubert and Johnnie and in consequence irretrievable damage was done to personal relationships in the army. Fergusson was one who found himself the target for abuse and Hogg was attacked for inducing his officers to withdraw their resignations. Hubert played no small part in villifying his critics and opponents and regarded Philip Howell with the deepest suspicion. Another victim was Colonel Sir Philip Chetwode, who had accepted temporary appointment to Hubert's command but had never actually left England: the very fact that he had been willing to go to Dublin was enough to earn him general opprobrium from the Gough faction. Much of the invective was directed at French and Paget and the violence of Hubert's language in describing them was unabated as late as July. But, of course, it was not all one way and Hubert was hardly popular in all quarters. Wilson's reputation for intrigue was also much enhanced.

Ironically, one personal relationship permanently blighted was that of Wilson and Johnnie through the belief of the Gough brothers that Wilson had not done as much as he might when he had learned of the proposed military movements at an early stage. Reference has already been made to Hubert's letter to Nora on 22 March in which he wrote that Wilson was only acting under pressure from Johnnie. It has also been suggested by Hubert's biographer (although without apparent evidence to support it) that during the breakfast conference of 22 March Johnnie had playfully 'hotted' Wilson by 'pretending to understand that Wilson was immediately adding his own resignation to theirs'. A letter from Hubert to Major-General A. J. Godley on 28 April also protested that Wilson had 'never raised a finger, till everybody else did. He was however useful in various ways, but did not mean to risk his own skin, & was very glad to help us pull out the chestnuts for him'. Consequently, as Hubert wrote in his memoirs, Johnnie 'refused ever to speak to Wilson again'. It was a breach Oliver tried but failed to heal.[24]

Fortunately, Ireland was relatively quiet in the immediate aftermath of the events of March but tensions again increased with a successful gun-running attempt by the UVF at Larne on 24 April. The renewed prospect of the army's involvement was most unwelcome since it raised the spectre of troops being called out 'in aid of the civil power', the trap that Gough had anticipated in March. However, French had been succeeded as CIGS by Sir Charles Douglas and confidence was placed in Douglas' ability to prevent the army being used. Certainly, any questions of troop movements in Ulster were treated with the utmost caution by the military authorities in both London and Dublin and discreet enquiries made in April demonstrated conclusively that the army was still too deeply disaffected to be used in any capacity. In effect, the divisions in the army ruled out any question of coercion and, with the situation no better on 4 July, the Army Council adopted a paper drafted by Wilson which pointed out in no uncertain terms that any operations in Ulster would require the mobilisation of the entire expeditionary force with serious consequences for home and Imperial defence. Discipline had been thoroughly undermined, Fergusson for one expressing his doubts on 14 July as to how far he could trust two of his infantry battalions. Recruiting had also been affected.

But, if the personal animosities forged within the army and the disciplinary difficulties were serious enough, the crisis had also had the most unfortunate results in terms of the relationship between soldiers and politicians. Some like Fergusson had feared that when greater dangers loomed at home and abroad the army would be dragged into the political arena over Ulster to such an extent that radicals in Asquith's party might force and win a general election on the cry of 'the people versus the army'. Others including even Hubert subscribed to the view, as he expressed it to Johnnie in a telegram of 26 March, that the army should not 'become tools of either political party'. This was the theme of remarks by Haig to his immediate subordinates, including Johnnie, at Aldershot on 25 March. Johnnie also felt that the army should avoid politics but had had to act to prevent civil war. Using the pseudonym, 'Soldier', he wrote to *The Times* on 25 March:

We dislike politics and have no desire to be mixed up in anything so unsavoury.

We, in common with most of our fellow subjects, do not want civil war. We are determined that the Army shall not be used for political purposes. If the country wants civil war then let the question be decided by the votes of the people at a general election, or by means of a referendum. Of one thing we may be quite sure i.e. civil war will destroy the Army & the Empire and will turn this country into a very hell.

We are firmly convinced that the action of officers in accepting dismissal has saved the country from civil war, and we devoutly hope that no government will ever again attempt to employ the army for party purposes.

But, at the same time, Johnnie was perhaps deluding himself for those like Roberts, Wilson and Rawlinson had had every intention and every expectation of bringing down Asquith's government. Thus, the contempt routinely showered on politicians by officers was wholly cynical in the context of the army's real political victory. It had effectively paralysed government policy towards Ireland, strengthening the hands of those in the Cabinet opposed to the use of force but ensuring a resigned acceptance of the continued existence of the paramilitary sectarian organisations. Only compromise was possible and, while an unamended Home Rule Act would be passed in September 1914, it was immediately suspended for the duration of the war with the promise of an amending bill at that time to exclude Ulster. It boded ill for Ireland's furture. It had also been a result achieved at the price of poisoning civil-military relations on the eve of war and of almost destroying the army as an institution. And whatever the depth of his feelings on Ulster, Johnnie had ultimately been willing to see the army destroyed.[25]

The strain of events on Johnnie was understandably considerable for he fully realised the consequences of his actions. Indeed, at times he had shouldered the burden of Hubert's own doubts, and on his return to Dublin on 24 March Hubert was duly grateful:

When my heart began to fail & my resolution to waver, as it did under the strain sometimes, you held me up & I can never be grateful enough to you for doing so. You did for me what Aaron & Hur did for Moses during the battle against the Amalekites!! All I can pray is that if, & when, you are in a crisis, that you will find me as prompt & as resolute in your support as you were in mine.

As a memento Hubert asked Johnnie, MacEwen and Parker to provide recent photographs which he then framed with his original letter of resignation drafted for Friend in Dublin but apparently never sent and the lines from Exodus (Chapter 17, verses 11 and 12) to which he had referred in his letter to Johnnie. Later, during the war, Johnnie remarked to Hubert that he had not yet experienced any moment as anxious as during 'your March show'. Johnnie was obviously still under strain in April for Hubert's former ADC in South Africa (and Wilson's brother-in-law), Captain Llewellyn Price-Davies, V.C., recorded that he ran into Johnnie at the large Unionist demonstration in Hyde Park and that Johnnie 'was in a fearful rage at the way the government had treated Ulster & the army'. It seems likely, therefore, that the events of

March contributed to the serious and sudden illness that seized Johnnie on 24 May.

The nature of his collapse is unclear other than that it required an immediate emergency abdominal operation. It may have been a lingering legacy, too, of the Somaliland campaign since a letter from Roberts and Oliver's account in *Ordeal by Battle* suggests that the surgery carried out by Sir Berkeley Moynihan 'restored him after several years ill health'. Roger Keyes learned that Moynihan had said that Johnnie 'could not have lived three months' without the operation. The King made especial enquiries as to Johnnie's progress, Wigram obtaining full details from Moynihan of the 'very serious operation'. On behalf of the King and Queen, Wigram then wrote to Dorothea that they 'know how his pluck and courage will be a great assistance to overcoming all obstacles to a state of convalescence'. Haig was also concerned and, in fact, young Diana had been taking tea at Haig's home when news was brought of Johnnie's collapse. Haig wrote to Dorothea that Johnnie should not attend the autumn manoeuvres and he also wrote to Moynihan so the surgeon would 'be able to arrange to keep him quiet so as to ensure thorough recovery from the operation'. Johnnie was not able to see visitors for some time, Dorothea relating to Eva Keyes that the patient was 'bored stiff' and, although frail, was 'very cheerful'. By 16 June Johnnie was able to sit up out of bed but there was no question of him attending exercises at Aldershot and in early July he, Dorothea and Diana went to stay with Roger and Eva Keyes at Fareham House.

Later in the month, Johnnie also undertook a short trip to Ireland against the advice of some of his friends who feared reopening controversial matters. Johnnie took no notice and even appears to have reviewed (presumably in mufti) UVF troops, Wilfred Spender later writing after Johnnie's death that Johnnie had said he felt he could lead them anywhere. He also attended a so-called Ulster Volunteer Service on 26 July. In fact, Johnnie had also visited Ireland at Easter, before his collapse, fishing at the Bagwell home at Marlfield near Clonmel with Hubert and others who included the Treasury Remember-ancer in Ireland and an old friend of Dorothea, Maurice Headlam.

As a further aid to convalenscence Oliver arranged a six-weeks shooting and fishing holiday in Sweden. Johnnie was by now anxious to get to the autumn manoeuvres but Moynihan 'forbade this, on the grounds that even by that time, he would not be fit to sit for a whole day in the saddle'. So, it was arranged to start the Swedish holiday in early August.[26] Other events were to intervene.

9

Chief of Staff, 1914–1915

OF all the peoples plunged into war in August 1914, the British had the least time in which to react to the crisis that had developed in European relations. The assassination of an Austro-Hungarian Archduke by a Serb in Sarajevo on 28 June seemed of little consequence compared to the continuing tensions in Ireland. Indeed, following the gun-running attempt by Irish nationalists at Howth on 26 July, troops had become involved in a crowd at Bachelors' Walk in Dublin and opened fire: three people had been killed. Moreover, when the final act in the drama of Europe's 'July Crisis' was being played out, Britain was enjoying an August Bank Holiday weekend blessed by glorious sunshine.

It was not until 27 July that the Foreign Secretary, Sir Edward Grey, brought the possibility of British intervention in a general European war before the Cabinet. Initially, he had felt it probable that a diplomatic compromise would arrest the drift towards hostilities between Austria-Hungary and Serbia. However, with that prospect rapidly failing, Grey still had to convince many of his colleagues that Britain should stand by the understanding reached with the French. While staff conversations had been held with the French in early 1906 (and, briefly and unsuccessfully, with the Belgians), it had not been until 1911 that a British Expeditionary Force (BEF) had been firmly written into French mobilisation plans. To a large extent this had been the achievement of Henry Wilson as Director of Military Operations and Wilson had received the sanction of the Committee of Imperial Defence for the army's continental strategy in August 1911. Few ministers had known of the original staff conversations and it was not until October 1911 that the Cabinet as a whole was appraised of Wilson's plans for British mobilisation. At that time the Cabinet was given to understand that the agreements were not binding and, at least in theory, there was no legal commitment of Britain to France in August 1914.

As Grey laboured to win over the waverers, the pace of events in Europe increased dramatically. Austria-Hungary declared war on Serbia on 28 July secure in the knowledge that she had the backing of Imperial Germany. Therefore, when Imperial Russia mobilised in support of the Serbs on 30 July this automatically triggered German mobilisation with a German declaration of war on Russia following on 1 August. In turn, the constraints of German military planning dictated that she would not attack Russia first but strike at Russia's ally France with the intention of delivering a knockout blow before the large but ponderous Russian war machine could mobilise fully. Germany's Schlieffen Plan for the defeat of France necessitated German troops advancing through both Luxembourg and Belgium, Britain being a guarantor of the latter's neutrality under a treaty of 1839. With German troops entering Luxembourg on 2 August, Grey was finally able to rally the Cabinet behind him for the loss of only two ministers through resignation. That evening news reached London that Germany intended to invade Belgium. On 3 August – Bank Holiday Monday – Britain sent a somewhat mildly worded ultimatum to Berlin demanding the neutrality of Belgium while, that same day, Germany declared war on France. When no reply was received to the ultimatum by the prescribed time of midnight on 4 August (11 p.m. British time), Britain, too, was at war with Germany.

On 27 July, Grey had at least managed to secure from the cabinet agreement on issuing warning orders for a 'precautionary period'. These went out two days later. On 1 August, Churchill on his own authority mobilised the Royal Navy. It was thus apparent to military men that a war might well ensue. When Frederick Oliver and his family arrived at Farnborough on Friday, 31 July, to stay with Johnnie and Dorothea for the holiday weekend he therefore found that Johnnie regarded war as inevitable:

He was in two moods on this occasion. He was as light-hearted as a schoolboy who is unexpectedly released from school; the reason being that the Army Medical Office had that morning passed him as physically fit to go abroad . . . his other mood was very different. The war which he had foreseen and dreaded, the war which in his view might have been avoided upon one condition, and one only – if England had been prepared – had come at last. I don't think I have ever known anyone – certainly never any anti-militarist – whose hatred and horror of war gave the same impression of integrity and reality as his. Not metamorphically, but as a bare fact, his feelings with regard to it were too deep for words; he would suddenly break off speaking about things which had occurred in his own experience; in particular about loss of friends and comrades.

Typically, while confiding his true feelings to a trusted friend like Oliver, Johnnie's public image was one of supreme confidence as recalled by Oliver's daughter, Beatrix.[1] Indeed, Johnnie's ability to project calm irrespective of his private views was to be a significant contribution at dark moments in the months to come.

As mobilisation proceeded, Haig was summoned to London on 5 August to a specially convened 'War Council' at which twelve leading soldiers were invited to discuss British strategic options. The six infantry divisions of the

BEF immediately available constituted a tiny force compared to the huge continental conscript armies, but it had been considered that the British could still make a decisive contribution either in defence of Belgium or on the French left flank. Accordingly, in September 1911, Wilson had agreed to a French request for the concentration of the BEF at Mauberge close to the Belgian frontier. All mobilisation schedules were based on this assumption. However, the War Council demonstrated a certain lack of commitment to the implications of continental strategy by discussing all manner of alternatives. Recalled to favour as Commander-in-Chief of the BEF, Sir John French preferred a descent on Antwept while Kitchener, who had been appointed Secretary of State for War that day while on home leave from Egypt, suggested a concentration at Amiens. Eventually the view of Lord Roberts that the French General Staff should make the decision prevailed. Even then it was not until 12 August that Kitchener finally agreed to a concentration on Mauberge.

Another issue discussed was how many divisions should be sent to France since an enquiry by the Committee of Imperial Defence in 1907 had resolved that two of the six regular divisions should be retained in Britain as a defence against possible German invasion. The War Council elected to retain only one division, but on the following day Kitchener prevailed on the Cabinet to keep two divisions at home after all, so reducing the BEF to just four infantry divisions. Haig at least had also gone to London with the intention of discussing wider issues and sought out Kitchener to discuss both the position of the Territorial Force and the threat posed to British possessions in East Africa from hostile forces in German East Africa. Haig had been briefed on the latter by Johnnie who gave him 'a few notes on the military situation in those parts. He urged the immediate capture of Dar-es-Salaam'.[2]

Johnnie's own preparations for the forthcoming campaign were as meticulous as ever. When he travelled to London with Haig on 10 August to meet with the mobilised General Headquarters (GHQ) staff of the expeditionary force in the Hotel Metropole, Johnnie took the opportunity to call at his publishers, Hugh Rees, to purchase a map measure, three fold map case and a pocket book. He accumulated a variety of maps for his personal use, War Office and French booklets on the German Army and a handy guide to French and Belgian regulations on requisitioning billets. The latter was especially prescient since his first problem upon arrival in France was to deal with billeting problems. Dorothea was also provided with a list of items to be forwarded every fortnight and every second fortnight. The former comprised a tin of toothpowder, a cake of soap, a packet of thick chocolate and a stick of shaving soap while the latter comprised a toothbrush, a silk handkerchief, a tin of brown boot polish and a tin of saddle soap. With mobilisation completed smoothly and a visit by the King to Aldershot accommodated on 11 August, Johnnie then motored down to Southampton with Haig and the latter's ADC, Baird, on the evening of 13 August. On the following day

Haig's party enjoyed a lunch at the Dolphin Hotel at which toasts were drunk to success and a safe return before embarking at 8 p.m. on the *Comrie Castle* for Le Havre. Johnnie's new pocket book, in which he had already scribbled arrangements for the King's visit to Aldershot, recorded his berth as number 23.

Johnnie carried a telegram sent to the Dolphin by Dorothea and Diana – 'Loving thoughts go with you' – which he was always to keep in his breastpocket and there was also an envelope with 'lucky feathers'. It had been the first parting since Johnnie's journey to Somaliland five years previously and he felt it keenly. Towards the end of the mobilisation period, Johnnie had briefly seen Angela Malcolm waiting to collect her husband Neill from his office. Johnnie 'only said about two sentences when he said goodbye, but he was so kind & encouraging – wished *me* good luck & said, "Remember you have the hardest time".' Again, as he was about to leave for Southampton Johnnie remarked to Charteris, 'These partings – after all, they are the worst things in the whole war.'

Disembarking at Le Havre on 16 August, Johnnie and Haig were immediately caught up in the popular excitement at the arrival of British troops. Everywhere they went they were saluted by all and sundry while children pursued them to grasp their hands. Later they settled into a first class compartment in the train for Amiens. At around midnight they were rudely disturbed by a tremendous jolt at a station, Haig recording that, 'Gough's portmanteau placed in overhead rack (contrary to my advice) came down with a bang, luckily on the floor of the carriage'. Another more unfortunate interruption in the journey next morning was the news that Haig's counterpart commanding II Corps, the portly but highly capable Lieutenant-General Sir James Grierson, had died of a heart attack in the train following immediately behind. That same day, 17 August, Haig and Johnnie established I Corps' first French headquarters at Wassigny and both then motored to GHQ at Le Cateau on 18 August to learn French's operational intentions. On their return they discovered the men of the 4th (Guards) Infantry Brigade in 2nd Division suffering the effects of typhoid inoculations that had not been authorised. Johnnie hastened to stop the inoculations but it would be some days before the Guardsmen were fully fit again. It would also not be until 22 August that all artillery and supporting units joined I Corps.[3]

Nevertheless, the majority of the corps was now concentrated with Major-General Lomax's 1st Division around Le Nouvrion, Boue, Esqueheries and Lavaqueresse and Major-General Monro's 2nd Division around Wassigny, Mennevret, Longchamps and Lesquielles. In theory, each division had an establishment of 18,073 men and 5,592 horses divided between three infantry brigades (each of four battalions with two machine guns per battalion), three field artillery brigades (each of three batteries with six 18-pounder field guns), a field howitzer brigade (of three batteries each with six 4.5" howitzers), a heavy battery (with four 60-pounders), two Royal Engineer field companies, a signal company, a divisional supply train, an ammunition column, a cavalry squadron and a field ambulance section. I Corps head-quarters had an establishment of 89 officers and men and 51 horses, five motor cars and two motor vans. In fact, it was slightly over-establishment with 20 officers and 80 other ranks and, in addition, there was an attached signal company of 67 officers and men with two 30cwt lorries, 16 horses and twelve motorcycles under the overall command of Major M. G. E. Bowman-Manifold as Assistant Director for Signals. There was also a liaison section comprising four French officers and 13 French other ranks drawn from the army and gendarmerie.

The two main departmental heads under Haig were Johnnie as Brigadier-General, General Staff and Colonel (temporary Brigadier-General) P. E. F. Hobbs as Deputy Adjutant and Quartermaster General (DA&QMG). Hobbs' section divided into two with Lieutenant Colonel Raymond Marker as Assistant Adjutant and Quartermaster General (AA&QMG), assisted by Major Travers Clarke as Deputy Assistant Adjutant and Quartermaster General (DAA&QMG), responsible for personnel matters, discipline, pay and postal services while the Assistant Quartermaster General (AQMG), Colonel H. S. Sargent, was responsible for transport and supply including ammunition, remounts and veterinary services. However, by far the most important department was that run by Johnnie as BGGS with an Operational Section manned by Colonel Hugh Jeudwine as GSO1 and Lieutenant Colonel Neill Malcolm as GSO2 and an Intelligence Section with Major Herbert Studd as GSO2 and Major A. Hinde as GSO3. The latter section subdivided into responsibilities for gathering information and intelligence through such activities as reconnaissance, examination of captured documents or interrogation of prisoners and a topographical subsection providing information on the theatre of operations through maps and sketches. The operational section also divided into a records subsection keeping documentary records and circulating others and a plans subsection headed by Jeudwine responsible for all movements, security matters, camps, halting places and billets and both for co-ordinating activity with all other staff functions and also for the issue of all orders. Brigadier-General Henry Horne and Brigadier-General S. R. Rice were attached as B-G, Royal Artillery and Commanding Engineer (CRE) respectively to advise on the action of artillery and mining and engineering problems. Other key staff included Major E. 'Micky' Ryan as Deputy Director for Medical Services (DDMS) and Colonel S. B. Jameson as Camp Commandant. Haig also had his two ADCs, Charteris and Baird, and for a short time a third ADC in the person of Captain C. M. Yates. By December there was a second Royal Army Medical Corps officer, an ASC Supply Officer and an AVC officer.

In practice, while Hobbs, Horne and Rice were technically equal advisers to Haig as corps commander, Johnnie was 'chief of staff' – he was usually described in contemporary documents as Senior General Staff Officer (SGSO)

— and reigned supreme in that capacity. He was responsible for providing the principal military advice to Haig on the basis of information generated by the remainder of the staff and then was responsible for executing Haig's plans in his own name. Most orders to subordinate commands within I Corps would bear Johnnie's signature rather than that of Haig although orders are occasionally found bearing the initials of Jeudwine or his successor, Neill Malcolm. Johnnie also had the responsibility of co-ordinating the movement of I Corps with the rest of the BEF and he rather than subordinates would frequently be required to go personally to GHQ for orders from the BEF's Chief of Staff, Lieutenant-General Sir Archibald Murray, recently promoted from command of 2nd Division. However, the fact that Johnnie had to go to GHQ so often at night in the company of the chiefs of staff to II Corps and the Cavalry Division for verbal orders was also an indication of GHQ's general lack of grip in the opening campaign of the war. Likewise, Johnnie represented Haig in contacts with neighbouring French commanders.

It also appears that Johnnie wrote some of the corps' operational narratives himself rather than have them drafted in the records subsection. Certainly, Haig remarked in a letter to Dorothea in April 1915 that he was not sending her any narratives as 'I fancy Johnnie sent on to you the copies which he used to get of them and also of some later editions which he himself wrote'. Moreover, there is a pencil draft of the operational narrative for the period from 12 to 19 November in one of Johnnie's notebooks and the carbon copy in his papers bears the pencilled addition to Dorothea, 'This might interest you – I wrote it'.

What is abundantly clear is just how far Haig relied solely on Johnnie's professional judgment, Haig writing to Dorothea on 4 March 1915: 'He was my only military adviser, and we discussed, planned & executed all operations with one mind. I had no military secrets from him'. Part of Johnnie's value was that 'active in mind and body and with a charming nature, he made everything go smoothly and ensured orders being cheerfully obeyed,' but at the same time he 'took such a wide view of everything that was going on both *naval* and military'. Haig also remarked that Johnnie and the two ADCs were his only regular messing companions while his diary entry for 26 December 1914 when he and Johnnie transferred to the new First Army headquarters mentions that Haig had decided 'to retain my small mess of General Gough, 2 ADCs and myself as being more convenient'. Similarly, the account published after the war in diary form by Charteris (but actually based on wartime letters to his wife) shows that when Haig established an advanced headquarters in Ypres in October 1914 he took only Johnnie, Charteris (by then GSO2) and one ADC while leaving everyone else six miles back at Poperinghe.[4]

Generally, the importance of the chiefs of staff at corps (BGGS) and, later, at army (Major-General, General Staff or MGGS) level during the Great War has been underestimated. Yet, it must be recognised that many of the problems faced by Hubert when he commanded Fifth Army later in the war derived from the particular characteristics of Neill Malcolm, who acted as Hubert's MGGS from May 1916 to December 1917. Hubert himself acknowledged this after the war and in turn was highly critical of John Vaughan who began the war as Allenby's chief of staff in the Cavalry Division. Similarly, there was general postwar criticism of all Johnnie's successors as Haig's chiefs of staff and of Archibald Montgomery (later Montgomery-Massingberd) as Rawlinson's chief of staff in Fourth Army from February 1916 to November 1918. Indeed, the official historian, Sir James Edmonds, was to call Montgomery a mere 'bottlewasher' in conversation with Basil Liddell Hart. Another unsuccessful choice as a chief of staff was the abrasive Major-General W. P. Braithwaite who acted in this capacity to the Mediterranean Expeditionary Force between March and October 1915. By contrast, much of the perceived success of Herbert Plumer's Second Army was seen to be that of his MGGS from June 1916 to April 1918, Charles 'Tim' Harington.[5]

When Sir John French had first informed Haig on 13 August that the BEF would move beyond Mauberge to the area between Le Cateau and Wassigny, little was known about the military situations in France and Belgium. The French were primarily interested in their own pre-arranged offensive – Plan XVII – and their First and Second Armies were launched into Lorraine on 14 August notwithstanding the possibility that the Germans might make rapid progress through Belgium. Even when the latter became a reality, the French Commander-in-Chief, General Joffre, still chose to conform to Plan XVII by also launching his Third and Fourth Armies into the Ardennes on 21 August in the belief that he could break through the German centre and strike at the southern flank of those German forces in Belgium. The French had seen the BEF's role as acting on the left flank of General Lanrezac's Fifth Army along the Sambre on what had been anticipated as being the extreme right of the German line. In reality, the entire thrust of the Schlieffen Plan was through Belgium with the German *First, Second, Third* and *Fourth Armies* executing a vast encircling movement pivoting on Verdun which was designed to throw the *First Army* around the French capital. The German *Fifth, Sixth* and *Seventh Armies* south of the Ardennes would have the task of holding the French offensive before advancing themselves towards the south-eastern sweep of *First Army* around Paris. Accordingly, the German *First* and *Second Armies* had entered Belgium on 4 August and, although delayed by the Belgian fortress system around Liège, had occupied Brussels by 20 August and pushed the main Belgian field army back into Antwerp.

Far to the South the Germans had already destroyed the French Lorraine offensive and would shortly accomplish the same in the Ardennes. Lanrezac, who had glimpsed the daunting truth at an earlier stage than most, attempted to convince Joffre of the threat to the French left flank. On 15 August Joffre did authorise a limited advance by Fifth Army towards the confluence of the Sambre and Meuse rivers at Namur. In effect, since the BEF would of necessity have to conform with Lanrezac's advance, the decision ensured that the British would run headlong into General von Kluck's German *First Army* advancing between Charleroi and Mauberge.

The BEF began its own forward movement on 21 August, by which time Lanrezac's leading elements were already engaging in desultory skirmishes with German advance guards. Allenby's Cavalry Division scouting ahead of the BEF also came into contact that day and Haig and Johnnie undertook their own forward reconnaissance towards Givry, discussing the tactical value of the ground traversed: they were seen riding together by John Bloomfield Gough of Hubert's 3rd Cavalry Brigade. Johnnie was particularly exercised by the problem for his marching arrangements posed by the proximity of the French fortifications around Mauberge and by French march plans. Troops were already becoming exhausted by marching in sweltering heat while carrying heavy loads: orders arrived late on 22 August to move 1st Division towards a line from Fauroeulx to Haulchin and 2nd Division to the line Havay to Quevy le Petit, but the latter could not comply since it had already dispersed into billets. Johnnie had reconnoitred a defensive position around Villers-sire-Nicole for 23 August but the new orders frustrated this and 2nd Division would have to move forward beyond this line on the 23rd to conform to the movement it had failed to execute on the previous evening. Those orders themselves recognised the perilous position of the BEF in view of cavalry and aerial reconnaissance reports revealing the proximity of large bodies of Germans.

French had decided to give battle along the line of the Mons to Condé canal with I Corps extending his line to the east of the drab industrial suburbs of Mons. II Corps, which had dug in along the canal, came under heavy attack early on Sunday 23 August, but 6th Infantry Brigade of 2nd Division did not become engaged until mid-afternoon. Major-General Sir Hubert Hamilton commanding 3rd Division in II Corps asked for Haig's assistance and 4th (Guards) Infantry Brigade was extended to the west to release more of Hamilton's own troops for the desperate struggle around the awkward salient formed in the British line by the town of Mons itself. During the day, Haig and Johnnie drove up by car close to Mons despite the press of civilian refugees heading in the opposite direction and they were able to walk over fields to a slight promontory offering a view over the battlefield.

At 6.30 p.m. Grierson's successor as GOC, II Corps, General Sir Horace Smith-Dorrien, arrived at Haig's headquarters in Bonnet to ask for more assistance and 5th Infantry Brigade was sent to help close a gap between Smith-Dorrien's 3rd and 5th Divisions. Half an hour later while Haig was again forward near the firing line Johnnie was summoned to GHQ 35 miles distant at Le Cateau. The overwhelming strength of the Germans – at least 200,000 men – was clear and von Kluck had as yet hardly committed two of his four corps. Moreover, Lanrezac, with whom Sir John French had manifestly failed to establish any kind of rappport, was already retreating. Consequently, when Johnnie reached Le Cateau he discovered that French intended to withdraw to a line from Jerlain to Mauberge. Johnnie realised that an early disengagement was desirable and even before travelling to GHQ he had begun preparations for a withdrawal, the pocket book purchased in London containing a brief note for this day, 'See Lomax and arrange all spare wheels to be about Bettingavies or further west & arrange for *point d'appui* on Lomax' right.' Thus, knowing that he could not possibly get back to Bonnet before the early hours, Johnnie telegraphed the withdrawal orders through to Haig. This enabled Haig to issue orders for retirement at 2 a.m. with I Corps away by 5 a.m. and at its destination five hours later. By contrast, Smith-Dorrien's chief of staff, George Forestier-Walker, chose to return to II Corps headquarters at Sars-la-Bruyere without telegraphing ahead and it was not until 3 a.m. that Smith-Dorrien even learned of the orders.[6]

II Corps had suffered by far the majority of the 1,638 British casualties at Mons and was in a far more exhausted state than Haig's command. Smith-Dorrien was therefore anxious that his troops should get an opportunity to recuperate and at noon on 24 August he visited Haig to try to get I Corps to cover his own retirement. However, thanks to Johnnie's precaution in telegraphing ahead, Haig's movements were all but completed by this time. It was the view of Sir James Edmonds that the speed of I Corps' withdrawal when German troops were advancing across its front to strike at Smith-Dorrien owed much to the mutual antagonism between Haig and his counterpart and that 'neither of them would have been particularly sorry to see the other take a knock, and would not have made much effort to avert it'. Unfortunately, Johnnie did not contribute to the harmony that should have prevailed between the corps headquarters since Edmonds also partly ascribed the poor communications that developed – all contact between I Corps and II Corps was lost between 26 August and 1 September – to an 'even stronger' antagonism between Johnnie and Forestier-Walker. The events at the Curragh where Forestier-Walker had been Paget's chief of staff may not have helped, of course, but Hubert appears to have maintained good relations with Forestier-Walker at that time. Far more likely, therefore, is that the antagonism went back to Somaliland, its beginnings conceivably indicated by Forestier-Walker's comments on Johnnie's first official report.[7]

As I Corps settled itself into new positions around Bavai with headquarters at Vieux Mesnil, Johnnie was again called to GHQ where he received orders to continue the retreat towards Landrecies and Le Grand Fayt, the location of the Forest of Mormal across the BEF's line of retirement necessitating that I Corps should pass to the east and cross the Sambre close to Mauberge while II Corps marched to the west. The march resumed at 2 a.m. on 25 August and was again hampered by French troops endeavouring to use the same roads. Much baggage was lost and some documents had to be destroyed. The new

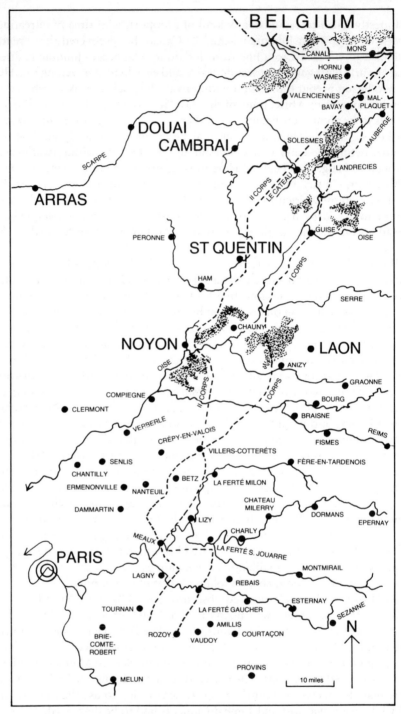

THE RETREAT FROM MONS 23rd AUG.–5th SEPT., 1914

corps headquarters was established at Landrecies where the 4th (Guards) Infantry Brigade was also quartered. News of German activity at around 5.30 p.m. prompted Haig to send Charteris to investigate but it proved a false alarm. Meanwhile, Johnnie 'thought the Guards were very sleepy and that the measures taken were rather half-hearted', so Haig himself went to impress the need for vigilance on Brigadier-General Scott-Kerr. Half an hour later an outlying picquet at Maroilles came under attack and after dark German troops apparently disguised in French uniforms tried to enter Landrecies itself.

Haig was suffering from diarrhoea and appears to have panicked, Edmonds recounting to Liddell Hart in 1933 that Haig could be seen 'standing on his doorstep, revolver in hand, saying "We must sell our lives dearly".' Indeed, Haig decided to withdraw his headquarters to the location of the 3rd Infantry Brigade at Le Grand Fayt and he, Johnnie and Charteris left Landrecies by car at 11.30 p.m. for a somewhat hair-raising ride through the darkness without lights. Haig later told Edmonds that he had only left Landrecies after the initial German attack had been repulsed and with the town well organised for defence. However, one of Edmonds' other postwar informants, Major J. C. Furness of 19th Field Ambulance recalled Haig arriving at Le Grand Fayt and announcing that the Guards were heavily engaged, the BEF was surrounded and they would all be annihilated. According to Furness, Haig ordered Brigadier-General Landon of 3rd Infantry Brigade to 'take your Brigade and fight to the last for the honour of old England'. It seems highly unlikely that Johnnie would have panicked and there was nothing but praise for his conduct and 'great work' during the retreat but, of course, he would have had little option but to comply with Haig's decision to flee Landrecies.

In fact, the Guards managed to repulse repeated German attacks during the night, the two actions at Maroilles and Landrecies costing only 270 British casualties, but Haig was so concerned that in the early hours of 26 August he even suggested that II Corps come to his assistance. Haig had ordered the retreat to continue at 12.30 and in such a way that I Corps would not now recross the Sambre as French had intended but create an even wider gap between the two British corps. Smith-Dorrien meanwhile had decided he must halt and make a stand at Le Cateau on 26 August. The day was to cost the BEF some 8,482 casualties but a sharp jolt was administered to the German pursuers which undoubtedly saved the BEF as a whole. I Corps, of course, had no idea of events at Le Cateau, Haig and Johnnie spending that night in a small inn on the road west of Iron dining on fried eggs and stewed rabbit.[8]

By this time, GHQ was subsiding rapidly into a deep pessimism. One manifestation was Henry Wilson, the Sub-Chief of Staff, telling Hubert on 26 August that he could please himself what he did. Subsequently, Hubert whose brigade had become detached from Allenby's division – deliberately so according to Allenby – happened to come across one of Johnnie's staff officers in a car. Hubert purloined all the maps the officer was carrying since he had only one of his own cut from the wall of a French mayor's office and he sent the officer back to Johnnie with what news he had and a request to pass under Haig's orders. This was officially approved and for the next few days Hubert was able to appreciate 'clear, precise and practical' orders.

Another manifestation of the state of GHQ was the order to both corps emanating from Wilson on 27 August – Murray had collapsed altogether under the strain – to ditch all ammunition and impedimenta and to use the transport to carry the men. While Smith-Dorrien merely countermanded the order, Johnnie was so incensed that he tore it up. He then made arrangements to double bank the transport on the road through Guise and Mont d'Origny so that it would only take up half the space. To ensure the fighting troops were free of encumbrances, Johnnie detached all transport except one ambulance per division and ordered the transport to double march to the rear. He considered that simply to abandon equipment would have the worst possible effect on morale. As it was, the men were so exhausted that the day's march on 27 August was delayed until 6 a.m., corps headquarters moving back to Mont d'Origny.[9]

On the following day, early mist gave way to the oppressive heat that was to characterise much of the retreat. Johnnie got the transport away at 2 a.m. and the infantry two hours later. Anxiety, fatigue and lack of time in which to prepare hot food were all taking their toll of the marching columns and some troops did not reach their assigned billets until 1 a.m. on 29 August. Fortunately, however, I Corps had not been pressed closely, although the 2nd Connaught Rangers of 5th Infantry Brigade were cut off at Le Grand Fayt on 26 August and the 2nd Royal Munster Fusiliers of 1st Infantry Brigade similarly trapped at Oisy on the following day. Haig initially declined to help Lanrezac mount a counter-attack on 28 August but then appears to have changed his mind. But Sir John French was now intent on withdrawing the BEF entirely from the line of battle and the successful attack by the French Fifth Army at Guise was accomplished without British help.

That evening, Haig and Johnnie travelled to see French at Compiegne, a distance of 35 miles over bad roads, to be told to continue the retreat towards Soissons. Haig took a leaf out of Johnnie's book and telegraphed orders to his headquarters for the transport to march off at 9 p.m. that night and the infantry at daybreak. On this occasion the heat was so oppressive that supply transport had to be ordered back to carry men. Corps headquarters was established at Vauxbuin, two miles south east of Soissons and on 31 August I Corps crossed the Aisne, more transport being released to carry men through the expedient of sending away half the ammunition. It seemed they had shaken off all pursuit, but on 1 September when the heat had caused the day's march to be terminated as early as 10 a.m., the rearguard of 2nd Division became engaged along the line Puiseux to Vivieres and had to fall back on 6th

Infantry Brigade. In the action that followed around Villers Cotterets the dead included Ian Hogg from Hubert's cavalry brigade – both Arthur Parker and Maurice MacEwen had already been wounded – and Johnnie's fellow Staff College luminary, the Hon. George Morris.

Johnnie was becoming irritated at the continuing retreat, Haig recalling the evening of 1 September in his diary after Johnnie's death:

Only once throughout the whole war did I have to say a sharp word to him. It was during the retreat on the night after the action at Villers Cotterets. After dinner at Mareuil he in his impetuous way grumbled at my going on 'retreating and retreating'. As a number of the staff were present I turned on him rather sharply, and said 'that retreat was the only thing to save the Army, and that it was his duty to support me instead of criticising'.

It was characteristic of Haig to remember such an incident, when Johnnie had obviously transgressed against Haig's demand that his staff show the utmost loyalty to him in public, at such a time. Yet Haig was also beginning to become annoyed at the retreat. Haig's soldier servant recalled Johnnie saying at one stage, 'It looks as though Joffre doesn't mean to make a stand until he reached the ramparts of Paris!' to which Haig replied, 'Why Paris? It looks more like Marseilles to me at this rate!'

Lanrezac was certainly convinced that all was lost and Sir John French was persuaded not to pull the BEF out of line and to retire to the Channel coast only by the personal intervention of Kitchener, who crossed to France in Field Marshal's uniform to interview French at Paris on 1 September and order him to remain. On 2 September – the day the French government abandoned Paris for Bordeaux – the BEF was ordered to take up a position between the outer Paris defences and La Ferte-sous-Jouarre, I Corps pulling back behind the Seine near Melun to conform on 4 September. But the Germans were also suffering, not least from logistic problems with their forward elements far distant from the railheads and their limited motor transport breaking under the strain of plugging the gap. Von Kluck's *First Army* had also become separated from von Bülow's *Second Army* with the result that von Kluck was ordered to swing east rather than west of Paris, a movement revealed to the Allies by aerial reconnaissance on 3 September. This now exposed the German right flank to Allied counter-attack and on 4 September Joffre resolved that the moment was ripe. A general advance was ordered next day.

In thirteen days of almost continual retreat, I Corps had covered 160 miles over mostly indifferent roads in difficult climatic conditions and virtual isolation, suffering 2,261 casualties from all causes. Johnnie, however, had come through the experience very well, Haig writing to his wife on 4 September that while others had cracked, Johnnie had not: 'Gough, too, is first rate and a great help to me'. Johnnie also appeared remarkably fit notwithstanding the operation so few months before, Roger Keyes writing of his brother-in-law, 'I am sure the gallant spirit within him keeps him so. On the 6th [September], and before the tide had really turned, and after that awful gruelling they had had, he wrote full of buoyancy and confidence to my sister'.[10]

Certainly spirits lifted as the BEF, now reinforced by III Corps under Lieutenant-General W. P. Pulteney, moved forward towards Montmirail. By 8 September it had reached the Marne and was pushing into the gap between von Kluck and von Bülow. The Germans appeared to be neither holding nor destroying the Marne bridges, although there were still fierce rearguard actions. On 9 September, for example, John Bloomfield Gough was killed when his RHA battery came under German counter battery fire: it was a bitter blow to both Hubert and Johnnie, but merely the first to Bloomfield Gough's family since John's two brothers, Owen and Rupert, would both also die during the war on active service. On the following day, a day on which Haig again sang Johnnie's praises in a letter home – 'Gough too has kept v. fit and is a great help to me – always cheery & full of sound advice' – the direction of what was now an Allied pursuit changed from north to north-east. The German High Command had taken the decision to withdraw on the previous day with a general retirement ordered on the line Noyon to Verdun. By 12 September the BEF had closed up to the Aisne, I Corps covering 70 miles in seven days and taking over 1,000 prisoners. However, Haig was inclined to be cautious and despite reports of only small German rearguards refused to cross the river that day. He preferred to wait until II Corps came up on his left and contact was made with the French Fifth Army, now commanded by General Franchet d'Esperey, on the right.

The line of the Aisne itself posed a formidable barrier to further progress. Most of the bridges had been destroyed – ironically by the French rather than by the Germans. This left an unfordable fast flowing river some 40 to 60 yards wide backed by heavily wooded bluffs leading to a high plateau some 480 feet above the river level and along which ran the Chemin des Dames road. The Germans had commanding fields of fire over the approaches. Thus, when beginning to work their way across on surviving bridges or improvised rafts on 13 September, all three British corps came under heavy fire. Ordered to force a crossing at Pont Arcy, Bourg and Chavonne opposite the German *Seventh Army*, I Corps found the Pont Arcy bridge partially intact and a precarious temporary trestle bridge across the Aisne at Chavonne. GHQ having ordered an advance to the line Athies to Laon for 14 September, I Corps struggled to seize the Chemin des Dames on that second day. Over 3,460 casualties were sustained for a gain of 4,000 yards at most.

That night Johnnie went to GHQ, returning at 12.15 a.m. on 15 September with orders for I Corps to dig in to consolidate. Considerable damage continued to be done by German artillery as efforts were made to put pontoons across the river but fighting was not to reach the same intensity as it had on 14 September. Writing to Roger Keyes, Dorothea reported that she had a few pencilled lines from Johnnie dated 17 September: 'He said they had fought a great fight which was still proceeding, & that our troops had been

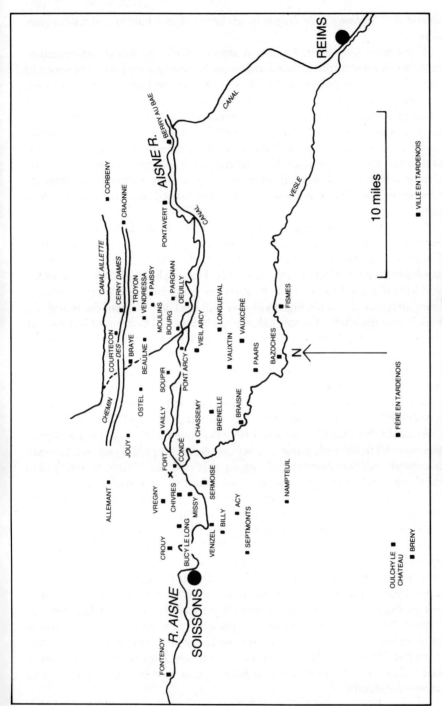

THE AISNE BATTLEFIELD, SEPTEMBER 1914

splendid – "*nothing in history* is much better than what our 1st Corps have done".'

There were only limited German attacks while the British attempted to reply to German artillery bombardments by use of aerial reconnaisance to spot the German positions. In I Corps, Horne and an officer from each division was stationed at the RFC airstrips to receive instant notice of reconnaissance information. By 20 September losses in I Corps over the past six days amounted to 1,382 and Haig sent Johnnie to ask French if the troops could be withdrawn for food and rest. As it happened, French arrived at Haig's headquarters and agreed to the request in Johnnie's absence. Thus, 1st Division was pulled back from exposed positions around Chivy on 21 September and, where possible, reliefs were carried out over the next four days.[11]

Johnnie's only surviving war letter – written to Frederick Oliver on 25 September – dates from this period of relative quiet on the Aisne. At the time Haig's headquarters was situated in a former flour mill close to the river, the available accommodation being shared by Haig, Johnnie, Marker, Charteris and Malcolm and heated and lit by acetyline gas cylinders. Professing himself living in terror 'that a big high explosive will land on the top of the house and knock over my chief', Johnnie calculated that while I Corps had lost heavily since crossing the Aisne, the Germans must have taken at least 7,000 casualties of their own. Johnnie recognised that the BEF was hardly in a good position with its back to the river and that officer casualties in particular would be difficult to make up. Moreover, while 'England seems to have quite woken up as regards "recruits" ', what was wanted was soldiers. Johnnie also wondered 'how this vast multitude is going to be equipped & trained'.

At about this time Charteris recorded that one night, while the headquarters was still in the mill, Johnnie woke everyone except Haig when a German counter-attack was rumoured. Nothing occurred and Haig was annoyed at the display of 'nerves'. Johnnie also had a disagreement with Charteris over the value of intelligence, remarking that during the war in South Africa, 'the intelligence only had one office box and he didn't see why we wanted any more'. It may be significant, therefore, that Charteris also wrote to his wife, 'Gough by the way, is very far from well. He has violent attacks of sickness which he tries to conceal. I only discovered it by accident and he forbade me to mention it to D. H. I hope it will pass off, for though he is a bit jumpy at times, he is altogether excellent and quite cool when things are really serious.' Interestingly, only a few days before Oliver had written to his brother that Johnnie 'has been a good deal handicapped by not having properly recovered from his very severe operation in June but I hear he is distinctly better this last fortnight. He has been doing very well.' Similarly, Dorothea had reported to Roger Keyes on 19 September that Johnnie had 'said he was very well & he wrote confidently'.[12]

Clearly, Johnnie was suffering in September, but it would be altogether characteristic of him to conceal the true nature of any difficulties and it does not appear to have seriously interfered with his professional duties. Indeed, on 27 September he submitted a memorandum to GHQ on the lessons to be learned from British and German tactics during the Aisne battles. While he felt that British troops were generally superior man for man, Johnnie pointed to the skilful use by the Germans of machine guns and artillery in defensive positions. He considered the German artillery observation far superior to that of the Royal Artillery, notwithstanding the successful experimentation with aerial reconnaissance, and he wanted to see the artillery shield the infantry more in attacks. Above all, he detected that the lessons of South Africa had been forgotten and he recommended for the infantry 'loose and irregular formations with men at 8 or 10 paces interval disposed so as to adapt themselves to any inequalities of ground' in order to minimise casualties yet retain effective strength in attack. Nor did any illness detract from his continuing value to Haig whose despatch of 5 October covering the period up to 5 September referred to Johnnie as 'an officer of character and of great military ability. It is impossible for me to speak too highly of the help which I have received from Brigadier-General Gough . . . throughout these difficult operations'.[13] As a result Johnnie was mentioned in despatches by French in the *Gazette* of 19 October.

As the fighting on the Aisne subsided into stalemate with both sides coming to appreciate the value of entrenchments, thoughts turned to the possibility of regaining the initiative by outflanking the other elsewhere. Neither side could afford to be outflanked by the other in turn. Thus began the so-called 'Race to the Sea'. Sir John French had in any case considered that the BEF would be better employed closer to the Channel ports on which it depended for supplies and on 1 October Joffre agreed to release it from the Aisne. II Corps was the first to move north, detraining at Abbeville on 8 October, with III Corps detraining at St Omer three days later. A new IV Corps under Henry Rawlinson also came into being at Ghent on 8 October, the Royal Naval, 7th and 3rd Cavalry Divisions having previously landed at Antwept and Dunkirk between 3 and 6 October. II Corps in particular became heavily engaged as it pushed forward towards Givenchy and the La Bassée canal and ran into the German *Fourth Army*, which was itself aiming to drive on Calais.

As the new Flanders campaign unfolded, Haig and Johnnie were involved in often frustrating negotiations with the French XVI Corps of Sixth Army in order to complete their own disengagement from the Aisne. The relief of Brigadier-General Ingouville-Williams' 16th Infantry Brigade proved especially troublesome and it was not until 16 October that I Corps went north. Haig, Johnnie and Baird established the new headquarters at St Omer with the corps concentrating between there and Hazebrouck on the extreme left of the British line. French's orders to Haig on 19 October were to advance through Ypres towards Bruges and Ghent but this coincided with a renewed German determination to make a decisive breakthrough to the Channel ports. Accordingly, German *Fourth Army* was reinforced by *III Reserve Corps* from the siege of Antwept with a further four fresh corps of young recruits en route to Belgium. German *Sixth Army* to the south was also committed to the offensive.

On 21 October 1st Division advanced on Poelcapelle and 2nd Division towards Passchendaele with IV Corps to the right and French forces to the left. The latter not only interfered with the British line of march but rapidly disappeared as ever larger numbers of Germans were encountered. That night the French, who were being co-ordinated by General Ferdinand Foch as Commander of the Northern Group of Armies, expressed the intention of mounting a major attack which they expected I Corps to support with an advance into the Houthulst Forest. The news of this projected attack reached Haig and Johnnie at 11 p.m. but it was clear that Foch had no idea of the actual positions of British troops and would be attempting to pass his men through the British lines. Johnnie hastened to GHQ at 2.30 a.m. on 22 October to try to get the attack postponed, being accompanied by Rawlinson's chief of staff, Montgomery. Jeudwine was despatched to discover the precise orders issued to General de Mitry commanding the French Cavalry Corps, while Malcolm made a similar mission to General d'Urbal who had been placed by Foch in overall command of the French offensive.

Johnnie was unable to get the French movements postponed, but in the event the attack failed to materialise and the day was marked by repeated French withdrawals. I Corps had to commit its last reserve battalion around 6.30 p.m. to restore the front. Clearly, the confusion of British and French forces could not be allowed to continue and on 23 October it was decided to concentrate all British troops to the east of the Ypres to Zonnebeke road with I Corps passing into reserve behind 7th Division of IV Corps. However, this could only occur once I Corps had been relieved by French cavalry – 'those damned fellows with their hair down their backs' was Johnnie's unflattering description. Nor did Johnnie have much regard for Foch's abilities, although he later came to appreciate the Frenchman's resolve. The relief was not finally completed until 25 October with 1st Division concentrated at Zillebeke and 2nd Division ordered to concentrate around Becelaere. Haig's small advanced headquarters was now established in Ypres with the rest of the staff at Poperinghe.

German pressure was now mounting steadily and 7th Division was forced back. I Corps was therefore ordered to support 7th Division which passed under Haig's orders on 27 October, by which time it had taken 162 officer and over 4,500 other rank casualties in nine days. 7th Division now held the line from Zandvoorde to the Menin road, 1st Division from the Menin road to Reutel and 2nd Division from Reutel to the Moorslede to Zonnebeke road. A limited counter-attack was attempted against the Germans but ran into heavy opposition on 28 October. During the afternoon, news also reached Haig's headquarters, now moved to the White Château near Halte, that a message had been intercepted ordering the German *XXVII Reserve Corps* and *Bavarian Reserve Division* to join in a major assault next morning. Aerial reconnaissance had also spotted German transport columns moving up. Warning orders were issued, but by 8 a.m. on 29 October 1st Division was being forced to give ground and GHQ had to be told that I Corps was bound to exceed its allotted daily artillery quota of 30 rounds per gun. Indeed, between 21 October and 22 November I Corps would expend 54 per cent of all 18-pounder shells, 53 per cent of all 4.5″ howitzer shells and 57 per cent of all 60-pounder shells it fired off between August and November 1914.

Haig decided that 2nd Division should still attempt to continue the counter-attack begun on the previous day, but by 11.30 a.m. the situation was so serious that the corps reserve had been totally committed. It was at this point that timely assistance was received from Hubert, newly promoted to Major-General and to the command of 2nd Cavalry Division. Allenby, himself elevated to the Cavalry Corps command, was apparently loath to weaken his own line, but the despatch of five of Hubert's squadrons and an RHA battery to Klein Zillebeke was arranged by personal contact between Hubert and Johnnie. It proved decisive and Johnnie was able to release Hubert's cavalrymen at 5 p.m. Johnnie had at once written to Hubert:

Very many thanks for your support. It was like you. I have been up to the front and organised a big counter-attack of close up to 8,000 to 12,000 men!!! I fancy this will do the trick. Things look better than they did already.

Johnnie had actually been out of corps headquarters when Hubert's cavalrymen arrived and Neill Malcolm had been the first to send a note of thanks to Hubert, adding that 'Johnnie, I need hardly say, is splendid on these occasions'.[14]

The most critical stage of the battle for Ypres was now at hand. On 30 October a new German *Army Group Fabeck* including *XIII, XV* and *II Bavarian Corps* was thrown into the struggle and made some progress in forcing back Hubert from Hollebeke and the 7th and 3rd Cavalry Divisions from Zandvoorde. Haig had some expectation of regaining the ground on the following day but the British counter-attack could make no headway against German artillery and massed infantry columns. By noon on 31 October 1st Division had lost Gheluvelt, 7th Division was in danger of being enveloped and it seemed nothing could prevent *Group Fabeck* from breaking into Ypres. Matters deteriorated even further at about 12.50 p.m. when a German shell burst in the very room in Hooge Château in which the staff of 1st and 2nd Divisions were conferring. Seven officers were killed outright including Johnnie's old friend George Paley serving as GSO2 in 1st Division. The divisional GOC, Lomax, was also so badly hurt that he never recovered and died of his injuries in April 1915.

Having heard the news, Johnnie ordered up Brigadier-General E. S. Bulfin of 2nd Infantry Brigade to take command at 1.50 p.m.:

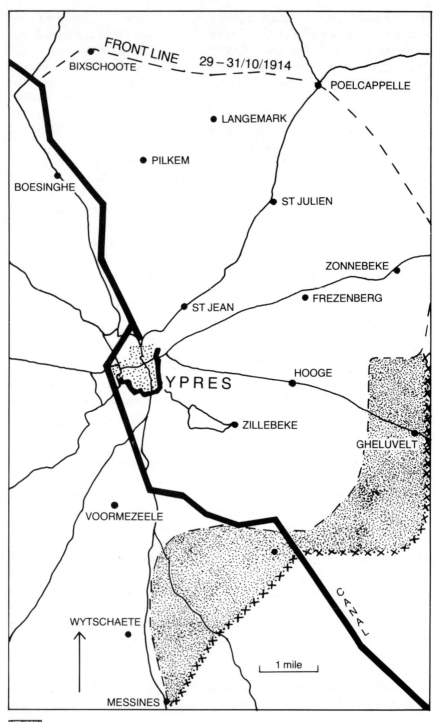

FRONT LINE 29 – 31/10/1914

BIXSCHOOTE

POELCAPPELLE

LANGEMARK

PILKEM

BOESINGHE

ST JULIEN

ZONNEBEKE

FREZENBERG

ST JEAN

Y P R E S

HOOGE

ZILLEBEKE

GHELUVELT

VOORMEZEELE

C A N A L

WYTSCHAETE

1 mile

MESSINES

The attack of the Army Group Fabeck on Oct. 31st 1914

FIRST YPRES 1914

Regret things very bad. 1st Division knocked about and retiring down road passed (sic) Hooge. Come up line yourself at once leaving Lord Cavan to take over your command. General Lomax wounded & Kerr [GSO1, 1st Division] killed & you must take over command but Sir D. Haig wants to see you first. Tell Cavan hold on tight with right to canal and to throw left back northwards towards Hooge. Keep French informed on your left.

In the circumstances, it was a remarkably clear and concise order for all that it was hastily scribbled in pencil. Indeed, during the day the British liaison officer at French General Headquarters, Sydney Clive, passed the White Château and noted in his diary, 'Johnny Gough was there – an absolute model of a GSO.'

It was another of those occasions when Johnnie's calm confidence was of the utmost importance. He had taken the precaution of placing secret papers in Haig's car ready for 'an emergency flit', but he was also intent on arranging Bulfin's counter-attack and obtaining additional support from the British cavalry. According to a later account by Edmonds of the 'inner truth' of 31 October, Haig again lost his head and had drawn up plans for a general withdrawal, only for 'one of his staff' – Edmonds did not identify who but it seems more than likely that it was Johnnie – to recall all copies and order them destroyed. At about 2 p.m. Sir John French appeared at the White Château. His later account actually confused the White Château with Hooge Château but he wrote of seeing Haig and Johnnie 'in one of the rooms on the ground floor; pouring over maps and evidently disconcerted'. Their news made sufficiently grim listening for French to believe that all was lost and he had made a somewhat undignified exit to his car, which he had left a 100 yards or so up the road: in the haste to get away French's car allegedly almost knocked down the CRE of 7th Division.

Just as French left at about 2.40 p.m., however, Rice who had been sent up to verify the situation at Hooge rode up to announce that the 2nd Worcesters had made a quite remarkable counter-attack that had carried Gheluvelt Château and restored the front. Haig's new ADC, Lieutenant G. H. Straker, was sent off to tell French and caught the C-in-C up before the latter reached his car although it does not appear to have prevented French's hasty departure. According to Rice, a retirement was still contemplated but Haig now intended to issue any necessary orders verbally once he had seen the situation for himself and he, Johnnie and the other staff mounted their horses and rode along the Menin road to steady the troops. Bulfin's counter-attack got under way at about 4.00 p.m. Jeudwine, who had been liaising between Bulfin and Cavan and was finally sent for reinforcements, found Haig and Johnnie soon after this beyond Hooge near the eastern end of what became known as Sanctuary Wood.[15]

The counter-attack by no more than five battalions and with reinforcements of only 80 or so men succeeded miraculously in driving the Germans back towards Messines. Accordingly, Haig wanted to press forward again next morning and at 11.15 p.m. Johnnie issued orders for a renewed push at 4 a.m. with French support. However, Bulfin believed this impossible and rode over to the White Château at 1 a.m.:

I found Johnnie Gough in bed in the château. I told him he must cancel the order, that if we were able to hold our line tomorrow it was as much as we could do, but to advance was madness and we would lose all the ground and Ypres into the bargain. He said all right, the order was cancelled, and I left him falling off to sleep at 1.30 a.m.

Fortunately, the following day saw no German counterblow. Indeed, it would not be until 10 November that a hastily organised German *Army Group Linsingen* would mount a renewed and last effort along the Menin road.

By this time, I Corps had been partially relieved, Johnnie having gone to GHQ at Bailleul on 4 November to urge the immediate relief of 1st and 7th Divisions. 1st Division was reduced to only 92 officers and 3,491 men and on 9 November Johnnie told a contact of Frederick Oliver 'that our men were so dead beat that they could only just hang on and he did not believe they had the physical strength to retreat to the next prepared position, and if the Germans made yet another attack he did not see how they could stand up to it'. Oliver put this down to 'over-depression' stemming from Johnnie's illness but he had to acknowledge that Johnnie's letters were actually 'of the most cheerful character' and he should have known that such a statement did not reflect Johnnie's public image. Neill Malcolm, for example, later wrote of Johnnie at Ypres:

There was no apparent limit either to his courage or to his resource. He had a truly wonderful instinct for the essential, and always seemed to have a solution for every difficulty.

According to Malcolm, Johnnie well knew the perils of any retreat from Ypres but 'kept his anxieties to himself and gave a brave lead to the rest of us'.

This familiar quality of Johnnie was also recognised by Hubert who wrote to Dorothea on 2 November that Johnnie 'was very fit, & doing a lot to keep up courage & resolution in others'. One way in which Johnnie appears to have had such an impact on morale was in the choice of an apt phrase for the moment that men long afterwards remembered. After Johnnie's death, Charteris wrote to his wife that he would never forget one remark by Johnnie in November 1914. Another version of these same remarks was used by the *Sunday Pictorial* as a rallying call in the even darker days of March 1918:

As he watched the enemy swarming over a low ride one of his staff said the fight was decided. Gough turned with his eyes ablaze and exclaimed: 'God will never let those devils win.'

Similarly, at a difficult period in the Second World War in April 1941 Major-General R. J. 'Jack' Collins, a former GSO3 in I Corps, broadcast on the BBC how his spirits had been uplifted by Johnnie at Ypres when his heart 'was in his boots':

'By George,' he said, 'I am sorry for the Huns on the other side of that hill. They must have had a terrible day. I think they are beat.' He was right; they were beat. But it took a man like General Gough to realise, that though things looked black enough for us, they were worse still for the Germans.

Collins was referring to the commitment of the *Prussian Guard* to the final German effort at Ypres on 11 November but this marked the end of the battle and things gradually quietened down.[16]

It had been a traumatic experience for the BEF as a whole and Johnnie had lost many friends apart from George Paley. On 4 November Raymond Marker had been mortally wounded and five others killed when I Corps headquarters was shelled and it had to be withdrawn to the Château des Trois Tours at Brielen. Two days later Hugh Dawnay had also been killed. He had often been close to Johnnie in his capacity as GHQ liaison officer with corps but had returned to a field appointment commanding 2nd Life Guards in 7th Cavalry Brigade. The brigade was sent to help extract Lord Cavan's infantry and French troops retiring from Zillebeke and Dawnay was killed – reports varied – either leading a squadron to clear the village of Zwarteleen or trying to rally demoralised Frenchmen. There had been other changes as well in I Corps. Charteris had taken over as GSO2 in the intelligence section on 16 September when Studd was posted to the Coldstream Guards and he was replaced as ADC by Straker. In turn, Marker was replaced by Travers Clarke moving up to AA&QMG and Clarke was replaced by Captain C. G. Liddell.

The post of GSO2 in the operations section also fell vacant when Jeudwine went as GSO1 to 1st Division and Neill Malcolm moved up to replace him in I Corps. The first officer appointed on 6 November was Major C. B. Thomson, later as Lord Thomson of Cardington and a Labour Secretary of State for Air to die in the R101 disaster in 1930. Thomson, who had been British military attaché in Serbia before the war, had a reputation for being politically radical and almost 'un-English'. What made it worse was not only that Thomson was a protégé of Henry Wilson but also that he was a convinced 'easterner' anxious to see the army pursue a Balkan strategy rather than remain committed primarily to the Western Front. Thomson's proximity to Wilson alone would have given him a rough passage in I Corps, another observer recording how he was 'astonished and upset' at the vehemence of the hatred for Wilson among I Corps staff. However, Thomson's advocacy of a Balkan front proved even more anathema to Johnnie with whom Thomson simply 'didn't hit it off'. Johnnie was especially critical of Thomson submitting memoranda on the Balkans:

General Gough did not think that fell to the province of a comparatively junior staff officer, and accused him of 'piaffing about', a figure taken from the repertoire of the Spanish riding school.

Consequently, Thomson tried to find a billet where his views 'would secure a more supportive (sic) audience' and he endeavoured to exchange appointments with Captain Archibald Wavell who was equally dissatisfied with a posting to the intelligence section of IV Corps. While Thomson's attempt to escape hardly increased his popularity in I Corps, the Military Secretary at GHQ was prepared to accept the exchange. However, since Collins had been appointed as GSO3 in the intelligence section to replace Hinde, who went off sick on 27 October, and was senior to Wavell, it could not be countenanced. Wavell subsequently secured the appointment of Brigade-Major to 9th Infantry Brigade while, on 4 December, Thomson managed an exchange with Major Sir Thomas Montgomery-Cuninghame, Bt., ironically another Wilson protégé, who was acting as a liaison officer with the French army.[17]

As the weather turned distinctly cold, conditions in the trenches deteriorated and tired infantry had great difficulties even in keeping rifles clean. In the three weeks between 30 October and 20 November, I Corps had 15,083 men evacuated sick or an average of 717 a day. It was then relieved and on 21 November Haig, Johnnie and Baird dined with Sir John French at St Omer prior to Haig and Johnnie's departure for England to represent the considered view that the time had come to create two British armies in France and Flanders. At 7 a.m. next morning Haig's party left Hazebrouck for London. Johnnie's mention in despatches had appeared the previous month and Haig had also asked French to promote Johnnie to Major-General. French had declined because Johnnie was too junior but during the meeting at St Omer he made a firm promise that Johnnie would indeed be promoted in due course.

Johnnie accompanied Haig to the War Office on 23 November when Haig was interviewed by Kitchener, but he was not present at Haig's second meeting with the Secretary of State for War or at Haig's interviews with the King and Asquith. Instead, Johnnie was able to enjoy the company of Dorothea and Diana, and he found time to see Frederick Oliver, who wrote:

He looks extraordinarily fit, and when he is in the company of his wife, and generally when there are people present, he is extraordinarily cheery. When I spoke to him alone, however, it was rather different – not that he was a bit less cheery and confident about the general outlook, or that he was any less proud of the achievements of the army than at other times, but when he talked to me about our mutual friends who have been killed and generally about the suffering of the army, one could see how great the strain had been and how deeply he felt the personal loss.

All too soon the respite was over and Johnnie took leave of his family. Diana recalled being promptly removed from the railway carriage after pleading to go to France as Johnnie's ADC, and indeed earlier, in October Dorothea had reported to Roger Keyes that Diana 'is most martial & signs her name everywhere as Tom Gough – in a flowing hand. She says she is 20 & is going to the "very front" immediately'. But, at the same time, young Diana naturally welcomed Johnnie's renewed presence in her life, writing to him after he had returned to France, 'Having you back was the happiest time in my life'.[18]

Haig and Johnnie arrived back at Hazebrouck on 27 November having again passed through St Omer to see Sir John French. There followed a routine of visits to units in which Haig was usually accompanied by Johnnie and Straker, Baird having left to be GSO2 in the Cavalry Corps. On 3 December the King visited I Corps at Hazebrouck and later, on 19 December, Haig and Johnnie paid a visit to Hubert's 2nd Cavalry Division, Hubert writing to Roger Keyes that Johnnie looked 'better than he has ever been since he first went to India in 1891'. Johnnie also penned some guidelines to divisions in I Corps on firing at hostile aircraft since the results to date had been lamentable with men generally failing to appreciate that they must aim well ahead of a fast moving aircraft.

On 21 December I Corps was ordered to move back into the line around Givenchy where the Indian Corps had been struggling to hold a local German attack. Haig was given responsibility for the sector on the following day and a corps conference was convened on Christmas Eve both to discuss how to hold the line taken over from the Indians and also the possibility of future offensive operations. Then on Boxing Day it was announced that the BEF would be divided into two armies and that Haig would take over the new First Army embracing I, IV and the Indian Corps. Johnnie would go with Haig as chief of staff and, although technically the post was for an MGGS, he would have to settle for remaining a Brigadier-General for the time being. Hobbs, Rice, Ryan, Charteris, Straker, Baird's replacement, Major Alan Fletcher, and three clerks were also retained. The new headquarters was established initially at the château of Lillers on 27 December but was moved to Moulin le Comte on 1 February 1915 when the former proved too small.

Johnnie threw himself into his extended responsibilities with enthusiasm. As early as 27 December he drafted a memorandum to GHQ on what he thought the correct relationship to be established between divisions, corps and armies, recommending that while GHQ should continue to deal direct with corps on most matters, operational directives should always pass through army headquarters. He also made tours at corps, divisional and brigade level. Visiting the Indian Corps on 29 December, for example, he recommended more attention being paid to march discipline and that artillerymen and infantrymen should not be segregated in billets. On 15 January 1915 he went to see the 3rd Infantry Brigade to get an account of its recent actions and the next day he was visiting 25th Infantry Brigade. Four days later he was with 2nd Infantry Brigade. On 25 January Hubert wrote to Dorothea that Johnnie had come to see his division:

Johnnie come over today to criticise & help us in practising the Infantry attack & tactics. We had the 5th [Cavalry] Brigade trying to fight their way through a thick wood in the morning for him & the other two attacking a village in the afternoon. But he was recalled before lunch by news of a severe attack on Givenchy & s of it.

Next day Johnnie was drafting a note on the lessons of the attack that had interrupted his visit to Hubert. He was critical of the lack of British artillery support for 1st Infantry Brigade, which had been the target of the attack, and he urged a proper system for local defence and counter-attack as 'only the ABC of soldiering and we cannot afford to neglect such simple precautions'. On 28 January, Johnnie together with the Master General of the Ordnance, Sir Stanley von Donop, attended a trench mortar demonstration at Rawlinson's IV Corps headquarters.[19]

Principally, however, Johnnie was involved in the detailed planning for what would be the BEF's first independent offensive in France and Flanders. Haig and Johnnie had visited I Corps on 6 January to discuss operational possibilities in the La Bassée area and eight days later Johnnie had met the King of the Belgians and his British liaison officer, Tom Bridges, at Furnes to review the potential of similar operations towards Ostend. The Allied Conference at Chantilly then approved the concept of a British offensive on 21 January and on 26 January Johnnie went to see the new chief of staff at GHQ, Sir William Robertson, whom he was delighted to see had replaced the ailing Murray. On 8 February Johnnie was visiting observation posts opposite the German lines at Neuve Chapelle which was fast becoming the favoured location for the attack. Indeed four days later Haig firmly recommended Neuve Chapelle since a successful push on the exposed German salient there would not only enable the British to quit waterlogged trenches on low ground for the superior tactical position of the Aubers ridge but would also lay open Lille by threatening communications between Lille and La Bassée. It is not clear whether Johnnie shared the confusion of tactical and strategic objectives that marked Haig's conception of the scheme in hand but it appears the uneasy compromise that emerged occurred only after Johnnie's death.

Initially, it had been anticipated that the British would be supporting a French offensive, but when denied use of the regular 29th Division by Kitchener, Sir John French was forced to renege on an agreement to take over more of the French line; Joffre retaliated by cancelling the wider offensive. Nevertheless, Robertson was determined to go ahead regardless and wrote to Johnnie on 13 February that he would press Sir John to accept the Neuve Chapelle option rather than another scheme suggested for the Messines area provided that Johnnie could give some details for 'it will be a great step in advance if we can put *some* plans definitely prepared, and which serves, for the next few weeks, as a *policy* to work on. It is time we made a plan of our own and ceased to dance attendance on French plans'. Johnnie was promised the 1st Canadian Division, one of two cavalry corps now with the BEF, two or three 9.2″ guns and possibly two 6″ howitzer batteries.

What Robertson described as his 'plot' succeeded and French approved the outline plans on 15 February, instructing that the offensive should begin as soon after 9 March as possible, ground state permitting. That same day, Haig convened the first detailed planning conference. Robertson and GHQ's artillery adviser came over to see Haig and Johnnie on 16 February and, on the following day, Robertson was able to confirm to Johnnie that mining engineers, two 15″ guns and two 9.2″ guns were all on their way from England. Robertson was also anxious that Rawlinson, whom Johnnie had told on 13 February would command the attack, had openly referred in a letter to 'our push at Neuve Chapelle' and he asked Johnnie to have a quiet word with the IV Corps commander. Since observation was difficult from the ground in front of Neuve Chapelle and Aubers ridge, Johnnie's preparations also included at least one flight in a reconnaissance aircraft over the German line, probably on 16 February. On hearing Johnnie had been up in an aircraft, Dorothea chided him, 'My dear, fancy you reconnoitring in an aeroplane! I hope you didn't get a chill!' In fact, Johnnie did, Haig's diary for 17 February recording that Johnnie 'has been in bed all day with a cold, but Ryan says it is slight, and that he will be all right in a few days'.[20]

The plan evolved for Neuve Chapelle between Haig, Johnnie and Rawlinson and his subordinates – notably the CRA of 8th Division, Brigadier-General (later Lieutenant-General Sir) Arthur Holland – had unique features befitting the first major offensive launched out of a defensive trench system. Artillery including 66 heavy guns was available in far greater strength than hitherto and in fact was deployed in a greater density than at any time previously. Experimentation on a distant section of German line and dummy positions behind the British line suggested a required ratio of five HE shells or 288 lbs shell weight per yard of trench attacked. Such a density was not again surpassed until 1917. Artillery was also required to register targets secretly with every battery given a role in a co-ordinated fireplan to deliver a short and precise opening barrage on the German trenches before lifting to put down a curtain to block the approach of German reinforcements. The aerial reconnaissance in which Johnnie had participated was also novel in terms of its scale and the use made of new aerial cameras, which enabled photographs of the objectives to be widely distributed down to battalion level before the attack. Despite Robertson's fears security was maintained and the area chosen proved to be comparatively lightly defended with only an estimated three German battalions facing 48 British and Indian battalions. The German second line defences were also incomplete. Subsequently, the attack on 10 March saw the defenders dazed by the short 35-minute hurricane bombardment – in fact a compromise between the ten minutes suggested by Haig and the two and a half hours suggested by Holland – and a breakthrough to a depth of 800 to 1,000 yards was achieved over a frontage of 4,000 yards around the village of Neuve Chapelle.

Unfortunately, the experimental network of telephone communications broke down and led to delays in which opportunities were missed. Problems were encountered through the late arrival of the promised 6″ howitzer batteries and the failure of the 18-pounders to cut the German wire in all sections, itself an experimental feature of the artillery programme. The failure to cut the wire was particularly regrettable since it tended to convince observers that the answer was a longer preliminary bombardment. Thus, the advantage of achieving surprise through a short bombardment on a narrow front was discounted and not revived for another two years. Moreover, Rawlinson did not fully absorb the lesson of the artillery ratios attained and dissipated the weight of artillery fire at Aubers Ridge and Loos in subsequent months. Such success as was achieved was perceived as Johnnie's legacy by some contemporaries and it is possible that his presence might have made a crucial difference. Certainly, it seems likely that he could have done something to reconcile the differences that developed between Haig and Rawlinson in early March as to how the battle should be conducted. That this was not to be was the result of developments that coincided with the planning of the Neuve Chapelle operation.

Early 1915 was a time of slow realisation that the war would not be won quickly and that the previously despised 'Kitchener armies' of volunteers raised in August and September 1914 and training in England would be needed in France. But, as yet, they were unready to take the field. The Territorial Force had done relatively well in 'plugging the gap' until the 'New Armies' were trained but regulars continued to believe that the former were not up to the task. There had been criticism in I Corps of the recuperative powers of the London Scottish, which had suffered enormous casualties in helping to hold the line around Messines in November 1914, and French declined the offer of the 46th (North Midland) Division, TF instead of the 29th Division for the forthcoming Neuve Chapelle operation. Johnnie, of course, had demanded 'soldiers' when writing to Oliver in September and this clearly continued to be a theme of his correspondence. Oliver recalled in December 1915, for example, that at this time the year before Johnnie had kept writing, 'Yes, you are getting plenty of recruits, but it is not recruits you want; it is trained soldiers.' It was a common enough plea of regulars at the time. Nevertheless, Johnnie was not unhopeful that the formations training in England could be made into good material and he had taken an interest in the 36th (Ulster) Division raised from the Ulster Volunteer Force and had written to them on a number of occasions with exhortations such as 'We want iron discipline; and, above all, we want all ranks instilled with a determination to win'.[21]

Some of the New Army divisions were now close to being brought overseas and it was thought that they would benefit from 'fighting soldiers' in command rather than the elderly 'dug outs' and others who had raised them. Consequently, a number of appointments were being discussed in February 1915. Haig believed that Johnnie would be an ideal choice, writing to Lady Haig, 'He will be a great help in training the keen troops on practical lines, and he will at once become a Major-General & soon after a Lieutenant-General if he gets a chance of a fight.' Later, Haig wrote along similar lines to Dorothea that Johnnie 'would have put energy & life into the new troops; but also his practical knowlege of war & its requirements would have been invaluable to those now striving after efficiency at home'. Consequently, on 13 February an offer of a divisional command was made to Johnnie and he was given 24 hours to make up his mind. Seeing Sir John French at St Omer on the following day, Johnnie was told that it would be recommended that he bring out one of the first New Army divisions ready for active service. If Johnnie found that it was not intended to send his new command to France before June or July 'then he had only to send Sir John a private letter, and he would arrange to have him sent out for some appointment here'.

According to Charteris, commanding a division would have been 'the dream' of Johnnie's ambition and two surviving letters sent by Dorothea to Johnnie do suggest that this was so, although Johnnie was obviously keen to see through the Neuve Chapelle operation. Haig asked Robertson if he could keep Johnnie until after the offensive but there appears to be no foundation in Hubert's later claim in conversation with Liddell Hart that Haig had been jealous of Johnnie and 'made no attempt to keep him'. Indeed, it seems that for all that both Johnnie and Charteris concurred that Haig often acted as his own chief of staff, Haig was extremely reluctant to part with Johnnie and only agreed in the interest of the army as a whole. Charteris concluded that 'we cannot well get anyone better or as good as Gough' and with two favoured candidates for Johnnie's replacement – Kiggell and Whigham – unavailable, Haig had to settle for Richard Butler who was commanding 3rd Infantry Brigade. Which division was intended for Johnnie is not clear. On 18 February Dorothea speculated that it might be either the 9th (Scottish) or 11th (Northern) Division. The 9th was indeed the first New Army formation to come out to France in May 1915 followed shortly by the 12th (Eastern) and 14th (Light) Divisions, but only the 12th, 13th (Western) and 15th (Scottish) Divisions received new commanding officers in March 1915, followed by 21st Division in April, which went to Smith-Dorrien's chief of staff, Forestier-Walker. The 12th Division therefore seems the likely choice but it is impossible to confirm.[22]

Forestier-Walker left Second Army for home on 22 February. However, although Dorothea clearly anticipated a wire from Johnnie at any moment announcing his imminent departure for England, he would almost certainly have remained until mid-March at the earliest. It is therefore not entirely correct to suggest as some have done that Johnnie was wounded while 'saying goodbye' to his old battalion although there was probably an element of this in his visit to 2nd Battalion, Rifle Brigade on 20 February. The battalion was now commanded by Reginald Stephens, the only one of the trio of Johnnie, George Thesiger and himself who would survive the war – Thesiger was killed at Loos in September 1915, only days after taking command of 9th Division. The battalion was part of 'Joey' Davies' 8th Division in Rawlinson's IV Corps occupying positions at Fauquissart opposite Neuve Chapelle. Consequently, it was in an area from which the forthcoming offensive would be launched and one reason Johnnie chose to visit the battalion was to have an opportunity of seeing the ground once more. Secondly, Stephens had written on 19 February inviting Johnnie to view a 'new breastwork' the battalion had constructed, since Stephens had come into conflict with his superiors over the strength of the sector's defences. There had been a suggestion that it was not desirable to erect a formidable barrier to any German attacks since the position would then be more difficult to recapture if it was lost, breastworks in low ground being usable from either direction. This had struck Stephens as unduly defeatist: 'To refuse to make your first line as strong as possible because you may be driven out of it is a confession of weakness and if you start with that idea you are bound to be beat.' He hoped, therefore, that Johnnie could intervene and proposed Johnnie visit between 19 and 21 February, 22 and 24 or 25 and 27 February when the battalion would be in the line, adding 'you can go round in the daytime quite fairly safely'.[23]

Johnnie received the letter on the morning of Friday, 20 February, and proposed to go for lunch that day. Haig had no objection although, according to his account, he told Johnnie 'to be careful and not run unnecessary risks by going too far forward'. The battalion headquarters was located in a house beside the Tilleloy road east of Fauquissart crossroads and 200 or 300 yards behind the British front line. Due to the nature of the ground – 'practically bare open plough land' and invariably waterlogged – the front line consisted of a parapet and not a trench system. On the way up before lunch, Johnnie and Stephens had come by way of a muddy track across a field to the rear of the headquarters building. Some shelling had occurred and when Johnnie expressed a wish to see his old company – A Company – after lunch he, Stephens and the battalion adjutant, Lieutenant R. C. J. Chichester-Constable, chose to walk along the Tilleloy road to A Company headquarters in a building at the crossroads. It was a route regularly used by Stephens and his officers and there was no thought of danger since it was not in direct sight of German positions save for a ruined factory 700 or 800 yards beyond the British parapet.

Returning to battalion headquarters by the same route at about 1 p.m., they passed a ruined wooden shed just past Fauquissart church, which was on the opposite side of the ten-yard-wide road, and about 120 yards behind the parapet. Remarking to Stephens, 'I can't see anything of the German lines from here. Let's stop & look,' Johnnie paused to look towards the Aubers ridge, leaning against the shed door post while Stephens stood behind him just inside the building. Later, a distraught Stephens wrote to Dorothea, 'I ought to have not allowed him to stop but all was very quiet and I never dreamt of danger.' A single shot was fired, apparently from a loophole in the top floor of the factory which was some 1,100 yard distant from where Johnnie was standing. Stephens thought it hit the British parapet, though years later Chichester-Constable told Roger Keyes he believed it hit the iron rim of a wheel on an old farmcart nearby. Either way the bullet then ricocheted off the Tilleloy road and struck Johnnie 'in the left side about the

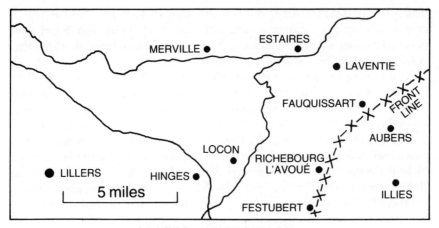

LILLERS–AUBERS RIDGE

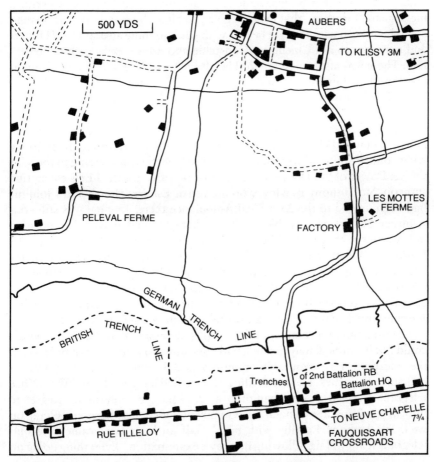

SKETCH TO SHOW FAUQUISSART CROSSROADS WHERE JOHNNIE GOUGH WAS
MORTALLY WOUNDED ON 20-2-1915 AND THE FACTORY IN THE GERMAN LINES
FROM WHICH THE SHOT WAS FIRED.

belt'. At the distance fired, the velocity was all but spent and it was a desperately unlucky circumstance, although both Haig and Rawlinson believed it unnecessary for Johnnie to have exposed himself and that Stephens was equally culpable for allowing Johnnie to stop.

As it happened, the battalion's medical officer, Byatt, had been standing outside battalion headquarters watching the party approach and he hurried to help. A few more shots were now fired without effect and Johnnie was carried the 200 yards back to A Company headquarters at the crossroads. Seeing that the wound was to the stomach Byatt felt it was 'everything not to move him' and Johnnie was kept in the house until a motor ambulance could be brought up to fetch him just after dusk at 4 p.m. According to Stephens, 'Johnnie was very bad at first and I think Byatt our doctor thought he would die then. But he rallied tremendously during the afternoon and when he left we hoped that he might live. He was in great pain at first but the doctor gave him morphia and he got much better and talked to me a little.' Johnnie had realised at once that he was seriously hurt and asked Stephens to send a message to Dorothea, 'that I was to give you all his love and say that no man could have been happier than he was with you'. Johnnie also spoke of Hubert and managed to ask Chichester-Constable about his service with the battalion. There was also a message for Haig 'to tell me "how grateful he (Gough) was for all my kindness to him"'.' Johnnie asked for water which Chichester-Constable had to deny him, but once the morphine took its effect he grew more drowsy.[24]

Stephens had at once written a brief note to Dorothea giving the bare facts and he had wired Haig. Haig immediately sent off Charteris and Ryan to see what could be done while writing himself to Dorothea and wiring to the War Office. Davies of 8th Division had meanwhile wired for the BEF's consulting surgeon, Sir Anthony Bowlby, who arrived at Estaires shortly after Johnnie had been moved to the 25th Field Ambulance there. Johnnie was still conscious and Charteris was able to tell him that news had arrived that morning in his absence that he had been gazetted a Companion of the Bath on 18 February. Dorothea had been especially angry that Johnnie had not so far figured in the honours distributed to the BEF and Johnnie's only comment to Charteris was 'I would get that now anyhow, even without a war!' Another arrival was Hubert who drove the 25 miles from his own headquarters to find Johnnie stretched out on a table awaiting examination but 'perfectly calm'.

The preliminary examination by Bowlby suggested that the bullet, which could not be immediately located, had gone upwards and had not penetrated the intestines. His favourable opinion was duly reported to Haig and, of course, to Dorothea. Her first inkling of what had happened was a War Office telegram received at Littlehampton at 9.34 p.m. that evening, 'Regret to inform you Brigadier-General J. E. Gough wounded this afternoon. Going on well. Sir Anthony Bowlby with him.' Half an hour later came a second telegram sent by Haig following Bowlby's examination, 'Everything going on satisfactorily.' Lady Keyes was staying with Dorothea at the time and while Diana was quickly sent off to the Oliver home at Checkendon – she wrote a short note for her father, 'Darling Daddy, I hope that German was killed who wounded you' – it was decided that Adrian Keyes should accompany Dorothea to France.

Quite fortuitously, Sir Berkeley Moynihan, who had operated on Johnnie the previous year, was due in France that very weekend to examine Johnnie's stomach as, once more, he 'had not felt well lately'. Moynihan was already en route when Johnnie was wounded and arrived at Haig's headquarters at 1 p.m. on Saturday 21 February to be promptly sent off to Estaires in a car with Straker. While Johnnie had had a reasonable night and his pulse was seemingly normal, Bowlby had concluded at his morning examination that damage had been done to the intestines after all and he decided on an exploratory operation as soon as Moynihan arrived. The surgeon attached to 25th Field Ambulance, who had had a pre-war practice in Plymouth, was also very highly regarded and there were two good nurses available as well. The operation that afternoon showed that the bullet had indeed done damage to the small intestine, specifically to the jegurnam and the tail of the pancreas. However, in what was regarded as a brilliant piece of surgery, Moynihan extracted the bullet, which had lodged near the spine, and closed the wounds successfully. While Johnnie would have remained a permanent invalid there seemed every chance he would live. Indeed, Haig sent a note with Straker to meet Dorothea at Boulogne where she was due to arrive at 5 a.m. on 22 February, 'Everything is now going on satisfactorily and Johnnie has every chance of making a good recovery'.[25]

As well as Hubert, Rawlinson and Davies were also in close attendance but early on that morning Hubert's trenches had come under attack, the Germans exploding a mine under positions held by the 16th Lancers. As a result he was compelled to leave: 'I told John I must go, and he said, "Of course, get on with your job," and so I left him never to see him alive again.' At midnight all was still well and Haig, who had been kept closely informed by Bowlby, received a telegram from Estaires stating 'Small but distinctly marked improvement.' Moynihan had said that 'if his heart would stand it he had a chance', but at 5 a.m. on Sunday, 22 February, Johnnie's heart failed 'and he died quite quietly and peacefully.' He was just 43.

It was the hour Dorothea should have been arriving at Boulogne, but her boat was delayed until 6 a.m. Having delivered his message from Haig, but since Hubert had also sent his ADC and cousin, Captain Owen Gough, with a car, Straker returned to Haig at 7.30 a.m. to learn that Johnnie was already dead. Unfortunately, Owen's car broke an axle and suffered a puncture and poor Dorothea did not reach Estaires until 11 a.m. where she had expected to move into a private house Hubert had obtained use of with two nurses for a fortnight. Instead, she and Owen 'were met with the news which a fool of an orderly blurted straight out to Dorothea before she was out of the car'.[26]

The funeral was held at 4 p.m. that afternoon, the sky overcast and a mist approximating to a fog all but defeating the efforts of a photographer present. Johnnie was buried in the communal cemetery at Estaires, the 2nd Battalion, Rifle Brigade, which had come out of the trenches that morning, in attendance and providing a firing party from A Company under the command of Chichester-Constable. Haig rode over after a further planning conference for Neuve Chapelle, but he did not wish to intrude upon Dorothea's grief 'so I did not speak to her'. He did talk to Stephens who, according to Eva Keyes, 'felt like a murderer'. Adrian Keyes had stayed at Boulogne that morning when it seemed Johnnie was recovering but he had not yet caught a boat so he was able to take Dorothea back to England with Johnnie's effects.

Understandably, it was a terrible blow to Dorothea who succumbed to suspected diptheria two days after her return. A special nurse had to be engaged and when Lady Keyes had to return to London from Littlehampton, Dorothea's sisters, Phyllis and Katherine, took over. Dorothea was no better by the end of March and Phyllis then accompanied her to Checkendon to stay with the Olivers. Johnnie's death also had a profound impact upon Harriette, who went into a considerable decline before eventually dying in April 1916. For Hubert the loss of any friend was bitter, but 'when that friend is also a loved and only brother, then bitter moments must ensue before their place can be taken by noble memories'. Indeed, shortly after Johnnie's death the Frenchman attached to Hubert's staff as interpreter, Paul Maze, saw his commanding officer sitting in a garden at his headquarters lost in thought.[27]

The army as a whole had also suffered a grievous blow in the view of many of Johnnie's contemporaries, not least in the context of planning for Neuve Chapelle. According to his wife, Haig was 'dreadfully upset' and Charteris also testified that it was the only occasion during the war when Haig allowed any personal incident to interrupt his normal routine. Sir John French had also sent an immediate telegram to Johnnie once he heard of his wounding and, as testified by his letter to Mrs Bennett, was also personally touched by Johnnie's death. For French's military secretary, Brigadier-General the Hon. Billy Lambton, Johnnie was a loss 'as he is a good hard fighter' and to Rawlinson the army had 'lost one of its very best leaders'. There was a letter of condolence to Haig from General de Maud'huy of French Tenth Army expressing his regrets at the death of an 'admirable' chief of staff and even Henry Wilson, who had been about to confront Johnnie regarding the hostility to himself in First Army, recognised the blow: 'A great loss although lately he has not been nice to me or about me.'[28]

Writing to Dorothea, Robertson felt he could 'truly say that no officer who has lost his life in this wretched war will be so greatly missed' and the phrase that occurred most frequently in the letters of condolence Dorothea received was that Johnnie's death was a 'national loss'. Typical of the messages was that from the King and Queen, Wigram telegraphing to Dorothea that 'His Majesty always held him in high esteem and feels that by his death the Army had lost one of its most promising and distinguished generals'.[29] In all, obituaries or notices of Johnnie's death appeared in 129 newspapers or journals. While many concentrated on how he had won the Victoria Cross, others spoke of the value of his services during the retreat from Mons and at Ypres.

Haig was determined to do something more to mark those services. He clearly recognised that Dorothea thought little of the CB and explained that this was less than might have been expected because it only covered Johnnie's services to early October and because he was about to be promoted to Major-General. Haig wrote to Robb, who was now Military Secretary at the War Office, on 4 April recommending the posthumous award of a KCB for Johnnie's work since October and a special pension to Dorothea. The King had decided that there should be no posthumous admissions to or promotions within the orders of chivalry unless 'for services of an altogether exceptional nature'. However, on 15 April, Robb was delighted to be able to write to Dorothea that the King considered Johnnie's case to be such an exception and that he would be posthumously knighted. Wigram reported to Rawlinson that 'it was a great pleasure to the King' to be able to do so and the announcement came in the *Gazette* on 22 April. Three days earlier Dorothea had been granted a pension of £470 per annum and a gratuity of £900, while for Diana she received a pension of £30 per annum and a gratuity of £300. Once Johnnie had died she had also automatically received a small pension from the Madras Military Fund as the daughter of Sir Charles Keyes. These sums were welcome since Johnnie left a relatively modest £2,860 gross in unsettled property and £1,824 net personally. But, of course, the recognition of the knighthood was a far more fitting tribute to his services. On 14 April, too, the *Gazette* had published French's despatch of 5 April mourning the loss of 'one of our most promising military leaders of the future'.[30]

Through the succeeding years that memory of a national loss was sustained by Johnnie's friends and colleagues. When Hubert was appointed to command 7th Division in IV Corps in April 1915, for example, Rawlinson noted, 'I would of course sooner have had poor Johnny Gough'. Roger Keyes, to whom Dorothea entrusted Johnnie's watch, frequently bemoaned Johnnie's death as he contemplated the disastrous efforts of lesser soldiers to break through the Turkish positions at the Dardanelles. Hubert, too, naturally kept the faith, reporting to Diana how proud he was to take command of I Corps in July 1915 because Johnnie had served in it. Hubert, who took over Johnnie's servant and horses, always sent Dorothea a letter on the anniversary of Johnnie's death and he kept watch over the grave at Estaires. Flowers were regularly placed on it and Hubert consoled Dorothea when the fighting of 1918 spilled around the cemetery area. Roger Keyes visited Estaires in January 1919 and was able to report that while there were many shell holes in the vicinity, the grave itself was untouched save for a small bullet hole in the cross. The grave remains, of course, but there is also a memorial tablet, designed by Eric Gill, in Winchester Cathedral and Johnnie's name appears on memorials in Eton College, Sandhurst and at the Staff College, Camberley. In 1922 Dorothea also presented a shield to the 2nd Battalion, Rifle Brigade to be awarded the best company each year in memory of Johnnie. There was further memorial in the form of Frederick Oliver's dedication and foreword to his book, *Ordeal by Battle*, published in 1915, which commemorated both Hugh Dawnay and Johnnie as fellow riflemen: 'We value our friends for different qualities, and would have their tradition fulfil itself in different ways. Those of us who counted these two – 'Johnnie' Gough and Hugh Dawnay – among our friends will wish that our sons may be like them, and follow in their footsteps'.[31]

Some of those others who wrote to Dorothea after Johnnie's death attempted to define just what it was that had made him seemingly indispensable. For Charteris Johnnie might be 'irritable when things were quiet' but 'never when there was a crisis' and he 'was at his very best when battle fighting' in which he showed 'tireless energy, calmness in crisis and a courage and confidence equal to Haig's own'. Similarly, 'Jack' Collins and Neill Malcolm, who had worked so closely with Johnnie at Ypres, also recalled his strength of character in crises. Malcolm wrote that 'when times were bad, as they sometimes were, and things began to look a little gloomy, Johnnie's resolution and resource were always beyond praise,' while Collins doubted 'if ever again we shall see such an exhibition of indomitable pluck and endurance'.[32]

Malcolm in particular wondered how Haig would fare without Johnnie at his side and this was echoed by both Rawlinson and Oliver, even though Johnnie would have taken his leave of Haig immediately after Neuve Chapelle. Haig himself wrote to Dorothea, 'For myself, I can only say that it is impossible for me to find anyone to replace my old friend' and, in a very real sense, he never did. Through Johnnie's death Haig lost a sounding board which was highly constructive yet far from uncritical. Had Johnnie gone on to command a division then it seems almost certain that, as predicted by so many contemporaries, he would have risen much further in the army. Johnnie was a convinced 'westerner' in strategic terms and a 'fighting general'. The army high command's commitment to the Western Front and to strategic offensives on that front would not have changed had Johnnie lived, but as he had demonstrated in his Staff College days he was a supreme realist and the conduct of these offensives might well have been modified by his influence with and, especially, by his ability to relate to Douglas Haig.[33]

In that sense Johnnie's career was unfulfilled. And yet, of course, he had had a spectacularly successful military career by any standards. At times he had benefitted from patronage, be it that of his father or of others such as Manning and Roberts. He would not have been able to enter either Sandhurst or the Staff College without such assistance but he profitted perhaps no more and no less than many others from the way the system operated in the

Victorian and Edwardian army. It was a system of inequalities and it undoubtedly bred rivalry and mutual antagonisms from which Johnnie was far from immune. But if it could produce a soldier as talented as Johnnie, then it is arguable that the system worked. This was especially so in the case of Johnnie who was remarkably free of any desire to push himself into the limelight.

Naturally enough, Johnnie had his faults and his prejudices, the latter abundantly clear at the time of the Curragh incident, but these were more than outweighed by his qualities. Frederick Oliver detected a 'virtue' akin to that of a radium 'which enabled it to affect adjacent objects with its own properties and to turn them, for a time, and for certain purposes, into things of the same nature as itself'. Johnnie was thus 'an alchemist who made fine soldiers out of all sorts and conditions of men, and whose spirit turned despondency out of doors'. Certainly, whatever his own doubts, Johnnie had always been able to inspire confidence in others. He has also fulfilled his duty when often physically unwell. The persistent neuralgia and fevers of his early campaigns had been followed by the serious illness in Somaliland and the complete collapse of May 1914. His recovery in order to go out with the BEF in August was a remarkable tribute to the sheer willpower which carried him through recurring illness in France. Oliver additionally wrote that Johnnie's watchwords were 'duty, discipline, self-discipline and the joy of life'. Hubert also summed up Johnnie's qualities in similar terms when writing to Dorothea in July 1915: 'Although Johnnie was so independent of character, & fearless, & never would submit to coercion, he had such an extraordinary *cultivated* as well as innate, sense of *duty* that he always did the right thing, however contrary to his own wishes'.[34]

Roger Keyes believed that there was something to be thankful for in that Johnnie had been able to 'prove his worth in this war' despite his illness. He even hazarded that Johnnie 'died the death he would have chosen'. That is conceivably so, although Johnnie died at a moment when he had so much more to offer his country and with consequences all but incalculable for the army. Johnnie had no fear of death and had comforted Lady Susan Dawnay when Hugh was killed by writing to her, 'How can the few years left of life here compare with eternity?' He had always believed in kismet and, shortly before his death, had spoken with a chaplain named Gibbon who had asked about Johnnie's religious views.[35] Johnnie had replied:

I may stand before God at my time and I know I have done many things I ought not to have done, but I think God will say to me, 'Gough, have you when you thought you knew what your duty was, not done it?' and I shall be able to look him in the face and say 'I may not have done my duty but I can honestly say I have always tried to'.

Let that be his epitaph.

Appendix:

Johnnie Gough's Awards and Medals

Victoria Cross
K.C.B. (Military)
C.B. (Military)
C.M.G.
Central Africa Medal with bar, Central Africa 1894–98
Queen's Sudan Medal
Queen's South Africa Medal with bars, Defence of Ladysmith, Laing's Nek, Belfast
King's South Africa Medal with bars, South Africa 1901, South Africa 1902
Africa General Service Medal with bars, Somaliland 1902–4, Somaliland 1908–10
1914 Star with bar, 5th Aug. – 22nd Nov. 1914
British War Medal
Victory Medal with bronze oak leaf emblem
Khedive's Sudan Medal with bar, Khartoum

Notes

Abbreviations used in Notes

AMOT	Army Museums Ogilby Trust
BL	British Library
DAG (K)	Dorothea Gough MSS
DG (P)	Diana Gough MSS
HPG	Hubert Gough MSS
IWM	Imperial War Museum
JEG	Johnnie Gough MSS
LHCMA	Liddell Hart Centre for Military Archives, King's College, London
NAM	National Army Museum
NLS	National Library of Scotland
OFH	*Official History of the Great War: Military Operations in France and Belgium*
PRO	Public Record Office
RA	Royal Archives
RBC	*Rifle Brigade Chronicle*
RGJ	Royal Greenjackets Museum
SRO	Scottish Record Office

Chapter One

1 IWM, 75/46/1, French MSS, French to Mrs Bennett, 24/25 February 1915; author interview with Mrs Beatrix Rabagliati, 18 December 1985.
2 HPG, Hubert to Nora, 22 March 1914; JEG, Haig to Dorothea, 4 March 1915.
3 IWM, G.36; Sir William Robertson, *From Private to Field Marshal* (Constable, London, 1921), p. 173; Sir George Aston, *Memories of a Marine* (John Murray, London, 1919), pp. 240–241; Sir Hubert Gough, *Soldiering On* (Arthur Barker, London, 1954), p. 121; *The Times*, 11 July 1933.
4 JEG, Roger Keyes to Dorothea, 22 April 1915; Brigadier-General John Charteris, *Field Marshal Earl Haig* (Cassell, London, 1929), p. 134; Brenda Gough, *A History of the Gough Family* (privately printed, nd), passim.
5 NAM, 6309–1–1,2; JEG, Charles to Laura Gough, 4 May 1880.
6 Gough, *Soldiering On*, p. 21; HPG, Charles to Laura, 26 September 1885; JEG, Harriette to Johnnie, 14 May 1885 and 28 October 1889 and Charles to Johnnie, 29 October 1889.

7   JEG, Harriette to Johnnie, 14 May 1885 and 28 October 1889; Gough, *Soldiering On*, pp. 22–23.
8   HPG, Charles to Laura, 26 September 1885; JEG, Charles to Laura, 5 February 1883 and Harriette to Johnnie, 14 May, 21 May and 1 June 1885.
9   JEG, Harriette to Johnnie, 7 May 1885 and Charles to Johnnie, 26 July and 9 August 1885; HPG, Charles to Hubert, 28 June 1885; *Eton Calendar*, 1885–87; *Eton College Chronicle*, 16 December 1885; Eton College Archives, LXX A16, James Housebook, 16 July 1887; *Liverpool Daily Post*, 27 February 1915.
10 JEG, Charles to Johnnie, 7 May 1885 and Harriette to Johnnie of 14 May 1885, February 1888 and fragment of 27 February 1888.
11 HPG, Charles to Hubert, 31 May 1885; JEG, Charles to Johnnie, 29 October 1889 and Harriette to Johnnie of 28 October, 12 November, 13 November and 25 December 1889.
12 PRO, WO 151/4; A. F. Mockler-Ferryman, *Annals of Sandhurst* (William Heinemann, London, 1900).
13 John Keegan, 'Regimental Ideology', in G. Best & A. Wheatcroft (eds.), *War, Economy and the Military Mind* (Croom Helm, London, 1976), pp. 3–18.
14 Arthur Bryant, *Jackets of Green* (Collins, London, 1972), pp. 156–157, 215–216.
15 RGJ, Draft Reminiscences of Francis Howard, p. 47; PRO, WO 76/273; *RBC*, 1892–1896, passim.

Chapter Two

1   JEG, Diary for 1896 and Johnnie to Harriette, August 1896; Gough, *Soldiering On*, pp. 40–41.
2   JEG, Diary 3–10 September 1896; Johnnie to Sir Charles, 26 August and Johnnie to Harriette, 29 August and 5 September 1896.
3   JEG, Diary 17–20 September and Johnnie to Harriette, 15 September 1896.
4   JEG, Diary 25–28 September and Johnnie to Sir Charles, 28 September 1896.
5   JEG, Diary 3–26 October, Johnnie to Sir Charles, 12 October and Harriette, 22 October 1896.
6   JEG, Diary 28 October and Johnnie to Hubert, 12 November 1896; I. Linden, 'The Maseko Ngoni at Domwe, 1870–1900' in B. Parchai (ed.), *The Early History of Malawi* (Longman, London, 1972), pp. 237–251; B. Parchai, *Malawi, The History of the Nation* (Longman, London, 1973), pp. 15–40.
7   JEG, Diary 1–9 November and Johnnie to Harriette, 22 October and 13 November; Johnnie to Sir Charles, 29 October and 8 November; Johnnie to Hubert 12 November 1896.
8   JEG, Diary 16–25 November and Johnnie to Sir Charles, 29 October and 2 December 1896 and 8 February and 29 April 1987; Johnnie to Harriette, 13 November 1896 and 7 May 1897; Johnnie to Hubert, 12 November 1896 with postscript, 19 November.
9   JEG, Diary 1 November 1896–13 January 1897 and Johnnie to Sir Charles, 2 December 1896.
10 JEG, Diary 1–6 November and Johnnie to Sir Charles, 2 December 1896 and 23 August 1897; Johnnie to Harriette, 17 August 1897.
11 JEG, Diary 6–13 November and Johnnie to Harriette, 13 November and Johnnie to Sir Charles, 2 December 1896.
12 JEG, Diary 6 November 1896 – 11 January 1897; Johnnie to Sir Charles, 29 October 1896 and 8 January 1897; Johnnie to Hubert, 13 December 1896 and Johnnie to Harriette, 17 January 1897.

13 JEG, Diary 19 November 1896–8 January 1897; Johnnie to Sir Charles, 2 December 1896 and 8 January 1897 and Johnnie to Harriette, 25 August 1897.
14 JEG, Diary 9–10 January and Johnnie to Sir Charles, 8 January 1987.
15 JEG, Diary 28 October 1896–14 January 1897; Johnnie to Hubert, 12 and 13 November; Johnnie to Sir Charles, 2 and 14 December; Johnnie to Harriette, 17 January and Johnnie to parents, 4 February 1897.
16 JEG, Diary 10 November 1896; Johnnie to Harriette, 29 August and 13 November 1896 and 17 January 1897; Johnnie to Sir Charles, 28 September and 2 December 1896, 8 January, 8 February, 8 and 21 April, 3 June, 8 July, 3 August and 28 September 1897 and Johnnie to Hubert, 22 March, 22 April, 7 July and 10 September 1897.
17 HPG, Hubert to Laura, 25 November 1896; JEG, Diary 12 November 1896; Johnnie to Harriette, 29 August and 13 November 1896 and 17 January and 27 May 1897; Johnnie to Sir Charles, 29 October 1896, 8 February, 8 April, 20 May and 3 June 1897; Sir Charles Gough and A. D. Innes, *The Sikhs and the Sikh Wars* (Innes, London, 1897).
18 JEG, Johnnie to Sir Charles, 28 September and 29 October 1896, 17 February, 29 April, 13 May, 3 June and 8 July 1897; Johnnie to Harriette, 28 February, 7 May, 17 and 25 August 1897.
19 JEG, Diary 9 November 1896–3 February 1897; Johnnie to Hubert, 12 November 1896; Johnnie to Sir Charles, 14 December 1896; Johnnie to Harriette, 17 January and Johnnie to parents, 4 February 1897.
20 JEG, Johnnie to Sir Charles, 8 January, 8 February, 14 March, 20 May and 8 July 1897; Johnnie to Hubert 22 March, 19 May and 7 July 1897; Johnnie to Harriette 7 and 27 May and Johnnie to Mrs Bagwell, 21 May 1897.
21 JEG, Diary 19 October 1897; Johnnie to Sir Charles, 8, 21 and 29 April, 13 and 20 May, 11 June, 23 August, 9 September, 20 October and 4 November 1897; Johnnie to Harriette, 28 February and 7 May; Johnnie to Hubert, 22 March, 22 April, 19 May, 8 June, 7 July and 10 September; Johnnie to parents, 17 February and Johnnie to Mrs Bagwell, 21 May 1897.
22 JEG, Johnnie to Harriette, 29 August and 13 November 1896, 17 January, 28 February and 17 August 1897; Johnnie to Hubert, 12 November and 13 December 1896, 22 March, 19 May and 7 July 1897 and Johnnie to Sir Charles, 2 and 14 December 1896, 8 January, 8 and 17 February, 14 March, 21 April and 23 August 1897.
23 JEG, Diary 5–14 August 1897; Johnnie to Hubert, 7 July and 16 August 1897; Johnnie to Sir Charles, 3 and 23 August and Johnnie to Harriette, 17 August and 28 October 1897.
24 JEG, Diary 1–14 October 1897 and Johnnie to Sir Charles, 21 April, 9 and 28 September and 20 October 1897.
25 JEG, Johnnie to Harriette, 28 October and Johnnie to Sir Charles, 14 November 1897.
26 JEG, Manning to Sharpe, 29 November 1897; Sharpe to Salisbury, 1 December 1897 and Bertie to Johnnie, 8 February 1898.

Chapter Three

1 JEG, Diary 10 June–6 July 1898.
2 JEG, Diary 6–12 July 1898.
3 JEG, Diary 15–27 July and Johnnie to Hubert, 30 July 1898.
4 JEG, Diary 27–31 July; Johnnie to Hubert, 30 July and Johnnie to Harriette, 31 July 1898.

5   JEG, Diary 1–5 August and Johnnie to Harriette, 6 August 1898.
6   JEG, Diary 6 August 1898.
7   JEG, Diary 7–21 August and Johnnie to Hubert, 17 August 1898.
8   JEG, Diary 22–31 August 1898.
9   JEG, Diary 1–2 September 1898; Johnnie to Sir Charles, 3 September and Johnnie to Harriette, 5 September 1898.
10 JEG, Diary 3–4 September and Johnnie to Hubert, 17 August 1898.
11 JEG, Diary 5–9 September 1898.
12 RGJ, Howard Reminiscences, pp. 88–95; PRO, Cab 37/44/17 and 37/45/34; H. C. C. D. Simpson, 'With the International Field Force in Crete, 1897', *Minutes of the Proceedings of the Royal Artillery Institution* XXVI, 1899, pp. 519–539; Arthur Evans, *Letters From Crete* (Privately printed, Oxford, 1898); B. Bennett, 'The Cretan Medal', *Journal of the Orders and Medals Research Society* Spring 1987, pp. 10–12.
13 RGJ, Howard Reminiscences, p. 106; JEG, copies of deeds 25 May and 8 June 1899 (from the collection of Dr M. S. Mackrakis); D. G. Hogarth, *Accidents of an Antiquary's Life* (London, 1910) pp. 67–68.
14 JEG, Chermside to Johnnie, 17 June 1899 and MSS extract reproducing Chermside to Salisbury, 10 December 1898.
15 JEG, Chermside to Johnnie, 29 June 1899.
16 W. E. Davies, 'The 2nd Battalion in Crete, 1899', *RBC* 1942, pp. 186–202.

Chapter Four

1   JEG, Johnnie to parents, 30 Sept. 1899.
2   JEG, Johnnie to parents, 30 September 1899; Johnnie to Sir Charles, 7 and 18 October and Johnnie to Harriette, 28 October 1899; Diary 2 October 1899.
3   JEG, Diary 26–28 October 1899; Johnnie to Sir Charles, 27 October and Johnnie to Harriette, 28 October 1899.
4   JEG, Diary 30 October; HPG, Johnnie's Siege Letter, 10 November 1899.
5   JEG, Diary 31 October–28 November; HPG, Siege Letter, 10 and 11 October 1899.
6   JEG, Diary 17 November–1 December 1899; Johnnie to Sir Charles, 29 October 1901 and 12 January 1902; HPG, Siege Letter, 22 November 1899.
7   JEG, Diary 12–23 November; HPG, Siege Letter, 12 November 1899.
8   JEG, Diary 24 November – 1 December; HPG, Siege Letter, 25 November and 1 December 1899; Thomas Pakenham, *The Boer War* (Weidenfeld & Nicolson, London, 1979), p. 269.
9   JEG, Diary 5 December; HPG, Siege Letter, 10 December 1899.
10 JEG, Diary 8 December 1899.
11 JEG, Diary 10–11 December; HPG, Siege Letter 10–12 December; RGJ, Thesiger Diary, 10–11 December 1899.
12 JEG, Diary 19 December 1899; Deneys Reitz, *Commando* (new edition, Faber and Faber, London, 1983), p. 58.
13 JEG, Diary 19–23 December; HPG, Siege Letter, 22 December 1899.
14 HPG, Hubert's Diary, 1 November and Hubert to parents, 15 and 19 November; Siege Letter, 5 and 26 December 1899.
15 JEG, Diary 27 December 1899–3 January 1900; HPG, Hubert to parents, 2 and 5 January 1900.
16 JEG, Diary 15 January 1900; HPG, Siege Letter, 16 January 1900; Gough, *Soldiering On*, p. 72; Sir Nevil Macready, *Annals of an Active Life* (Hutchinson, London, n.d.), I, p. 90.

17   JEG, Diary 15–21 January 1900; RGJ, Howard Reminiscences, pp. 126–130.
18   JEG, Diary 21–30 January; HPG, Siege Letter, 26 January 1900.
19   JEG, Diary 14–24 February 1900; RGJ, Howard Reminiscences, pp. 126–130; *RBC* 1900, p. 211; Hugh Dawnay, 'The Siege of Ladysmith', *RBC* 1900, pp. 68–93; W. E. Davis, 'The 2nd Battalion, Rifle Brigade in South Africa, 1899–1902', *RBC* 1944, pp. 142–176.
20   JEG, Diary 27 February and 5 March 1900; HPG, Hubert's Diary, 4 March and Siege Letter 2 March 1900; Gough, *Soldiering On*, p. 80.
21   JEG, Diary 5 March and Johnnie to Harriette, 10 March 1900; HPG, Hubert's diary, 4–29 March and Hubert to parents, 5 March 1900; Gough, *Soldiering On*, p. 71.
22   Gough, *Soldiering On*, p. 71; HPG, Metcalfe to Sir Charles, 26 October 1900; Johnnie to Sir Charles, 9 September and 17 November 1901; *London Gazette* 8 February 1901.

Chapter Five

1   HPG, Hubert's Diary, 6 April 1900; RGJ, Thesiger Diary, 1 July 1900.
2   HPG, Johnnie to Sir Charles, 4 and 11 July 1900; *RBC* 1900, passim.
3   E. T. Aspinall, 'Reminiscences', *RBC* 1936, p. 242; ibid, 1937, pp. 188, 197, 204–205.
4   Aspinall, *RBC* 1936, pp. 204–205; NAM, 8111–52, Verney MSS, letters of 17 and 19 July 1900; RGJ, Thesiger Diary, 5 August; HPG, Johnnie to Sir Charles, 18 and 19 July and Metcalfe to Sir Charles, 26 October 1900.
5   HPG, Johnnie to Sir Charles, 25, 29 and 31 July 1900 and Hubert to Sir Charles, 1 August 1900.
6   HPG, Johnnie to Sir Charles, 31 July and 5, 15, 20 and 24 August 1900.
7   Aspinall, *RBC* 1934, pp. 197–198; HPG, Johnnie to Sir Charles, 29 August, 3, 8 and 11 September and Metcalfe to Sir Charles, 26 October 1900.
8   HPG, Johnnie to Sir Charles, 11, 15 and 20 September 1900.
9   HPG, Johnnie to Sir Charles, 11 and 29 July, 15 and 20 August, 20 and 24 September and Hubert to Sir Charles, 22 September 1900.
10   HPG, Johnnie to Sir Charles, 2, 24 and 29 October 1900.
11   HPG, Johnnie to Sir Charles, 4, 7, 17, 22, 25 and 30 October and 11 November 1900.
12   Aspinall, *RBC* 1935, p. 184; HPG, Johnnie to Sir Charles, 17 and 21 November, 2, 6, 14 and 23 December 1900 and 2 January 1901.
13   Aspinall, *RBC* 1935, p. 191; Davies, *RBC* 1953, p. 59; HPG, Johnnie to Sir Charles, 11, 12, 17, 21 and 25 November, 2, 6 and 23 December 1900, 9 and 18 January, 1 February and 12 and 19 March 1902.
14   HPG, Johnnie to Sir Charles, 21 and 25 November, 14 and 23 December 1900 and 3 and 11 January 1901; JEG, McIntyre to Sir Charles, 29 May 1903.
15   HPG, Sir Charles to Hely-Hutchinson, 3 November 1899; Johnnie to Sir Charles 30 October and 6 and 14 December 1900; JEG, Wolseley to Sir Charles, 13 July 1899, 9 June and 10 November 1900; Howard to Sir Charles, 2 December 1900; Roberts to Sir Charles, 31 December and Gretton to Sir Charles, 31 December 1900.
16   HPG, Johnnie to Sir Charles, 9 and 17 August and 25 November 1901; Johnnie to Harriette, 23 August and 29 October 1901; Wood to Sir Charles 6 September and Roberts to Sir Charles, 20 October 1901; Staff College Library, *Report on the Examination for Admission to the Staff College held in August 1901* (HMSO, London, 1901).

17 HPG, Johnnie to Sir Charles, 9 October, 12, 17 and 25 November and 8 December 1901 and 12 March 1902; Johnnie to Harriette, 6 November and Hubert to Sir Charles, 2 October 1901.
18 HPG, Johnnie to Sir Charles, 11 November 1900, 23 August, 9 and 23 September, 27 December 1901, 9 and 12 January 1902 and 14 and 25 February 1902; Johnnie to Harriette, 6 November 1901 and Johnnie to Hubert 6 February 1902; PRO, WO 32/8090.
19 JEG, Milner to Johnnie, 26 November 1901; HPG, Johnnie to Sir Charles, 1 and 8 December 1901, 6 January, 6 and 8 February, 4 and 12 March, 27 April and 13 May 1902; Johnnie to Harriette, 29 October 1901; PRO, WO32/8110.
20 *RBC* 1901, passim; HPG, Johnnie to Sir Charles, 31 January, 18 February, 4, 12, 13, 19, 25 and 27 March, 28 April and 5 May 1902.
21 HPG, Johnnie to Sir Charles, 5 June 1902; Alan Gough to Sir Charles, 24 August 1900; Johnnie to Sir Charles, 1 December 1901 and 3 January and 13 May 1902; JEG, Davidson to Johnnie, 15 July 1902; Park to Sir Charles, 20 August and 15 September 1902; HPG, Seymour to Sir Charles and Kelly-Kenny to Sir Charles, both 19 March 1902.
22 HPG, Johnnie to Sir Charles, 29 October, 25 November 1901 and 8 February 1902; JEG, telegrams to Johnnie of 27 and 30 October 1902; Johnnie to parents, 28 October; Sir Charles to Laura, 25 October; Johnnie to Harriette, 4 December 1902.

Chapter Six

1 JEG, Johnnie to Sir Charles, 2 and 28 November 1902 and 8 February 1903; Johnnie to Harriette, 10 November 1902.
2 JEG, Johnnie to Sir Charles, 2 and 12 November 1902 and 8 February 1903; Johnnie to Harriette, 10 and 15 November 1902; Johnnie to Hubert, 18 November 1902; NAM, 6702/91/24, Melliss Diary, 13 November 1902; Sir Tom Bridges, *Alarms and Excursions* (Longman, Green & Co., London, 1938), p. 39.
3 JEG, Johnnie to Hubert, 18 November; Johnnie to Harriette, 22 November, 4 and 13 December 1902; Johnnie to Sir Charles, 28 November, 17 and 22 December 1902.
4 JEG, Johnnie to Sir Charles, 22 December 1902, 3 and 18 January and 1 February 1903; Johnnie to Harriette, 8 and 24 January 1903.
5 JEG, Johnnie to Sir Charles, 8 and 15 February 1903; Johnnie to Hubert, 16 February and Johnnie to Harriette, 22 February 1903.
6 India Office Library, L/MIL/5/703, Staff Diary Base and LOC, Berbera-Bohotle, 3 March 1903; JEG, Johnnie to Sir Charles, 7, 13, 18/19 March and 2 April 1903; Johnnie to Harriette, 1 April 1903.
7 JEG, Johnnie to Hubert, 4/7, 13 and 21 April and Johnnie to Sir Charles, 20 April 1903; NAM, 7610–7–3, Pope-Hennessy Diary, passim.
8 JEG, Bridges to Johnnie, 29 April and Cobbe to Johnnie, 8 May 1903; Bridges *Alarms and Excursions*, pp. 40–43; *Official History of the Operations in Somaliland, 1901–04* (HMSO, London, 1907), I, pp. 153–171.
9 JEG, Johnnie to Harriette, 23 April; Johnnie to Hubert, 3 May 1903; Draft report on Daratoleh 28 April and 17 May; Johnnie's personal account, 12 September and Johnnie to Sir Charles, 30 May 1903; *Official History* I, pp. 173–180, 326–329; *London Gazette*, 7 August 1903; *The Times*, 10 August 1903; *The Scotsman*, 11 August 1903; *The Daily Graphic*, passim; IWM, G36; H. Moyse-Bartlett, *The King's African Rifles* (Gale & Polden, Aldershot, 1956), pp. 181–182; C. E. Callwell, *Small Wars* (HMSO, London, 1906), p. 395; D.

Jardine, *The Mad Mullah of Somaliland* (Herbert Jenkins, London, 1923), pp. 106–114.

10 JEG, extract of Lenox-Conyngham letter 26 April 1903; Hussain to Johnnie, 17 March 1905; Johnnie to Hubert, 16 February and 3 May 1903; Johnnie to Sir Charles, 5 May and telegrams to Sir Charles, 27 April 1903; Sir Charles to Laura, 27 April; Bridges to Johnnie, 29 April 1903; *London Gazette*, 7 Aug. 1903; India Office Library, L/MIL/5/703, 25 April 1903.

11 JEG, Johnnie to Sir Charles, 5 and 10 May and Johnnie to Harriette, 15 May 1903.

12 JEG, Johnnie to Sir Charles, 24 and 31 May, 5 and 14 June; Johnnie to Harriette, 30 May 1903.

13 JEG, Johnnie to Sir Charles, 20 and 27 June; Orders by Swann 13, 19 and 22 June; Note by Johnnie, 23 June; Copy of Mullah's letter (Also L/MIL/5/703) 19 June 1903.

14 JEG, Johnnie to Sir Charles, 27 June, 14 and 26 July, 3 August; Johnnie to Harriette, 20 July 1903.

15 JEG, Johnnie to Harriette, 5 and 22 August; Johnnie to Sir Charles, 24 May, 20 June, 14 July, 10 and 30 August 1903; Macmillan to Johnnie, 16 January 1904; *The Times*, 10 August 1903; NAM, 7712–55–2, Walker MSS, Brodrick to Walker, 7 August 1903.

16 JEG, Johnnie to Sir Charles, 30 August, 6 and 30 September; Johnnie to Harriette, 16 September and Johnnie to Hubert, 4 October 1903.

17 JEG, Johnnie to Harriette, 7 October; Johnnie to Sir Charles, 12, 16 and 27 October, 25 November, 6, 12, and 18 December 1903; Johnnie to Hubert, 26 November 1903.

18 JEG, Johnnie to Sir Charles, 18 December 1903 and 12 January 1904.

19 JEG, Johnnie to Sir Charles, 12 October and 25 November 1903; Sir Charles to Laura, 27 April 1903; *London Gazette*, 15 January and 2 September 1904; *The Times*, 16 January 1904; MOD (MS1b), VC Register, III, pp. 104–105.

20 PRO, WO 32/8438 (also NAM, 6309–1–3/5).

21 JEG, Sir Charles to Laura, 5 February; Sir Charles to Harriette, 29 February; Macmillan to Johnnie, 29 February 1904; Willoughby Verner, 'The Operations in Somaliland, 1902–03', *RBC* 1903, pp. 42–59.

Chapter Seven

1 John Gooch, *The Plans of War* (Routledge and Kegan Paul, London, 1974), pp. 32–61; Edward Spiers, *The Army and Society, 1815–1914* (Longman, London, 1980), pp. 236–264; Ian Beckett, 'H. O. Arnold-Forster and the Volunteers' in Ian Beckett and John Gooch (eds.), *Politicians and Defence* (Manchester University Press, 1981), pp. 47–68.

2 Gough, *Soldiering On*, pp. 93–94; JEG, French to Dorothea, 8 March 1915; Aston, *Memories of a Marine*, pp. 240–241; 'Four Generations of Staff College Students', *Army Quarterly* LXV, 1, 1952, pp. 42–55; A. R. Godwin-Austen, *The Staff and the Staff College* (Constable, London, 1927), pp. 235–262; Brian Bond, *The Victorian Army and The Staff College* (Eyre Methuen, London, 1972), pp. 181–211.

3 Staff College, Honour Boards and Cricket Scoring Books; LHCMA, Isacke MSS, Diary for 1905, passim; JEG, Sir Charles to Laura, 23 March 1905.

4 Bridges, *Alarms and Excursions*, p. 55; Anthony Farrar-Hockley, *Goughie* (Hart-Davis, MacGibbon, London, 1975), pp. 73–74; JEG, Sir Charles to Laura, 5 February 1904; Sir George Aston, *Mostly About Trout* (Allen and Unwin,

London, 1921), pp. 112–120; ibid, *Memories of a Marine*, pp. 240–241.

5 Elizabeth Muenger, 'The British Army in Ireland, 1886–1914', unpub. PhD,
   Michigan, 1981, pp. 70–84, 114–120, 182–188; Sir Neville Lyttelton, *Eighty
   Years* (Hodder and Stoughton, London, n.d.), pp. 173–181; JEG, press cuttings;
   LHCMA, Burnett-Stuart draft autobiography, p. 47; *Eton College Chronicle*, 30
   March 1915; *Alahabad Pioneer*, 17 May 1915.

6 *The Globe*, 14 August 1907; *The Army and Navy Gazette*, 17 August 1907;
   Daily Telegraph, 14 August 1907; JEG, Johnnie to Sir Charles, 26 July 1903;
   Interview with Mrs Diana Pym, 12 December 1985; DAG(K), Dorothea to Lady
   Keyes, 16 January 1906.

7 Sir Terence Keyes and L. G. Pine, 'The Family of Keyes' unpub. typescript, 1961;
   C. Aspinall-Oglander, *Roger Keyes* (Hogarth Press, London, 1951), pp. 1–13;
   interview with Mrs Diana Pym, 12 December and Mrs Beatrix Rabagliati, 18
   December 1985; DAG (K), Sir Charles Keyes to Dorothea, 24 October 1883;
   Charles Keyes to Dorothea, 28 April 1896, 31 August 1898 and 22 February
   1900; Keyes Family MSS, Antrobus to Lady Keyes, 6 September 1901.

8 DAG(K), Oliver to Dorothea, 28 September 1901 and 3 June 1903; Austen
   Chamberlain to Dorothea, 1 and 4 September 1900; NLS, Oliver MSS,
   7726/123/7, Dorothea to Katie Oliver, 11 July 1901; 7726/104/6, 10, Oliver to
   Katie Oliver, 9 and 15 July 1901; DAG(K), Dorothea to Lady Keyes, 2, 6 and 27
   November 1902, 25 May, 26 and 27 July 1903, 17 and 23 January, 17 and 19
   February, 1 and 2 May, 5 and 12 June, 28 August 1904 and 10 March 1905.

9 Interviews with Mrs Pym and Mrs Rabagliati, 12 and 18 December 1985;
   DAG(K), Oliver to Dorothea, 28 September 1901; Visitors' Book of Dorothea
   Gough; JEG, press cuttings; Grille's Hotel to Dorothea, 26 September 1907.

10 PRO, CO 534/6, f. 162–166, 188–191, 205, 240, 350–354; CO 534/7, f. 38–47,
   196; CO 534/5, f. 79–80, 502.

11 PRO, CO 534/7, f. 172–178; ibid, Cab 11/116, CDC paper on KAR reduction,
   July 1910; Randolph S. Churchill, *Winston S. Churchill* (Heinemann, London,
   1969), II Companion Part II, pp. 715–724; Moyse-Bartlett, *The King's African
   Rifles*, pp. 137–140, 147–148.

12 PRO, CO 533/37, f. 209, 273–274; ibid, Cab 8/5 (Also Cab 38/15/7, 12); G. H.
   Mungeam, *British Rule in Kenya, 1895–1912* (Oxford University Press, 1966),
   pp. 171–180.

13 PRO, CO 534/6, f. 220; CO 534/7, f. 57–73, 81; DAG(K), Dorothea to Lady
   Keyes, 5 June 1904; author interview with Mrs Pym, 12 December 1985; JEG,
   East African Notebook.

14 JEG, Johnnie to Harriette, 14 December 1907 and 13 January 1908; Dorothea to
   Sir Charles, 15 December 1907 and 3 January 1908; Dorothea to Harriette, 26
   December 1907; Dorothea to Lady Keyes, 26 December 1907; Joint Diary, 18
   December 1907–6 January 1908.

15 JEG, Johnnie to Harriette, 13 January 1908; Dorothea to Lady Keyes, 3 January;
   Dorothea to Harriette, 14 January; Johnnie to Sir Charles, 23 January; Johnnie
   to Dorothea, 17 April; Joint Diary 5–16 January 1908; PRO, CO 534/8, f.
   118–126, 129–132, 361; CO 533/43, f. 4–210; Mungeam, *British Rule*, pp.
   171–175.

16 JEG, Dorothea to Lady Keyes, 3–23 January; Dorothea to Harriette, 14 and 23
   January and 11 February; Johnnie to Sir Charles, 23 January; Joint Diary, 16–31
   January; Dorothea to Sir Charles, 5 February; Johnnie to Sir Charles, 16/18
   February 1908; PRO, CO 533/43, f. 585–587 and CO 533/44 passim.

17 JEG, Johnnie to Sir Charles, 16/18 February; Johnnie to Dorothea, 5 and 17
   April and 14 May; Dorothea to Harriette, 30 April and Dorothea to Sir Charles,
   31 May 1908.

18 JEG, East African Notebook; Johnnie to Dorothea, 17 April; Dorothea to Sir Charles, 5 February 1908; PRO, CO 534/5, f. 310–311; CO 534/8, f. 158–172, 198–235, 391–414; 534/9, f. 58–81, 293–332; 534/10, f. 94–114; CO 533/44, f. 648–747; WO 106/24; Moyse-Bartlett, *The King's African Rifles*, pp. 140–148.
19 PRO, CO 534/8, f. 71–94; 534/9, f. 187; 534/10, f. 94–111, 171–173, 548–560; 533/44, f. 628–646, 748–810; Moyse-Bartlett, *The King's African Rifles*, pp. 146–148.
20 JEG, Dorothea to Sir Charles, 5 February and 31 May 1908; Dorothea to Harriette, 30 April 1908; DAG(K), Visitors' Book; PRO, CO 534/9, f. 220–227; 534/10, f. 92–93.
21 Moyse-Bartlett, *The King's African Rifles*, pp. 148–150, 190–194; Jardine, *Mad Mullah*, pp. 156–196; PRO, Cab 37/89/84; 37/96/165–6.
22 PRO, CO 535/13, Johnnie's 'The Situation in Somaliland', 30 June 1908 and notes by Johnnie of 25 September and 1 October; ibid, Johnnie's 'Considerations Affecting the Organisation and Composition of a Force for Operations', 8 October; CO 535/11, Note 2 October; 534/10, f. 169–170; 534/9, f. 384–388.
23 PRO, CO 535/13, Johnnie's 'The Situation in Somaliland', 17 November with notes by Read, Antrobus and Crewe; ibid, CO to Cordeaux, 30 November 1908.
24 PRO, CO 535/14, Johnnie to Cordeaux, 10 January 1909 and Cordeaux to CO, 15 January; WO 106/24 (also CO 534/11); Keyes Family MSS, Eva to Roger Keyes, 14 January 1909; PRO, CO 535/14, Somaliland Staff Diary; ibid, Johnnie to Cordeaux, February 1908 and 4 and 22 March; Johnnie's 'The Military Situation in Somaliland', 15 March 1908; *London Gazette*, 17 June 1910, pp. 4260–4262.
25 PRO, Cab 41/32/6; CO 535/14; CO 535/15; CO 534/11, f. 410–412; CO 535/15, Johnnie's memoranda for 6 September and 21 October 1909; Cab 37/100/107 (also CO 535/17); WO 106/24, Johnnie's 'Military Policy in Somaliland', 4 October (also JEG); JEG, Wingate to Johnnie, 23 May 1909; Crewe to Johnnie, 18 September 1909; Univ. of Durham Sudan Archive, Wingate MSS, 288/6/52, Johnnie to Wingate, 22 September 1909.
26 PRO, Cab 41/32/34, 39, 53, 54; CO 534/11; CO 535/15; *London Gazette*, 17 June 1910; JEG, Sir Charles to Johnnie, 25 June 1910; Univ. of Durham Sudan Archive, Wingate MSS, 289/3/7, Johnnie to Wingate, 4 December 1909 and 290/1/45, Johnnie to Wingate, 9 January 1910.
27 IWM, DS/MIL/80, Wilson Diary, 28 September, 5, 6, 9, 22, 24 and 26 October, 24 November, 18 and 26 December 1909, 4 February, 11 June and 28 July 1910; ibid, 73/1/17, passim; Godwin-Austen, *Staff and Staff College*, pp. 235–262; Bond, *Victorian Army*, pp. 244–298; Sir William Robertson, 'The Staff College, Camberley', *Army Review* III, 2, 1912, pp. 403–412.
28 JEG, Wilson to Johnnie, 31 July 1910; Robertson, *Private to Field Marshal*, p. 173; Sir George Barrow, *The Fire of Life* (Hutchinson, London, n.d.), pp. 116–121; Gough, *Soldiering On*, p. 121; R. J. Collins, *Lord Wavell* (Hodder and Stoughton, London, 1948), pp. 50–51; JEG, Robertson's report, 1912 and Richardson to Johnnie, 20 December 1912.
29 *Eton College Chronicle*, 30 March 1915; J. E. Gough, 'Peace Training for Command', *Army Review* I, 2, 1911, pp. 241–246; ibid, 'Local Counter-Attacks', *Army Review* VII, 1, 1914, pp. 39–50; ibid, 'The General Reserve: A Letter to a Young Officer', *Army Review* VI, 2, 1914, pp. 372–384; JEG, Mil. Educ. Committee to Johnnie, 1 January 1914 and Pope-Hennessy to Johnnie, n.d. [April 1914]; J. E. Gough, *Fredericksburg and Chancellorsville* (Hugh Rees, London, 1913).
30 Gough, *Fredericksburg*, pp. xv–xvi; *JRUSI* LVIII, 1914; PRO, CO 534/44, f. 648–679; CO 534/11, f. 470; F. S. Oliver, *Ordeal by Battle* (Macmillan, London,

1915), pp. xxvi–xxxv; Ian Beckett, 'The Nation in Arms' and 'The Territorial Force' in Ian Beckett and Keith Simpson (eds.), *A Nation in Arms* (Manchester University Press, 1985), pp. 1–36, 127–164.

31   DAG(K), Visitors' Book; Staff College Library, Cricket Scoring Books; *United Service Gazette*, 5 December 1912; JEG, Hubert to Johnnie, 24 March 1914; ibid, Miscellaneous financial papers; Rees to Johnnie, 25 January 1913 and Johnnie's accounts with Rees; Ruthven to Johnnie, 2 February 1914; Oliver, *Ordeal by Battle*, p. xxxi; *The Times*, 11 July 1933.

Chapter Eight

1   JEG, WO to Johnnie, 31 July and Haig to Johnnie, 6 August 1913; S. Gwynn (ed.) *The Anvil of War* (Macmillan, London, 1936), p. 245; G. J. de Groot, 'The pre-war life and military career of Douglas Haig', unpub. PhD, Edinburgh, 1983, passim; Tim Travers, *The Killing Ground* (Allen and Unwin, London, 1987), pp. 85–126; E. K. G. Sixsmith, *Douglas Haig* (Weidenfeld & Nicolson, London, 1976), pp. 87–88

2   Gough, *Soldiering On*, p. 121; A. Duff Cooper, *Haig* (Faber & Faber, London, 1935), p. 138; NLS, Haig MSS, Acc 3155/100, Diary 22 February 1915; Travers, *Killing Ground*, pp. 103–123; JEG, WO to Johnnie, 18 August 1913; *Daily Telegraph*, 23 August 1913.

3   Staff College Library, *Reports of General Staff Conference, 1906–14*, 1910, p. 79; 1914, pp. 5–12, 15, 21–22, 37, 42, 60, 71–72, 77, 83–84; *Irish Times*, 3 July 1915.

4   JEG, 'The Army and Home Rule', account written June or July 1914; RA, K 2553(2)/77.

5   Oliver, *Ordeal by Battle*, p. xxx–xxxv; Monro of Williamwood MSS, RH4/84/4, Ewart autobiography, pp. 11–12; Sir George MacMunn, *Behind the Scenes in Many Wars* (John Murray, London, 1930), p. 106; *Liverpool Post*, 1 April 1916; NLS, Oliver MSS, Acc 7726/95 f. 176–177; F. S. Oliver, *The Alternatives to Civil War* (John Murray, London, 1913); HPG, Howard to Hubert, 25 March 1914; JEG, Howard to Johnnie, 30 March 1914.

6   JEG, 'Army and Home Rule'; IWM, DS/MISC/80, HHW 22 Wilson Diary, 26 December 1913.

7   Ian Beckett, *The Army and the Curragh Incident, 1914* (Bodley Head for Army Records Society, London, 1986), pp. 1–11, 57–78.

8   Ian Beckett and Keith Jeffery, 'The Royal Navy and the Curragh Incident, 1914', *Bulletin of the Institute of Historical Research*, 62, 147, 1989, pp. 54–69.

9   JEG, Hubert to Johnnie, 19 March 1914 and Account by Hubert 7 April 1914 (also NAM, 7101–23–202; ibid, 800–6–4; RA, GV F.674/83; BL, Keyes MSS, 3/17); Fergusson MSS, Account by Fergusson 27 March (also RA, GV F.674/44[a]; Bodleian, Ms Asquith 40, f. 104–106; PRO, WO 35/209[g]).

10 JEG, Hubert to Johnnie, 20 March; NAM, 7101–23–202, Roberts MSS, Brett to Rolt, 21 March (also in Fergusson MSS; RA, GV F.674/38); Beckett, *Army and Curragh*, pp. 11–16, 25.

11 Queen's Royal Irish Hussars, Pragnell MSS, Note by Pragnell, Feb. 1933; RA, GV F.674/17; Pragnell MSS, Account by Hogg, 25 March; NAM, 7101–23–202, Roberts MSS, Account by Breeks, 28 March (also JEG; NAM, 8001–6–6; House of Lords RO, Bonar Law MSS 39/2/20; Birmingham Univ. Lib., AC 14/3/8; RA, GV F. 674/83; BL, Keyes MSS 3/17); NAM, 8001–6–7, MacEwen MSS, account by MacEwen (also JEG; NAM, 7101–23–202; Pragnell MSS; House of Lords RO, Bonar Law MSS 39/2/20; Churchill College, WMYS

2/5; RA, GV F.674/83; BL, Keyes MSS 3/17); NAM, 8001–6–3, MacEwen MSS, fuller account by MacEwen, April 1914; Nuffield College, Ms Mottistone 22, f. 206 (also RA, GV F.674/18; Pragnell MSS).

12   JEG, Johnnie to Hubert, 20 March (also HPG); NLS, Haig MSS, Acc 3155/91(h), Johnnie to Haig, 20 March; IWM, DS/MISC/80, HHW 23, Wilson diary, 20 March; JEG, Johnnie to Oliver, 8 April and Hubert to Johnnie, 20 March 1914.

13   JEG, Johnnie to Hubert, 21 March; Johnnie to Oliver, 8 April; Johnnie to Franklyn, 21 March; Haig to Johnnie, 21 March (also NLS, Acc 3155/91[h]); House of Lords RO, Bonar Law MSS 32/1/38, Lugard to Law, 21 March; HPG, Hubert to Daisy, 22 March; JEG, Chamberlain to Dorothea, 24 March; Birmingham Univ. Lib., AC 14/3/1–2, Dorothea to Chamberlain and Johnnie to Chamberlain, both 25 March; IWM, DS/MISC/80, HHW 23, Wilson diary 21 March; Bodleian, Ms Dawson 64, f. 23–27; Ian Beckett, 'A Note on Government Surveillance and Intelligence during the Curragh Incident, March 1914', *Intelligence and National Security* I, 3, 1986, pp. 435–440.

14   JEG, Hubert to Johnnie, 21 March; Account by Hubert, 16 April (also NAM, 7101–23–202; ibid, 8001–6–9; RA, GV F.674/83); IWM, DS/MISC/80, HHW 23, Wilson diary 21 and 22 March; HPG, Hubert to Daisy, 22 March; RA, GV F.674/17; NAM, 8001–6–3, MacEwen account, April 1914.

15   HPG, Brooke to Hubert, 6 April; *Liverpool Post*, 1 April 1916; NAM, 7101–23–202, Roberts MSS, Hubert to Aileen Roberts 10 April (also NLS, Oliver MSS, Acc 7726/147); Bodleian, Ms Asquith 40, f. 35–37.

16   NAM, 8001–6–3, MacEwen account April 1914; SRO, RH4/84/3, 126 Ewart diary, 22 March; Bodleian, MsAsquith 40, f. 69–72; JEG, Account by Hubert 16 April (also NAM, 7101–23–202; ibid, 8001–6–3; RA, GV F.674/83); Nuffield College, Ms Mottistone 22A, f. 3–15, Account by Nicholson.

17   Nuffield College, Ms Mottistone 22A, f. 3–15; HPG, Jolliffe to Hubert, 10 April; JEG, Johnnie to Franklyn, 22 March (also Nuffield College, Ms Mottistone 22, f. 217–219 and Churchill College, DRBK 3/7).

18   IWM, 73/1/18, Rawlinson to Wilson, 22 March and Roberts to Wilson, 23 March; NAM, 7101–12–125–3, Note by Roberts on conversation with Chamberlain, 22 March; JEG, Johnnie to Oliver, 8 April; NLS, Haig MSS, Acc 3155/91(h), Johnnie to Haig, 21 March and Haig diary for 21 and 22 March; HPG, Dorothea to Daisy, 23 March; Beckett, *Army and Curragh*, p. 21.

19   Beckett, *Army & Curragh*, pp. 22–25, 263–311; JEG, MacEwen to Johnnie, 2 April; Parker to Johnnie, 25 March; Robertson to Johnnie, 23 March; Hill to Johnnie, 24 April; NAM, 8001–6–3, MacEwen account, April; BL, Keyes MSS 3/17, Hubert to Lady Keyes, 5 April; HPG, Hubert to Daisy, 22 March 1914.

20   JEG, Bridges to Johnnie, 22 March; Howard to Johnnie, 30 March; Dawnay to Johnnie 26 March; Daly to Johnnie, 2 April; Verner to Johnnie, 25 March; *RBC* 1915, pp. 113–117; HPG, letters to Hubert from Cobbe, Howard, Daly, French, Paley, Thesiger, Stephens, Malcolm, Dawnay, De Pree, Hayter, Hailliday, Reed, Maxwell and Gwynn.

21   NLS, Haig MSS, Acc 3155/2(m), Diary 23 March; NAM, 8001–6–3, MacEwen account, April; JEG, Johnnie to Oliver, 8 April and Hubert's account 16 April (also HPG; NAM, 7101–23–202; ibid, 8001–6–9; RA, GV F. 674/83); SRO, RH4/84/3, 126 Ewart diary, 23 March; IWM, DS/MISC/80, HHW 23, Wilson diary 23 March; Nuffield College, Ms Mottistone 22A, f. 3–15; Monro of Williamwood MSS, Hubert to Ewart, 23 March and memorandum given to Hubert (also JEG; HPG; NAM, 8001–6–8; Nuffield College, Ms Mottistone 22, f. 230–232; IWM, French MSS, 75/46/4; Pragnell MSS); Pragnell MSS, Account by Hogg, 25 March; Oliver, *Ordeal by Battle*, pp. xxx–xxxv; *Correspondence Relating to Recent Events in the Irish Command* (Cmd. 7318 and 7329, 1914).

22   Beckett, *Army & Curragh*, pp. 20–22; JEG, Seely to Johnnie, 26 March; Haig to
     Johnnie, 26 March and Hubert to Johnnie, 24 March 1914.
23   JEG, Repington to Johnnie, 25 March; Oliver to Johnnie, 26 March; Dorothea
     to Oliver, 17 April; Johnnie to Oliver, 8 April; 'Jack' to Johnnie, 22 April;
     Beckett, *Army & Curragh*, pp. 22–29, 263–311.
24   JEG, Hubert to Johnnie, 3 April; Beckett, *Army & Curragh*, pp. 22–29; Farrar-
     Hockley, *Goughie*, p. 106; IWM, Godley MSS, Hubert to Godley, 28 April;
     Gough, *Soldiering On*, p. 171; interview with Mrs Rabagliati, 18 December
     1985.
25   Beckett, *Army & Curragh*, pp. 22–29, 333–386; JEG, Hubert to Johnnie, 26
     March; Johnnie to *The Times* 25 March; NLS, Haig MSS, Acc 3155/2(m), Haig
     diary 25 March 1914.
26   JEG, Hubert to Johnnie, 24 March; Keyes Family MSS, Roger to Eva Keyes, 2
     June and Eva to Roger, 5 June; AMOT, Price-Davies MSS, Diary 4 April; Gough,
     Soldiering On, p. 121; JEG, Haig to Dorothea, 24 May; Wigram to Dorothea,
     24, 26 and 28 May; Haig to Moynihan, 26 May; Roberts to Johnnie, 16 June
     1914; *Naval and Military Record and Docklands Gazette* 20 May and 3 June
     1914; Keyes Family MSS, Visitors' Book; JEG, Spender to Dorothea, 24 Feb-
     ruary 1915; Philip Orr, *The Road to the Somme* (Blackstaff, Belfast, 1987), p. 41;
     Maurice Headlam, *Irish Reminiscences* (Robert Hale, London, 1947), p. 141;
     Oliver, *Ordeal by Battle*, pp. xxx–xxxv.

Chapter Nine

1   Oliver, *Ordeal by Battle*, pp. xxxii–xxxiii; interview with Mrs Rabagliati, 18
    December 1985.
2   Robert Blake, *The Private Papers of Douglas Haig* (Eyre and Spottiswoode,
    London, 1952), pp. 69–70; P. T. Scott, 'From Precaution to Mobilisation', *Army
    Quaterly and Defence Journal* 109, 4, 1979, pp. 447–456.
3   JEG, Johnnie's account with Rees; Marker to Johnnie, 15 August; list of items to
    be forwarded to France; Dorothea and Diana to Johnnie, 14 August; Angela
    Malcolm to Dorothea, 5 March 1915; NLS, Haig MSS, Acc 3155/98 Diary
    10–16 August; Brigadier-General John Charteris, *At GHQ* (Cassell, London,
    1931), p. 8; PRO, WO 95/588; Duff Cooper, *Haig*, p. 138; JEG, Corps Opera-
    tional Narrative (hereafter CON).
4   *Staff Manual: War (Provisional)* (War Office, 1912); P. T. Scott, 'The Staff of the
    BEF', *Stand To!* 15, Dec. 1985, pp. 44–61; PRO, WO 95/596; JEG, CON 12–19
    November; Haig to Dorothea, 5 April 1915; Johnnie's Notebook; Haig to
    Dorothea, 4 March 1915; Charteris, *At GHQ*, p. 49; PRO, Cab 45/129,
    Vaughan to Smith-Dorrien, 24 June 1919; NLS, Haig MSS, Acc 3155/100, Diary
    22 February 1915.
5   LHCMA, Liddell Hart MSS 11/1929/15; 11/30/15; 11/1935/58; 11/1935/72;
    11/1935/107; 11/1935/14; 11/1936/31; 11/1937/4; 11/1936/31.
6   J. B. Gough MSS (in possession of Tony Allen), Diary 21 August; T. Secrett,
    Twenty-Five Years with Haig (Jarrolds, London, 1929), pp. 78–79; JEG, John-
    nie's Notebook; CON 22–24 August; NLS, Haig MSS, ACC 3155/215(c); ibid,
    3155/98, Diary 22–24 August; PRO, WO 95/588; *OFH*, Volume I, 1914
    (HMSO, London, 1922), pp. 97–98; Sir Horace Smith Dorrien, *Memories of
    Forty-Eight Years Service* (John Murray, London, 1925), p. 388; Charteris, *At
    GHQ*, p. 16.
7   LHCMA, Liddell Hart MSS, 11/1937/4.
8   LHCMA, Liddell Hart MSS, 11/1933/26; NLS, Haig MSS, Acc 3155/215(c);

ibid 3155/98, Diary 25–26 August; PRO, WO 95/588; JEG, CON; *OFH* Volume I 1914, p. 115; PRO, Cab 45/129, Haig to Edmonds, 18 December 1919; ibid, Cab 45/196, Accounts by Keppel and Furness, n.d.

9 Sir Hubert Gough, *The Fifth Army* (Hodder and Stoughton, London, 1931), p. 33; Gough, *Soldiering On*, p. 117; LHCMA, Allenby MSS, 6/VI/26, Chetwode to Wavell, 20 June 1928; 6/VI/10, Barrow to Wavell, n.d.; Charteris, *At GHQ*, p. 21; JEG, CON; PRO, WO 95/588.

10 JEG, CON; PRO, WO 95/588; NLS, Haig MSS, Acc 3155/98, Diary 29 August; 3155/100 Diary, 22 February 1915; 3155/141, Haig to Lady Haig, 4 September 1914; IWM, DS/MISC/80, Wilson MSS, Diary 29 August; Secrett, *Twenty-Five-Years*, p. 82; P. G. Halpern (ed.), *The Keyes Papers I: 1914–18* (Navy Records Society, London, 1977), p. 34.

11 PRO, WO 95/588; JEG, CON; Gough, *Fifth Army*, p. 45; NLS, Haig MSS, Acc 3155/141, Haig to Lady Haig, 10 September and 3155/98, Diary for 15 September; LHCMA, Liddell Hart MSS, 1/259/64–64A; Duff Cooper, *Haig*, p. 183; BL, Keyes MSS, 15/30, Dorothea to Roger Keyes, 19 September 1914.

12 NLS, Oliver MSS, Acc 7842/2, Johnnie to Oliver, 25 September; Charteris, *At GHQ*, p. 37; NLS, Haig MSS, Acc 3155/141, Haig to Lady Haig, 19 September; Gwynn, *Anvil of War*, p. 77; BL, Keyes MSS, 15/30, Dorothea to Roger Keyes, 19 September 1914.

13 PRO, WO 95/588; JEG, Extract from Haig's Despatch, 5 October 1914.

14 PRO, WO 95/588; NLS, Haig MSS, Acc 3155/215(c); 3155/99, Diary 16 October; JEG, CON and papers concerning French attack, 22 October; Charteris, *At GHQ*, p. 49; Gwynn, *Anvil of War*, p. 77; *OFH* Volume II 1914 (HMSO, London, 1925), pp. 183–184; IWM, MISC/3/43; Gough, *Fifth Army*, pp. 62–63.

15 NLS, Haig MSS, Acc 3155/99, Diary 31 October; IWM, MISC/3/43; PRO, WO 95/588; Cab 45/140, Bulfin Diary, 31 October and other correspondence of Bulfin, Rice, Straker and Malcolm with Edmonds; CAB 45/182, Edmonds correspondence with Jeudwine; *OFH* Volume II 1914, p. 326; Field Marshal Lord French. *1914* (Constable, London, 1919), p. 249; LHCMA, Clive MSS, II/1, Diary 31 October; Liddell Hart MSS, 11/1931/4; Secrett, *Twenty-Five Years*, p. 100; C. D. Baker-Carr, *From Chauffeur to Brigadier* (Ernest Benn, London, 1930), p. 50.

16 NLS, Haig MSS, Acc 3155/215(c); French, *1914*, p. 265; *OFH* Volume II 1914, p. 379; DAG(K), Hubert to Dorothea, 2 November; Gwynn, *Anvil of War*, pp. 50–51; *Eton College Chronicle* 30 March 1915; *Sunday Pictorial* 24 March 1918; Charteris, *At GHQ*, pp. 76–77; JEG, Collins to Dorothea, 24 April 1941; PRO, Cab 45/143.

17 JEG, Papers on death of Hugh Dawnay; NAM, 5201–33–17, Rawlinson MSS, Rawlinson to Wigram, 10 November; *OFH* Volume II 1914, p. 379; JEG, CON; Collins, *Wavell*, p. 67; John Connell, *Wavell: Scholar and Soldier* (Collins, London, 1964), pp. 97–98; Sir Thomas Montgomery-Cuninghame, *Dusty Measure* (John Murray, London, 1939), pp. 169–170; PRO, WO 95/596.

18 JEG, CON; NLS, Haig MSS, Acc 3155/99, Diary 21–27 November; IWM, DS/MISC/80, Wilson Diary 22 November; PRO, WO 95/589; JEG, Haig to Dorothea, 4 March 1915; Gwynn, *Anvil of War*, p. 56; interviews with Mrs Rabagliati and Mrs Pym, 18 and 12 December 1985; JEG, Diana to Johnnie, 6 December; BL, Keyes MSS 15/30, Dorothea to Roger Keyes, 2 October 1914.

19 NLS, Haig MSS, Acc 3155/99, Diary 28–30 November, 8–29 December 1914; PRO, WO 95/589; Halpern, *Keyes Papers*, p. 67; PRO, WO 95/154; DAG(K), Hubert to Dorothea, 25 January 1915; NAM, Rawlinson MSS; 5201–33–25, Diary 29 January 1915.

20   PRO, WO 95/154; WO 158/181, Haig to GHQ, 12 February 1915; Gwynn, *Anvil of War*, p. 85; JEG, Robertson to Johnnie, 13 and 17 February; Dorothea to Johnnie, 18 February; Keyes Family MSS, Eva to Roger Keyes, 18 April 1915; NLS, Haig MSS, Acc 3155/100, Diary 17 February 1915.

21   DAG(K), Roger Keyes to Dorothea, 22 April 1915; DG(P), Hubert to Diana, 10 March 1916; JEG, Stephens to Dorothea, 31 July 1915; S. Bidwell and D. Graham, *Firepower* (Allen & Unwin, London, 1982), pp. 73–77; JEG, CON, 14 November 1914; Gwynn, *Anvil of War*, pp. 128–129; NAM, Rawlinson MSS, 5201–33–17, Notes on Attack on Neuve Chapelle and Points for Consideration, both 18 February 1915; ibid, 5201–33–25, Diary 13–22 February; JEG, Spender to Dorothea, 24 February 1915.

22   NLS, Haig MSS, Acc 3155/141, Haig to Lady Haig, 14 February; 3155/100, Diary 13–14 February; JEG, Haig to Dorothea, 4 March; Dorothea to Johnnie, 17 and 18 February; Charteris, *At GHQ*, pp. 74–77; Duff Cooper, *Haig*, p. 225; LHCMA, Liddell Hart MSS, 11/1936/31

23   IWM, Smith-Dorrien MSS, p. 365, Diary 23 February; JEG, Dorothea to Johnnie, 18 February; Stephens to Johnnie, 18 February; NLS, Haig MSS, Acc 3155/100, Diary 20 February 1915.

24   NLS, Haig MSS, Acc 3155/100, Diary 20 February; PRO, WO 95/1724; JEG, Stephens to Dorothea, 20 February and 31 July 1915; Stephens to his wife, 20 February; Owen Gough to Dorothea, 24 February; Keyes Family MSS, Eva to Roger Keyes, 24 February; Gwynn, *Anvil of War*, pp. 90–91; RA, Q2522/21, Rawlinson to Wigram, 21 February; JEG, Roger Keyes to Dorothea, 17 October 1933.

25   JEG, Stephens to Dorothea, 20 February; Haig to Dorothea, 20 February; Diana to Johnnie, 20 February; Haig to Dorothea, 21 February; NLS, Haig MSS, Acc 3155/100, Diary 20–22 February; 3155/141, Haig to Lady Haig, 20–21 February; Charteris, *At GHQ*, pp. 76–77; PRO, WO 95/1703; Keyes Family MSS, Eva to Roger Keyes, 21, 22 and 24 February 1915.

26   Gough, *Fifth Army*, p. 76; NLS, Haig MSS, Acc 3155/100, Diary 21 February; 3155/141, Haig to Lady Haig, 23 February; Keyes Family MSS, Eva to Roger Keyes, 23 and 24 February; PRO, WO 95/1731; WO 95/1703.

27   JEG, Pilkington to Taylor, n.d.; Keyes Family MSS, Eva to Roger Keyes, 26, 28 and 29 March and 15 April 1915; NAM, Rawlinson MSS, 5201–33–25, Diary 22 February; Gough, *Fifth Army*, p. 77; Paul Maze, *A Frenchman in Khaki* (Heinemann, London, 1934), p. 100.

28   *OFH* Volume I, 1915 (HMSO, London, 1927), p. 81n; PRO, WO 158/181, Robertson to Haig, 21 February; Lady Haig, *The Man I knew* (Moray Press, Edinburgh & London, 1936), p. 126; Charteris, *Haig*, p. 134; JEG, French to Johnnie, 21 February; RA, Q832/220, Lambton to the King, 21 February; RA, Q2522/22, Rawlinson to Wigram, 22 February; Sir Frederick Maurice, *The Life of General Lord Rawlinson* (Cassell, London, 1928), pp. 125–126; Montgomery-Cuninghame, *Dusty Measure*, p. 187; IWM, Wilson MSS, DS/MISC/80, Diary 22 February 1915; NLS, Haig MSS, Acc 3155/100, de Maud'huy to Haig, 22 February 1915.

29   JEG, Robertson to Dorothea, 23 February; Furse to Dorothea, 23 February; Malcolm to Dorothea, 23 February; Chamberlain to Dorothea, 24 February; Beddington to Dorothea, 23 February; Robb to Dorothea, 15 April; Wigram to Dorothea, 22 February; Owen Gough to Dorothea, 24 February; Gwynn, *Anvil of War*, pp. 90–91; Headlam, *Irish Reminiscences*, pp. 141–144; JEG, Grenfell to Dorothea, 25 June 1915.

30   JEG, Obituaries File; Haig to Robb, 4 April; Robb to Dorothea, 15 April; Haig to Dorothea, 17 April; WO to Dorothea, 19 April 1915; NAM, Rawlinson MSS,

5201–23–66, Wigram to Rawlinson, 26 April; *London Gazette* 14 April 1915.

31 RA, Q2522/27, Rawlinson to Wigram, 22 April; Halpern, *Keyes Papers*, pp. 97, 125, 253, 273, 280; DG(P), Hubert to Diana, 23 July 1915; DAG(K), Hubert to Dorothea, 7 April and 27 October 1915, 22 February and 3 June 1916, 22 February and 12 April 1918; Owen Gough to Dorothea, 2 March 1915; Roger Keyes to Dorothea, 29 January 1919; Gill to Dorothea, 19 January 1921; Buxton to Dorothea, 16 July 1922 and 27 March 1924; Crosbie to Dorothea, 19 Oct. 1922; Oliver, *Ordeal by Battle*, p. xxxv.

32 Charteris, *Haig*, p. 134; ibid, *At GHQ*, pp. 76–77; JEG, Malcolm to Dorothea, 23 February and Collins to Dorothea, 1 March 1915.

33 RA, Q2522/21, Rawlinson to Wigram, 21 February 1915; Gwynn, *Anvil of War*, p. 102; DAG(K), Hubert to Dorothea, 29 July 1915.

34 Oliver, *Ordeal by Battle*, pp. xxxiii–xxxiv; DAG(K), Hubert to Dorothea, 29 July 1915.

35 Halpern, *Keyes Papers*, p. 93; JEG, Lady Susan Dawnay to Dorothea, 24 February 1915; note on Johnnie's comments to Gibbon (in Hubert's handwriting), n.d.

Bibliography

1. Manuscript Sources

Official Papers
India Office Library: L-MIL/5/703
Public Record Office: Cab. 8, 9, 11, 37, 38, 41, 45
                        CO. 533, 534, 535
                        WO. 32, 35, 76, 95, 106, 151, 158

Private Papers
Allenby MSS (Liddell Hart Centre for Military Archives)
Asquith MSS (Bodleian Library)
Bonar-Law MSS (House of Lords Record Office)
Burnett-Stuart MSS (Liddell Hart Centre for Military Archives)
Chamberlain MSS (Birmingham University Library)
Clive MSS (Liddell Hart Centre for Military Archives)
Dawson (Robinson) MSS (Bodleian Library)
De Robeck MSS (Churchill College)
Edmonds MSS (Liddell Hart Centre for Military Archives)
Ewart MSS (Scottish Record Office)
Fergusson MSS (Sir Charles Fergusson, Bt.)
French MSS (Imperial War Museum)
Godley MSS (Imperial War Museum)
Gough (Sir Charles) MSS (Mrs Denise Boyes)
Gough (Diana) MSS (Mrs Diana Pym)
Gough (Dorothea) MSS (Mrs Diana Pym)
Gough (Hubert) MSS (Mrs Denise Boyes)
Gough (Johnnie) MSS (Mrs Diana Pym)
Gough (Lucy) MSS (Tony Allen)
Gough Victoria Cross Files (National Army Museum)
Haig MSS (National Library of Scotland)
Howard MSS (Royal Greenjackets Museum)
Isacke MSS (Liddell Hart Centre for Military Archives)
James House Books (Eton College Archives)
Keyes MSS (British Library)
Keyes Family MSS (Lord Keyes)
Kiggell MSS (Liddell Hart Centre for Military Archives)

Liddell Hart MSS (Liddell Hart Centre for Military Archives)
MacEwan MSS (National Army Museum)
Marker MSS (British Library)
Melliss MSS (National Army Museum)
Monro of Williamwood MSS (Sir Hector Monro)
Mottistone MSS (Nuffield College)
Oliver MSS (National Library of Scotland)
Pope-Hennessy MSS (National Army Museum)
Pragnell MSS (Queen's Royal Irish Hussars)
Price-Davies MSS (Army Museums Ogilby Trust)
Rawlinson MSS (National Army Museum/Churchill College)
Roberts MSS (National Army Museum)
Robertson MSS (Liddell Hart Centre for Military Archives)
Royal Archives (Windsor Castle)
Smith-Dorrien MSS (Imperial War Museum)
Snow MSS (Imperial War Museum)
Stephens MSS (Imperial War Museum)
Thesiger MSS (Royal Greenjackets Museum)
Verney MSS (National Army Museum)
Victoria Cross Files (Imperial War Museum)
Victoria Cross Registers (Ministry of Defence)
Walker MSS (National Army Museum)
Wester-Wemyss MSS (Churchill College)
Wilson MSS (Imperial War Museum)
Wingate MSS (University of Durham Sudan Archive)

2. Memoirs and Biographies

Aspinall-Oglander, C., *Roger Keyes* (Hogarth Press, London, 1951)
Aston, Sir George, *Memories of a Marine* (John Murray, London, 1919)
Aston, Sir George, *Mostly About Trout* (Allen & Unwin, London, 1921)
Baker-Carr, C. D., *From Chauffeur to Brigadier* (Ernest Benn, London, 1930)
Barrow, Sir George, *The Fire of Life* (Hutchinson, London, n.d.)
Blake, Robert, *The Private Papers of Douglas Haig* (Eyre & Spottiswoode, London, 1952)
Bridges, Sir Tom, *Alarms and Excursions* (Longman, Green & Co., London, 1938)
Charteris, John, *Field Marshal Earl Haig* (Cassell, London, 1929)
Charteris, John, *At GHQ* (Cassell, London, 1931)
Churchill, Randolph S., *Winston S. Churchill* (Heinemann, London, 1969), Vol. II.
Collins, R. J., *Lord Wavell* (Hodder & Stoughton, London, 1947)
Connell, John, *Wavell: Scholar and Soldier* (Collins, London, 1964)
Duff Cooper, A., *Haig* (Faber & Faber, London, 1935)
Evans, Arthur, *Letters from Crete* (Privately printed, Oxford, 1898)
Farrar-Hockley, A., *Goughie* (Hart-Davis, MacGibbon, London, 1975)
French, Field Marshal Earl, *1914* (Constable, London, 1919)
Gough, Brenda, *A History of the Gough Family* (Privately printed, n.d.)
Gough, Sir Hubert, *The Fifth Army* (Hodder & Stoughton, London, 1931)
Gough, Sir Hubert, *Soldiering On* (Arthur Barker, London, 1954)
Grenfell, Field Marshal Lord, *Memoirs* (Hodder & Stoughton, London, n.d.)
Gwynn, Stephen(ed), *The Anvil of War* (Macmillan, London, 1936)
Haig, Countess, *The Man I Knew* (Moray Press, Edinburgh and London, 1936)
Halpern, Paul(ed), *The Keyes Papers I: 1914–1918* (Navy Records Society, London, 1977)

Headlam, Maurice, *Irish Reminiscences* (Robert Hale, London, 1947)
Hogarth, D. G., *Accidents of an Antiquary's Life* (London, 1910)
Holmes, Richard, *The Little Field Marshal* (Cape, London, 1981)
Howard, Francis, *Reminiscences, 1848–90* (John Murray, London, 1924)
Keyes, Sir Terence (with L. G. Pine), *The Family of Keyes* (Typescript, 1961)
Lyttelton, Sir Neville, *Eighty Years* (Hodder & Stoughton, London, 1927)
MacMunn, Sir George, *Behind the Scenes in Many Wars* (John Murray, London, 1930)
Macready, Sir Nevil, *Annals of an Active Life* (Hutchinson, London, n.d.) 2 volumes.
Maurice, Sir Frederick, *The Life of General Lord Rawlinson* (Cassell, London, 1928)
Maze, Paul, *A Frenchman in Khaki* (Heinemann, London, 1934)
Montgomery-Cuninghame, Sir Thomas, *Dusty Measure* (John Murray, London, 1939)
Oliver, Frederick, *Ordeal by Battle* (Macmillan, London, 1915)
Robertson, Nora, *Crowned Harp* (Allen Figgis, Dublin, 1960)
Robertson, Sir William, *From Private to Field Marshal* (Constable, London, 1921)
Secrett, T., *Twenty-Five Years with Haig* (Jarrolds, London, 1929)
Sixsmith, E. K. G., *Douglas Haig* (Weidenfeld & Nicolson, London, 1976)
Smith-Dorrien, Sir Horace, *Memories of Forty-Eight Years Service* (John Murray, London, 1925)
Terraine, John, *Douglas Haig: The Educated Soldier* (Hutchinson, London, 1963)
Thornton, L. H. and Fraser, P., *The Congreves* (John Murray, London, 1930)

3. Secondary Works

Official Histories and Publications
Official History of the Operations in Somaliland, 1901–1904 (HMSO, London, 1907) 2 vols
Official History of the Great War: Military Operations in France and Belgium
Volume I 1914 (HMSO, London, 1922)
Volume II 1914 (HMSO, London, 1925)
Volume I 1915 (HMSO, London, 1927)
Correspondence relating to Recent Events in the Irish Command (Cmd. 7318 and Cmd. 7329, 1914)
Report on the Examination for Admission to the Staff College held in August 1901 (HMSO, London, 1901)
Reports of General Staff Conferences, 1906–1914 (Bound for the Staff College)
Staff Manual: War (Provisional) (War Office, London, 1912)

Other Books

Beckett, Ian F. W.(ed), *The Army and the Curragh Incident, 1914* (Bodley Head for Army Records Society, London, 1986)
Beckett, Ian F. W. and Gooch, John (eds), *Politicians and Defence* (Manchester University Press, Manchester, 1981)
Beckett, Ian F. W. and Simpson, Keith, *A Nation in Arms: A Social Study of the British Army in the First World War* (Manchester University Press, Manchester, 1985)
Bidwell, S. and Graham, D., *Firepower* (Allen & Unwin, London, 1982)
Bond, Brian, *The Victorian Army and the Staff College* (Eyre Methuen, London, 1972)
Bryant, Arthur, *Jackets of Green* (Collins, London, 1972)
Callwell, C. E., *Small Wars: Their Principles and Practice* (HMSO, London, 1906)
Clark, Alan, *The Donkeys* (Hutchinson, London, 1961)
Farrar-Hockley, A., *Death of an Army* (Arthur Barker, London, 1967)

Godwin-Austen, A. R., *The Staff and the Staff College* (Constable, London, 1927)
Gooch, John, *The Plans of War* (Routledge & Kegan Paul, London, 1974)
Gough, Sir Charles and Innes, A. D., *The Sikhs and the Sikh Wars* (Innes, London, 1897)
Gough, J. E., *Fredericksburg and Chancellorsville* (Hugh Rees, London, 1913)
Jardine, D., *The Mad Mullah of Somaliland* (Herbert Jenkins, London, 1923)
Mockler-Ferryman, A. F., *Annals of Sandhurst* (Heinemann, London, 1900)
Moyse-Bartlett, H., *The King's African Rifles* (Gale & Polden, Aldershot, 1956)
Mungean, G. H., *British Rule in Kenya, 1895–1912* Oxford University Press, Oxford, 1966)
Oliver, Frederick, *The Alternative to Civil War* (John Murray, London, 1913)
Orr, Philip, *The Road to the Somme* (Blackstaff, Belfast, 1987)
Pakenham, Thomas, *The Boer War* (Weidenfeld & Nicolson, London, 1979)
Parchai, B. (ed), *The Early History of Malawi* (Longman, London, 1972)
Parchai, B., *Malawi: The History of the Nation* (Longman, London, 1973)
Spiers, Edward, *The Army and Society, 1815–1914* (Longman, London, 1980)
Terraine, John, *Mons* (Batsford, London, 1960)
Travers, Tim *The Killing Ground* (Allen & Unwin, London, 1987)
Young, F. W. *The Story of the Staff College* (Gale & Polden, Aldershot, 1958)

4. Articles

Aspinall, E. T., 'Reminiscences', *Rifle Brigade Chronicle* 1934, pp. 163–201; 1935, pp. 155–202; 1936, pp. 209–244; 1937, pp. 184–229; 1938, pp. 202–223; 1939, pp. 87–130; 1940, pp. 96–113; 1945, pp. 166–181; 1951, pp. 86–94.
Beckett, Ian F. W. and Jeffery, Keith, 'The Royal Navy and the Curragh Incident', *Bulletin of the Institute of Historical Research* (forthcoming)
Beckett, Ian F. W., 'A Note on Government Surveillance and Intelligence during the Curragh Incident, March 1914', *Intelligence and National Security* I, 3, 1986, pp. 435–440
Bennett, B., 'The Cretan Medal', *Journal of the Orders and Medals Research Society* Spring 1987, pp. 10–12.
Davies, W. E., The 2nd Battalion in Crete, 1899', *Rifle Brigade Chronicle* 1942, pp. 186–202.
Davies, W. E., 'The 2nd Battalion, Rifle Brigade in South Africa, 1899–1902', *Rifle Brigade Chronicle* 1943, pp. 150–172; 1944, pp. 142–176; 1945, pp. 182–204; 1946, pp. 128–148; 1953, pp. 53–70.
Dawnay, Hugh, 'The Siege of Ladysmith', *Rifle Brigade Chronicle* 1900, pp. 68–93.
De Groot, G. J., 'Educated Soldier or Cavalry Officer: Contradictions in the pre-war career of Douglas Haig', *War and Society* 4, 2, 1987, pp. 51–69.
Edmonds, J. E., Franklyn, H. E., Braclay, C. N. and Wedderburn, D. M. A., 'Four Generations of Staff College Students', *Army Quaterly* LXV, 1, 1952, pp. 42–55.
Gough, J. E., 'The British Central Africa Protectorate', *Rifle Brigade Chronicle* 1897, pp. 136–143
Gough, J. E., 'Peace Training for Command', *Army Review* I, 2, 1911, pp. 241–246.
Gough, J. E., 'Local Counterattacks', *Army Review* VII, 1, 1914, pp. 39–50.
Gough, J. E. (Anon), 'The General Reserve: A Letter to a Young Officer', *Army Review* VI, 2, 1914, pp. 372–384.
Keegan, John, 'Regimental Ideology' in Best, G. and Wheatcroft, A. (eds), *War, Economy and the Military Mind* (Croom Helm, London, 1976), pp. 3–18.
Robertson, Sir William, 'The Staff College, Camberley', *Army Review* III, 2, 1912, pp. 403–412.
Scott, Peter, T., 'From Precaution to Mobilisation', *Army Quarterley and Defence*

Journal 109, 4, 1979, pp. 447–456.

Scott, Peter T., 'The Staff of the BEF', *Stand To* 15, December 1985, pp. 44–61.

Simpson, H. C. C. D., 'With the International Field Force in Crete, 1897', *Minutes of the Proceedings of the Royal Artillery Institution* XXVI, 1899, pp. 519–539.

Verner, Willoughby, 'The Operations in Somaliland, 1902–3', *Rifle Brigade Chronicle* 1903, pp. 42–59.

Verner, Willoughby, 'Brigadier-General J. E. Gough, V.C.', *Rifle Brigade Chronicle* 1915, pp. 67–70, 113–117.

5. Theses

De Groot, G. J., 'The pre-war life and military career of Douglas Haig', Unpub. Ph.D., Edinburgh, 1983.

Muenger, Elizabeth, 'The British Army in Ireland, 1886–1914', Unpub. Ph.D., Michigan, 1981.

6. Newspapers and Periodicals

Army Review
Eton College Chronicle
Eton Calendar
Daily Graphic
London Gazette
Rifle Brigade Chronicle
The Times

Index

Note: in the majority of cases the military rank of soldiers listed in the index is that held at the close of their service career.